# DEADLY DOZEN
# 3

Also by Robert K. DeArment

*Bat Masterson: The Man and the Legend* (Norman, 1979)
*Knights of the Green Cloth: The Saga of the Frontier Gamblers*
   (Norman, 1990)
*George Scarborough: The Life and Death of a Lawman on the Closing
   Frontier* (Norman, 1992)
(ed.) *Early Days in Texas: A Trip to Hell and Heaven* (Norman, 1992)
*Alias Frank Canton* (Norman, 1996)
*Bravo of the Brazos: John Larn of Fort Griffin, Texas* (Norman, 2002)
*Deadly Dozen: Twelve Forgotten Gunfighters of the Old West* (Norman,
   2003)
(ed. and anno., with William Rathmell) *Life of the Marlows: A True
   Story of Frontier Life of Early Days* (Denton, Tex., 2004)
*Jim Courtright of Fort Worth: His Life and Legend* (Fort Worth, Tex.,
   2004)
*Broadway Bat: Gunfighter in Gotham : The New York City Years of Bat
   Masterson* (Honolulu, Hawaii, 2005)
*Ballots and Bullets: The Bloody County Seat Wars of Kansas* (Norman,
   2006)
*Deadly Dozen, Volume 2: Forgotten Gunfighters of the Old West*
   (Norman, 2007)

*Forgotten*

# *Gunfighters*

## *of the Old West, Volume 3*

# DEADLY DOZEN

### ROBERT K. DeARMENT

Foreword by Roger D. McGrath

UNIVERSITY OF OKLAHOMA PRESS • NORMAN

Library of Congress Cataloging-in-Publication Data
DeArment, Robert K., 1925–
Deadly dozen : forgotten gunfighters of the old W est, volume
3 /Robert K. DeArment ; foreword by Roger D. McGrath.
p. cm.
Includes bibliographical references and index.
isbn 978-0-8061-4076-6 (hardcover)
ISBN 978-0-8061-9207-9 (paper)

1. Outlaws — West (U.S.) — Biography. 2. Frontier and pioneer life — West
(U.S.) 3. West (U.S.) — Biography. 4. West (U.S.) — History — 1860–1890.
5. West (U.S.) — History — 1890–1945. I. Title.
F596.D385 2010
978'.020922 — dc22
[B]    2009019588

The paper in this book meets the guidelines for permanence and
durability of the Committee on Production Guidelines for
Book Longevity of the Council on Library Resources. ∞

# Contents

# Illustrations

# Foreword

Robert K. DeArment writes often and writes well on the characters who made the Old West wild and woolly. With the exception of his fine study of Bat Masterson, DeArment's books, particularly his *Deadly Dozen* series, have been devoted to gunfighters less well known. This is a special treat. Those who think they have a comprehensive knowledge of gunfighters will be excited by DeArment's introduction of shootists known only tangentially by some and known not at all by most. This is especially true of *Deadly Dozen, Volume 3*. In a sense, "dozen" is a misnomer. While DeArment focuses principally on twelve gunfighters, he brings to light dozens more. After having read about everything I could on gunfighters, including DeArment's first two *Deadly Dozen* volumes, I was surprised to find characters I had never heard of in this current volume. Moreover, a few who were familiar to me are more fully developed here than in any other source.

Bob DeArment was a gunfighter himself, although his field of battle was not the Old West but the European theater of World War II. His weapon was not a six-shooter but a machine gun. He understands that there is nothing more dramatic than a man fighting for his life and nothing more courageous than a man hearing the snap and crack of bullets about his head yet coolly and deliberately returning fire. This is what the gunfighters of the Old West did, and some did so on several occasions. DeArment has spent dozens of years exhaustively researching every extant source to reveal the derring-do of these men. Some of his lesser known figures just might rank with the more publicized gunslingers in grit and deadliness. This volume makes a compelling case for their inclusion in any discussion of those men in the frontier West who stood their ground with six-shooter in hand. As one cowboy put it, "I'll die before I'll run."

As with the legendary gunfighters, DeArment reveals that hyperbolic and wholly fictional tales have also been spun about the less well known shootists. He conscientiously and carefully separates fact from fiction. Even when some tales are left in the dust, those that remain are astounding—especially when considering that the tales involve gunfighters unknown to most fans of the Old West. A sandy-haired terror from a large Texas family, Porter Stockton may have shot to death more than a dozen men in gun battles and easily wounded that many more. Most of the time Stockton was acting in the role of wild cowboy, but during one period he was town marshal of Animas City. He shot to death his first man in Cimarron. He would kill another man in Cimarron and others in New Mexico and Colorado before he was through. His younger brothers were nearly as wild and fearsome. Although tangentially involved in the Lincoln County War, Ike Stockton made a name for himself in an equally violent range war that saw a year of shootouts, killings, horse theft, and cattle rustling on the border of New Mexico and Colorado. Sam Stockton shot to death a Texas Ranger and escaped from jail before vigilantes hanged him.

Unique in one way but otherwise typical of the gunfighters was Jim Levy. He is the only known Jewish gunfighter in the Old West. Like many others, however, he was born in Ireland and immigrated with his parents to New York City. By 1860 he was in California but soon left for silver strikes in Nevada. In Pioche, he came to idolize Irish immigrant Richard Moriarty, who was the town's premier shootist and chief bad man. Levy ambushed his first victim, but since the man had earlier threatened him and had managed to get off a shot, Levy successfully pleaded self-defense. The encounter left Levy with a bullet-scarred face, giving him a sinister appearance. He would rack up another kill in Pioche in a dispute over a mining claim. When the veins pinched out and Pioche declined, Levy was off, first to Virginia City and then to Deadwood. However, it was in Cheyenne that he engaged in his most celebrated gunfight. Charley Harrison made disparaging remarks about Levy, not because he was Jewish but because he was Irish. Harrison paid for the epithets with his life. Levy was in Tombstone during its heyday in 1881. The next year he would die in a hail of gunfire in Tucson.

Although Jim Masterson was involved in far more shooting scrapes than his brother Bat, he got none of the national attention of the latter. Born into a growing Irish Catholic farm family in Canada, Jim, like his brothers, would spend his adult life not behind a plow but as a lawman and gunfighter in the American West. He first followed his brothers onto the plains of Kansas to hunt buffalo and, then, when Ed became town marshal of Dodge and Bat became sheriff of Ford County, Jim became a policeman and a sheriff's deputy. He got into some hot-lead action almost immediately. While patrolling Dodge with another policeman, Wyatt Earp, two Texas cowboys galloped by, hooting and firing their six-shooters wildly. Masterson and Earp fired at the wild Texans, and one of them later dropped from his horse dead. This was the beginning of nearly two decades as a lawman, gambler, and hired gun for Bat's younger brother. James Patrick Masterson was one of the rare shootists, though — at least among those who remained in the profession for any significant amount of time — who did not die with hot lead in his belly. Tuberculosis took him at age forty-nine.

The name "Whispering Smith" has a familiar ring to it, but only because several writers of fiction loved its sound and used the moniker for their chief western character. The real man behind the name has gained little attention. He began his career in New Orleans as a policeman shortly after the Civil War and quickly rose through the ranks to detective. By 1876, however, he had left the Crescent City to become a railroad detective with the Union Pacific. Railroad detectives had authority that seemingly extended everywhere. Smith pursued outlaws through states, territories, and Indian reservations. He was not only involved in shootouts aplenty but brought seemingly untouchable outlaw gangs to bay, including a gang that took gold bullion worth a million dollars in today's money from an express office before it could be loaded on the Union Pacific. The early 1880s found him chief of Indian police on the Mescalero reservation in New Mexico. By the middle of the decade he was a range detective — essentially a hired gun — for the Wyoming Stock Growers Association. He was in the thick of the battle between the cattle barons and the pioneer settlers. Later years found him back with the railroads and then with a mining company. He never stopped fighting and shooting — and drinking ever more prodigious amounts of whiskey.

The Stocktons, Levys, Mastersons, and Smiths are the characters who fill this third volume of the *Deadly Dozen*. As with his earlier works, Bob DeArment brings to life these violent, deadly, and recklessly brave men who ensured that the Old West will remain legendary for generations to come.

Roger D. McGrath
Thousand Oaks, California

# Acknowledgments

I must acknowledge all the help I received from other Old West writers, researchers, and buffs who had already dug into the histories of some of the characters in this book and generously passed along the information they had uncovered, thereby saving me hundreds of hours of research. Many of them are friends of mine of many years standing; others I have come to know through the work on this book, and I am pleased to include them now in my list of friends.

Bob Alexander of Maypearl, Texas, biographer of Dave Allison, provided information on Allison and his killer, Hillary Loftis. Tom Bicknell of Crystal Lake, Illinois, longtime student of the careers of Ben and Billy Thompson, was able to confirm my suspicion that the accounts of Porter Stockton's association with the brothers was hokum. Photos of Porter Stockton were generously provided by Pam S. Birmingham. John Boessenecker of San Francisco passed along valuable information on Jim Levy and Dave Neagle. The late Msgr. Stanley Crocchiola (F. Stanley) in his final days gave me what information he had on the passing of Jim McIntire. Phil Earl of Reno, Nevada, sent me material on Langford Peel I had not seen. Fred Egloff of Chicago provided a source document on Dave Neagle I had been unable to locate. Nevada lawmen historian Bob Ellison of Minden, Nevada, shared information he had on Langford Peel. James Fenton of Lubbock, Texas, who has researched Hillary Loftis for years, opened his files to me and critically read a draft of the Loftis chapter. William Gorenfeld of Ventura, California, a military historian, provided me valuable information on Langford Peel. Chuck Hornung of Odessa, Texas, sent along important details on Porter Stockton's activities in Otero, New Mexico. Roger Myers of Larned, Kansas, helped me with information on Jim Masterson. Fred Nolan of Bucks, England, sent me an artist's depiction of Ike Stockton of which I was unaware. Chuck Parsons of Luling, Texas, sent me infor-

mation on the last days of Milt Good, cohort of Hillary Loftis. Chris
Penn of Norfolk, England, helped me with the research on Langford
Peel and Jim Masterson. James S. Peters of Edgewater, Colorado,
shared with me research he had done on the Stockton brothers and
Jim Masterson. Larry Reno of Denver also provided valuable material
on Jim Masterson and Whispering Smith. Gary Roberts of Tifton,
Georgia, gave me the benefit of his research on Billy Brooks and
Masterson. Bob Rybolt of Washington, D.C., aided me considerably
with the story of Whispering Smith. William B. Secrest of Fresno,
California, was of great help in sorting out the careers of Dave Neagle
and Jim Levy. The late Carol Wahl of Fillmore, California, was generous in sharing information she had gathered on Port and Ike Stockton. Roy Young of Apache, Oklahoma, sent me valuable information
on the killing of Jim Levy.

To them all, and any others I may have inadvertently overlooked,
I extend my heartfelt thanks.

# DEADLY DOZEN
# 3

# Introduction

In this, my third volume devoted to the careers of forgotten gun-fighters of the frontier West, may be found accounts of a dozen more formidable wielders of the six-shooter. The stories cover eight decades of American western history, from the California and Colorado gold rushes of the 1850s to the 1920s, when one of the last of the breed gunned down his last two victims, another man and then himself.

In the 1860s, several decades before the term "gunfighter" came into vogue, a young newspaperman named Samuel Clemens at Virginia City, Nevada, recognized in that "Comstock Commotion" the emergence of a distinctive class of frontiersmen, a species he called the "long-tailed heroes of the revolver." In later years the perspicacious Clemens, of course, would become a world-renowned author and social commentator under his pen name, "Mark Twain."

The histories of Langford Peel, Jim Levy, and Dave Neagle, three of the many gunmen who populated the early Nevada mining camps of the 1860s, are recounted here. Peel, who during the 1850s had been driven out of Salt Lake City by the Mormons after a bloody gunfight, became "chief" or top gunman at Virginia City in the 1860s, and then moved on to the new mining districts of Montana, where he fell before the gun of another notable pistoleer, John Bull.[1]

Levy's violent career included sojourns in the boomtowns of the Dakota Black Hills and Colorado before he died in a hail of gunfire at Tucson, Arizona, in 1882.

During the 1870s, Neagle would be a presence to be reckoned with in a number of Nevada, California, and Arizona boomtowns, including a stint as city marshal at Tombstone in the early 1880s when the town was awash with much more publicized gunfighters, including the brothers Earp, Doc Holliday, John Ringo, et al. But it wasn't until later in that decade that his name was splashed across newspaper

3

headlines throughout America when he shot and killed a nationally prominent former justice of the California Supreme Court in a railroad station dining room.

There were two gunfighting gamblers named Charley Harrison. One would die in a famous gun battle with Jim Levy at Cheyenne, Wyoming. The other, like Langford Peel, barely escaped the wrath of the Salt Lake City Mormons in the 1850s to turn up in the raw new mining camp at Denver, Colorado, where he would remain the dominant figure of the sporting crowd until the Civil War brought his violent demise.

The buffalo hunting trade and the developing cattle business of the 1870s introduced a new group of gunfighters to the plains of Texas, Kansas, and Wyoming, including four whose careers are recounted here: Billy Brooks, Jim Masterson, James ("Whispering") Smith, and Jim McIntire.

The candle of Brooks burned brightly in Kansas during the 1870s but was extinguished before the end of the decade as he dangled at the end of a rope.

Masterson would go on from the buffalo ranges and the deadfalls of Dodge City to further adventures in Colorado, New Mexico, and Oklahoma during the 1880s and 1890s.

Whispering Smith would become a legendary figure in Wyoming, Nebraska, Utah, and Colorado in a lengthy career covering four decades before suffering an excruciating death by swallowing lye and taking his own life in a jail cell.

Having also survived numerous adventures in Texas, New Mexico, and Oklahoma in the 1880s and 1890s, Jim McIntire published a book of his experiences in 1902 before fading into obscurity.

The escapades of Port and Ike Stockton grabbed newspaper headlines in Colorado and New Mexico for several months in 1881, but after both brothers died in separate gunfights that year they were mainly forgotten.

Ed Short first came to prominence during the bloody county seat wars of western Kansas in the late 1880s, but moved on to Oklahoma, where in 1891 he died in a celebrated shootout with a notorious bandit.

Born in 1870, Hill Loftis arrived late on the scene of the gunfighter era, but for thirty years he proved to be a dangerous gunman in Texas,

New Mexico, and Montana before ending his own life, and figuratively the gunfighter era, with a self-inflicted bullet.

As might be expected, these quick-triggered men, living in tumultuous times and places and associating with others every bit as dangerous and violence-prone, quite often came to abrupt and violent ends. Of the twelve men depicted here, only three — Neagle, Masterson, and McIntire (presumably) — died from natural causes. The other nine met violent and untimely deaths. No fewer than five — Peel, Levy, Short, and Ike and Port Stockton — were shot dead by enemy gunmen or officers of the law. Harrison was killed by Indians, struck by a bullet from an Osage's rifle and skewered by a lance. Brooks was hanged by vigilantes. Whispering Smith and Hill Loftis took their own lives.[2]

In this book, I have sketched the careers of a dozen more Old West gunfighters who were notorious in the West in their day, but whose stories have been ignored for the most part by later writers. Perhaps the reader will find these histories of long-forgotten practitioners of the fine art of draw and shoot as interesting as the Hickoks, the Earps, the Billy the Kids, and their other more highly publicized compatriots.

# — I —

## FARMER PEEL
### 1829–1867

*Peel was noted as being one of the quickest men with a gun in the West.
He could pull his gun and discharge with accurate aim in a fraction of
a second and with the same movement, and his handiness with a six-
shooter gave him the reputation of being an exceedingly dangerous man.*
— *Elko (Nevada) Daily Independent*

Many western gunfighters honed their skill with weapons in military
units, most often as participants on one side or the other in the Civil
War, but few had actually been professional soldiers. Langford Peel
was one of the few.

Born in Belfast, Ireland, in 1829,[1] Peel came to America while still
a small child. Little is known about his parentage, other than his
mother, Rachel, gave birth to him at the age of seventeen, and his father was a soldier.[2] Evidently the father died before Langford reached
his teens, for by 1841 Rachel had married another career soldier, an
armorer named John Lyons. Amazingly, Langford Peel at the tender
age of twelve entered the U.S. Army that year with the approval and
assistance of his mother and stepfather. On September 20 at New
York City he was sworn in by First Lieutenant Darling of the Second
Dragoon Regiment for a five-year enlistment. Darling, as the recruiting officer, certified that he had inspected the applicant and found him
"entirely sober," "of lawful age," and "duly qualified to perform the
duties of an able-bodied soldier." How a blue-eyed, light-haired, fair-
complexioned boy, only four feet five inches tall and twelve years of

age, as plainly described on the enlistment papers, could be expected to perform the duties of an able-bodied man was not explained.[3]

On the enlistment form was an addendum, signed by Lyons and attested to by a justice of the peace: "I hereby certify that I give my consent for my son, Langford M. Peel, to enlist in the U.S. Dragoons to serve for five years to learn music."[4]

It was a fairly common practice for the army at the time to accept young boys into the service to be trained as musicians. They were sent to Governor's Island, New York, for some basic training and then shipped off to Carlisle Barracks, Pennsylvania, for education in music. Peel followed this path. The army trained him as a bugler until October 24, 1842, when, after thirteen months of service, he was discharged at Carlisle Barracks.[5]

The army life must have appealed to the youngster, for he signed up again for a five-year enlistment. By 1845, although still only sixteen years old, he was on active duty at Fort Atkinson, Iowa, assigned as bugler for Company B, First Regiment of United States Dragoons, commanded by Captain E. V. Sumner.[6]

First sergeant of Company B during the early years of Peel's enlistment was Ben Bishop, and it was under Bishop that the young man experienced his first combat on the plains of Kansas in the spring of 1846. When Indians drove off a herd of four hundred oxen in present-day Pawnee County, Sergeant Bishop led a detachment of twenty dragoons, including Peel, in pursuit. A vicious firefight erupted at the mouth of Coon Creek on the Arkansas River. Twelve soldiers were killed or wounded before the Indians retreated. An arrow pierced Bishop's body, but he survived. Bugler Peel captured the attention of his older comrades and earned their respect when he personally accounted for three of the Indian dead.[7]

Bishop left the army in 1849, and Percival G. Lowe succeeded him as first sergeant of Company B. Lowe became quite friendly with Peel over the course of the next few years as the two shared the hardships and perils of frontier army duty together and fought side by side in several Indian battles. On Lowe's unreserved recommendation, Peel was later promoted to sergeant. Lowe described Peel as "the best specimen of 160 pounds, five feet, nine inches, naturally bright, clear headed, cheerful and helpful always; as keen as an Indian on the trail, well up in every branch of prairie craft, a perfect horseman, possessing unlimited courage and endurance, he was a man to be relied on and trusted in every emergency. A full set of such noncommissioned officers under a good commander would make a troop invincible against any reasonable odds."[8]

Lowe recorded several skirmishes with Indians in which Peel accredited himself well.

In September 1849 a Pawnee war party attacked a wagon train on the Little Blue River near Fort Kearny, Nebraska. They killed one man and wounded a dozen others. Peel was a member of a patrol from the fort that pursued the band and in a sharp clash slew two of the Pawnees.[9]

A month later, on October 29, scouts advised Captain and Brevet Major R. H. Chilton, in command at Fort Kearny, that a Pawnee war party was camped on an island in the Platte River only two miles from the post. Chilton led a force of twenty men, including Peel, in a raid on the camp. Anxious to take prisoners for use in negotiations with the tribal chiefs, Chilton instructed his men to capture the Indians alive and shoot only if necessary, an order with which Peel strongly disagreed. When Peel and three noncommissioned officers, Sergeant Martin and Corporals Cook and Haff, cornered four braves, the soldiers attempted to follow Chilton's order and motioned the Indians to throw down their arms and surrender. The Indians, however, had no such ideas and bolted.

Lowe said Haff followed one Indian and dispatched him, and Cook shot and killed another as the warrior "gave his final war-whoop" and fired his rifle, missing the corporal.

Meanwhile, Sergeant Martin and Bugler Peel were confronting the other two braves. "One Indian escaped in the brush," wrote Lowe, "while Martin was trying to carry out the Major's orders, and Peel, seeing that the other Indian was about to fire, shot him near the heart and he fell on his face, immediately raised himself on one elbow, fired, and shot Martin through the heart, and fell dead. Martin fell from his horse and was borne back to the post to a soldier's grave, a victim of obedience to orders. If he had taken Peel's advice, all four of the Indians would have been killed, and Martin would have lived."

Martin, a veteran who had fought with Chilton in the Mexican War, was the oldest man in the troop. He was very popular with the dragoons, who lamented his death, which they considered unnecessary.[10]

In July 1850 Peel, now twenty-one years of age, was enumerated in the U.S. Census, taken at the U.S. Arsenal at St. Louis, under the name Langford P. Lyon. His mother, listed as Rachel C. Lyon, was also present, working at the military base as a laundress.[11]

When his five-year enlistment was up in 1853, Peel signed up for a third tour of duty with the dragoons. He took another important step that year; at St. Louis on March 18 he entered into marriage with German-born Josephine Lay, a "lady of very good family."[12] Soon thereafter Josephine took up residence in Leavenworth, Kansas, to be close to the fort where her husband was stationed. In 1854 she gave birth to a son, named Langford after his father. A second son born in 1856 was named Percival in honor of Peel's close friend and associate, Percival Lowe.[13]

During the summer of 1853 Peel had a narrow escape from death at the hands of hostile Indians. While his company was camped on the Pawnee Fork of the Arkansas River, he and another soldier went out on a buffalo hunt. They had dropped a buffalo apiece when suddenly fifty or more warriors appeared over a rise. As Lowe related the story, Peel was half a mile west of his comrade and almost a mile and a half from the Indians when he spotted the warriors. He could have escaped by fleeing to the camp, but with scarcely one chance in ten of saving his companion, he took that chance at the risk of his own life. "One iota of weakness would have induced Peel to abandon his friend and save himself," said Lowe, but he stayed with his pal, and the two men hid in a thicket behind a little bluff. The warriors passed without seeing them, and then Peel and his friend raced to a point on the river where Cook, now a sergeant, had earlier arranged to meet them with a wagon and two other soldiers. The Indians attacked, but the five men fought them off, killing two horses and wounding several of the braves, until a strong force from the main camp arrived and the Indians retreated.[14]

Soon after this engagement the men of Company B went on a long march to Fort Union, New Mexico. They were camped near Raton Pass, when Peel, out on a lone hunting expedition, took the opportunity to display his remarkable shooting ability. Shortly after he left camp, a sudden thunderstorm came up, and he sought shelter in a copse of pines. There he was joined by a flock of turkeys also seeking haven from the rain, hail, and strong winds. While the gale raged,

Peel sat quietly and picked off the turkeys, one by one, shooting all of them in the head to avoid damaging the meat. He killed seventeen before the few remaining realized their danger and flew off. "Peel came into camp about dark," said Lowe, "with all that his mule could stagger under."[15]

After Company B returned east to its station at Fort Leavenworth, Peel became involved in a search for a deserter. The incident had humorous aspects, but it led to serious trouble with the civil authorities and ultimately the end of Peel's army career.

When Lieutenant David H. Hastings received information that the deserter was hiding with his wife at a house outside Weston, a small town across the river from the fort, he and Sergeant Peel took a squad of dragoons to the town. As he approached the house, Peel spotted a man he recognized as the deserter run inside. He followed and searched the house without finding his quarry. Several people, including the deserter's wife, were sitting at a table preparing to eat. The wife wore one of those big hoop skirts, which were the fashion of the day, and Peel eyed her suspiciously. The man he sought was small, and Peel became convinced that he was hiding under those skirts. He told the woman he was determined to find her husband "if he had to go under her skirts." But before he carried out his threat, Lieutenant Hastings arrived and berated Peel, saying he had no authority to invade a civilian's house without a search warrant. On the lieutenant's order, the dragoons retreated across the river without their quarry. Although Peel did gain some measure of satisfaction when a month or so later the deserter gave himself up and confessed that he was indeed hiding under his wife's skirts when Peel was after him, the incident led to problems with the civil authorities at Weston, who brought an indictment against Peel for invasion of a private civilian's dwelling without a warrant. By avoiding Weston, Peel managed to avoid arrest and prosecution, but the army brass at Fort Leavenworth were so embarrassed by the affair that on March 22, 1855, they discharged Peel from the service.[16]

During his three enlistments and fourteen years of military service Peel had grown to robust manhood and developed a high degree of proficiency in the use of arms. He had also become expert in gambling, the major pastime for soldiers during the long periods of inactivity at army posts, and in civilian life he turned to the gambling table for his livelihood.

The fortunes of the professional gambler, he discovered, ebbed and waned as certainly as the tides, but without their predictability. For a time he did quite well at Leavenworth, near his old military post, where he was accounted "a prosperous citizen,"[17] but following the extremely hard winter of 1856 money dried up in many of the pioneer towns of Kansas, including Leavenworth. Peel was generous with his monetary contributions for the relief of many financial sufferers, including a pair of gamblers named Dave Conley and Oliver Rucker,[18] who were in "a state of complete destitution."[19] He welcomed them into his house and provided for their needs throughout that awful winter.

Nathaniel P. Langford (1832–1911), pioneer and early historian of the frontier, in his book *Vigilante Days and Ways* devoted a full chapter to Peel, in whom he may have developed a particular interest because Peel's first name was the same as Nathaniel's last. Peel, he said,

> was regarded as one of those strange compounds who unite in one character the extremes of recklessness and kindness. In his general conduct there was more to approve than condemn, though his fearless manner, his habits of life, and his occupation as a gambler, gave him a doubtful reputation. Among people of his own class he was especially attractive, because of his great physical strength, manly proportions, undoubted bravery, and overflowing kindness. To these qualities he added a repose of manner that gave him unbounding influence in his sphere. No man was more prompt to make the cause of a friend his own, to resent an injury, or punish an insult. His dexterity with the revolver was as marvelous as the ready use he made of it when provoked. His qualifications as a rough and ready borderer bespoke a foreground in his life of much exposure and practice.[20]

In search of greener pastures (or greener gambling victims), Peel moved west in 1857. The fall of the following year found him in Great Salt Lake City, Utah, financially strapped after a long losing streak at the tables. Badly in need of a stake, on September 9, 1858, he looked around town for other, more prosperous members of the gambling fraternity and found Dave Conley, the gambler he had aided during that hard winter in Leavenworth two years earlier. Conley was acting as lookout at a faro table when Peel approached him and asked for the loan of $25. Conley refused the request.

Infuriated by this inexplicable display of ingratitude, Peel's face grew hard, and he snapped, "Great God! Is it possible that there is not a man in the country who will lend me twenty-five dollars?"

The faro dealer, a man named Robinson who had never before met Peel but knew him by reputation, saw the mounting fury in Peel's eyes and quickly offered to lend him $25 or any amount he wanted. Never taking his gaze from Conley, Peel said, "This is all I want," and took five half-eagles from the dealer's bank and pocketed them. Then, with a swift move, he grabbed the case-keeper from the table and hurled it at Conley's head. Conley ducked, and the apparatus crashed against the wall. Conley fled the building as Peel pulled out a pistol and seemed bent on pursuit when Robinson grabbed his arm and pleaded: "Stay your hand, Peel. For God's sake, don't make any disturbance."

Calming down a little, Peel explained to Robinson why he had been so angered by Conley's ungratefulness. He thanked Robinson for his trust and promised to repay the loan as soon as his luck turned.

Leaving the building, he headed straight for a gambling house on Commercial Street, where he had been informed Oliver Rucker, the other man he had aided in Leavenworth, was dealing a game. Sitting down at Rucker's table, Peel placed some of his borrowed coins on a card on the faro layout. Rucker contemptuously pushed the money away, saying, "I don't want your game."

Again Peel flew into a rage. Grabbing a chair, he flung it across the table. Just as his friend Conley had done, Rucker ran out of the room, exited the building through a rear door, and entered the adjoining store of A. B. Miller.[21] Peel stalked after him and found Rucker, pistol in hand, crouching in a dimly lit room.

The guns in the hands of the two gamblers exploded almost simultaneously. Both men were wounded, but as they tumbled to the floor they continued to cock and fire their weapons until they were empty. Peel was hit in the cheek, the thigh, and the shoulder; Rucker had been struck by every one of Peel's bullets.[22]

According to an account of the battle in an 1881 history, Peel, bleeding from three bullet wounds and his pistol empty, put an end to the fight by crawling to Rucker's side and driving a bowie knife into his heart.[23]

Another version was related some years later by W. D. Weir, who said he was in the store when Rucker, holding a pistol and a fistful of money, ran in, closely followed by Peel, also armed with a revolver, and the shooting erupted. Weir thought as many as a dozen shots were fired as he ran from the room. When the shooting stopped, he returned to the smoke-filled room to find the two combatants, both conscious, stretched out on the blood-soaked floor. A doctor was called and, after examining the fallen men, gave them only a few minutes to live and advised them to make their wills.

Rucker, still grasping the money from his faro game in his bloody left hand, mumbled: "I've got $5,000 here. Send it to my old mother down in Tennessee. Tell her I'm dead but for God's sake don't break her heart telling her I went like this."

Peel was still full of anger and unashamed that he was dying in battle. "Damn you!" he blurted at Rucker. Then, looking at the doctor, he said, "I've got a wife in Leavenworth City. Write and tell her I fit till the last minute; aye, and I fit till the last minute."[24]

Rucker expired within moments as predicted, but Langford Peel defied both the doctor and the Grim Reaper. Taken to the Salt Lake House, he received treatment for his wounds and began a long recovery. Rucker's friends clamored for Peel's arrest, and city officials seemed inclined to acquiesce to their demands when he had recovered enough to be moved. On September 29, twenty days after the shooting, Richard J. Ackley filed an affidavit in Great Salt Lake County probate court swearing that "on or about the ninth day of September A.D. 1858 . . . one Langford H. Peel did kill H. Rucker by shooting him with a pistol in violation of the statutes of the Territory."[25]

But Peel had friends also, and for $45 they hired "a Mormon dignitary of high standing in the church" to convey him in the dead of night to a secret hiding place twelve miles from town. There he was to remain until he healed sufficiently to make the final escape from the Salt Lake country. He was to be provided "female apparel and a fast horse" when the time came for the dash.

He made one attempt to leave, but too weakened by his wounds, was forced to return. He had been seen, however, and city officers were sent to arrest him. The Mormon clergyman came to the rescue again, moving Peel to the ranch of a man named Johnson, who secreted him for several more weeks.[26]

While Peel was recovering, according to one newspaper account, his enemies posted a large reward — not for his capture, but for his death — and some unscrupulous characters delivered a dead body and claimed the reward. Josephine Peel, reading the published reports of her husband's death, and hearing nothing from him to disprove them, is said to have remarried two years later.[27]

When he was strong enough to undertake the arduous trip on horseback across country, Peel went to California "by the southern route, passing through San Bernardino and Los Angeles," said Nathaniel Langford.

> From the moment of his arrival on the Pacific coast, his downward career was very rapid. He associated only with gamblers and roughs, among whom the height of his ambition was to be an acknowledged chief. He was a bold man who dared to dispute the claim to this title with him. . . . Expert in pistol practice, desperate in character, Peel was never more at home than in an affray. His wanderings at length took him to Carson City, in Nevada, where his shooting exploits, and their bloody character, form a chapter in the early history of the place. It is told of him by his associates, as a mark of singular magnanimity, that he scorned all advantage of an adversary, and, under the bitterest provocation, would not attack him until satisfied that he was armed.[28]

In the western custom of dubbing individuals with completely inappropriate nicknames, calling rotund men "Slim" or bald-headed men "Curly," for instance, Peel somewhere in his western travels acquired the sobriquet "Farmer," probably because he looked so little like a man of the soil. Many who knew him in Nevada, including Mark Twain, never learned his name was Langford and invariably referred to him as "Farmer." Peel struck Virginia City, Nevada, in 1863 when that camp was establishing itself as the queen city of the fabulous Comstock Lode. Shortly before his arrival a desperado named Sam Brown, generally recognized as "chief" of the town's pistoleers, was killed by a shotgun blast, so the position was open.

Mark Twain, who began his remarkable literary career as a newspaperman in Virginia City during this period, explained in his early work *Roughing It* the high regard gunmen were held in that silver camp:

The first twenty-six graves in the Virginia cemetery were occupied by murdered men, so everybody said, so everybody believed, and so they will always say and believe. The reason why there was so much slaughtering done, was that in a new mining district the rough element predominates, and a person is not respected until he has "killed his man." That was the very expression used. . . . It was tedious work struggling up to a position of influence with bloodless hands; but when a man came with the blood of half a dozen men on his soul, his worth was recognized at once and his acquaintance sought. . . .[29]

The desperado stalked the streets with a swagger graded according to the number of his homicides, and a nod of recognition from him was sufficient to make a humble admirer happy for the rest of the day. The deference that was paid to a desperado of wide reputation, and who "kept his private graveyard," as the phrase went, was marked, and cheerfully accorded. When he moved along the sidewalk in his excessively long frock-coat, shiny stump-toed boots, and with dainty little slouch hat tipped over left eye, the small fry roughs made room for his majesty; when entering the restaurant, the waiters deserted bankers and merchants to overwhelm him with obsequious service; when he shouldered his way to a bar, the shouldered parties wheeled indignantly, recognized him, and—apologized. They got a look in return that froze their marrow. . . .

The best known names in the Territory of Nevada were those belonging to these long-tailed heroes of the revolver. Orators, Governors, capitalists and leaders of legislatures enjoyed a degree of fame, but it seemed local and meager when contrasted with the fame of such men as Sam Brown, Jack Williams, Billy Mulligan, Farmer Pease [*sic*], Sugarfoot Mike, Pock-Marked Jake, El Dorado Johnny, Jack McNabb, Joe McGee, Jack Harris, Six-Fingered Pete, etc., etc. They were brave, reckless men, and traveled with their lives in their hands. To give them their due, they did their killing principally among themselves, and seldom molested peaceable citizens, for they considered it small credit to add to their trophies so cheap a bauble as the death of a man who was "not on the shoot," as they phrased it. They killed each other on slight provocation, and hoped and expected to be killed themselves — for they held it almost shame to die otherwise than "with their boots on," as they expressed it.[30]

This, then, was the real beginning of the era of the western gunfighter, although that expression did not come into general usage until some years later.

"With Sam Brown's death there was considerable excitement among the 'bad men' as to who would succeed him as 'Chief' at Washoe," wrote a Comstock historian.[31] Peel, described as "a noble-looking youth with mild blue eyes and long golden beard [who] had already proved his prowess, as the six notches on his gun-butt could testify," was a notable candidate for the honor.[32]

"Of all the desperadoes that scourged the Comstock, Sam Brown excepted, no one ever attained the distinction of Farmer Peel," said another chronicler. "He came to Virginia City with a record of five murders. Within a year or two he had added as many more and with his comparative youth and vigor promised an abundant continuation of the harvest." Decidedly prepossessing with his blond beard and pleasant manners, he was indeed a singular character. "When sober, he was as mild and agreeable a gentleman as one could wish to meet; but when in liquor he was a demon. But, drunk or sober, his instinct was to kill."[33]

Peel proclaimed himself "chief" at Virginia City. The first to challenge that claim was Dick Paddock, a sporting man who, as one newspaper put it, "would rather look down the barrel of a gun than waste wind."[34] Late in September 1863 Paddock provoked a quarrel with Peel in a saloon, and, as recorded by an early Comstock historian, after "a few hard words" between the two, the following exchange took place:

Said Paddock to Peel: "Do you want to take it up?"

"I haven't any objections," replied Peel quietly.

"Very well," said Paddock. "What's your game?"

"Your game is mine," Peel answered amiably.

"Come right outside," said Paddock.

In the street they took positions and opened fire. Paddock missed, but Peel's bullets struck his adversary in the right hand and chest.[35]

An account of the gunfight was telegraphed to newspapers in San Francisco and given wide publicity. It was said that Paddock and Peel "agreed to go out in the street and fight, and neither to make complaint against the other. Nine bullets were discharged, one of which struck Paddock on the right side and passed through his liver, coming out at the back, and another passed through his right wrist, shattering it. The surgeons think the first wound is fatal. The other man was not injured."[36]

As recounted in a later publication, "Farmer Peele [sic], a bad man with a gun . . . , skillfully perforated Dick's exposed edges while the latter was seeking shelter behind an awning post. The farmer was very quick on the draw, could shoot as well drunk as he could sober, and altogether was a man against whom it was well to take precaution."[37]

Despite the severity of his body wound and the doctor's unfavorable prognosis, Dick Paddock survived this encounter and, after acknowledging Peel as "chief" at Washoe, lived on for a few more years before being shot dead by a Virginia City police officer.[38]

Another saloon tough with aspirations of attaining "chief" celebrity was John Dennis, known familiarly in Virginia City as "El Dorado Johnny," who went up against Peel on October 24, 1863.[39] According to one chronicler, Dennis, in order to look his best when facing off against Peel, went into a barbershop and announced: "Fix me up fit. I'm going after a bad man." After getting his hair cut, his whiskers trimmed, and his boots polished, he sought out Peel in his favorite hangout, Pat Lynch's (Lannan's?) Saloon.

"Any 'Chiefs' about?" he called out, loud enough for everyone to hear.

Peel turned from the bar. "You probably intend that remark for me."

"Any one can take it up that likes," Johnny replied.

"Very well, we'll settle it right now," Peel said with a sigh. "Come out into the street."

Johnny walked into the street and wheeled around to fire, but Peel, who had stopped at the doorway, raised his gun and killed him with a single shot.[40]

Nathaniel Langford told it much the same. He said that after sprucing up, El Dorado Johnny walked into Lannan's saloon and asked the proprietor, "Pat, what sort of a corpse do you think I'd make?"

"You don't look much like a corpse now, Johnny," replied Lannan, laughing.

"Well, I'm bound to be a corpse or a gentleman in less than five minutes," replied Johnny, passing on.

When he found Peel he confronted him, "half drawing his pistol," and shouted, "Peel, I'm chief."

"You're a liar," snapped Peel, whipping out his revolver and shooting Dennis dead.[41]

One Virginia City old-timer related a different version, saying that "when Johnny reached the opposite side of the street he squatted and was taking aim with his pistol on his left arm, when Peel, standing in the doorway of the saloon, raised his pistol and fired, shooting Johnny squarely between the eyes and killing him instantly."[42]

All agreed El Dorado Johnny "made as pleasant a looking corpse as the roughs ever turned out to bury."[43]

Nathaniel Langford said that Peel was arrested, tried, and acquitted for the killing of John Dennis,[44] but this appears to be untrue. According to Comstock historian George D. Lyman, many Virginia City folks thought Peel was providing a public service by eliminating some of the saloon riff-raff. Peel, he said, was not punished for the Dennis killing or for "any of the other five which 'El Dorado's' friends forced him to commit soon after. He was not even arrested. The taking off of each one whom he shot or stabbed added to the feeling of general security. Those who were in favor of law felt that Peel was making a greater contribution than any edicts could accomplish. He was 'cleaning house' by getting rid of a class better dead than alive." Lyman added that none of the community's police, including the redoubtable marshal John L. Blackburn, evidenced any desire to meddle with "Chief" Peel.[45]

Another Comstock chronicler related one memorable encounter Peel did have with the law. When his behavior became so outrageous that "a unanimous demand went up for his arrest," the apprehension was accomplished by a number of citizens with some difficulty. Taken before Justice of the Peace Davenport, Peel was given a choice: a fine of $100 or twenty days in the city jail. Peel said he had no money to pay the fine, but if released on his own recognizance, he would raise the amount. Judge Davenport, "a mild man with an excessively long beard, of which he was excessively proud," consented. A half an hour later Peel, "his blue eyes glittering and his blond beard bristling," returned. He was loaded, not with cash, but with a fresh ingestion of alcohol.

"Quick as a flash, Peel seized Davenport's long chin whiskers in both hands and pounded his head against the wall until he was almost dead. Half a dozen officers were in the room, but made no remonstrance. That gun-butt demanded respect." Peel then walked calmly out of the courtroom. He paid no fine and served no time.[46]

On occasion, when in his cups, Peel was prone to this type of brutal and lawless behavior, but for the most part he was considered a mild-mannered, albeit an extremely dangerous, sort. "Peel never hunted a fight; neither did he run away when a fight was offered him," wrote Myron Angel, the first Comstock historian. "He was brave and cool, which made him a dreaded enemy."[47]

James Marber, a Comstock pioneer who knew him well in Virginia City, described Peel as a "cool, polite, carefully speaking, determined man, as thin as a rail and brave as a lion. His thinness was of advantage to him in his shooting matches, for even a good marksman may miss a slim man togged out in loose clothes which hide the outline of his figure." Peel, he said, usually allowed his opponent to fire the first shot before "plugging him before he could fire a second. This may have come from the deliberation with which he aimed, for when the other man missed, as most always he did, Farmer Peale [sic] didn't, and the fight ended with a funeral that wasn't his."[48]

Another historian recounted an encounter Peel had with newspaperman Dan DeQuille of Virginia City's *Territorial Enterprise*. Hearing that Peel had taken umbrage at DeQuille's account of one of his killings and was threatening vengeance, DeQuille sought out the "chief" in his favorite saloon.

DeQuille wasted no time on preliminaries. "I hear you are looking for me," he blurted.

Seeing at a glance that the young reporter was not afraid of him, Peel admitted having been nettled by DeQuille's account of the shooting, but after a second reading found it to be mainly accurate and so had decided he had no grounds for complaint. And there the matter ended.

"Whatever were his failings, and notwithstanding the general belief that bullies are cowards," concluded the writer, "Peel was really a brave man, and in Dan DeQuille he recognized an equal in the only realm of which he had any conception. That episode established Dan's reputation for intrepidity, and won the respect not only of Farmer Peel, but all of his kind."[49]

In addition to his well-known fearlessness, Peel's often-demonstrated sense of fair play contributed to the high regard in which he was held by all classes in Virginia City. A story told James Marber is illustrative of both qualities.

One night Peel was dealing faro when a young teamster from a freighting outfit sat down at his table and, with a phenomenal run of luck, parlayed a $10 stake into $600. Although his case-keeper and lookout grumbled when the fellow asked to cash in his chips, Peel complied with the request, saying, "The young man has a perfect right to quit the game if he sees fit."

After buying a round of drinks for the spectators, the lucky winner left for his camp. But the eagle-eyed Peel noticed that two disreputable-looking characters followed him out. Turning over his faro box to another, Peel also followed.

At a deserted stretch outside town the two ruffians drew revolvers and held up the young man. They were in the act of going through his pockets in search of his winnings when from out of the dark came Peel's voice, ordering them to drop their weapons and hold up their hands. Instead of complying, both fired in the direction of the voice. Peel returned the fire with five shots, and the robbers fell dead.

Marber said he attended an inquest into the death of the two men before a coroner's jury the next day and heard the story as told by Peel and the young man. The jury took only twenty minutes, he said, to render a verdict of justifiable homicide. "Peale [sic] gave the coroner $50 to pay for burying the men, and the proceedings were closed."[50]

Peel left Virginia City in the spring of 1865 to check out gambling opportunities in the new mining districts of Idaho. The editor of the *Gold Hill News*, for one, welcomed his departure: "Langford Peel, alias Farmer, left yesterday for Idaho Territory, where we trust he may avoid the scenes of riot and bloodshed he so freely participated in in Virginia City. We could cheerfully recommend several others to that congenial clime."[51]

Somewhere in his travels Peel teamed up in his gambling operation with an English émigré, appropriately named John Bull. At thirty years of age, Bull was seven years younger than Peel, but already was a veteran of several frontier boom camps and reckoned a clever gambler and dangerous gunman by the sporting fraternity. The two became familiar figures in mining camps throughout the West. Sometime in the spring of 1867 the partners quarreled, apparently over their next move. Bull wanted to transfer operations to Salt Lake City, but Peel, for good reason considering his history, was reluctant to go there. But Bull argued that nine years had passed since Peel had killed Oliver Rucker and barely escaped the wrath of Rucker's friends and the law. Much had happened in Mormon Utah during those years, including a national furor over the infamous Mountain Meadows Massacre of 1857. The killing of Rucker long years before, Bull contended, would certainly be forgotten. He finally managed to convince Peel, and in May 1867 the partners moved into Salt Lake City. But they did not remain long, as the word soon spread through the gambling halls that Helena, Montana, was the hot new camp for the sporting fraternity, so to Helena they went.

They did not travel together, however. Bull, accompanied by a female consort, went first, and before Peel arrived, decamped again for the site of a new mining excitement on Indian Creek. He reportedly even took a job as stagecoach driver there for a while.[52] When Peel showed up in Helena with his mistress, he was surprised and angered to find that his partner was not there.

The name of Bull's mistress has been lost to history, but Langford Peel's inamorata was Belle C. Neil, a slick gambler in her own right. Remembered by Helena pioneers as the handsomest woman to strike the town up to that time, she had no problem picking up a job as faro dealer in John Chase's gambling saloon.

A couple of stories have survived about Peel's gambling activities at Helena. With a reputation as a "square" gambler who abhorred crooked play at the tables, he is said to have stood quietly one night and watched a faro game in which six miners were consistently losing their stakes to a dealer. Finally he stepped forward and asked each player in turn what he had lost to that point. Then, turning to the dealer and dropping his hand to his gun, he ordered him to return that amount to the losers. After the dealer, trembling with fear of the renowned gunman, complied, Peel turned over the faro box, showing exactly how the miners had been cheated with a rigged dealing mechanism.[53]

John McDonald, another man with a gunfighting reputation, had also joined the rush of the sporting crowd from Salt Lake City to Helena. Riding a hot streak at the tables and his poke bulging with gold dust, he walked into the Bank Exchange Saloon one day and traded some of his dust for a large stack of chips. His luck held and his stack was growing when Peel walked up to the faro table and, without asking permission, began pulling chips from McDonald's pile and placing bets on the layout for him. His wagers lost, and quickly McDonald's stack of chips began to shrink.

"Farmer," McDonald said, understandably indignant, "you spoiled my luck."

Spectators scattered, believing bullets were about to fly. But nothing of the sort happened, as McDonald backed off, deciding it was better to lose several hundred dollars than his life.[54]

Since Peel was an honest gambler and could not depend on the certain returns of braced games, he often ran into streaks of bad luck and went busted. When that happened he did not hesitate to demand a loan from other, better fixed members of the gambling fraternity. It was a practice that had precipitated the bloody gunfight with Rucker back in Salt Lake. Now in Helena he employed the same tactics.

The gamblers got together and agreed not to be intimidated by Peel and to form a solid combine to resist his bulldozing. Hearing of this, Peel reacted in typical straightforward fashion. Meeting the proprietor of the biggest gambling establishment in Helena on the street, he demanded an immediate loan of $50. Taken aback by the effrontery, the gambler mumbled something about not carrying that much money on his person. Locking the man's eyes in a cold-stone stare, Peel spoke quietly: "Make that seventy-five dollars."

After staring into those icy blue eyes and reflecting on Peel's reputation as a killer of men for a few tense moments, the gambler withdrew his wallet. With trembling hands he counted out $75 in greenbacks and handed them over. Witnesses to this incident lost no time in spreading the word, and soon it was the main topic of conversation in every saloon and gambling house in Helena. The combine to defy Peel quickly dissolved, and he had no more difficulty borrowing operating capital.[55]

In an article appearing in the *Helena Independent* some fifteen years later the editor called Peel "the most notorious desperado of the mountains [who] had killed some seven or eight men. He could fire at the drop of a hat and hit a dollar [at] ten paces every time. He was consequently cock of the walk in the early days of Helena and no one dared to dispute his supremacy."[56]

He was, said a contemporary Montana paper, "a noted character in this territory and through Utah, Nevada and California, [where he] had the reputation of being one of the coolest and most desperate men in the country. . . . He was a man of many generous impulses, princely in his dealings with his friends and to his enemies implacable. Altogether he was one whom few cared to have any dealings with and he was shunned by his own associates, as such men usually are."[57]

When John Bull finally showed up in Helena, Peel, still fuming over the man's behavior, refused to renew their partnership or even to speak to him. The stage was set for a violent confrontation between the two gamblers, both of whom were recognized as expert gunmen.

The flash point came on the night of July 22, 1867. Bull and a friend named William Knowlden were sitting in the Bank Exchange Saloon when Peel and Belle Neil came in. Walking past them, Peel muttered something to the effect that Bull was "a dirty dog."

Bull immediately leaped to his feet and snapped: "Peel, you don't want to talk to me in that way. I won't stand for it."

"Jump out!" Peel retorted in gunfighter jargon, meaning Bull should go for his gun.

Bull replied: "I haven't got a thing in the world," meaning he was unarmed.

"Go and heel yourself and come back," said Peel, at the same time slapping Bull in the face.

"I'll come soon," Bull promised.

Peel: "Go, and when you come, come a-fighting."[58]

Bull left and went to his rooms, where he wrote letters to his family and friends with instructions for the disposition of his property if he were killed. He carefully loaded his six-shooter and walked back into the night.

Peel waited an hour in the saloon, keeping a watchful eye on the door. When Bull failed to appear, he became convinced that his erstwhile partner, after careful consideration of Peel's awesome reputation, had decided, like many before him, that discretion was the better part of valor and had reneged on his promise to return. Believing the affair was over, Peel left the saloon.

There are several versions of what happened next. The editor of the *Helena Independent* printed one as related to him by John Bull fifteen years later. Offering Belle his arm, Peel walked out the door. Suddenly Bull appeared before them.

"There he is, Langford," Belle cried, instinctively tightening her grip on her companion's arm.

"The desperate men both were quick as lightning. But the woman holding the arm of Peale [*sic*] placed him at a disadvantage, and before he could fire, Bull's unerring bullet had crushed through his brain."[59]

The contemporary press reported that after arming himself, Bull returned to the saloon and met Peel and Belle coming out. Seeing him, "Peel drew his revolver, when Bull immediately fired at him three shots. The first shot went through Peel's heart, the second was in the left side of his neck, and the third entered his cheek, the pistol being held so close that the cheek was burned. Peel fell at the first fire and never fired a shot."[60]

A man named John R. Drew, who claimed to have witnessed the shooting, told it differently. "When they came out on Main Street," he said,

the woman was holding Peel's right arm. They started toward the restaurant and had gone only a little way, when, from behind a pile of dry goods boxes, a shot was fired which struck Peel in the side. He reached for his hip pocket to get his own pistol, but the badly frightened woman held to his arm with an iron grip. Before he could jerk his arm loose, a second shot was fired and Peel fell to the ground. Then Bull stepped from behind the boxes, and standing directly over Peel, fired a bullet into his head. So close was the weapon held that Peel's face was all powder stained.[61]

A circus was playing in town at the time and many residents, including John Xavier ("X") Beidler, the celebrated Montana vigilante and lawman, were in attendance. After seeing the show, Beidler stopped in the John Ming Saloon, where he first learned of the shooting from the bartender, Len Robinson. When Robinson told him John Bull had killed the famous gunfighter Langford Peel, Beidler could not believe it. "I asked him if he was in earnest," he later said, "as Peale [*sic*] was such a rattler that I didn't think he would be killed."[62]

Beidler's difficulty in accepting the fact that Peel had been gunned down was shared by many. Historian Walter R. Curtin, whose father ran a store directly across Helena's Main Street from the site of the shooting, wrote: "Among the old time desperadoes there was a belief that some men have such a tenacity of life that they cannot be killed. This was believed of Peel, which made him so feared, and he believed it himself, which gave him confidence. 'Someone may get me from behind when I'm not looking,' he boasted: 'But I'll get him before I drop.'"[63]

But hard as it was for many to accept, Peel had indeed been shot to death, and John Bull was his killer. Beidler hunted Bull down, arrested him, and locked him up in the county jail. Bull was deathly afraid of a vigilante raid on the jail and a lynching bee. He had good reason to be fearful, for Peel's many friends and admirers in Helena attempted to incite just such a vigilante action, but Beidler and his fellow officers held them off.

Bull was indicted and tried for the killing, but the jury, standing nine for acquittal and three for conviction, was hung, and he was freed. He wasted little time getting out of Helena. He returned once, fifteen years later and, interviewed by the editor of the *Helena Independent*, went over the details of his shooting of Langford Peel, one of the most notable events of the town's early history.[64] Bull then went back to the gamblers' circuit, which he followed throughout his adventurous life. For many years wherever he went he was invariably pointed out by the sporting crowd as the killer of the deadly gunman Langford Peel.[65]

Friends of Peel arranged for his funeral and burial at Helena. The wooden headboard placed over his grave contained a strange inscription:

Grave marker of Langford Peel, Helena, Montana. Courtesy of the Montana Historical Society, Helena.

SACRED

TO THE

MEMORY

OF

LANGFORD PEEL,

BORN IN

LIVERPOOL.

DIED

JULY 23RD 1867

AGED

36 YEARS

IN LIFE BELOVED BY HIS FRIENDS

AND RESPECTED BY HIS ENEMIES.

VENGENCE IS MINE

SAYETH THE LORD.

I KNOW THAT MY REDEEMER LIVETH.

ERECTED BY A FRIEND.

The age and place of birth of the deceased were both in error, and the biblical quotations cited were ambiguous. Curious about the significance of the scriptural quotations, Nathaniel Langford "found that the friend had the idea that, as Peel did not have fair play, the Lord would avenge his death in some signal manner. The other sentence was thought to properly express the idea that the man was living who would redeem Peel's name from whatever obloquy might attach to it, because of his having 'died with his boots on.'" "Could there be a more strange interpretation of the scriptures?" Langford asked.

At some point after the burial, the headboard disappeared, and the location of the grave was lost. After reading about the headboard in Langford's book more than seventy years after Peel's death, historian Curtin, who had been raised in Helena and whose father had known Peel well, determined to try and find the marker and photograph it for posterity. "After prowling around some of the deserted grave yards of the pioneers near Helena without success," he said,

> I remembered that when I was a small boy I had heard of skeletons being plowed out on the site of the new Helena High School. With this clue and the help of Mr. Leslie Jorud of Helena, who took the picture for me, the headboard was located. It had been removed from the grave of Peel by a pioneer citizen of

Helena, W. F. Sanders, who had been the attorney aiding the Vigilantes at Virginia City, Montana, when they cleaned out Sheriff Plummer's band of road agents. The headboard lay in Sanders' attic for thirty or forty years and at his death was sent to the Historical Museum in Helena, where it now is [1943]. It was taken out and set up for the taking of the picture. What was done with the skeleton of Peel and those of the other old timers buried near him no one knows. Junked in some ditch by the contractors and forgotten, probably.[66]

And forgotten today is Langford M. Peel, soldier, Indian fighter, gambler, "chief" of the sporting element in several rough-and-ready western towns, and gunfighting pioneer.

# — 2 —

## CHARLEY HARRISON
### 1833–1863

*Then I commenced shooting at him, but for the smoke I could not tell whether I hit him or not, until just as I was going to shoot for the fourth time, Mr. Hill let go of his pistol and fell, as my pistol went off.*

— Charley Harrison

Dirty, bedraggled, and bone-tired, Charles Harrison and a companion rode double-mounted on an equally begrimed and weary horse into the new mining town of Denver, Kansas Territory, in the fall of 1859. Their arrival probably evoked no particular interest among the inhabitants of the infant town, all recent arrivals themselves, other than a mild curiosity as to why the double-mounting and admiration for the horse they rode, an obviously well-bred bay gelding built for speed. But over the next two years Charley Harrison, a professional gambler and gunfighter, would play an important role in the early history of Denver.

Born in Edgefield County, South Carolina, in 1833, the son of Heartwell and Mary Ann Polly Key Harrison, he was christened Charles Harrison Harrison.[1] As a youth he left the Old South to seek his fortune in the boom camps of the frontier West. Early on he eschewed the back-breaking labor of extracting wealth from the streams and diggings of the mining districts and turned to the green felt tables and gambling for a career. He was generally close-mouthed about his past, and rumors about him soon flew around Denver. It was said that he had come from Utah, that he was a Mormon "Avenging Angel," that he had killed five men and had participated in the Mountain Meadows Massacre.[2]

To friends he made in Denver he admitted that he had come from Utah, but was hardly an "Avenging Angel," as he and his pal and gambling partner, Tom Hunt, had barely escaped with their lives from the wrath of the Mormons. At Salt Lake City, he said, the Mormons had charged Hunt with a heinous crime. A lynching party was in the process of stringing him up when Harrison, astride Border Ruffian, a prize racehorse he had stolen, and leading Hunt's big sorrel, charged into the midst of the mob and whisked their intended victim out from under their noses. The two gamblers galloped off, with the Mormons in hot pursuit.

They rode east toward Denver and, better mounted than the Mormons, managed to lose them in the mountains. But sometime later they were accosted by a gang of bandits, intent on robbing them. In a running gunfight they succeeded in driving off the outlaws, but Hunt's sorrel was wounded and had to be abandoned. Then, double-mounted on Border Ruffian, they went on to Denver.

Harrison related this story to twelve-year-old Eugene H. Teats, a recent arrival from Michigan, who came to idolize the swashbuckling gambler.[3] Eugene was the son of Robert Teats, who worked at the Denver House, where Harrison settled in on his arrival. Several months later the elder Teats would take over management of the combination hotel, restaurant, saloon, and gambling house; enlarge it; and rename it the Elephant Corral. But it was still the Denver House when journalist Albert D. Richardson stopped there in 1859. He described it as "a long low one-story edifice, one hundred and thirty feet for thirty-six, with log walls and windows and roof of white sheeting. In its spacious saloon, the whole width of the building, the earth was well sprinkled to keep down dust. The room was always crowded with swarthy men armed and in rough costumes. The bar sold enormous quantities of cigars and liquors. At half a dozen tables the gamblers were always busy, day and evening." He characterized the gamblers as "entertaining in conversation [with] curious experiences to relate." They "evinced great knowledge of human nature, and were specially kind to each other in misfortune. Some were gentlemanly in manners. Like all men who gain money easily, they were open-handed and charitable."[4]

Charley Harrison was of the latter class of gamblers. Eugene Teats described him as "compactly built, with dark hair and well-kept silky beard," and guessed his age as "about forty years old."[5] Actually, Harrison was only twenty-six, but with his worldly ways, wealth of experience, and prematurely balding head, seemed much older to the young boy. Eugene was impressed by the gambler's generosity: "He would give his last dollar to a friend. Often I would find myself short of funds, and only a hint was sufficient. He would generally ask how little I could get along with. If I said a couple of dollars, it was likely to be twenty."[6]

The boy's eyes widened especially watching Harrison perform with the two pearl-handled cap and ball .45-caliber Colt's revolvers he carried. Eugene said Harrison spent many hours on the banks of the Platte practicing with the guns he called his "pets." The boy would toss a tin can in the air and watch in amazement as Harrison put two or three holes in it before it struck the ground, "and that with either hand, or with both guns at once."[7]

Denver was full of violent men during this early period, and it behooved a man, especially a gambler like Harrison, to be able to defend himself and react with deadly force on a moment's notice. "Denver society was a strange medley," wrote Richardson, composed of

> Mexicans, Indians, half-breeds, trappers, speculators, gamblers, desperadoes, broken-down politicians and honest men. Almost every day was enlivened by a shooting match. While the great gaming saloon was crowded with people, drunken ruffians sometimes fired five or six shots from their revolvers, frightening everybody pell-mell out of the room, but seldom wounding any one. . . . Firing at the bartender was a common amusement among the guests. At first he bore it laughingly, but one day a shot grazed his ear, whereupon, remarking that there was such a thing as carrying a joke too far and that this was "about played out," he buckled on two revolvers and swore he would kill the next man who took aim at him. He was not troubled afterward.[8]

Legend has it that during his two-year stay in Denver, Harrison contributed mightily to the violence in the town, bearing responsibility for four violent deaths, three by his deadly revolvers and one by hanging.[9] Young Teats said he witnessed the first of the shootings:

One morning, some fellow from the gold fields with an over-load of booze pulled his gun and began popping it off in the street. Leaning against the porch posts of the Elephant Corral was the colored cook of the Ford Brothers' gambling saloon. . . . One of the stray bullets found a vital spot in his frame, and he was a cook in our town no longer. . . .

Just then Harrison came walking along. . . . [He] pulled his old reliable, and although he was some distance away, dropped the rowdy from the pony with one shot. Harrison did not even wait to learn what had happened. But that was his disposition. He would walk a long way to avoid trouble, but if he thought he was in the right, no one ever lived who could intimidate him. He feared neither God, man, or devil, was the way his friends put it. He was never known to take advantage of any man, gambling or shooting. Never could anyone get a drop on Harrison if he had an equal or an almost equal show, and never would he shoot without giving his opponent the call, "Pull your iron!"[10]

That Harrison was a gunfighter of nerve, skill, and ability would by amply demonstrated during his two-year residence in Denver, but strangely, his career has been confused by later writers with other gunmen of the same name. In an article written in 1907 W. B. ("Bat") Masterson, a noted gunfighter in his own right and therefore an authority to be respected, wrote of Charley Harrison, "one of the best known sporting men west of the Missouri River," and the most expert man with a pistol he ever saw.[11] Masterson was referring to another gambler-gunman named Charley Harrison who came to the fore two decades later,[12] but in recent years writers, evidently unaware of the two Charley Harrisons, have quoted him, assuming incorrectly that his comments referred to Charley Harrison of Denver.[13]

According to gambling historian Herbert Asbury, another sporting man with gunfighting credentials named Harrison was a contempo-rary of Charley Harrison of Denver. A son of New York City gam-bling house proprietor Jack Harrison, this fellow reportedly went west about 1854 and killed several men in the California mining camps. Driven from San Francisco by the second Vigilance Commit-tee in 1856, he went to Kansas, where he added to his unsavory reputation as a killer:

One day while walking with a friend in Leavenworth he counted on his fingers eleven men he had killed.

"By God!" he cried. "I'll have a jury of my own to try me in Hell!"

For no better reason than that he drew his pistol and shot an old German shoemaker sitting peacefully at work in the open window across the street.[14]

This story sounds suspiciously familiar to one told about Charley Harrison of Denver: "He is said to have carried a pistol with eleven notches filed on one side of the barrel for the number of men he had killed, and three notches on the other for his woman victims, once remarking that 'counting the three women as equal to one man, there would be a competent jury waiting to try him in Hell.'"[15]

Although no doubt apocryphal, the stories are examples of how myths attaching to one legendary figure can easily be transplanted to another.

On July 12, 1860, Harrison was in Cibola Hall, a popular Denver watering hole, conversing with three leading men of the community: postmaster William Park ("Bold Thunder") McClure, probate judge Seymour W. Waggoner, and attorney J. Bright Smith. Sitting at a nearby table engaged in a poker game with Harrison's old partner, Tom Hunt, and several desperate types, known in Denver as "Bummers," was "Professor" Charles Stark. A big, powerful, dark-skinned former slave of apparent African and Mexican antecedents,[16] Stark, after purchasing his freedom, had worked on Mississippi riverboats, owned a barbershop in Omaha, and kept a blacksmith shop in Denver. He had acquired the title "professor" in Denver because of his penchant for elegant clothing.

Stark was losing in the poker game, and he called out to Harrison at the bar: "Hey, Charley, I'd like to sit in a game with you. I know you're honest, but these God damn' fellows are swindlers."

Harrison immediately took umbrage at what he viewed as the black man's impudence. "Who are you to address me as Charley and these gentlemen as swindlers?" he barked.

Angered by this response, Stark leaped to his feet and pulled out a bowie knife. "I'll show you who the hell I am," he growled, advancing on Harrison with knife upraised.

Backing away, the gambler whipped out one of his pearl-handled "pets," fired, and three bullets slammed into Stark, who tumbled to the floor. Bystanders carried the stricken man to a rude cabin, where a doctor ministered to wounds in his thigh, shoulder, and chest. He lingered in critical condition for more than a week before finally expiring on July 21.[17]

Harrison, concerned that there might be negative reaction to his shooting, is said to have ridden out of town and remained at the ranch of a friend for several days until the thing blew over.[18]

Harrison couldn't afford to stay out of Denver long, for at this time he was negotiating with Ed Jump, owner of the Criterion, another well-attended resort, for purchase of the place. Originally called Jump's Hall, after its owner, the Criterion was a two-story, white frame building with accommodations for hotel guests, dining, drinking, dancing, and gambling. With frosted-glass front windows adorned with delicate flower designs, it was considered in roughhewn Denver to be the ultimate in ornate splendor. At the time of the Stark affair Harrison was in the process of having the second floor remodeled into a theater with a seating capacity of 650 and planning to pirate the Converse and Petrie Ethiopian Minstrels from Apollo Hall to entertain his guests on grand opening night, scheduled for August 15, 1860.[19]

Although Harrison and his admiring supporters claimed from the outset that the shooting of Stark had been a plain case of self-defense, William N. Byers, feisty editor of the *Rocky Mountain News*, was doubtful. The death of Stark brought to a head his growing concern about the increasing audacity and violent eruptions of the Bummers in town, and his paper four days later carried a scathing editorial in which he attacked Harrison as the leader of the desperadoes. The shooting of Stark, he charged, was

> wanton and unprovoked; in short, a cold-blooded murder — if called by its right name — scarcely less enormous than the several others that have occurred recently. The man who has shot down an unarmed man, and then repeats his shots while his victim writhes at his feet until the charges of his pistol are exhausted — even if justified in the first act, is unfit to live in, and an unsafe member of a civilized community. . . . Murder is murder, whether committed upon the body of an unknown and unrespected human being, or on the highest citizen of the land.

In another column Byers issued a thinly veiled threat of vigilante action against the Bummers:

The rowdies, ruffians, and bullies generally that infest our city had better be warned in time, and at once desist from their outrages upon our people. Although our community has borne their lawless acts with fortitude very nearly akin to indifference, we believe that forbearance has ceased to be a virtue, and that the very next outrage will call down the vengeance of an outraged people in a wave that will engulf not only the actors, but their aiders, abettors and sympathizers whoever they may be. One more act of violence will at once precipitate the inevitable fate; and the terrors that swept over the fields of California at various times, and first purified its society, will be reenacted here with terrible results to outlaws and villains, or else we are no judge of the determined countenances, compressed lips and flashing eyes that we have so frequently met in the last few days.[20]

Stirred by the strong language in the *News*, angry townsmen began talking of forming a vigilance committee. Unrepentant Bummers, heavily armed, congregated at the Criterion. War seemed eminent.

Cooler heads, led by the thirty-year-old probate court judge Seymour Waggoner and attorney J. Bright Smith, stepped into the breach. Waggoner sought out Charley Harrison and asked for a two-hour respite to see if he could calm the explosive situation. Harrison agreed. A delegation led by Waggoner, Smith, Harrison, and several other well-regarded townsmen, followed by a mixture of curious citizens and saloon toughs, marched to the *News* office and confronted Byers. Judge Waggoner made a strong argument in defense of Harrison, citing eyewitnesses to the Stark shooting—including himself, Smith, and Park McClure—and demanded an apology and public retraction. This, he said, was only fair to Harrison, but, more important, it might prevent a bloody battle in which many lives could be lost. He convinced Byers, who immediately published a handbill entitled "Justice," which he circulated throughout the town. It contained the arguments of Judge Waggoner over his signature and his own apology. Byers said that after conversations with Judge Waggoner and Smith,

Newspaper editor William N. Byers, who owed his life to Charlie Harrison and came to admire him greatly. Courtesy of the Western History Department, Denver Public Library, Denver.

both of whom were in the immediate vicinity at the time of the killing, we learn unmistakably that the first insult was given by Stark and that he was the first to draw arms and make an attack. We had before understood that Stark was unarmed, and such was not the case. He drew a heavy bowie knife . . . and made two or three lunges at Harrison before the latter fired. Stark continued his attack until the knife was knocked from his hand by the pistol of Harrison.

Mr. Harrison [is] anxious to have an investigation before the people's tribunal, and stands ready at any moment to vindicate his cause. We had hoped that such a trial would have been given, but the public seems so well satisfied of the justification of Mr. Harrison, that we presume nothing will be done. We cheerfully make this explanation in justice to Mr. Harrison.

[The explanation of] Judge Waggoner presented quite another complexion to the unfortunate transaction of the 12th inst. We await the result of the investigation instituted today, hoping Mr. Harrison will be acquitted of all blame, and shall, in our next, give a report of the same.[21]

With this mea culpa by Byers the Harrison-Stark affair became a dead issue, but crime and rampant violence continued. In response townsmen organized Denver's first vigilance committee and held the initial meeting on the morning of July 28. They tried a confessed horse thief named Samuel Dunn, convicted him, and imposed a sentence of twenty-five lashes and banishment from the city. Saloon bartender Bill Bates, tried for the murder of Martin Hadley, gained acquittal when he convinced the tribunal the shooting was accidental.[22]

The formation of a vigilance organization troubled the Bummers hanging out in the Criterion a great deal, of course. The vigilante leaders were unknown to them, as membership remained secret, but the Bummers blamed Byers of the *News* for the current crackdown on lawlessness. On July 31 five of them — Carl Woods, William Harvey, John Rooker, James Innes, and George Steele — moved on the editor. They invaded the *News* office, grabbed Byers, and, holding the other newspapermen at bay with drawn guns, hustled him out and on up the street to the Criterion, two blocks away.

Byers knew by the surprised look on Harrison's face that he had no part in this affair. He offered his hand, and the gambler shook it. Byers was in a tough spot, certain that his life could be snuffed out at any moment in that den of cutthroats; his only hope was the help of Charley Harrison, a fellow Mason, who held a degree of power over the ruffians.

Harrison, also aware of the gravity of the situation, acted quickly. Telling the crowd that he wanted to speak to Byers privately, he ushered him through a doorway into the kitchen. There, out of sight of the ruffians, he hurried Byers out a back door and walked briskly with him back to the newspaper office. Byers never doubted, then or later, that Charley Harrison saved his life that day.

When the Bummers learned what their leader had done, the five who had originally seized Byers went on the warpath. They attacked the *News* office, but Byers and his staff drove them off with a hail of bullets. The only casualty was George Steele, who in the exchange of gunfire suffered a minor buckshot wound. As he rode off, Steele was confronted by policeman Tom Pollock, also mounted and carrying a shotgun. Both men raised their weapons to fire, but Pollock, a split second quicker, blasted away most of the desperado's face.[23] With an "entire side of his head blown away and his brain feely exposed," a diarist recorded, Steele survived for several hours before dying.[24]

Carl Woods was collared later, tried by the vigilantes, and banished from Denver. The other three Bummers — Innis, Harvey, and Rooker — fled the town and were not seen in those parts again.

The action taken by Harrison in defying the Bummers and saving the life of Byers greatly enhanced his stature in Denver. Within a short time his Criterion was no longer viewed as a rendezvous of ruffians, and the better element of the town began to patronize his establishment. Despite their opposing convictions with regard to the critical question dividing the nation that summer of 1860 — the Southern-born gambler was a strong adherent of states' rights and an advocate of secession, while the newsman was an equally fervent Unionist — Harrison and Byers maintained a strong bond of friendship.

Denver, with a population split over the national issues of slavery and states' rights, the secession debate became even more divisive following the election of Abraham Lincoln to the presidency in November 1860.

Another hot issue had the attention of residents of the gold fields at the same time. There was a vigorous campaign under way to remove the Pikes Peak region from the western reaches of Kansas Territory and establish a new governmental entity to be called Jefferson Territory. When a provisional legislature for the new territory met in Denver to organize and elect officers, they chose the theater above the Criterion for their meetings. During their frequent breaks in deliberations, when they adjourned to the bar and gambling tables downstairs, delegates found Charley Harrison a most accommodating and convivial host. Jealous of Harrison's windfall, several representatives who had financial interests in saloons and gambling halls in Golden City launched a successful campaign to transfer the deliberations to that community.

A Golden City resident named A. B. Riley, after a number of drinks at the bar of the Criterion, boasted too loudly of his town's victory. He aroused the wrath of Harrison, who had the man thrown out into the street, none too gently.

The next day two of Riley's friends called on Harrison and presented him with a note. "Sir," it read, "I demand from you an apology by the hands of the bearers of this note, or by some other friend whom you may select; for the ungentlemanly manner in which you treated me yesterday, Believing myself to be entirely justified in my course, I do hereby pronounce and post Charles Harrison a liar and a coward." It was signed simply "Riley."

Park McClure, who was with Harrison when he received this challenge, wrote the gambler's dictated response:

Friday, November 23, 1860
Mr. Riley: It is my pleasure to reply in request to the challenge forwarded by your friend to me this very day. As I see no reason for making any public apology in your behalf at this time or any other time for this matter, I accept your challenge on the following terms: Tomorrow, November 24, Saturday morning, at ten o'clock at a point one-half mile south of Warren's ferry along the north bank of the Platte River. Both parties to be armed with heavy duty Navy Colt revolvers and a bowie knife; to be placed only ten paces asunder; to advance and fire until all six shots are exhausted, and if neither has fallen, the bowie knife is to finish the work.

W. P. McClure
For
Charles Harrison.[25]

Hundreds of excited spectators on hand at the appointed spot the next morning to witness the scheduled bloodletting were disappointed. At 9:30 Edward W. ("Ned") Wynkoop, a deputy sheriff and also a bartender in the Criterion, rode up and announced that there would be no duel. "Friends of Mr. Harrison and Mr. Riley," he said, "have at last successfully reconciled the differences between them in a manner satisfactory to both parties. Mr. Riley has publicly proclaimed that he was wholly in the wrong from the beginning and has asked Mr. Harrison to disregard any remarks he may have made."[26]

In his account of the affair editor Byers of the *Rocky Mountain News* added the observation: "It is reported that the Golden City individual failed to put in an appearance, and the matter blew over. We sincerely hope and trust the matter will not be again revived."[27]

The duel "blew over," but there was an aftereffect that resulted in another Harrison shooting.

Many who came to Denver for the express purpose of witnessing the duel drowned their disappointment in drinking sprees that soon developed into drunken brawls. One of these broke out in front of the Elephant Corral, where Harrison and Deputy Sheriff Wynkoop were having their Saturday evening supper. In helping the officer quell the disturbance Harrison had to draw his weapons.

One of the drunks who resented this interference was a rancher named James Hill. An imposing figure of a man, standing over six feet tall and weighing more than two hundred pounds, Hill, in his ankle-length coat trimmed in wolf skins and his shaggy black hair and beard, resembled the proverbial wild man down from the hills. After berating Harrison with shouted threats, Hill withdrew to continue his drunken binge. Harrison merely shrugged and went back to his meal. As a saloonkeeper he had heard a lot of drunken talk and alcoholic warnings, but knew these were generally forgotten after a sobering night's sleep.

But Jim Hill never slept that night. He was still on his monumental two-day toot the next day when he determined in his alcohol-fogged mind to kill Charley Harrison. A man named J. J. Thomas fifty years later recalled that he and a friend named Mitchell ran into Hill on that Sunday afternoon and found him "loaded to the collar with booze," flourishing a six-shooter, and on his way to the Criterion "to take a few shots at Charlie [*sic*] Harrison" because Harrison had killed one of his friends.[28] "We tried to get him to forego his purpose and come with us," said Thomas, "but he wouldn't, so we left him, thinking his talk was all blow anyway, and that he would back down as he met Harrison, for Harrison was a notorious 'gun man,' and quick to shoot at any or no provocation."[29]

But Hill continued on to Harrison's Criterion and started a ruckus with Rocky Thomas, Harrison's bartender, who, because of Hill's obvious inebriation, refused to serve him a drink. Hill flew into a rage. Wynkoop and Harrison, who were both present, tried to calm him, but the man was beyond reason. Pulling a gun, he called the bartender a son of a bitch. That was enough for Harrison, who later explained in detail what happened next:

> On my coming up to Mr. Hill, I told him I did not allow any man to call my barkeeper a sonofabitch, for I kept no such men in my employ. Mr. Hill said if I took his part, I was not better than him, and shoved me off with one hand and raised his pistol in range of my body. I grabbed his pistol and tried all in my power to get it from him, but he tried to get in range [of] me, and I shall always believe when this was done he meant to fire at me. My fingers caught before the trigger and behind the guard of his pistol, and when he let go of it my finger was benumbed, and all the skin rubbed off by the guard. I had no use of my finger for some time. . . .
>
> When I went up to Mr. Hill I had no intention of killing him, nor did such a thought enter my brain for one moment, until I saw he was determined on killing me if he could. Then I commenced shooting at him, but for the smoke I could not tell whether I hit him or not, until just as I was going to shoot for the fourth time, Mr. Hill let go of his pistol and fell, as my pistol went off.[30]

Despite horrendous wounds, Hill lingered for several hours, finally succumbing at three o'clock on the morning of Monday, November 26. A warrant was issued for Harrison's arrest, but, fearing that officers of the People's Court could not protect him from a vengeful mob already forming on the streets, he refused to submit and barricaded himself in the Criterion, surrounded by heavily armed supporters.

A mob bent on hanging Harrison was marching on the Criterion when Sheriff William Middaugh stepped into the breach. With only his young son, Asa, to back him up, he stood atop his carriage and addressed the angry throng. They might storm the saloon and take Harrison, he said, but the gambler and his friends would exact a heavy price, and many in the crowd would die in the attempt. He asked for time to talk to Harrison and convince him to surrender and avoid a certain bloodbath. The crowd accepted Middaugh's logic, and he entered the saloon and conversed with Harrison. The gambler liked and trusted Middaugh, and when the sheriff pledged his own life and that of his son to protect him from the mob, he agreed to surrender. Flanked by the Middaughs, father and son, Harrison walked out through the ranks of the tense and restive crowd.[31]

He remained in jail as a coroner's jury determined that James Hill met his death from a gunshot wound he had inflicted, and a hastily convened grand jury indicted him on a charge of first-degree murder. The next day he was released on $1,000 bail to face trial before the People's Court one week later.[32]

On November 4, 1860, the trial opened before County Judge William M. Slaughter. The chief prosecutor was James E. Dalliba, who had never lost a case. Representing Harrison was a battery of legal talent, including two judges, Hiram P. Bennett and George W. Purkins. Hamilton R. Hunt, a real estate broker and rancher as well as an attorney, and J. Bright Smith, "a tall and handsome man of polished manners and splendid voice," rounded out the defense team.[33]

Major witnesses for the prosecution were Frederick J. Stanton and Henry P. A. Smith, eyewitnesses to the shooting, who testified that Hill had no pistol in his hand when he went down under Harrison's fire. Cyrus H. McLaughlin and John Cavell said they had seen Hill draw his pistol on Wynkoop, but he had then holstered it before the confrontation with Harrison.

Other witnesses to the shooting called by the defense gave completely contradictory testimony. Deputy Sheriff Wynkoop said he "saw Hill reaching for his pistol, then Harrison drew his and advanced, commencing to fire. Hill fell from the second shot. Four shots were fired. I seized Harrison's arms and his pistol fell to the floor." Rocky Thomas said Hill reached for his gun and Harrison grabbed his hand. James D. Rice said Harrison "thrust out his hand, seized Hill's hand and commenced firing. I could see the deceased's right hand across his chest, and in that hand a gun. . . . I was about fifteen feet from the parties, but after the shooting started, the smoke from the discharged pistol was so thick it immediately obscured my vision. Right after that I ran out the back door." Bill Greer said, "Harrison then caught Hill by the hand in which was a pistol, and shot him. . . . Hill had a pistol in his hand. I think he had it in his hand all the time from the first trouble with the barkeeper Thomas." Dr. A. F. Peck, who ministered to Hill, and C. A. Cromwell and Chat Dubray testified that they heard the dying man admit he had drawn a gun first. Other witnesses—A. S. Blair, Charles Buford, and Ed Higgins—testified to having heard Hill threaten Harrison's life earlier in the day during his tour of the town's saloons. Harrison took the stand in his own defense and repeated the story he had told many times before.

Significantly, J. J. Thomas and his friend Mitchell, who had heard Hill declare that he was going to the Criterion that Sunday afternoon to kill Harrison, were never called by the defense. "Mitchell and I were in the court room every day," Thomas said. "Our evidence would have cleared Harrison if we had chosen to give it, for Hill had been the aggressor and had gone out to kill Harrison, and we knew Harrison had shot in self defense. But we kept mum and said nothing, for we wanted to see Harrison hang. [He] richly deserved to swing."[34]

After deliberating fourteen hours the jury reported that they stood ten to two for acquittal but were hopelessly deadlocked. Prosecutor Dalliba, perhaps with a thought to preservation of his perfect record, moved to drop the case; the judge agreed, and Harrison walked free.[35]

The case was closed, but immediately wild stories and rumors swept Denver. Harrison's paramour, bagnio madam Ada Lamont,[36] it was said, had shelled out $5,000 to members of the jury to ensure an acquittal.[37] Another story circulated by the famous newspaperman Horace Greeley had it that after dark the jurors dangled a rope from the window of the jury room to friends below and hauled up a basket filled with bottles of whiskey. This led to drunken fights between the jurymen and made agreement on a unanimous verdict impossible.[38] J. J. Thomas, the man who had heard James Hill say he was going to kill Harrison but never gave that testimony, said he and his friend Mitchell personally witnessed the passing of the booze-filled basket to the jurors.[39]

Byers of the *Rocky Mountain News*, commenting editorially on the trial and its outcome, said the case had been most remarkable and singular, with eyewitness testimony so contradictory. "No two sets of eyes saw alike," noted Byers, but enough men were present to disarm and prevent one drunken man from doing harm. It would seem from Harrison's remarks that he did not consider his life threatened, but simply reacted with fatal consequences against a patron calling his employee a "sonofabitch." "If that is sufficient provocation to justify the taking of human life," Byers opined, "it is time for the people of Denver to know it. Let every citizen realize how cheaply life is held."[40]

The next edition of the paper carried Harrison's "card" in which he again recounted his version of the events on the night of November 25: how he had been insulted by Hill, who pulled a gun; how he grabbed the weapon and "benumbed" his finger in preventing its use; and how he finally had to shoot the man bent on killing him.[41]

Harrison's public statement may not have convinced others of his innocence, but it apparently had an effect on Byers, who suddenly seemed to remember the debt he owed Harrison for saving his life the previous July. In an introduction to Harrison's "card," he said he published it "most cheerfully," adding that if the public agreed that Harrison acted only in self-defense, he, as editor, "would be most pleased to announce such a gratifying state of public sentiment. It would enable us to discharge an obligation we owe Mr. Harrison for a service rendered us on a former occasion in a more acceptable way than by any other method. But we owe a duty to the public as well, and it was in the discharge of this duty that we made our comments of yesterday. No injustice was intended towards Mr. Harrison; and we are gratified with the assurance that he did not so regard it."[42]

As the Christmas season approached, any differences between the editor and the gambler seemed to have completely resolved. Byers noted in his paper: "One of the most elegant as well as acceptable holiday presents we have been favored with was presented to us this afternoon by Charles Harrison . . . , a huge cake, ornamented in the highest style of the confectionary art . . . and a copious supply of splendid old cognac to 'wash it down.' "[43]

As a token of his friendship, Harrison would later present Byers with a handsome ring of gold, emblazoned with the Masonic emblem.

The editor always counted it as one of his most cherished possessions and wore it the rest of his life.[44]

One of the reasons for Byers's change in attitude toward Harrison was the major role played by the gambler in the solution of the mysterious murder of Thomas Freeman, a fellow Masonic Lodge member. When Freeman disappeared and his blood-stained wagon was found, Pat Waters, a man known to have been in the missing man's company, was suspected of murdering Freeman and hiding his body. Under questioning Waters adamantly denied the allegation. At a meeting of Masons held in the Criterion, a resolution was adopted:

> Whereas, it was reported that Mr. Freeman, a member of our fraternity, has been murdered some thirty miles from this place, and his body thrown into the river, buried, or otherwise disposed of, and,
> Whereas, a man by the name of Patrick Waters has been apprehended and arrested under suspicion of being in some way connected with the murder of our brother; Therefore — Resolved, that this meeting appoint a committee of five to ascertain how the body of our deceased brother was disposed of for the purpose of finding and bringing it to this city for decent interment.[45]

Named to the five-man committee were John Wanless, William Byers, Ned Wynkoop, C. W. Pollard, and John J. Thomas. Eight others, including Charley Harrison, who had earlier initiated a fund drive to apprehend Freeman's killer, volunteered their assistance. Byers and Harrison rode together in the wagon that also contained the suspect, Pat Waters.

At the location where Freeman's wagon was found Harrison forcefully interrogated Waters, who remained unwavering in his denial of any knowledge of the murder. Finally, Harrison threw a rope over a tree limb and dropped a noose around the suspect's neck. Under the threat of lynching Waters broke down and led the party to where he had hidden Freeman's body.

The Masons returned to Denver with the prisoner and the body. Waters was held in a room above the Criterion and provided for at Harrison's expense while the lodge members attended to the funeral and burial of their brother. Then they turned their attention to the trial of the accused murderer.

Charley Harrison interviewed the prisoner in private and managed to secure a complete confession. Waters was tried, convicted, sentenced to death, and summarily executed on December 21.[46]

The Waters case seems to be the basis for the story that Harrison hanged a man in Denver. According to this mythical tale, because Freeman was a fellow Mason and his accused killer was a Catholic, Harrison, at the head of a vigilance committee composed of gamblers, conducted the investigation, trial, and execution of Waters. The judge and jury, all "gentlemen of the cloth," found him guilty and sentenced him to hang. Harrison was given responsibility for the execution, so went the story, and he arranged for a nine-foot drop, "almost sufficient to separate the man's head from his body, but instead of the head coming off, the neck stretched until it was fully eighteen inches long" — the most gruesome sight he ever beheld, according to the young Asa Middaugh.[47]

Actually, Pat Waters was the first man formally indicted in the history of Jefferson Territory, and his trial was conducted in People's Court with due decorum and respect for law. A notice in the *Rocky Mountain News* of December 18 called all citizens to be present at a special meeting to be held in front of the Criterion the next morning "to take measures regarding the trial of Patrick Waters." There a temporary court was organized with Colonel William Person as presiding judge and E. H. Hart and General F. J. Marshall, the former governor of Kansas, as associates. Ned Wynkoop was appointed city marshal to summon a jury panel. General L. L. Bowen prosecuted, and C. C. Carpenter and C. P. Hall conducted the defense. All these men were prominent in the town's business circles and would have been appalled to have been categorized as gamblers. Charley Harrison testified but played no other part in the proceedings.[48]

The execution, under the direction of City Marshal Wynkoop and his deputy, W. T. Shortridge, was performed shortly after three o'clock on the afternoon of December 21 on a scaffold specially constructed on the west side of the South Platte River. Waters would be the last man hanged by the People's Court.[49]

Despite Byers's observation that the trial "would have been highly credible to the highest legal tribunal in the States," the story that the

Criterion gamblers had orchestrated the entire affair and that Harrison had personally hanged a man persisted.[50]

In May 1861 Harrison was at the center of another exciting event in Denver's early history. At a big celebration to welcome William Gilpin, first governor of newly created Colorado Territory, the main feature was to be a race between two prize racehorses of the region, Border Ruffian and Rocky Mountain Chief. Harrison, who had arranged and promoted the race, solicited donations in gold for a winner's purse, which he then took to the Clark and Gruber mint and had melted down into a nugget valued at $95,000.

On May 29, the day of the race, a huge crowd congregated at a rude track built just for the event. It was estimated that fully 70 percent of the entire population of the Pikes Peak region came to see the great race. Border Ruffian, the fine mount that had saved Charley Harrison and Tom Hunt from the Utah Mormons back in 1859, was now the property of veteran gambler Colonel A. B. Miller. His rider in the race was Jim McNassar, son of James McNassar, another sporting man. Bill Greer, a St. Joseph, Missouri, gambler, owned Rocky Mountain Chief and had hired Tom Hunt as the Chief's trainer. Eugene Teats, idolizer of Harrison, was to ride the animal.

Three heats of one mile each were to be run, with the $95,000 gold nugget going to the winner of two of the heats. Side bets abounded, of course, and an estimated $100,000 was wagered on the first heat alone.

Charley Harrison's judgment of horseflesh and his gambling instincts overcame any affection he may have felt for Border Ruffian; his money was on Rocky Mountain Chief. Tom Hunt, on the other hand, although employed as the official trainer of the Chief, secretly bet a wad on Border Ruffian, as he could not forget that he and Harrison owed their lives to the gallant steed.

When the gun sounded to start the first heat, Hunt held on to the Chief's bridle for an instant, long enough for Border Ruffian to take a lead that he never relinquished. Backers of the Chief protested loudly, and there were calls for Hunt's immediate lynching, but in the end he was banished from the field and told to get out of town before nightfall.

Odds against Rocky Mountain Chief winning the last two heats and capturing the gold nugget ran as high as twenty to one. Charley

Harrison, taking all those bets he could find, told young Teats he was depending on him to boot the Chief home in front, and not to spare the whip.

At the halfway point of the second heat the horses were neck and neck, and Teats had not gone to the whip. Harrison leaped on a horse and galloped to the final turn, where the racers, still side by side, were starting into the final stretch run. Pulling alongside young Teats, Harrison leveled a gun at the young rider. "Whip that horse, boy," he ordered, "or I'll fill you full of lead."

The youngster needed no further urging. His whip flashed, and the Chief surged forward. A desperate Jim McNassar also used his whip, striking the opposing jockey across the face, but Teats held on, and Rocky Mountain Chief drove home in front.

Now the Ruffian's backers set up a howl, claiming Harrison had interfered, and all bets should be canceled. The judges, guarded by two burly prizefighters, conferred and announced their decision: Harrison's actions had not affected the outcome and, anyway, McNassar had fouled Teats. They declared Chief the victor in the second heat.

Fistfights erupted in the crowd, and the judges hunted cover. But as calm was restored and preparations made for the final heat, Colonel Miller, still fuming over the turn of events, removed Border Ruffian from the track and refused to let him run. Eugene Teats raced Rocky Mountain Chief alone around the oval, and Bill Greer was awarded the $95,000 golden nugget.

That night Greer and Harrison celebrated together in the Criterion. Late in the evening they sat down together and engaged in a game of high-stakes poker. By the next morning Charley Harrison was the owner of the $95,000 nugget as well as most of the money wagered on the day of the great race.[51]

The day marked the acme of Charley Harrison's Denver period. Momentous events were happening in the East that would dramatically change the course of his life. The clash between the Northern and Southern states, long simmering, had finally erupted in violence. "MOST EXCITING NEWS!" read the headline of the *Rocky Mountain News* on April 18, 1861. "COMMENCEMENT OF HOSTILITIES! BATTERIES OPEN ON SUMTER!"

On the morning of April 24 the Confederate flag appeared atop Wallingford & Murphy's general store, next door to the Criterion. Both establishments were known hangouts of Southern sympathizers. The flag's appearance almost set off an armed conflict between Union loyalists and secessionists, led by Charley Harrison, postmaster Park McClure, and Mayor John C. Moore. Only a last-minute compromise, permitting the flag to be flown until sunset and then taken down, never to be raised again, prevented bloodshed.

Throughout that spring and summer skirmishes broke out between the two factions. The arrival on August 21 of a company of First Colorado Volunteers, recruited in the outlying mining camps, only aggravated the tense situation. The militiamen were billeted in a building directly behind the Criterion, within shouting (or shooting) distance of the Rebel headquarters. On that very first night some of them got into a ruckus with a few "sesesh" in Ada Lamont's bordello and manhandled them severely. Seeking revenge, a group from the Criterion beat up the sentry guarding the militia barracks. The man would later claim that his attackers were led by Charley Harrison and John Cody, uncle of the yet-to-be-famous William F. ("Buffalo Bill") Cody. U.S. Marshal Copeland Townsend, newly appointed for Colorado Territory, had Harrison and Cody arrested. They were released on bond at a hearing the next day.

Tensions mounted, and on the night of August 24 there was an explosion. When a bunch of militiamen crowded into the Criterion, Harrison denied them service and ordered them out. They refused to leave, a squad of bouncers moved in to enforce the ejection, and a donnybrook erupted. Before it was over, the Criterion was a shambles, and Charley Harrison was livid. The word went out that he sought vengeance.

Shortly after midnight gunmen in the Criterion opened a barrage into the nearby barracks, wounding two militiamen. Other soldiers grabbed rifles and began pumping lead into the windows of the Criterion. A bugler blew "assembly," and the entire company fell out and quickly surrounded the saloon. They wheeled a cannon into position in front of the entrance, loaded it, and waited for orders to fire.

Following two hours of negotiations, Harrison submitted to arrest by civil authorities. Officers led him and several of his followers in shackles from the Criterion and held them for trial on charges of complicity in rebellion. Harrison's lawyer, J. Bright Smith, petitioned for his release on a writ of habeas corpus, but the request was denied on the grounds that traitors and rebels were not entitled to the privilege. Hearing this, the gambler's supporters grew more vociferous in their demand for his release, even threatening to march en masse to the jail and release him by force. A rumor spread that secessionist sympathizers from outlying settlements were preparing to converge on Denver, join forces with the Criterion gang, free Harrison and his fellow prisoners, pillage the banks and business houses, and then burn the town to the ground. Panic set in. Military guards patrolling the streets were doubled, and another company of volunteers from outlying districts began a forced march to protect the city.

Struck with fear that their decision to hold Harrison would lead to the destruction of their community, the civil authorities, claiming a lack of adequate jail facilities, reversed their earlier ruling and agreed to a habeas corpus hearing. After a brief meeting with Commissioner William Larimer, Harrison and his cohorts were freed on bonds of $1,000 each, pending trial before Benjamin F. Hall, chief justice of Colorado.

The trial, beginning on September 3, lasted two weeks. The prosecution, led by Colorado Attorney General James E. Dalliba, well aware of the heated atmosphere prevailing, realized that the conviction and imprisonment of Harrison on a charge of complicity in rebellion might lead to a violent uprising and widespread bloodshed. Reducing the charge to the lesser crime of obstructing proper officers of government, he gained a conviction. Harrison's sentence, as imposed by Judge Hall, was a $5,000 fine, a mandatory oath of allegiance to the United States, and banishment from the territory of Colorado for the remainder of his life. The judge gave Harrison two days to wind up his affairs and warned that if he were found in Denver after sundown on September 19, he was subject to arrest, imprisonment, and summary sentencing.

Harrison paid his fine and took the oath of allegiance on September 17. By the 19th he had sold the Criterion to the firm of Rice and Lewis and boarded an eastbound stagecoach, never to see Denver again.[52]

But he was destined to make one spectacular effort to return, an effort that would cost him his life.

The forced oath he had taken obviously meant nothing to him, for his objective in traveling east was to meet with leaders of the Confederacy and offer his services to the Rebel military. A commission was not long in coming; only two months later, on November 20, 1861, the *Daily Times* of Leavenworth, Kansas, noted his arrival in that community: "Charles Harrison, of Denver notoriety, is in town and rejoicing in the title of Captain Charles Harrison." The title was not an honorary one, but an actual military rank, as Harrison was now an officer in the Confederate army, commanding Company A of Colonel Emmett MacDonald's Fourth Missouri Cavalry. Not explained was what business a Confederate captain had in Leavenworth, Kansas, a Yankee stronghold.

Harrison had a distinguished military career, and his superior officer, Colonel MacDonald, commended him on several occasions for his fine leadership. Harrison's company fought at Cane Hill, Arkansas, on November 28, 1862, a battle in which the Confederates bested a larger force of bluecoats. "During the entire engagement Companies A and B fought nobly," reported MacDonald. "No company of officers and men ever fought better. Capt. Harrison . . . and the lieutenants in both companies deserved much praise."[53]

Harrison also distinguished himself about a month later at the battles of Reed's Mountain on December 4–6 and Prairie Grove, Arkansas, on December 7, when McDonald's cavalrymen captured forty supply wagons, two hundred horses, and 450 stands of arms. They took some two hundred prisoners, including a Union major, and helped rescue Confederate Colonel Joseph O. Shelby and his battery of light artillery, captured earlier by the Union army.[54]

Promoted to the rank of lieutenant colonel on January 6, 1863, Harrison was second in command to MacDonald when, with a force of less than two hundred men, the unit surprised and burned Fort Lawrence on Beaver Creek in Missouri, killing ten, capturing seventeen, and routing about 250. The Confederates captured two hundred horses, three hundred stands of arms, ten supply wagons, and a quantity of quartermaster and commissary stores. MacDonald's cavalry supported General John S. Marmaduke in the eight-hour Confederate attack on Springfield, Missouri, and later captured the fortified town of Marshfield and burned a Union fort at Hartville. In the fighting at Hartville MacDonald was killed and Harrison became a full colonel and assumed command of the regiment.

In February 1863 Harrison organized the six hundred cavalrymen of the Fourth Missouri into bands of sixty to eighty men each and for three months waged a guerrilla war against the five-thousand-man Federal army in southern Kansas, Missouri, Arkansas, and Indian Territory.

A report written on April 23, 1863, by T. T. Crittenden, then a Union lieutenant colonel of cavalry and later governor of Missouri, described an exchange of prisoners during which Harrison was almost killed:

> A few days since two of my best soldiers were captured by a gang of guerillas and taken to the camp of one Colonel Harrison (formerly lieutenant colonel of MacDonald's regiment, now its colonel) from whom I received a note stating that he had these men and would hold them until two of his men were released from the guard house in Springfield. From my previous knowledge of Colonel Harrison I believed I could affect [sic] the release of my soldiers and learn some other things that would be of importance to me at this place and the Government. I sent out a flag of truce to him. . . . My men arrived safely, but Col. Harrison was fired upon while under his flag . . . , his horse was shot under him. . . . Colonel Harrison seems to be in command of all the squads, bands and gangs abroad in the country.[55]

In May Harrison led successful attacks on Yankee strongholds in the vicinity of Sherwood, Missouri. Reportedly killed in one action, he survived.[56]

He then unveiled a plan for military action that, if successfully carried out, would achieve two goals he fervently desired — an important victory for the South and a devastating blow of vengeance against Denver, the town that had banished him. He proposed to lead a small force of Confederate officers into the Pikes Peak region, enlist the many secessionists he knew to be there, and create a fighting force to attack and loot Denver. In addition to arms, ammunition, horses, and wagons, all badly needed by the Confederate army, he knew Denver hoarded a commodity the South needed most: gold. He convinced his superiors that since very few Union forces stood between Missouri and the Colorado gold fields, the fighting unit he proposed to lead could cross the plains of Kansas unopposed and undetected.

In early May his plan was approved, and he set about enlisting those officers he wanted to accompany him. One of the first was Park McClure, who had left Denver with him and was now a Rebel captain. Other volunteers included Colonel Warner Lewis, nephew of the famous Meriwether Lewis; a full colonel, B. H. Woodson; a lieutenant colonel; one major; three captains besides McClure; and eleven lieutenants, for a total of twenty officers. On the morning of May 14, 1863, Harrison led his party of raiders out of camp and turned toward Denver, five hundred miles to the west. He was proudly leading his little force in what would be one of the boldest, most audacious attacks of the Civil War.

Harrison in his planning had failed to reckon with the Osage, who, having been driven from their homes in Texas and Arkansas by Confederates, were now roaming the Kansas prairie. Like most of the plains Indians, the Osage had no interest in the outcome of the Civil War, but harbored deep hatred for the men in gray for deposing them. On May 17 a hunting party of Osage under Chief Little Bear came on Harrison's force at Lightning Creek, a tributary of the Verdigris River in southeastern Kansas. Little Bear demanded to know who these men were and what was their mission. Harrison's efforts to convince the Indians that they were a Union scouting party met scornful disbelief. One of the whites panicked and fired on the Osage, killing one. The Indians rode off, but soon returned with large reinforcements. More than two hundred strong, they swooped down on the twenty Confederates.[57]

William L. Bartles, a trooper with a unit of the Ninth Kansas Cavalry investigating the scene some days later, described what had happened as disclosed by the evidence remaining:

> They struck the party of white men about five miles from a loop in the Verdigris River. Over that entire five miles there was a running fight. The little party of whites, hemmed in on all sides by the circle of death, were striving to beat off the Indians and reach the timber they could see in the distance. In this running fight the Confederates . . . lost two men. . . . Being well armed and in the open, they were able to keep the Osages at some

distance, and killed at least one. [Reaching the timber], they retreated, contesting every foot of ground. The odds were too great, and they found themselves forced to the bank of the river and out onto a sand-bar at the water's edge, under a terrible fusillade from the Osages, now concealed and protected by the timber. . . . To the last cartridge they held their enemy at bay, and when they had been fired the survivors stood in a little group, their dead around them, and met the rush of the Indians with clubbed carbines and revolvers, and fell one upon the other. It was brave blood that reddened the little sand-bar in the Verdigris that day.[58]

The bodies of the Confederate officers lay where they had fallen. Many were stripped of their clothing; all had been defiled and mutilated. Heads had been severed, as was the Osage custom, kicked far from the bodies, and the scalps taken. Harrison had been one of the first to go down in the initial attack. It appeared he had been first struck by a bullet and then pierced by an Osage lance. His balding head had not provided sufficient hair for the scalping knife of the Osage brave who counted coup on him, so Harrison's luxuriant black beard provided the trophy. The beard-scalp was later seen hanging from a lance in an Osage village.

Eighteen of the twenty officers were killed in the battle; only Colonel Warner Lewis and Lieutenant John Rafferty escaped. Hiding in the river thickets by day and traveling by foot at night, they worked their way back eastward. Three days later, after nearly eighty tortuous miles, they reached the safety of Missouri and told their story.[59]

So ended the dramatic, violent career of Charles Harrison, gambler, soldier, and deadly gunfighter.

# — 3 —

# WHISPERING SMITH
## 1838–1914

*A gunfighter of recognized standing in the fraternity and who, despite his fifty-seven years spent on the plains and in the mountains, is able to pick off the pennies at fifty yards.*

— *Denver Times*, February 7, 1905

Jim ("Whispering") Smith was one of those rare individuals whose fictional persona has overwhelmed and almost completely obliterated the memory of his actual life. When novelist Frank Spearman latched on to his catchy nickname and wrote a popular novel in 1906 extolling the frontier feats of a railroad detective called "Whispering" Smith, the adventures of this fictional character were picked up and exploited by other media, most notably in a 1948 motion picture entitled *Whispering Smith*, starring Alan Ladd. The name became firmly implanted in the public memory, but the actual story of the Wild West gunfighter whose sobriquet gave birth to the myth has been ignored by writers and virtually forgotten today.[1]

And yet according to contemporary newspaper reports and the testimony of old-timers, the man called "Whispering" Smith was a gunfighter of exceptional ability and figured prominently in bringing the rule of law to the Old West. A 1905 article in the *Denver Times* said he was "a gunfighter of recognized standing in the fraternity," whose six-shooters carried "many notches." After fifty-seven years on the frontier, he could still "pick off the pennies at fifty yards."[2] He was, said the *Rocky Mountain News,* "one of the most famous gunfighters [whose] fame as a sleuth and dead shot spread over the country."[3]

Edgar Beecher Bronson, who claimed to know Smith well, praised him as "one of the best peace-officers the frontier ever knew [who] wrote more red history with his pistol than any two men of his time. . . . He had enough dead outlaws to his credit—thirty-odd—to start . . . a fair-sized graveyard." A glance from his "great burning black eyes, glowering deadly menace from cavernous sockets of extraordinary depth," was enough to "still the heart-beat and paralyze the pistol hand." Bronson could not remember seeing Smith's thin-lipped mouth clamped between a tightly curled mustache and a stiff black imperial relaxed in a smile. Wide-shouldered and deep-chested, Smith was pantherlike in his movements. "The very incarnation of a relentless, inexorable, indomitable, avenging Nemesis," he was the most fearsome-looking man Bronson ever saw.[4]

As a professional gunman, Smith paid special attention to his lethal hardware. Bronson said Smith carried a full-length .45 in a breast scabbard and another with a cutoff barrel in a deep pocket of his sack coat. "He loved those guns I know, for often have I seen him fondle them as tenderly as a mother her first-born."[5]

The breast scabbard was "constructed so that a small, leather-covered piano wire fitted into the muzzle of the revolver, with a hand-spring circling the cylinder. When wanted, the gun would fairly leap into the hand." General Z. R. Bliss received it as a gift from his lifelong friend, " 'Whispering Smith' who had designed it and carried it for many years for the Santa Fe Railroad and who was rated one of the fastest gunmen of the early west."[6]

One of the major obstacles in the effort to trace the man's early history is his name; there were simply too many James Smiths around. Prolific western researcher and writer Ed Bartholomew in his book *Western Hard-Cases, or Gunfighters Named Smith* gave only a paragraph to the man under consideration here, but summarized the careers of five others named James Smith, including one James W. "Six-Shooter" Smith, who got twelve pages.[7]

James Louis ("Whispering") Smith was born in Maryland about 1838, the fifth child of Joseph and Lydia Smith.[8] Nothing is known of his childhood, and mystery surrounds his early adult years as reports of his activity conflict.

Jim Whispering Smith as sketched by a newspaper artist. *Denver Times*, February 7, 1905.

Although documentation is lacking, he reportedly served in the Union army during the Civil War and rose to the rank of captain.[9]

According to a newspaper report many years later, Smith had achieved some notoriety as a pistol-wielder even before the war. He was said to have engaged in a duel with an Australian gambler named Larry Boyle aboard the *Belle of Memphis*, a steamboat on the Mississippi.[10] Although unconfirmed with solid documentation, there may be some validity to this story, for it is consistent with other evidence that Smith was active on the Mississippi River during and after the Civil War. On October 8, 1862, one James L. Smith was appointed acting second engineer on the USS *Baron DeKalb*, an ironclad riverboat of the Mississippi Squadron, and later served on the USS *Rattler* as first assistant engineer until resigning his commission effective May 31, 1864.[11] If this was the man who would later become "Whispering" Smith, he could hardly have served in the Union army and risen to the rank of captain.

James Louis Smith, the man who would achieve a level of fame in the West as an intrepid lawman, slick with a gun, first pinned on a badge in New Orleans. He joined that city's Metropolitan Police Department shortly after its establishment in 1868. Promoted up through the ranks, by 1873 he was a detective on the force.[12] On St. Valentine's Day of that same year he married twenty-year-old Irish-born Anna Mannion. One of the witnesses to the ceremony was Smith's close friend and fellow detective, Thomas Devereaux.[13]

In 1874 Detectives Smith and Devereaux were involved in a shooting with burglar suspects. Munson Alexander, an escaped convict, and his brother Benjamin had teamed with James Bowman in a burglary gang. On May 21 Smith and Devereaux traced the Alexander brothers to a house at Seventh and Carondelet streets. When they entered, a gunfight broke out. Benjamin quickly surrendered to the officers, but Munson, although struck by three bullets, managed to escape.[14]

Two days later Smith and Devereaux, armed with double-barreled shotguns loaded with buckshot, staked out a house where they believed Munson Alexander was hiding. When Alexander appeared at three in the morning, according to their later testimony, they called on him to surrender, but he pulled a pistol and ran. Smith said he fired in the air, but Devereaux admitted unloading both barrels of his shotgun at the suspect, who fell dead. At a coroner's inquest Dr. C. P.

Ames determined that of the thirteen buckshot wounds in Alexander's body, ten were in the back. The body of the deceased also had three wounds from revolver bullets, received during the previous encounter with the officers. The coroner adjudged the shooting justifiable, released the body to relatives, and the matter appeared closed.[15]

Soon after this incident Smith received another promotion; he was made warden of the New Orleans Work House.[16]

Some folks in New Orleans expressed dissatisfaction with the resolution of the Alexander shooting. For eighteen months rumors circulated through the city that Smith and Devereaux had murdered the man in cold blood. Some claimed to have heard Smith brag around town that he was the one who had actually killed Alexander, while others insisted that Devereaux was the killer but had implicated his partner to extricate himself from a charge of wanton murder. Many were convinced there had been a grand conspiracy on the part of the metropolitan police to hide the true facts of the case from the public. Finally, on November 13, 1875, a hearing into the affair was held in Municipal Police Court. After a magistrate heard highly contradictory testimony given by some thirty witnesses, he bound Smith and Devereaux over to await action by a grand jury, but permitted their release on bail. The following January a grand jury failed to bring in a true bill against the defendants, and all charges against them were dropped.[17]

Perhaps the entire Alexander shooting affair and what he perceived as treachery by his best friend and fellow officer soured Jim Smith on the Crescent City. In any event, very shortly after his exoneration by the grand jury in January 1876, he and his wife left New Orleans and the Southland, and headed for the West.

Later that year they were settled in Omaha, Nebraska, where Smith was employed by the detective bureau of the Union Pacific Railroad, while Anna took in washing to augment the family income.[18]

"No company's police have a more distinguished past than the Union Pacific's," notes a student of law enforcement in the West. "Single guards and detectives certainly served the railroad when its first tracks reached out from Nebraska to Utah; Pinkerton men were regularly employed as police into the 1870s. By 1880 divisions along the line maintained undercover operatives and investigators such as M. F. Leech [Leach], N. K. Boswell, and James Smith.

Times were dangerous, stakes high, and the railroad policemen often worked alone."[19]

As pointed out by another writer: "If historians have slighted the work of the nineteenth century railroad police, so did writers of the time. Contemporary newspapers, for example, mentioned the railroad detectives inconspicuously, never with headlines." Notable members of the class were five special agents of the Union Pacific: N. K. Boswell, James L. Smith, George Eisley, W. C. Lykens, and M. F. Leach (or Leech).[20]

By early 1878 the Union Pacific had assigned Smith duty in Cheyenne, Wyoming, where, as was the practice with railroad detectives, he secured local law enforcement authority by obtaining appointment as a "special policeman."[21] Acting in this capacity he collared a man named Robert Johnson in February 1879 and locked him up on a charge of public drunkenness and creating a disturbance. After sobering up, Johnson accused Smith of taking several dollars from him during the arrest. No formal charge was filed, but Cheyenne mayor Lawrence R. Bresnahan thought the allegation against one of his officers sufficiently serious to warrant an internal investigation. When a witness, a *Cheyenne Daily Leader* editor named J. G. Mills, corroborated Johnson's story, the mayor revoked Smith's police authority. Union Pacific officials, embarrassed by the affair, transferred Smith to Sidney, Nebraska. He left, carrying bitter feelings against newspaperman Mills and a determination to get even. Several months would pass before he had that opportunity.

The railroad bosses sent Smith to the Pine Ridge Indian Reservation on the Nebraska-Dakota Territory line, where his assistance was needed to help quell outlawry there. Gangs of white outlaws led by "Doc" Middleton and "Lame Johnny" were taking refuge in the reservation while preying on stagecoaches operating between the Black Hills and Cheyenne. Their theft of Indian ponies was also the cause of considerable unrest on the reservation. An immediate crackdown on the criminal activity was believed necessary to prevent an Indian uprising and the resultant damage to the commercial interests of the railroad.

Valentine T. McGillycuddy, the agent at Pine Ridge, held an appointment as U.S. court commissioner, with powers to employ deputies, issue arrest warrants, and hold criminal hearings. His chief law enforcement officer was William H. H. Llewellyn, a twenty-seven-year-old adventurer from Wisconsin with a talent for garnering political largesse, but little or no experience as a man-hunting lawman. Llewellyn had recently secured appointment as a special agent of the U.S. Department of Justice, assigned to eradicate the Middleton and Lame Johnny gangs. Llewellyn, aware that he needed experienced help to accomplish his mission, suggested the call for Whispering Smith.[22]

Julia McGillycuddy, wife of the agent, clearly recalled the railroad detective who showed up at the agency as a gentle-voiced man who never drank liquor "but had no regard for human life and was known on the frontier as a killer."[23]

The first target of the Llewellyn outlaw eradication campaign was bandit chieftain Cornelius Donohue, who used the alias John Hurley but was known throughout that country as "Lame Johnny."

A coach carrying U.S. mail was held up and robbed near Dry Lake, Dakota, on June 9, 1879, by two bandits witnesses identified as Lame Johnny and Frank Harris. A few weeks later Agent McGillycuddy received a wire from Fort Robinson, outside Crawford, Nebraska, that two men, believed to be Lame Johnny and Frank Harris, had attempted to sell stolen horses as cavalry remounts. They were arrested and held in the post guardhouse. Jim Smith went to investigate and confirmed the two suspects were indeed Lame Johnny and Frank Harris.

Since he was acting alone and could only rely on the assistance of a stagecoach shotgun messenger in guarding the prisoners during their conveyance, Smith decided to take them individually to Rapid City for trial in federal court. Electing to transport Lame Johnny first, he caught the Sidney and Black Hills stagecoach at Red Cloud Station, just north of Fort Robinson. For the start of the trip he asked Jesse Brown, the shotgun guard, to sit in the coach with Johnny, while he rode up on the boot with the driver. Holding the reins was Ed Cook, who had no love for the Lame Johnny gang, having once been held up by them. Other passengers in the coach were Brown's wife and two daughters.[24] Later Smith and Brown exchanged seats.

As the coach approached Buffalo Gap Station in Dakota Territory on the night of July 1 it was halted by a party of eight armed men wearing masks. What happened then was detailed in the pages of the

*Black Hills Journal* of Rapid City from interviews with Smith and the other stage occupants.

Smith said it was obvious to him at once that this was no holdup, that the men were after Lame Johnny. Finding it useless to offer resistance against such a force, Smith stepped from the stage and gave up his weapons. The men then dragged Lame Johnny roughly from the coach and took him off the trail about a hundred yards. After allowing Smith to retrieve his handcuffs, they ordered him back to the stage. There he remained with the Brown family and Cook, he said, until the vigilante party finished its grisly business and he saw Lame Johnny dangling from a tree limb.[25]

Another paper reported that "the doomed robber resisted the vigilantes with all his strength and begged [Smith] for his revolver. He knew well his fate and wanted to sell his life as dearly as possible."[26]

According to another account, Lame Johnny died game. The vigilantes "demanded from him a confession and the names of his associates in crime. He replied that he had nothing to confess and never would betray a partner, whereupon they told him his hour had come, as they intended to hang him. He replied: 'Hang and be damned; you can't do it any too soon.' "[27]

Later there was talk that Smith had no intention of taking Lame Johnny safely to Rapid City, that he had conspired with vigilantes to pull off the lynching. He was said to have hinted to Agent McGillycuddy before he left on the mission that he might lose his prisoner along the way, and that he later sent a wire to the "Shotgun Brigade," as the local vigilantes were known, telling them when and where to stop the coach and string up Lame Johnny.[28] Conspiracy theorists generally believed Jesse Brown was a party to this scheme also, but no one ever explained why, if such a dangerous plot had been in the works, he would have taken his wife and children along on the trip.[29]

Lawmen of the region did not share the concern of some with regard to how Lame Johnny passed from this earth. In a letter to A. D. Hazen of the Post Office Department, Special Agent John B. Furay commented that Frank Harris and Lame Johnny "had been leading away some halters with horses in them," and, after he was apprehended, "Lame Johnny got so badly strangled with a rope . . . as he was being conveyed to jail, that he only lived a few minutes."[30]

In another letter to D. B. Parker, chief inspector of the Post Office Department, Furay said that Lame Johnny died by "strangulation." He quoted with obvious amusement the lines scratched onto a rude wooden slab someone had erected over Lame Johnny's grave at the site of his demise:

> Pilgrim, Pause! You're standing on
> The moldering clay of "Limping John."
> Tread lightly, stranger, on his sod
> For if it moved, you're robbed, by G——d.[31]

From Rapid City Smith returned to Fort Robinson for Frank Harris, the other suspect, and transported him without incident to Dakota, where Harris confessed to his crimes, was convicted, and was sentenced to seven years in prison.[32]

With Lame Johnny gone, another outlaw gang led by a notorious horse thief known as "Doc" Middleton became the focus of attention for law enforcement officials in Nebraska and Wyoming.[33] Responding to outraged complaints from ranchers, stage line operators, and Indian reservation agents, all of whom had suffered from the gang's crimes, the officers combined forces to hunt down the culprits. Jim Smith and other Union Pacific detectives played a major role in the effort. In March the *Cheyenne Sun* noted that Union Pacific detective J. L. Smith had organized a posse in North Platte to track down the Middleton gang. To assist him he had chosen "three of the best men in the police service of the Union Pacific," and led them in an exhausting but fruitless ten-day search.[34]

The various posses in search of Middleton and his gang kept the outlaws on the run for several weeks. Late in April Jim Smith's party of man-hunters, narrowing the chase, joined up with posses led by Sheriff Con Groner of Lincoln County and Sheriff Robert Hughes of Keith County. They were only a day behind the outlaws, who went into camp just west of Sidney.

Rather than attack the camp and trigger a long-range gun battle during which their main quarry, Doc Middleton, might escape, the officers decided to entice the gang leader into town. They employed a troublesome Texas hard case named J. C. ("Charley") Reed, who was languishing in the Sidney jail awaiting trial on several charges, as bait for their trap. They promised Reed to drop the charges against him if he brought Middleton into town, where the officers would be waiting with cocked guns. Reed went along with the plan and rode out to the outlaw camp.

Middleton, however, wary as a wolf, declined Reed's invitation to a celebratory round of the Sidney saloons, but allowed Joe Smith, a youthful gang member, to go.

As soon as Reed and Smith arrived back in Sidney shots rang out, and the young outlaw fell, mortally wounded. Taken into the Saratoga House and stretched out on a billiard table, Smith looked up at Reed and spoke his last words: "You're the son-of-bitch who gave me away." No one knows whose bullet killed the outlaw, but local tradition has it that it came from the gun of Detective James L. Smith.[35] Middleton and his cohorts, only a mile out of town, alerted by the sound of gunfire, quickly broke camp and mounted up. They were long gone by the time the officers assembled and rode out to the location.

The reprobate Charley Reed, now despised by both law enforcers and lawbreakers, went on a drunken binge of several days' duration. On May 1 he shot Henry Loomis, a popular local resident. Lynch talk rumbled through the town as Loomis's life hung in the balance for several days. When he died on May 5 a mob descended on the jail, dragged Reed to a telegraph pole, and hanged him. Local legend credits Whispering Smith with participation in this man's departure also. Following his suspected complicity in the Lame Johnny lynching, there was a widely held view that Smith "had a tendency to enforce his own sense of justice through the hangman's noose."[36]

In July 1879 William Llewellyn and Union Pacific detective William C. Lykens conspired with ex-convict and known Middleton associate Lyman Hazen to arrange a secret meeting with the outlaw leader. The idea was to offer Middleton the promise of a pardon from the governor of Nebraska in exchange for his peaceable surrender. The meeting on July 20 blew up in a roar of gunfire. Middleton and Hazen were both wounded, and Llewellyn was creased by bullets before all parties to the affair rode off in different directions.

Llewellyn regrouped at Fort Hartstuff, Nebraska, a military post some eighty miles to the south. There he organized a posse composed of a squad of infantry that included James L. Smith, fresh from his adventures and misadventures with Lame Johnny and Frank Harris.

On July 27 the Llewellyn posse caught up with Middleton at his hideout camp on Wyman Creek, where his wife was ministering to his injuries. One shot fired into the outlaw's tent convinced him to surrender.[37] The officers took Middleton to Sidney, where doctors treated his wound. Fearing that the prisoner had supporters in Sidney who might interfere with a trial held there, local officials decided to turn the prisoner over to Wyoming authorities. Transportation of Middleton to the railroad depot was reportedly conducted in dramatic fashion. "Smith and Llewellyn, well armed and alert, bore him on a stretcher, preceded by Lykens, armed with a double-barreled shotgun and two Colt 45s, having in the meantime sent word to the would-be rescuers that any demonstration on their part would result in the immediate death of their leader."[38]

Tried and convicted of horse theft in Cheyenne, Middleton was sentenced to a five-year term. Jim Smith was one of the guards who escorted the prisoners to a train for transport to the Nebraska State Prison.[39]

While attending the Middleton trial in Cheyenne, Smith took up the unfinished matter of J. G. Mills, the newsman who had figured largely in his embarrassing departure from the city seven months earlier. He quietly began an investigation of the man's background. From authorities in Lexington, Mississippi, he obtained a written statement that Mills had been a leader of a white supremacy organization there and had murdered a black man. Smith circulated the report around Cheyenne and waited for a reaction. It was not long in coming.

On November 11 Mills confronted Smith on the street and demanded that he retract his allegations. Smith asked if Mills was "heeled." The newsman replied that he was not. "Then," said Smith, "go and get your gun, and we'll have the amusement to ourselves out by the lake." Mills protested that he was not a duelist, but Smith would hear none of it and warned him again to get "heeled." Smith went out to the designated spot, but Mills failed to appear.[40]

According to the account in the *Leader*, which may have been written by Mills himself, later in the day Smith spotted Mills on the street carrying a shotgun. Turning white, he cried, "Great God, he's got a

shotgun. That's too big odds!" and jumped over a fence to get away.[41]
How much truth there was to this yarn no one can say. The behavior
ascribed to Smith in this instance was certainly not consistent with
any other action in his long career.

On March 10, 1880, a sensational gold bullion theft in Sidney,
Nebraska, brought Jim Smith hurrying back to his earlier headquarters and embroiled him in a complicated investigation that led ultimately to his involvement in two more shootings.

A large shipment of gold bullion from the Black Hills, with an
estimated value of between $119,000 and $125,000, had arrived in
Sidney the day before on "Old Ironsides," an armored coach with
half-inch steel plates and gun ports, and guarded by five of the toughest shotgun messengers in the West. The shipment had been delayed
by a snowfall and muddy roads and could not be transferred to a train
that day as planned. It became necessary to hold the treasure overnight. Scott ("Quick Shot") Davis, the guard in charge, ordered the
bullion locked up in the express office vault and assigned a double
guard to watch over it during the night. In the morning he had the
gold taken out and placed on a baggage cart in preparation for the
transfer to the train. The train was late, and at noon the station agent
assured Davis the treasure would be safe locked in the express room
while the guards repaired to a nearby hotel for lunch.

But on their return the guards were shocked to find that the gold
had disappeared, removed through a hole cut in the express office
floor. The depot had been constructed on pilings above the ground to
put it on a level with the train platform. Searching the space below,
Davis found four large gold bars, the bulk of the treasure, cached in a
coal pile. Still missing was about $13,000 in gold and currency.[42]

Davis got the recovered gold loaded on the next eastbound train.
Telegraph wires hummed, and officials of the Pacific Express Company and the Union Pacific Railroad hurried to Sidney to begin an
investigation of the theft. Arriving from Cheyenne with Superintendent Robert Law of the railroad's Mountain Division was Detective
James L. ("Whispering") Smith.

As a former resident of Sidney, Smith was well acquainted with
most of the town's residents. He was immediately suspicious of Cornelius M. ("Con") McCarty, a former Cheyenne County sheriff who
now owned the Capitol Saloon and Gambling Hall, the largest estab-

lishment of its kind in Sidney, and a group surrounding him. These included Patrick H. ("Patsy") Walters, a conman and gambler who had served as a deputy during McCarty's tenure as sheriff and now tended bar at the Capitol; Thomas Ryan, another one-time McCarty deputy who currently held the position of county assessor; Dennis L. Flannigan, the town barber and ex-convict, who wangled an appointment to the grand jury looking into the treasure robbery; and Chester K. Allen, the station agent.

Working with John M. Thurston, a Union Pacific attorney who had been appointed special prosecutor in the case, Smith developed a strong circumstantial case against McCarty, Walters, Ryan, and Allen. The prosecution was thwarted, however, by Flannigan's undermining of the case with other members of the grand jury and possible jury tampering by a county judge who also dealt faro in McCarty's Capitol Saloon,[43] and Thurston was only able to get Allen indicted.

Allen's trial was in progress on May 24, 1880, when Jim Smith tangled with one of the McCarty outfit. While taking a drink in one of the town's saloons he got into a heated argument with Patsy Walters. Both men went for their guns. Smith got his pistol, a Webley .45, into action first. He plugged Walters once in the belly and missed with a follow-up shot. Before falling to the floor, Walters triggered off several rounds. One of his bullets struck Smith's revolver and glanced off, injuring his hand.

Fearing retaliation by other McCarty gang members, Smith fled to the hotel where the bullion shipment guards, in town for the Allen trial, were staying. When Sheriff Robert C. ("Mose") Howard attempted to take him into custody, Scott Davis and Jesse Brown refused to turn him over. Smith finally negotiated a deal; after receiving treatment for his wound, he would surrender the next morning on condition that he be allowed to keep a loaded rifle in his cell and Davis and Brown be assigned to guard him.

Chester Allen was cleared of complicity in the bullion robbery, and when Patsy Walters recovered from his gunshot wound, a jury also accepted Jim Smith's plea of self-defense and acquitted him of attempted murder.[44]

Smith remained in Sidney the remainder of that year, attending the various trials and keeping a wary eye on his enemies in the Con McCarty camp. The word on the street was that Dennis Flannigan, in particular, was gunning for him. After a protracted New Year's Eve drinking spree during which he repeatedly bragged to saloon customers that he would put out Smith's light, Flannigan marched to the Lockwood House, where Smith roomed, and confronted his foe in his room. When shots rang out, other occupants of the hotel rushed to the scene to find Flannigan stretched on the floor, mortally wounded. He died shortly afterward, but not before making a statement in which he claimed he was unarmed and seated in a chair when Smith "got the drop" on him and shot him three times. Smith, on the other hand, said he was in bed when Flannigan, brandishing a cocked revolver, entered his room. Aware of Flannigan's earlier threats, Smith said he grabbed his pistol and fired in defense of his life.[45] Indicted for murder in the second degree, Smith once again was freed on his self-defense plea.[46]

Smith stayed on in Sidney, a town that was becoming notorious for its violence and criminality. Concerned citizens, moved to action, organized a vigilante committee called "The Regulators," and set out to rid the community of the worst of its lawless element. In concert with city officers, they stormed the worst nest of villains, the Capitol Saloon, rounded up Con McCarty and some of his henchmen, including Patsy Walters, and a suspected stagecoach robber named John McDonald, and threw them in jail. Several nights later, a group of Regulators, impatient with the turnings of the slow wheels of justice, marched on the jail. They took McDonald, who had taken a shot at one of the officers at the time of the Capitol raid and was most vocal in his remonstrations, threatening to burn down the town in revenge, and hanged him to a telegraph pole. They horsewhipped McCarty, Walters, and the rest of the crew and ran them out of town with the promise of another necktie party if they returned.

Perhaps not coincidentally, Whispering Jim Smith, who had been out of town, returned to Sidney the night of the McDonald lynching and McCarty gang exodus. When he quietly disappeared again for two days and nothing more was heard about the whereabouts of McCarty and his deposed gang, old-timers in Sidney nodded their heads knowingly; the Whisperer, they were sure, had dispatched some more bad actors.[47]

The months of stress occasioned by his battle with the McCarty crowd led to some heavy drinking by Smith at this time. The recurrent rumors that he had participated in the McDonald lynching and cold-bloodedly murdered his enemies seemed to put him in the same class as the criminals and did nothing to calm his frayed nerves. One night he got into an angry dispute with a couple of prominent townsmen. He pulled his gun and denounced them as no better than McDonald and deserving a similar fate. He was arrested and taken before a magistrate, who fined him $50 for public drunkenness and disturbing the peace. A delegation of Regulators then converged on him, ordered him out of town, and threatened a lynching if he returned. Smith caught the first train for Cheyenne.[48] On April 14, 1881, only a few days after his undignified departure, a notice, signed by sixty-four leading Sidney residents and businessmen, appeared all over town. Lawlessness in Sidney had run riot, it said. The lives and property of the best citizens had been threatened, robberies committed with impunity, and the rule of order and decency trampled underfoot. Law-abiding people had therefore found it necessary to organize and issue a stern warning, which was emblazoned in large letter: "ALL MURDERERS, THIEVES, PIMPS, AND SLEEK FINGERED 'GENTLEMEN' MUST GO."[49]

So the renowned railroad detective and nemesis of evildoers James L. ("Whispering") Smith had been thrown into the class of "murderers, thieves, pimps, and sleek fingered 'gentlemen.' " His services with the Union Pacific Railroad had also been terminated — whether at the request of the employer, the employee, or by mutual agreement is unclear — and it was definitely time to look elsewhere for employment.

In the spring of 1881 W. H. H. Llewellyn, with whom Smith had worked successfully in the Doc Middleton capture, took an appointment as agent at the Mescalero Apache Reservation, near Tularosa, New Mexico. Remembering the soft-spoken but hard-bitten detective in Nebraska, he sent for Smith and offered him a job as chief stock herder and chief of Indian police at the reservation. The salary was $75 a month, later increased to $100. Smith accepted, and began work on June 23, 1881.[50]

One of the problems plaguing the agency was assuring safe delivery of supplies from the nearest railroad point at Las Cruces, one hundred miles away. Raids on supply wagons by renegade Indians and outlaw gangs were a constant threat. Jim Smith detailed armed escorts of Indian police to guard the conveyances, and from August 22 on, when he personally led the first transport, there were no more plundering attacks.[51]

Raids on settlers by renegades from the reservation continued to be a serious problem, however. In September Smith and his Indian police joined a cavalry troop from Fort Stanton to attack the camp of Apache subchief Nantizli, where wanted fugitives Give-Me-A-Horse and Carpio were being sheltered. In a sharp engagement both renegades were fatally wounded by bullets reportedly fired by Chief of Police Smith.[52]

After an argument with Llewellyn in 1883 Whispering Smith left the Mescalero Reservation. Several causes of the rift between the two men have been suggested. Edgar Beecher Bronson said he talked to Smith in El Paso shortly after his departure, and Smith told him he resented the agent countermanding an order he had given his police. Smith pulled a gun on Llewellyn and threatened his life, according to this fanciful tale.[53] Another early writer hinted that Llewellyn was critical of Smith because he was "bloodthirsty."[54] A more recent writer has speculated that Smith was enraged when Llewellyn publicly bragged that he got $10,000 for the capture of Middleton and did not share it with the other lawmen.[55]

By early 1884 Smith had returned to Cheyenne, where on January 25 he took employment with the Wyoming Stock Growers Association (WSGA) as a "roving" range inspector, or detective.[56] He made his home in Cheyenne, near the headquarters of the WSGA, and lived at the Inter Ocean Hotel, according to the *Cheyenne City Directory for 1884*. His wife had not accompanied him to New Mexico, and the two were evidently estranged. Smith finally divorced Anna at Sidney, Nebraska, on November 9, 1885, claiming she had "willfully" been absent from him for over two years.[57]

It was common practice for stock inspectors, or range detectives as they were generally known, to obtain appointments as deputy sheriffs in the counties to which they were assigned, in order to make arrests of suspected cow thieves. As a "roving" inspector for an organization with widespread membership, Smith might be called on to travel throughout Wyoming, Nebraska, Dakota, Colorado, and Montana, and as far afield as Iowa and Minnesota, but for the most part he worked the area he knew best, the counties of Sioux, Dawes, and Cherry in northwest Nebraska, where local sheriffs deputized him.

In March 1885 Smith wrote Thomas Sturgis, secretary of the association, from Crawford, Nebraska, a little cow town just outside the Fort Robinson military post, where he had been sent to investigate claims by association members of cattle rustling in the area. Smith began by apologizing for being so brief in an earlier report, explaining that he had to "run a class in the Sunday school," an excuse that might have raised some eyebrows among his critics. He then said his investigation had disclosed a breakdown in law enforcement in the Fort Robinson area. He charged that local lawmen had done nothing to crack down on "hog ranches and ginmills [brothels and unlicensed saloons] . . . the resort of thieves and idle vagabonds, who have lived on range cattle." He claimed that his appearance in the district had already made a dramatic difference. Prior to his arrival, he said, stage stations and restaurants always had plenty of beef but had not purchased it from the post butcher. He cited the case of a man named McCoy, keeper of the Sidney and Black Hills stage station two miles east of the post, who regularly fed Deadwood-bound passengers, but had purchased no beef from the post for six months. "Since my arrival," said Smith, "he gets his beef regularly from the Post butcher. He has a lot of thieves laying around his place and last fall they stole three horses from the stage company . . . and some five or six weeks ago they held up the south bound stage. . . . McCoy leaves the first of April and goes to Chadron to run a hotel. I will give him my attention."[58]

The report of their "roving" detective convinced WSGA headquarters that a permanent stock inspector was needed at Fort Robinson and that Smith was the man for the job. In April he was given that assignment. He remained there until August, when Secretary Sturgis received reports of large-scale slaughter of stock belonging to association members in the Chadron district. Assuring Smith that he had "entire confidence in your doing everything that one man can do," he transferred him there.[59]

A letter from association member Bartlett Richards to WSGA secretary Sturgis in December 1885 was hardly meant to laud the work of Inspector James L. ("Whispering") Smith, the self-proclaimed Sunday school teacher.[60] When he sought Smith's aid in arresting a man who had killed one of his cows, Richards said, he found the inspector "drunk in bed at 10:30 a.m." and had to go the local sheriff for assistance. Richards also complained that Smith set a value of only

$25 on the animal killed, an amount insufficient to get a penitentiary sentence on conviction, so Richards had to have a new warrant issued, placing the value at $40 so that a penitentiary sentence could be imposed on the miscreant.[61]

Feeling that he had been unjustly criticized by rancher Richards, Smith, in a January 8, 1886, letter, pleaded his case to Sturgis, and in so doing gave clear evidence of the "macho" element that was an integral part of the western gunfighter's character. When a "hog ranch" opened in Chadron, he said, he avoided the place, as it was a notorious "resort of thieves and pimps." But when the word spread that he was afraid to enter the dive, he felt "duty bound" to go there, not just once, but for eight consecutive nights. To prove the toughs in the place held no terror for him, he said on the third night he deliberately slapped the faces of two of the pimps, fully expecting his action to precipitate gunplay, as they were armed. However, both ran, knocking down others in their flight. Only the charge that he was afraid to go there, he said, took him to the place, as he was never a hog ranch man and was now too old to commence.[62]

Secretary Sturgis seemed inclined to believe his stock inspector rather than the complaining cattleman. He wrote Richards, suggesting that he was in error with regard to the character of and valuable service of Smith and asking him to consult with the inspector personally.[63]

Although he did not mention it at the time, Jim Smith had another reason to hang out at the Chadron hog ranch. A friend of his, J. J. Hamlin, had been murdered some years earlier, and Smith, in investigating the case, had learned that men involved in the crime were notorious habitués of the dive. Smith began frequenting the place to pick up any information he could about the murder and the suspects.

When he was a railroad detective Smith had worked closely with Hamlin, a WSGA stock inspector, while stationed at Sidney. In December 1883 a man calling himself John H. Smith shot and killed Hamlin near Valentine, Nebraska, but got off on a claim of self-defense when three witnesses — Cherry County Sheriff-elect William H. "Billy" Carter; his deputy, Jesse Danielson; and a man named John Pierce — supported his story. It turned out that John Smith and Hamlin were brothers-in-law, having married sisters, and some folks around Valentine attributed the shooting to a family quarrel. But others, including Jim Smith, were convinced that Hamlin had been killed because he was about to expose the crimes of a rustling gang that included in its number John Smith, Carter, Danielson, and Pierce. Through the efforts of Whispering Smith and other honest Chadron lawmen, a Cherry County grand jury at the spring session of court brought indictments against all four men for the murder of Hamlin.[64]

Danielson and Pierce immediately skipped the country. Carter and John Smith were released on bail to await trial. Smith, described by one who knew him as a "Texas horse thief, a low, degraded, ignorant Texas hoosier,"[65] sold his property for $3,000, considerably less than it was worth, and also fled, leaving a wife and two children.

Cherry County posted a $200 reward for the capture of John Smith, and Jim Smith made a special trip to Omaha to convince William A. Paxton, president of the Omaha stockyards and a member of the WSGA executive board, to add to that amount.[66] As a result of his efforts, the WSGA did offer a $100 reward for John Smith, "dead or alive."

Following up on leads, Jim Smith learned in June that John Smith was in the vicinity of Nogales, Arizona. He wired George H. Miles, a friend in Nogales, to arrest and hold the fugitive until he could get down there for him, but "not to give Smith any more chance for his life than he would give a rabid dog."[67] Following instructions, Miles in August trailed John Smith fifteen miles into old Mexico, where he shot him dead.

The other three charged in the Hamlin murder were rounded up and tried. They came clear, but Jim Smith could take satisfaction in the knowledge that John Smith, recognized by all as the worst of the lot, had bitten the dust. The $100 bonus the WSGA gave him for avenging one of their own did not hurt either.[68]

While deeply involved in the Hamlin murder affair, Smith also found time to bring a civil suit against a man he contended had slandered him. It was a highly unusual procedure for a hotheaded gunfighter, notorious for resorting to more violent measures when verbally attacked. The target of his suit was a resident of Sidney, probably one of the enemy clique he had antagonized in that town. Smith explained in his report to the WSGA that after a stagecoach holdup near Sidney, a man named G. H. Jewett had spread the word around town that he — Jim Smith, who was attending court in Sidney at the time — was "the son of a bitch that robbed the stage." Smith said that only the fact that Jewett was "too insignificant to thrash" prevented him from doing so. Instead he filed suit for slander, asking $10,000 as recompense for the damage to his reputation, and announced publicly that any proceeds he received from the action would be turned over to the school fund.[69] Nothing further was heard of this contretemps, and the matter was evidently settled out of court with neither payment nor thrashing.

Following the disastrous winter of 1886 when cattle died by the thousands on the western plains and many ranchers went broke, the WSGA fell on hard times. It became necessary to lay off many of their inspectors, including Jim Smith. He was so well thought of as a guardian of their interests, however, that a group of cattlemen combined to set up a special fund to retain his services. The association kept him on and also requested the railroad to provide him the usual annual pass, saying, "Mr. Smith has always been a valuable man in our employ, and his very presence is a preventive of considerable crime."[70]

In 1887 Inspector Smith launched a battle against "grangers," small farmers and ranchers whose increasing numbers on the plains threatened the open range practice of the big cattlemen who employed him. He mounted a campaign to impeach a Sioux County judge whom he accused of unfairly favoring the grangers in his court decisions. Vilifying the grangers in a report to the WSGA, Smith found them an "ignorant and degraded gang of continental European paupers whose only stock in trade consists of a large number of ragged kids." The judge, he said, was "a descendent of this class," a man "void of any of the finer feelings that make up the human race. I have abused him in his own office with the most violent of epithets and have gone so far as to threaten to kick him out of the county."[71]

The officers of the WSGA were a little taken aback by their inspector's effrontery. In a letter to a friend the secretary pointed out that Smith had "undertaken a pretty large contract to impeach a county judge." He conceded that Smith was "a valuable man in his line, but I trust that he will not in his zeal overstep the bounds of prudence and get himself in trouble, and involve the Association is an unreasonable amount of expense."[72]

When admonished by the secretary to be careful in attacking a representative of the law, Smith replied that in order to prevent a granger from getting a constable's position, he had been compelled to accept the office himself. He then fired another barrage at the hated settlers. "These grangers," he said, "commit all kinds of depredations on stock and when arrested they cry and beg in order to obtain sympathy for their wives and families." He said he was aware that his attack on a county judge "would not be tolerated in well established communities," but pointed out that "in this thin settled jack rabbit" county without attorneys or a jail things were different.[73]

Smith was fighting a losing battle, however. In the end the settlers prevailed, for the day of the open range was fast closing, and the once powerful WSGA was in dire financial straits, as evidenced by an exchange of letters between Thomas B. Adams, the new secretary of the association, and Inspector Smith in the winter of 1888. When Smith requested a cash advancement, Adams replied that, much to his regret, "there is not one cent available . . . , and very little prospect of our being able to pay off outstanding warrants." Smith, in bad economic shape himself, answered: "If you can induce the gentlemen who agreed to pay half my salary for last year to settle the same, you will do me a great favor, as I am desperately short."[74] The WSGA closed out its detective-inspector bureau later that year, and it is not known if Smith ever received his back wages.

By the end of 1888 Whispering Smith had returned to his old occupation of railroad detective. He took a position with the Denver & Rio Grande (D&RG) line, and made his home in Castle Gate, Utah.[75] His sponsor was cattleman Alexander H. Swan, prominent member of the WSGA, who at this time was promoting the Emery County Railroad, connecting the D&RG with recently discovered coal deposits in the vicinity of Castle Gate. When Swan came into conflict with John R. Middlemiss, another investor, Smith (with the blessing of Swan) published a broadside accusing Middlemiss of all sorts of crimes. Calling on "all officers of the law whose business it is to hunt down and bring to justice rogues, frauds and traveling bilks" to provide him with any additional information they had on Middlemiss, he signed the bulletin "James L. Smith, Detective."[76]

When Smith and Middlemiss met on the street, hot words were exchanged before Smith chased the other man into a store and threw a lit cigar in his face. Middlemiss filed criminal libel charges against Smith, who was indicted and released on $2,000 bail posted by Swan and his business partners. Tried on May 28, 1890, Smith was convicted. His fine of $300 was also paid, no doubt by Swan and his associates.[77] Smith may have continued to harass Middlemiss. The *Ogden Standard* four months later noted: "Captain James L. Smith is in town. He is the gentleman that hunted down Captain J. R. Middlemiss to his hole more than once."[78]

Over the next few years, while still a detective with the D&RG, Smith prospected for mineral deposits. He filed on several coal claims, which he then sold to the Pleasant Valley Coal Company, an organization that later hired him as a security officer.[79]

In April 1897, while employed with the coal company, Smith was present at a meeting of the Carbon County commissioners at Price, where he presented a resolution attacking Sheriff Gus Donant for attempting to hire C. L. ("Gunplay") Maxwell as a deputy. Contending that Maxwell was a thief and a rustler who consorted with members of Butch Cassidy's outlaw gang, Smith demanded the sheriff's dismissal. The commissioners adopted the resolution, fired Donant, and named Charles W. Allred as his replacement.[80]

Jim Smith had a remarkable premonition or some inside knowledge, for only a few days later, on April 21, Butch Cassidy's Wild Bunch robbed the payroll of the Pleasant Valley Coal Company, getting away with $8,000. Strangely, no mention is made of the company's security officer, J. L. Smith, in accounts of the robbery.

In October 1897 the new sheriff, Charles Allred, appointed Smith special deputy, without pay, with responsibility for law enforcement at the Pleasant Valley Coal Company.[81] He later had good reason to regret this move, for Smith, increasingly addicted to drink during this period, was a constant source of trouble for the sheriff. On Christmas Day Smith got drunk and caused a disturbance. Allred took him to his rooms at the Mathis Hotel and left him to sleep off his binge. Soon he was called back by a Mrs. Hart, the hotel manager, who claimed Smith had insulted her and waved a revolver around, terrorizing her family. Allred arrested his deputy and took him before a justice of the peace. Smith pleaded guilty to public drunkenness and making a disturbance and was fined $5.[82]

Less than a week later Smith, inebriated again, attacked J. W. Warf, who had acted as attorney for the discharged sheriff and was now prosecuting attorney for the county. Encountering Warf at the Price railroad depot, Smith emptied his six-shooter at the lawyer without scoring a hit, a good indication of the advanced state of his intoxication. Warf pulled a revolver and fired back with equally ineffective results, before running to the courthouse to file a complaint against Smith, charging him with attempted murder.[83]

Sheriff Allred again arrested his deputy, who, after sobering up, filed a countercomplaint against Warf, saying that Warf had fired the first shot. Both men made bond and were released. A grand jury indicted Smith for assault with intent to murder and dismissed his complaint against Warf. At the trial Warf was both prosecutor and chief witness against the defendant. Smith's counsel argued successfully that was unlawful and got the case thrown out on the technicality.[84]

Discredited in the district because of his behavior, Smith lost the support of the coal company officials and ultimately his job. Through the influence of widely respected lawman C. W. "Doc" Shores, who came to Price to testify at the trial as a character witness for the defendant, Smith was rehired as a detective by the D&RG.

As the century turned, Whispering Smith had achieved a level of notoriety throughout the West as a dangerous gunman, unafraid to take on anyone in a contest of arms. At Denver, Colorado, the owners of the *Denver Post*, Harry Tammen and Fred G. Bonfils, and their protégés, sports editor Otto C. Floto and prize fighter Patrick ("Reddy") Gallagher, were locked in a battle with another legendary gunfighter, W. B. ("Bat") Masterson, over competing boxing clubs. They sent for Smith, and hired him to intimidate Masterson and drive him out of town, or, if need be, kill him. What happened when Smith showed up has been told in greatly contrasting versions by spokesmen for the two sides in the fight.

Masterson's close friend and supporter, the popular novelist and editor Alfred Henry Lewis, told one story in an article extolling Bat written seven years later. Reddy Gallagher, he said, "imported a desperate character, one Smith, for the wiping out of Mr. Masterson. . . . Mr. Masterson, when he heard, sent a 100-dollar bill to Mr. Gallagher, with word that the money was his if he would but walk down the streets as far as 'Murphy's,' with his importation."[85] According to Lewis, Gallagher refused the money, and "Smith made haste to explain that his purpose in coming to Denver was wholly innocuous."[86]

Masterson, in a newspaper column written at the time in his usual belligerent and pull-no-punches style, placed the responsibility for Smith's importation squarely on the shoulders of the owners of the *Post* and fired back an unambiguous warning. Bonfils and Tammen, he said, had "tried to hire someone to take a fall out of me, but so far have failed to find the right man. They won't pay the price, they are too rotten miserly. . . . They want to get a man killed for $2 and a $2 man is a dangerous man to do business with." He went on to advise the owners of the *Post* to be sure and hire the right man for the job, as "I am onto your every curve, and if your man misses me I will not miss either of you. This is official, final and irrevocable."[87]

Smith's account was given in an interview with a *Denver Times* reporter five years later. Calling Masterson a "four-flusher," who had an undeserved reputation as a gunfighter, Smith said he ordered Masterson out of Denver for circulating false stories about him, and he went. "It was not my intention to shoot him. That was not necessary. I would merely have kicked him down Seventeenth street and would have seen to it that he went aboard the train." Smith said he had been employed by two unnamed "blackmailers" who had had a "misunderstanding" with Masterson.[88]

The *Times* reporter completed the account, saying the two employers, fearful of Masterson, "cast about for a bodyguard who was not afraid, and Captain Smith was engaged." Hearing that Masterson had concluded Smith had been hired to assassinate him, "the captain" set out to talk the matter over with Bat, and followed him from one saloon to another. Masterson was obviously avoiding him, so Smith gave up and sent him a message "which, it is believed, caused Bat to suddenly decide he preferred the lights of Broadway."[89]

Whatever the truth of Jim Smith's claim that he sent Bat Masterson packing from Denver, it is true that, having lost his boxing club battle with the *Post* bunch, Masterson left Denver in the fall of 1900 and was gone for two years. He continued to maintain a residence there, however, and called Denver his home. He returned briefly in 1902 and then departed for good.[90]

W. B. Bat Masterson as he appeared about the time he was threatened in Denver by Jim Whispering Smith. Courtesy of the Western History Department, Denver Public Library, Denver.

Masterson's charge that Whispering Smith was given employment by Bonfils and Tammen gains some credence by the listing of James L. Smith in the *Denver City Directory of 1901*, wherein Smith's occupation was given as "watchman for the Denver Post."

The controversy over Smith's part in Masterson's departure from Denver was revived again in 1914 when Smith died. In recounting the dramatic story of Jim Smith's history, the Denver papers repeated his version of the happenings of fourteen years earlier, which prompted Masterson to fire off a letter from his office in New York to the editor of the *Rocky Mountain News*. "The fact is," he said, "the so-called Captain Smith never spoke to me in his life, nor did he ever act as if he desired to, and to be frank about it, if he had looked as if he even wanted to speak to me I would have shot him as if he were a mad dog, for the reason I believe it would have been hard for him to assassinate me."[91]

In the early years of the new century, Jim Smith, now in his sixties, continued to work in some type of law enforcement. The *Sidney Telegraph* of May 19, 1903, noted his passage through the town where he had many adventures: "Captain James L. Smith passed through this community today en route to Lincoln, where he has business with the Governor. He is currently in the employ of the secret service of the stockmen's association. Older residents will recall that he is the man who killed Flannigan here in self-defense and is known as one of the nerviest men ever to wear shoe leather."

In 1910, at the age of seventy-two, Smith was working as a guard at the Colorado State Reformatory at Buena Vista.[92] But the ravages of alcoholism continued to plague him, and the final years of his life were spent in abject poverty. In July 1914, homeless and penniless and desperate for food and shelter, he turned himself in to federal authorities, confessing falsely to having participated in criminal bootleg activity in Boulder County, Colorado. Bedeviled by delirium tremens after a two-week confinement in jail without alcohol, he slashed his throat in an unsuccessful suicide attempt.

On August 26, while still locked up in the Arapahoe County jail, he managed to obtain a quantity of lye kept for sanitary purposes, swallowed it, and died an agonizing death. No friends or relatives mourned his passing. His divorced wife, Anna, had long since died.

There were no children. He was interred in a pauper's grave in Denver's Riverside Cemetery.

The Denver newspapers marked his passing with lurid stories of the fabulous career of the man the *Post* called a "noted gun fighter,"[93] and the *Rocky Mountain News* called him a "noted duelist, a gunfighter feared by bad men."[94] But James L. ("Whispering") Smith was soon forgotten, only to have his name, if not his deeds, memorialized in a novel by Frank Spearman.[95]

# − 4 −

## JIM LEVY
### 1842−1882

*Jim Levy had more "sand" in one of his fingers than the three yellow-streaked curs [who killed him] had in their three bodies combined.*
— A. F. Banta, March 30, 1924

It is not at all surprising that the feared gunfighter James H. Levy was a native of Ireland — many Irish-born immigrants achieved renown in the West for their nerve in a fight and ability with weapons.[1] What made Levy unusual was the fact that he not a typical Irishman, of Celtic blood and Roman Catholic religion; Jim Levy was a Jew. As a representative of his heritage and faith in the gunfighting fraternity, Levy was certainly singular, if not unique.[2]

Born in Ireland in 1842, at the age of eight he sailed with his parents from Liverpool, England, aboard the vessel *Huguenot*, and arrived in New York City harbor on May 14, 1850.[3] As a very young man he journeyed west in search of fortune in the gold camps of California. When enumerated by the U.S. census-taker at Sacramento in June 1860, he gave his age as twenty-two, although he was several years younger. He was living in a hotel in Sacramento at that time and employed as a miner at one of the nearby diggings.[4]

When rich silver deposits were discovered in eastern Nevada in early 1868, Levy joined the rush to the new bonanza. Springing up almost overnight as the principal town of the new district was Pioche, named after San Francisco mining entrepreneur Francois Louis Alfred Pioche. Remotely located some three hundred miles from the more populated settlements of western Nevada, the town was notorious from the first for its bloodshedding.

Writing to his sister in Maine on November 3, 1870, college-educated Franklin A. Buck, an early Pioche merchant, emphasized that the frequent episodes of bloodshed usually resulted from altercations among the violence-prone gunmen and normally did not involve peace-loving citizens. "About one half of the community are thieves, scoundrels and murderers," he wrote. "You can go up town and get drunk and get shot very easily if you choose or you can live peaceably. I will send you a paper with an account of the last fight. I was in hopes that eight or ten would have been killed at least, as these fighting men are a pest in the community. . . . There is a fight every day and a man killed about every week. About half the town is whisky shops and houses of ill fame."[5]

One Nevada historian resorted to alliteration in writing: "Pioche was a pistol-popping pippin of a pioneer wild western mining town."[6] Although it cannot now be determined with certainty the exact number of victims of violence who ended up in the Pioche cemetery, estimates are it was more than two hundred. Legend has it that seventy-five men died violently in Pioche before a single death from natural causes.[7] "The first recorded killing occurred on March 29, 1868, just as the town was getting started. . . . Thompson and West's *History of Nevada, 1881* lists 36 of the subsequent 'important' killings through the years — too many to note the details of each, but enough to prove that Pioche was no place for the faint of heart or slow of draw during its swaggering days."[8]

Even the editor of the *Territorial Enterprise* over in Virginia City, a raucous boom town that had seen plenty of gunplay, marveled: "Pioche is overrun with a desperate class of scoundrels as probably ever afflicted any mining town and the law is virtually a dead letter."[9]

The violence intensified when a war developed between mine operators John Ely and W. H. Raymond and the Newland brothers, Tom and Frank, over mining rights to a certain lucrative property, and both sides began enlisting fighting men.

Miners willing and able to use lethal force against their fellow man, finding their services in demand, dropped the pick and shovel and took up the revolver.

Foremost among these mining men turned fighting mercenaries was Richard Moriarty, who, like Jim Levy, was an Irish immigrant. Moriarty, better known in Pioche under his alias Morgan Courtney, became "chief" of the Pioche mining district gun wielders. Levy came to look upon him as a hero and role model and patterned his life after the man.

Born at Cahirciveen, County Kerry, Ireland, in 1844, Moriarty came to the United States and, like Levy, found his way to the mining country of the West at an early age.[10] He was working as a miner at Virginia City in 1868 when he got into his first shooting scrape of record.

On the evening of November 14, 1868, he stopped in a saloon for a drink and got into an argument with one John O'Toole. As the debate grew heated, Moriarty stepped back, jerked a gun from a shoulder holster under his coat, and threw down on O'Toole. Other saloon patrons jumped in to prevent bloodshed. Several hustled Moriarty out a back doorway and into the street. But, his Irish temper aroused, Moriarty ran around the building, took aim through a window, and dropped O'Toole with a single shot. Three days later O'Toole died.[11]

On November 27 a grand jury indicted Moriarty for murder, but he had skipped out of town the night of the shooting and was not seen around Virginia City for the next three years. By the summer of 1870, when he turned up at Pioche, he was using the alias Morgan Courtney, a name that would soon become familiar throughout the camp.

Courtney arrived in Pioche just in time to become involved in the developing conflict between the Newland brothers and the Ely-Raymond mining concern. When embattled employees of the Newland brothers took over the Washington and Creole, a particularly productive mine owned by Ely and Raymond, and constructed a rude fort at the entrance to resist any attack, Courtney offered to expel the interlopers forcibly in return for the proceeds of a thirty-day production of the mine. The mine owners agreed, and Courtney rounded up several others with fighting reputations — Michael Casey, Barney Flood, and William Bethers.[12]

On November 9, 1870, Courtney stealthily posted his forces around the mine opening. He then sent a messenger bearing a case of whisky to the forted mine entrance. The booze, he told the guards, was a gift from their employers. The guards, of course, welcomed this display of generosity and imbibed with gusto.

Courtney waited until the mine's defenders were roaring drunk, then launched his attack, killing W. G. Snell, one of the Newland men, in a sharp engagement before taking possession. Suffering minor wounds were Thomas Newland, who came running when he heard the shooting, and Morgan Courtney himself.

Courtney and his followers worked the mine for the next month according to the terms of their agreement with the Ely-Raymond concern, and reportedly netted $60,000 over that period.[13]

There was a cursory investigation of the affair. Arrested and indicted for the murder of Snell, Courtney was freed on $5,000 bail posted by his employer, W. H. Raymond. Court records and newspaper files are incomplete, but it appears that later the charges were quietly dropped.[14]

Following the "Washington and Creole Mining War," as the conflict became known, Morgan Courtney was cock of the walk among the sports and gunmen of Pioche. Well fixed with money, he turned to the gambling tables for a profession. With his white linen spotless, his fingernails clean and manicured, and his six-shooter with notched handle prominently displayed, "the dandy of the desperadoes," as he was called, became a familiar figure in the saloons and gambling dens of Pioche. Among Courtney's many admirers was Jim Levy, who, seeing the sudden rise to affluence and celebrity of his fellow Irishman, vowed to some day achieve that exalted status himself.

But not everyone admired Morgan Courtney. A man named Thomas Coleman was vociferous in his condemnation of Courtney for the attack on the Newland forces and the death of Snell. When Coleman was found dead on a Pioche street, Courtney and pal Barney Flood were arrested on February 2, 1871, as suspects in the murder, but a grand jury declined to indict them.[15]

For more than a year Courtney enjoyed his acclaim as "chief" of the sporting men in Pioche. He apparently did well gambling, especially at faro, his favorite game. He invested in mining ventures, including a shaft appropriately named the "Faro Bank."[16] He reportedly killed a number of men during this period—estimates range from ten to twenty.[17] Although the court and newspaper records are incomplete, these unverified reports appear to be greatly overblown.

A deadly affray in which he engaged on the evening of June 8, 1872, has been confirmed, however. The difficulty began in Ginbey's saloon where he and Jim Sullivan got into a heated argument, which was continued on the street outside. When Sullivan pulled a knife, Courtney jumped back, unlimbered his revolver, and shot the man in the groin, inflicting a mortal wound. Arrested immediately, Courtney spent the next three months in jail. Considered an escape risk, he was denied bail. At his September trial he took the stand in his own defense and readily admitted shooting Sullivan, but claimed he acted in self-defense. The jury accepted his story and acquitted him.[18]

Again Courtney walked free, but this time did not walk far. During the course of the trial his real name had been revealed, and authorities back in Virginia City took action. A warrant was issued for the arrest of Richard Moriarty, alias Morgan Courtney, on the old charge of the murder of John O'Toole back in 1868. He was arrested by Story County deputies following his acquittal in the Sullivan case before he ever left the building and escorted back to Virginia City. But it was all for naught. Witnesses to the 1868 shooting could not be found, and District Attorney J. A. Stephens at an October 16 hearing requested dismissal of the charge.[19]

Courtney returned in triumph to Pioche, where his celebrity status among the sporting element was only enhanced by this latest episode. On a visit to the town a few weeks later the editor of the *Eureka Daily Sentinel* described the local chief: "He has the appearance of an amiable, mild-mannered individual. We do not believe he is naturally a vicious or bad man — circumstances have doubtless made him what he is. It sometimes happens that when a fellow kills his man in the rough camps of the frontier, he has then to keep up his 'lick' to save his own bacon. This seems to have been the case with Courtney."[20]

Morgan Courtney had less than a year to enjoy his fame and fortune. The gunmen of Pioche began killing each other off, and he was among the first to go.

His final battle was over the affections of a woman, a denizen of the red light district named Georgianna Syphers. Courtney had put his brand on Syphers, claiming her as his very own, but this was disputed by a fellow named George McKinney. According to saloon talk, McKinney was a tough customer indeed, having recently killed three Italian woodchoppers near Elko. Courtney and McKinney had words about the Syphers matter on several occasions, but the showdown came on August 1, 1873, when the two rivals argued heatedly in the Mint Saloon. Finally, McKinney stormed out of the place. Courtney remained, had another drink, and, some fifty minutes later, casually strolled out. He had not gone ten feet on the sidewalk when McKinney stepped out from behind a fruit stand and shot him in the upper chest. Courtney staggered and clawed at a pistol in his pocket, but McKinney continued firing, emptying his revolver. Five bullets struck Courtney, and he collapsed.

Deputy Sheriff Joseph R. Hoag arrested McKinney and escorted him to jail, while other spectators to the shooting carried Courtney to the drugstore of Dr. D. L. Deal, where he was attended by Dr. Henry Bergstein.

Courtney was conscious and in extreme pain. After examining the wounds, Dr. Bergstein gave him morphine to relieve the pain and advised him there was no chance of survival. Someone sent for Father Dominick Monteverde, a Roman Catholic priest, to administer the last rites for the dying man. A number of Courtney's friends and admirers gathered around their chief. Someone suggested he make a statement about the shooting, and he dictated the following: "I think I am going to die. I was walking down the street and McKinney shot me in the back. I started to run in order to get in a place to defend myself but he shot so fast that I could not do anything but run. I did not shoot at McKinney at all. I did not get any pistol out until he fired six shots. Georgie Scyphers [sic] told me that Frank Cleveland gave McKinney a pistol yesterday."[21]

Courtney lingered until just after noon the following day, when he finally died. In reporting his passing, the editor of the *Pioche Daily Record* was saddened that "one so young, so qualified to adorn an honorable station, should have been so suddenly cut off and ushered into the presence of his maker." Courtney, he said, was "feared by some, detested by others, and respected by a few." His violent death was a "verification of the prophecy that those who slay by the sword shall by the sword be slain."[22]

John Dennis, editor of the *Reese River Reveille* of Austin, Nevada, felt no such compassion for either the victim or his slayer. Courtney, he wrote, was "one of the most desperate and bloodthirsty characters that ever disgraced a mining town," but thought "immediate hanging" of McKinney would be advisable.[23] Buried in an expensive coffin with a silver engraving plate, Courtney was given a hero's funeral, escorted to his rest by a brass band and most of the town's population. The outpouring of sympathy for the gunman prompted another snort from editor Dennis over in Austin: "It is almost encouragement to people to die with their boots on, when such a fuss is made over their planting. Vive le humbug!"[24]

McKinney's trial for the murder of Richard Moriarty, alias Morgan Courtney, opened on September 10, 1873. Jim Levy was called as a prosecution witness and reluctantly admitted that he had heard Courtney threaten McKinney's life on at least two occasions.[25] McKinney, who testified in his own defense, swore he did not shoot until Courtney made a move to draw a gun. Then he shot and continued shooting. "I knew if I didn't he'd kill me—that if he got the first shot he'd kill me."

It took ten days to try McKinney; the jury took three minutes to acquit him.[26]

Jim Levy's idol had now gone the way of so many of his kind, but Levy, who had long since adopted the Courtney lifestyle, continued on, undaunted.

William Bethers and Barney Flood, Courtney's confederates in the Washington and Creole Mining War, had dropped from the Pioche scene. Bethers left town to be killed in Eureka, according to reports. Flood also departed Pioche hurriedly after stabbing a man in a quarrel.[27] Only Mike Casey remained. Like his leader, Casey was destined to die in a Pioche gunfight, and the circumstances of his demise drew Jim Levy into the story.

A few months after the battle at the Raymond and Ely mine, a dispute over money between Casey and well-to-do Pioche businessman Thomas Gorson escalated into gunplay. Casey, quicker with a gun, dropped Gorson with a mortal wound. Before he died, Gorson bequeathed all his money to friends, with the exception of $5,000, which was to go the man who avenged his death by killing Mike Casey.[28] Jim Levy decided to go after that $5,000 prize. In the saloons of the town he loudly proclaimed that Casey had shot Gorson down without giving him a show.

Casey took the bait. On May 29, 1871, he confronted Levy in a saloon. With his hand on his pistol butt, he demanded that Levy publicly retract his accusations. Levy, aware that he was at a fighting disadvantage, quickly protested that he was unarmed. "I have got nothing on me," he said, "but I will go and fix myself, and when I come back I will come fighting."[29]

He did come back fighting and, as the *Pioche Daily Record* reported, "our town was thrown into an intense state of excitement by . . . another one of those bloody affrays for which Pioche has of late gained such an unenviable reputation."[30]

Casey was standing in front of Freudenthal's store, conversing with a mining friend named David Neagle, when Levy approached through an alley. Catching his quarry unawares, he announced: "Casey, you son of a bitch, I am here!" and fired his pistol at the same moment. His bullet struck Casey in the head. As he fell, Levy shot him again in the back of the neck. Levy and Neagle then exchanged gunfire, and a ball struck Levy in the chin and "glanced round the jaw bone."[31]

Deputy Sheriff John Pattie, drawn to the scene by the gunfire, "covered Levy with his six shooter and ordered him to desist firing, which he at once did, after retreating into the alleyway. Levy and Neagle were then arrested and taken to jail."[32]

Both men were quickly released on bail. Levy went to his rooms in Hamilton's lodging house, where he was treated by a Dr. Foltz for his gunshot wound. The doctor found that "the ball which struck Levy entered a little to the right of the chin fracturing the lower jaw bone and lodged in the muscles of the neck."[33] The wound, painful but not life-threatening, would leave Levy with a sinister-appearing scar on his face for the rest of his life.

After the shooting Dr. Foltz had also attended Mike Casey, who had been taken first to a drugstore and then to his lodging house. Casey had two head wounds, one a bloody gash from being struck by the barrel of Levy's pistol, and another in the scalp where a bullet from that pistol had "grazed the skull and scooped out a small portion of the bone." Another bullet had struck him in the back of the neck and plowed a path downward along the spinal column. The doctor rated his survival chances at about fifty-fifty.[34]

Mike Casey lost that toss-up and died from his wounds. At a hearing into the shooting it was decided that since Levy had given fair warning he was coming after Casey "heeled," it was therefore a fair fight, and no further prosecution of the matter was necessary.[35]

So it was that Jim Levy joined the ranks of the man-killing shootists. He evidently collected without difficulty Thomas Gorson's $5,000 reward for putting Casey under the sod, for from that time on he became a full-fledged professional gambler and was never again forced to toil in the mines. During the next two years he followed his idol Morgan Courtney through the deadfalls of Pioche, risking his money at the gambling tables and his reputation as a man to be feared and respected.

Details of any fights he had during this period are sketchy. One man later recalled seeing Levy chase another with a pitchfork.[36] When, in January 1873, another mine claim battle erupted, he was suspected of killing a man named Thomas Ryan.

The Raymond and Ely mining concern was in conflict this time with the Pioche Phoenix mining company over ownership of a mine site. As was typical of this type of difficulty in Pioche, both sides employed gunfighters to protect their interests, and the dispute culminated in a gunfight in the depths of the disputed mine shaft. Ryan, a Pioche Phoenix man, was killed. In the frenzied confusion of the underground battle, no one could be certain who fired the fatal shot, but suspicion immediately fell on Jim Levy, a leader of the Raymond and Ely forces. The suspicion deepened when Levy disappeared from town immediately after the affair. Acting on information that the suspect was on his way to the neighboring mining camp at Hamilton, officers pursued and apprehended him on the road. They returned him to Pioche, where he was jailed. His feet, severely frostbitten during his flight, grew steadily worse, and later in the month the authorities transferred him from the jail to the county hospital. "He now remains in custody while the Grand Jury investigates the affair," said the *Pioche Daily Record*. "There is no surmising what the verdict will be."[37] There may have been insufficient evidence to bring Levy to trial, or, as one writer has suggested, "no one was foolish enough to testify against him,"[38] but Levy escaped indictment. The denizens of the sporting world were convinced, nevertheless, that he had killed his second man, and his reputation as a dangerous gunfighter went up a notch.

When Morgan Courtney was killed seven months later, Jim Levy could lay claim to the title of "chief" of the gunmen of the town, and no one seemed disposed to challenge that claim. Pioche reached its peak that year of 1873, attaining a population of almost 6,000, but then declined rapidly as the silver mines played out. Violence declined as the town shrunk. In its issue of December 13, 1873, the *Pioche Daily Record* pointed out that not a single murder had been committed in the preceding two months.[39]

It was time for Jim Levy, gambler and gunman, with his disfigured face and frostbitten feet, to move on. For a couple of years he worked Virginia City and the surrounding camps in the Comstock mining district. And then in 1876 he joined the rush to the new bonanza, the gold discoveries in the Dakota Black Hills and the boomtown of Deadwood.

Among the throng of sporting men arriving in the Black Hills in that boom year of 1876 was James Butler ("Wild Bill") Hickok, another professional gambler and part-time lawman whose notoriety as a gunfighter and slayer of men had already spread nationwide. Hickok would reach the end of the trail in Deadwood on August 2, 1876, when an assassin named Jack McCall put a bullet in the back of his head. Hickok was the most famous of the town's gunmen, but there were many more.

Wrote a contemporary newspaperman with only a degree of exaggeration: "Every man in Deadwood carries about fourteen pounds of firearms hitched to his belt, and they never pass any words. The fellow that gets his gun out first is best man, and they lug off the other fellow's body. . . . They don't kill him for what he has done, but for what he is liable to do."[40]

Deadwood pioneer Ellis T. ("Doc") Peirce recalled in 1925: "Whenever a gunman came along to the gulch the word was passed along as quickly as it would be at a ladies sewing society. . . . Deadwood was then hogwild; duels and gunfights in the streets, and often one had to duck or fall flat on the ground to escape a shower of lead." Gunfighter standouts Peirce remembered included Jim Levy, John Bull,[41] Billy Allen,[42] Tom Hardwick,[43] Joel Collins,[44] "Laughing Sam,"[45] C. C. Clifton,[46] and Boone May.[47] With the exception of Wild Bill, he rated Jim Levy "the top-notcher of them all."[48]

Peirce did not mention Wyatt Earp, who was also there but had not yet gained the stature as a gunman that would later make his name nationally known. In interviews with Stuart Lake, his biographer, Earp named other prominent Deadwood shootists: Seth Bullock, the sheriff; city marshals John Mann and Jerry Lewis; express guard Scott

Davis;[49] and gamblers Jim Levy, Tom Mulqueen,[50] Tom Dosier,[51] Charlie Rich,[52] Lew Schoenfield, Bill Hillman, Johnny Oyster,[53] Charlie Storms,[54] and "Colorado Charley" Utter.[55] "Of the group," he said, "Jim Levy, Charlie Storms, and Tom Mulqueen were possibly the outstanding six-gun artists."[56]

As far as is known, Jim Levy managed the get through his Deadwood period without gunplay. By early 1877 he was established as a resident gambler at Cheyenne, Wyoming, a one-time end-of-track, hell-on-wheels town that was now the jumping off place for the Black Hills mines. Cheyenne during these years was a gunman's rendezvous, accommodating those going to or coming from Deadwood as well as an abundant crop of its own. Hickok, the ace of them all, spent some time there before pushing on to the Black Hills, never to return. In the 1876–77 period Wyatt Earp, John H. ("Doc") Holliday, and W. B. ("Bat") Masterson, soon to attain national recognition as gunfighters, spent time in Cheyenne, where their gambling skills were tested, but not their shooting ability.

"Cheyenne at that time was wild and woolly," wrote James W. ("Doc") Howard, who had seen some mighty rough towns during his five year U.S. Army service on the frontier before joining the police force at Cheyenne. "It was a common occurrence to find a man shot down or strung up most any time. There were gambling joints, sixty saloons and three variety shows and dance halls."[57]

Jim Levy took up residence in the town soon to be dubbed "The Magic City of the Plains" and pursued his gambling vocation in the town's many dives. In Cheyenne he engaged in the gun battle for which he is best remembered.

Charley Harrison, another professional gambler celebrated in frontier sporting circles for his ability with shooting irons, was in Cheyenne at the time. Bat Masterson witnessed a demonstration of Harrison's accuracy and dexterity with revolvers and was impressed. Calling Harrison "one of the best-known sporting men west of the Missouri River, he said the man hailed from St. Louis but traveled throughout the West. "He was of an impetuous temperament, quick of action, of unquestioned courage and the most expert man I ever saw with a pistol," said Masterson. "He could shoot faster and straighter when shooting at a target than any man I ever knew; then add to that the fact that no man possessed more courage than he did, the natural conclusion would be that he would be a formidable foe to encounter in a pistol duel."[58]

Shortly after six o'clock on the cold, snowy evening of Friday, March 9, 1877, Harrison and Jim Levy entered the Shingle and Locke Saloon on Sixteenth Street in Cheyenne and sat down at a table. It was evident to other saloon patrons that both were well into their cups. Levy was loudly voicing his anger over an earlier high-stakes card game in which he claimed he had been "cinched," or cheated. Harrison, the beneficiary of Levy's loss, added fuel to Levy's fire by declaring the Irish were always poor losers.

Enraged, Levy jumped to his feet and drew his pistol, but Harrison spread his hands and protested that he was unarmed. However, he said, if Levy would allow him to get a weapon, he would certainly "give him a turn."[59] Levy agreed, and together the two walked out into the street, while excited onlookers placed bets on the outcome of the showdown. Harrison was the heavy favorite.[60]

Harrison entered the Senate Saloon and retrieved a revolver he had left there. When he emerged, Levy was nowhere to be seen, so Harrison, gun in hand, walked north up Eddy Street toward Dyer's Hotel, where he was staying with his wife and daughter. As he approached Frenchy's saloon, he spotted Levy across the street.

According to the story in the *Cheyenne Daily Record*, Harrison, on seeing his adversary, immediately snapped off a shot without taking careful aim. He missed. Levy responded with a shot that struck Harrison in the chest, and he tumbled to the snow-covered street, triggering another ineffectual round as he fell. Levy ran across the street, firing as he went. Then, at point-blank range, he shot Harrison again. The second bullet struck Harrison in the right hip, and took a circular course across the lower abdomen and lodged close to the surface in the left hip.

Friends of the stricken gambler carried him to his hotel room, where two doctors treated him. One of the physicians, a Dr. Joseph, said that when he reached Harrison he was cold and "life seemed extinct," but with the "prompt and proper use of restoratives [he] soon opened his eyes and loosened his tongue and limbs. At midnight he was sleeping quietly in the arms of morphine."[61]

A story of the affair in a Deadwood paper said that Jim Levy, following the shooting, coolly walked around the corner to the Oyster Bay Restaurant and ordered a meal. He was calmly eating when Laramie County Sheriff T. J. Carr arrested him. At a preliminary hearing on March 14 Levy was released on $1,000 bail, pending the outcome of Harrison's struggle to live.[62] Cheyenne policeman Doc Howard said that Levy's bondsmen were Charley Storms, late of Deadwood, and his partner, Dublin Trix, both of whom he characterized as "confidence and bunco men."[63]

The *Cheyenne Daily Leader* of March 16 reported that "Levy, the pistoliferous gambler, has procured bail and is at large. Harrison is reported as improving, his medical attendant stating that he will recover, with the loss of a portion of one leg."

In the following days Harrison's wife expressed confidence to reporters that her husband would survive. She said that he had been involved in gun scrapes in various cities, including a gun battle in Pittsburgh in which he killed a man and had been badly wounded himself. On three occasions he had been brought home with bullets in his body.[64]

But after a nearly two-week struggle, Charley Harrison lost this battle. On March 22 he died. Forty carriages followed the hearse from Dyer's Hotel to the cemetery, carrying "probably about 125 occupants, embracing a majority of the sporting fraternity, with their wives and other females."[65]

Bat Masterson in a 1907 magazine article cited the Levy-Harrison shooting affair as a classic six-gun duel, and said it exemplified his contention that deliberation was a necessary ingredient in a gunfight, every bit as important as courage, speed of hand, or accuracy in shooting. Harrison, said Masterson, "fairly set his pistol on fire, he was shooting so fast and managed to fire five shots at Levy before the latter could draw a bead on him." Levy finally triggered off a shot, and Harrison went down, mortally wounded. Harrison was as game as Levy without a doubt and proved he could shoot faster, said Masterson, but his lack of deliberation cost him his life. "Levy took his time. He looked through the sights of his pistol, which is a very essential thing to do when shooting at an adversary who is returning your fire."[66]

Despite the fact that Masterson may not have personally witnessed the gunfight and his description of it did not exactly conform to the accounts in the contemporary press — no mention is made, for instance, of Levy's running across the street to deliver the final fatal shot—later writers have quoted it extensively.[67] In so doing they have given Jim Levy a modicum of fame as a western gunfighter.

In his reporting of the affair, Herman Glafcke, editor of the *Cheyenne Daily Leader*, evidenced no admiration for either the winner of the gunfight or his victim. His first headline read: "THEY DIDN'T KILL EACH OTHER, BUT THE PEOPLE WOULD HAVE BEEN BETTER SATISFIED IF THEY HAD. A SHOOTING AFFRAY BETWEEN TWO DRUNKEN GAMBLERS, NEITHER OF WHOM WAS A GOOD MARKSMAN."[68]

The sporting fraternity objected to this disparaging treatment of two of their own. Three of them immediately announced they were canceling their subscriptions to his paper, and there was talk in the saloons of "a delegation of leading gamblers" making a call on the editor.[69]

Following Harrison's death, rumors spread throughout Cheyenne that Levy had fled the town, headed for Deadwood, but the *Leader* stilled these stories on March 24: "Levy, the man who shot Harrison, was in the city last evening, giving the lie to the report that he has gone north. He says he proposes to stay and stand trial."

The trial of Jim Levy, charged with manslaughter, began on June 19, 1877. Over the next three days twenty witnesses testified. Among the witnesses for the defense were A. C. McCalls and Oscar Harding, who claimed they witnessed the altercation between the gamblers in the Senate Saloon and heard Harrison abuse Levy "without stint, calling him a coward and various other names not proper to be mentioned in print." McCalls said Harrison dared Levy to fight and when Levy declined, left the saloon, saying he would "go and get his gun and make him fight."[70]

The testimony of M. N. Madison and M. M. Davis, who said they saw the fight, differed greatly from the initial press reports. Both stated positively that Harrison fired first, that he was still standing when the last shot was fired, and that no additional shots were fired after he fell.

Levy himself made a statement that was not very long, but was "in full accord with the great preponderance of testimony given on the trial."[71]

The jury was out only fifteen minutes before bringing in a verdict of "not guilty."[72]

Following his release, Levy lost no time shaking the dust of Cheyenne from his boots. He spent some time Leadville, a wild mining town high in the Colorado Rockies to which sporting men were flocking, and then headed south to the warmer climes of Arizona. By late 1880 he was at Tombstone, the burgeoning Arizona silver camp down by the Mexican border, where he must have run into Dave Neagle, the man who had disfigured his face and almost killed him in that little shooting match in Pioche a decade earlier. If any words passed between these two gunmen about the incident, they went unreported.

In Tombstone were a number of other familiar faces, including Charley Storms and his partner, Dublin Trix (or Lyons), who had gone Levy's bail after the Harrison shooting back in Cheyenne. This pair did not last long in Tombstone, however. On February 15, 1881, Luke Short, another professional gambler, extinguished Storms's light in a brief gunfight outside the Oriental Saloon. Two days later Luke Short's close friend and gambling associate Wyatt Earp ordered Dublin Lyons to get out of town, and he promptly complied.[73]

That same month Levy entered into a water rights partnership with several other prominent members of the gambling community: Richard ("Dick") Clark, a partner in the gambling operation at the Oriental Saloon and considered the "boss gambler" of Tombstone; Wyatt Earp; and Doc Holliday. Although the names of Earp and Holliday are undoubtedly the most widely recognized today, in 1881, according to western historian Gary Roberts, "Leavy [sic] was by far the best known of the quartet of investors who set out from Tombstone to stake water claims."[74] In early February the foursome staked out water claims at three locations and filed them as jointly owned with the recorder's office of Cochise County.[75]

Levy did not remain long in Tombstone, nor did he contribute to the sanguinary history of that violent town. By early 1882 he had moved on to Tucson, which was destined to be the last stop on his life journey.

On June 5, 1882, Levy entered the Fashion Saloon, a popular Tucson resort owned and operated by Eli B. Gifford, a noted sporting man,[76] and sat down at a faro table to buck the game of John Murphy. Levy and Murphy were on bad terms, having engaged in a squabble a week or so earlier. Levy had later been heard to boast that he would "shoot out Murphy's eye" and waltz on Murphy's faro layout and "shoot the checks from the table."[77]

The argument was renewed on the evening of the 5th, and, as both men had been drinking heavily, the dispute grew increasingly heated. Finally, Levy made the point-blank accusation that Murphy was running a crooked game. According to witnesses, Levy remained "perfectly cool and self-minded" during this exchange, while Murphy grew "exceedingly irate and threatened all manner of things."[78]

The quarrel finally ended in a mutual agreement to take the matter across the border into Mexico and fight a duel to determine if "either or both should measure his breadth on the daisies." A hat passed among the patrons and employees of the Fashion produced $30 to pay for a wagon to convey the combatants and their entourages to the scene of action. Since "both men had the reputation of being desperate characters, and both [had], at different periods, helped to increase the population of cemeteries at different points in the country," the news of the impending clash quickly caught the attention of members of the sporting fraternity, and the word spread throughout the saloons of Tucson.[79]

When Chief of Police A. G. Buttner got wind of the goings-on, he hurried to the Fashion and found Levy and Murphy still there. Adjudging the affair a "burlesque," he urged both men to go home and forget the matter.

But Murphy and two of his friends, Dave Gibson and Bill Moyer, did not consider the affair a burlesque. They followed Levy as he walked to the Palace Hotel on Meyer Street, where he lodged. Believing he had gone to arm himself, they waited outside. When he emerged a few moments later, they immediately began shooting. Hit by at least one bullet as he stepped from the doorway, Levy staggered out into the street, where several more shots struck him and he collapsed.

A writer for the *Arizona Daily Star* was among the throng of people who converged on the scene and reported seeing Levy stretched out on the sidewalk gasping his last breath as his lifeblood saturated his shirt. He said no weapon was evident on the body, which was quickly removed to the morgue, where a Dr. Holbrook pronounced Levy dead from a gunshot wound.[80]

Based on his knowledge of the arguments and threats voiced earlier in the Fashion by both Murphy and Levy, Chief Buttner arrested

Gamblers like Jim Levy and Charley Harrison "bucking the tiger" in a faro game in a Cheyenne saloon. From *Frank Leslie's Illustrated Newspaper*, 1877.

Murphy as the prime suspect in the shooting. The gambler readily acknowledged his involvement, telling Buttner, "Well, he got it good. I did it and don't deny it." His pistol, "a small-sized Smith & Wesson patent," contained two empty chambers.[81]

An inquest held the following day in the offices of Coroner W. B. Horton concluded that James Levy, a native of Ireland, about forty years of age, came to his death on June 5, 1882, "from pistol shots fired by pistols in the hands of William Moyer, Dave Gibson and John Murphy, with intent to kill said James Levy." Warrants were issued for the arrest of Gibson and Moyer, and Chief Buttner took them into custody and locked them up with their pal Murphy.[82]

A preliminary examination into the case began on June 8 before Judge Meyer. Prosecutor Hugh Farley called an impressive array of witnesses.

Dr. L. D. Lyford, who examined Levy's body, found five bullet wounds, one of which "had passed above the collar bone, entering in the right side, passing down the backbone and coming out the left side." Another had entered "the left side above the collar bone, passing through the backbone, coming out through the back on the right side." A third had passed "through the right side, going through the heart, lodging near the left shoulder." A fourth shot passed through the upper part of the brain. A bullet had also gone through the left arm. "I would state," said the doctor, "that all of the shots excepting the one through the left arm were necessarily fatal. I should judge that the shot through the left arm was made by a smaller bullet than the other wounds."[83]

W. B. Hopkins, a clerk at the Palace Hotel, testified that, having seen Murphy waiting in the street with a pistol in his hand, he had advised Levy to go out the back door rather than the front, but, being "quite drunk," Levy ignored the warning. Hopkins heard two shots fired almost simultaneously, and saw Levy start to run, "with his hands out and nothing in them, across the street." He saw Dave Gibson firing a revolver in the direction of Levy as he ran to the opposite sidewalk, where he fell.

Chief Buttner told of Murphy's admission to the shooting and the two empty chambers in his pistol. Police officer M. R. Johnson testified that no weapon had been found on Levy.

George H. Duncan, who said he had known Levy for seven or eight years in Virginia City, Cheyenne, Deadwood, and Tucson, stated that shortly before the shooting, Levy had told him he did not have a friend in the world and that he couldn't find anyone to second him in the duel. He didn't even have a gun, and tried to borrow Duncan's, but was refused. The witness said he saw Murphy fire the first two shots and Gibson fire two more. When the shooting began, he said he heard Levy cry out, "My God! Don't murder me, I'm not armed."

Witnesses Thomas B. Langley, T. M. Gale, W. D. Staley, John L. Story, and Michael Crowley testified to seeing Murphy aim his pistol at Levy and fire two shots. Before the firing began, Langley said he heard someone say: "Here's our game." Staley said he passed Murphy and Moyer on the street before the shooting and heard them cocking revolvers. He said he saw Moyer fire no less than five times. After the shooting he saw Gibson and Moyer walking away with revolvers in their hands and heard Gibson call out to Murphy: "I got him. He is over there on the sidewalk, they can go and get him."[84]

Henry Hicks said he saw both Murphy and Moyer fire. He thought there were seven to ten shots in all. When J. E. Latham saw Gibson after the shooting and asked him what the fuss was all about, Gibson replied that it was nothing of importance, but now Murphy was "chief." Louis Lepage said he heard Moyer say, about an hour after the shooting: "The damn son of a bitch is dead; he's been threatening my life for the past two weeks, and I put five bullets in his body."

Thomas Fitch, for the defense, called a number of witnesses who testified to Levy's unsavory character. Thomas Callahan, who said "Levy's reputation was bad, he being a dead shot and quarrelsome," heard Levy threaten to shoot Moyer two weeks earlier. Ely B. Gifford and A. G. Ryan agreed Levy's character was bad.

Charles Zimmer said he had known Levy for eleven years and had seen him at Pioche, White Pine, and Tombstone. He had seen him kill a man at Pioche and go after a man with a pitchfork at White Pine. He had recently heard Levy say he would shoot Moyer in the eye if he ever winked at him.

A former gambling partner of Levy's named Matthew J. Redding testified that he had known and worked with the deceased in Virginia City, Leadville, and Tucson. Although he was considered to be honest in money matters and "an honorable fighter," Levy, he said, was dreaded and considered dangerous in all those towns. For the last few months Levy's behavior had been erratic, and the witness suspected he was going crazy. When Levy complained that he hadn't a friend in the world, Redding loaned him $50 to buy a gun. Levy said he wanted the best gun in town to "hunt up and kill the damn son of a bitch [Murphy]." Redding warned Murphy to avoid a showdown with Levy, for if it came to a gunfight he would surely die.

John Green also said Levy had complained to him about nine days before the shooting that he was without friends or money and blamed Murphy and Moyer for his problems.

Gibson and Moyer had nothing to say in their defense, but Murphy made a statement. He told of the trouble at his faro table, where Levy denounced the game as crooked and called the dealer a cheat. Murphy said he assured Levy "his game had always been on the square, that he had never allowed a drunken man to play at his table, and that the man who said his game was a thieving one was a liar." The duel challenge followed this exchange. Murphy said when he encountered Levy in the hallway of the Palace Hotel, he saw Levy's right hand drop to his side as if to draw a weapon. "Then," he said, "I did the shooting."[85]

On June 10 Judge Meyer held that sufficient cause had been presented to bind all three defendants over for action of the grand jury, and they were returned to the confines of the Pima County jail.[86]

The shooting of Jim Levy and the resulting trial prompted the editor of the *Arizona Daily Star* in Tucson to pontificate about the gunfighters who had always been a part of the history of the western frontier. In an editorial entitled "The Men Who Kill," he wrote:

The professional bravo is not a desirable character in any community. The characterless adventurer, whose conduct is a perpetual menace to peaceable citizens, sooner or later terminates his career at the muzzle of the pistol. He defies the laws of society — is reckless of his own life and the lives of others — and for fancied or imaginary injuries is ready to kill on the slightest provocation. A dispute with a person of this description cannot be regarded in the light of a mere difference of opinion. It is more significant than a quarrel between ordinary people, because it carries with it the issues of life and death to one at least, and perhaps both of the disputants. The bravo stands alone in the community. He is alien to all humanizing feelings, reckless of all that other people most regard — a hero only in his capacity to kill — just as the wolf or the tiger is different from the animals upon whom they prey. Armed and menacing, his forbidding life threatened all with whom he came in contact. A social pariah — a cipher in moral economy, without domestic ties and alien even to the friendships which men most honor and respect, to weigh his life in the balance with better men, would be to give to it a value which neither justice nor magnanimity can accord it. Swept out of life, there is not even a regret to succeed him, or a ripple on the surface of the society which his life menaced. Dead, there is not a single virtue along the devious pathway of his checkered career to whiten the memory of an ill-spent life.

In the moral and social economies of border civilization we can afford to dispense with the bravo and the professional killer. They have been the darkest blotches upon society in Arizona.[87]

On the night of October 23 Murphy, Gibson, and Moyer overpowered their jailer and broke out of the Pima County jail, and in the process liberated six other prisoners. With arms and horses provided by friends on the outside, they vanished into the hills. Rewards totaling $900 were offered for their capture, but a posse led by Undersheriff H. Ward was unable to track the trio down.[88]

The jail breakout turned into a political squabble when charges were raised that leaders of the county Democratic Party had conspired in the escape in the hope that Sheriff Bob Paul's embarrassment would lead to his defeat at the polls in November.[89]

In November the *Tombstone Epitaph* reported that a farmer named T. J. Hazen arrived in Tombstone with the news that Murphy, Moyer, and Gibson, mounted on fine horses with pack animals and armed with Winchesters and revolvers, had ridden into his place in Apache County, looking for barley. They were camped, they said, in an inaccessible portion of the White Mountains while friends in Tucson worked to "square" things so they could return. Murphy was quoted as saying: "We three are about as hard a game as you can find anywhere, and if we are driven to desperation we will kick up the damnedest muss ever raised in Arizona."[90]

The fugitives were later captured and tried individually for the murder of Jim Levy. Amazingly, Murphy and Gibson were acquitted, and Bill Moyer alone was convicted and sentenced to life in prison.[91]

James Levy apparently never married, had children, or formed any sort of permanent family attachment during his two decades of life in the West. No one seemed to mourn his passing in Tucson, and he certainly did not receive anything like the elaborate send-off his victim Charley Harrison received in Cheyenne.

But he did have his admirers, as evidenced by a memoir written by old-timer Albert Franklin Banta more than forty years after Levy's death.[92] After relating the circumstances of Levy's death at the hands of what he termed "cowardly assassins," Banta wrote: "Jim Levy had more 'sand' in one of his fingers than the three yellow-streaked curs had in their three bodies combined. Given even half a show (and the curs knew it), Jim Levy would have cleaned up the three at one and the same time — if the cowardly curs had attempted to face the music. All three were bullies or 'four flushers,' and it is a notorious fact that class of cattle are notoriously 'yellow,' without a single exception."[93]

And that will have to do for James H. Levy's epitaph.

# — 5 —

## DAVE NEAGLE
1847–1925

*Fair Sarah and Terry*
*Thought Judge Field a Berry*
*At the table they give him a biff*
*But Neagle's good gun*
*Put a stop to the fun*
*And the Coroner sat on the stiff.*
— John Brown in "The Life and Times of David Neagle"

David Butler Neagle was an unimpressive little man, five feet seven inches tall, and never weighing more than 145 pounds. As a gun-fighter he had a single distinguishing feature: his left-handedness. He is forgotten today, but there was a period in 1889 when his name (often misspelled "Nagle") was emblazoned across headlines in news-papers from coast to coast. Later his name became forever immor-talized in a momentous decision of the U.S. Supreme Court.

Born on October 10, 1847, the son of a plasterer in Boston, Neagle was destined to spend all but the first few years of his life in the West. In 1852, when he was only five, his Irish-born parents, William and Bridget Neagle, took him and his six-year-old sister, Mercy, across the continent to California and settled in the Mission District of San Francisco. Perhaps due to the rigors of that journey, wife and mother Bridget died soon after their arrival. William Neagle placed his daughter in the city's Female Orphan Asylum and raised young David himself.[1]

David Neagle grew to manhood in San Francisco, and the mining boom camp excitement pervasive in that city during its early years clearly entered his blood and shaped his personality, endowing him with a zest for mining and an adventurous and aggressive nature that he retained, for good and ill, throughout his life. He attended private and public schools at Mission Dolores in San Francisco and at the age of ten entered the Roman Catholic school at Santa Clara, California, which later became Santa Clara University. But mining camp excitement drew him like a magnet, and, when only fifteen, he ran off to join the rush to the new strikes at Florence, Idaho. Returning to San Francisco in 1863 when his father died, he went back to school for a time, but soon left again to get in on the Comstock mining rush.[2] It was one booming mining town after another. In Nevada he was at Virginia City, the center of the great Comstock bonanza, Treasure City in the White Pine district, and Pioche, the chief camp of the Ely mining district.[3]

During this period he traveled to Salt Lake City, Utah, where he met and wooed Bertha Boesque, a pretty seventeen-year-old French girl, who soon became pregnant. A daughter named Louisa was born in 1870, and another daughter, Emma, came along the following year, but both died in childhood.[4] The couple apparently lived together until 1873, when they were married in California.[5]

At Pioche, one of the largest and rowdiest camps in Nevada, Neagle became involved in his first recorded gunplay in May 1871. He was standing on the town's main street conversing with gunman Mike Casey when Jim Levy, another pistoleer, attacked Casey from behind and shot and pistol-whipped him. Neagle appears to have been more than an innocent bystander, for he was armed and, in defense of Casey, unhesitatingly drew his weapon and triggered off four rounds. One bullet perforated both of Levy's cheeks and shattered his jaw.[6]

The story goes that Pioche lawmen arrested both Neagle and Levy and locked them up in the same cell. "The purpose behind this, Neagle suspected, was less to purify the civic sense than to tickle the Pioche sense of humor. [However], Jim Leavy [sic], with that hole through both cheeks, simply wouldn't be friends."[7]

In September 1871 a great fire swept Pioche, virtually destroying the town. Neagle was mentioned as one of the casualties of the blaze, but if he was anything, Neagle was a survivor, and he lived on after this disaster.[8]

Rumors of a promising silver strike in the Panamint Mountains, high above Death Valley, drew him back to California, and he headed for the new camp, called Panamint, arriving there on June 26, 1874.[9]

An early arrival at the raw new town emerging in Surprise Canyon, he pitched a tent, set up a board across two whisky barrels, and declared the Oriental Saloon open for business. From the start his place prospered, and as more material was freighted in he expanded his operation. Eventually he replaced the tent with a frame building and installed fixtures worth $10,000, including a billiard table, a black walnut bar, Inyo pine wainscotings finished to look like oak, a number of paintings of nude females, and two gambling rooms. He acquired an entire block on Main Street and soon was turning a handsome profit selling off lots.[10]

In an exuberant letter to a friend back in Pioche, Neagle sounded like a spokesman for the Panamint Chamber of Commerce. Extolling the town as "the richest mining camp on the Coast," he said he expected to have running soon "the finest saloon out of San Francisco," a place twenty by fifty feet with a splendid bar and the best stock money could buy. "Times are lively, money is plenty, and everyone is in high hopes and full of confidence [and] the population is increasing every day." His "honest impression was that Panamint would be a "second Washoe."[11]

He didn't mention that Panamint was a rowdy, shoot-'em-up town, evidently believing that fact to be self-evident to a fellow veteran of the region's raucous mining camps. To protect his customers from errant bullets flying on the streets of Panamint, Neagle reinforced the walls of his saloon with sheets of corrugated iron.[12]

The Oriental was more than just another Panamint saloon; it became a center of social and political activity in the town. There were no churches, but Neagle allowed the Reverend Orne of Owens Valley to conduct religious services in his saloon. Neagle brought theatrical troupes into town and presented shows on a little stage he built in the back of the place.[13]

Neagle envisioned a glorious future for Panamint, and, as one of the original pioneers, he anticipated that his personal prosperity would grow with the town. As an indication of his intention to settle down, he married Bertha and invested heavily in town lots and surrounding mining ventures. William Stewart, U.S. senator from Nevada and a big investor in mining enterprises, became a close friend and confidante.[14]

One of Neagle's more unusual business ventures during this period involved Senator Stewart; James Hume, renowned detective for Wells, Fargo and Company; and a pair of highwaymen named John Small and John McDonald. Between stagecoach holdups Small and McDonald did a little prospecting on the side. When in Panamint, they made their headquarters in Dave Neagle's Oriental Saloon and became quite friendly with the owner, who grubstaked their prospecting ventures. The partners hit a good-looking prospect just about the time Jim Hume got hot on their trail for stealing $4,000 from Wells, Fargo. Neagle, who knew Senator Stewart was interested in investing in a Panamint silver mine, arranged a meeting between the senator, the detective, Inyo County Sheriff Gilmore, the firm of Small & McDonald, and himself. A deal was worked out. Small and McDonald sold their mine to Stewart's company for $12,000. They repaid Wells, Fargo the $4,000 they had stolen, gave Neagle $4,000 for his grubstake, and kept $4,000 for themselves. All robbery charges were dropped. Everybody was pleased with the outcome, especially Dave Neagle, who had his $4,000 and the comforting knowledge that Smith and McDonald would probably drop the balance of the money in his establishment.[15]

In August 1875 Bertha gave birth to another child, a daughter named Winifred, called "Winnie" by the parents.[16] That year Neagle ventured into politics, leading an unsuccessful campaign to break the surrounding mining district away from Inyo County and form a new county with the seat at Panamint. He ran for county recorder and lost narrowly.[17]

Then came a series of calamities. First there was the Bank Panic of August 1875, and the bottom dropped out of the mining stock. Any hope that a railroad would build up Surprise Canyon was soon dispelled. In the spring of 1876 the mines surrounding Panamint showed signs of panning out, and the exodus began.

Dave Neagle joined it. He packed up and moved on, leaving his saloon and its accoutrements to the desert rats. It was reported, however, that he left the town with $20,000.[18] For a time he and Bertha stayed in Virginia City, where his sister Mercy lived, and there he opened a saloon called The Capital.[19]

But the boom camp itch was still in his blood, and for the next few years he was almost constantly on the move. After six or eight months he left Virginia City for Prescott, Arizona, where he took a job as a mine foreman, but still found time to work his own claims. The *Prescott Weekly Miner* in July 1877 noted that "Dave Nagel [*sic*], a good prospector and miner, is sinking a shaft on the Goodwin and is now down about 50 feet and considers the ore fair and his prospects flattering."[20]

Later that year while working a gold claim on Turkey Creek he suffered a serious leg injury in a fall. His leg became infected, and it was feared for a time that he would lose it, but his remarkable recuperative powers prevailed, and after being bed-ridden for four months he began to regain his health.[21] He went to the boom camp at Bodie but suffered a relapse and returned to San Francisco to recuperate. Regaining his strength, he headed for Nevada to check out the mining possibilities at Eureka. But after only six weeks he became ill again. There was a newspaper report that he had cancer.[22] Once again Neagle was forced to return to San Francisco.

When finally fully recovered, he resumed his tour of the far-flung mining camps. In Utah he took a job at the Horn Silver Mining Company for several months. From there he went to the headwaters of the Snake River. Hearing of mining excitement at placer diggings in Wyoming, he went there but was disappointed. Returning to Bodie, he worked mines and ran a saloon. Never long in one place, he mined in Arizona and took a job as foreman of a mine in Sonora, Mexico. He was at loose ends when the mine shut down, and John H. Behan, sheriff of Cochise County, Arizona, hired him as a deputy.[23]

Neagle had known Behan, a close friend and fellow Irish American, since Prescott days. Behan had been active in political circles around Prescott for years, having served as sheriff of Yavapai County and representative to the territorial legislature. When Behan moved to Tombstone with his young son on September 14, 1880, Neagle, his wife, and infant daughter were already there.[24] Both men would become deeply involved in the political struggles and violent history of the famous mining town.

Expanding rapidly, Tombstone, in Pima County, quickly became the largest community in Arizona. In recognition of that reality the territorial legislature split off a section of Pima to form a new county, Cochise; designated Tombstone the county seat; and authorized formal organization in January 1881. County officers were to be appointed by Governor John C. Frémont to serve until general elections scheduled for November 1882.

Wyatt Earp, his brothers Virgil and Morgan, and pal John H. ("Doc") Holliday, were early on the scene at Tombstone. Wyatt aspired for the lucrative job of tax collector and sheriff, and, as a Republican, had reason to believe that the governor, also a Republican, would favor him with an appointment. But John Behan, a Democrat, also coveted the post and had powerful friends in the capitol who successfully lobbied for his appointment. In the end Frémont tapped Behan for the job. Wyatt Earp did not accept this setback gracefully, and it was the beginning of a bitter enmity between the two men that contributed to the violent history of Tombstone that made its very name notorious.

Sheriff Behan named a political crony, Harry Woods, editor of the *Nugget*, one of the town's two newspapers, as his undersheriff. Among the deputies he selected was his friend from Prescott, David Neagle. Others given appointments were William M. ("Billy") Breakenridge, Dave Campbell, Frank H. Hereford, and Frank Stilwell.

The Earp brothers meanwhile secured employment with Wells, Fargo and Company as special stagecoach guards, appointments as city police, and deputy U.S. marshal commissions. In the months to come clashes between the various branches of law enforcement would add to the Tombstone turmoil.

During all those turbulent months Neagle trod a precarious line as a lawman. Sheriff John Behan was his boss and his friend, but Neagle never became too closely allied with him in Behan's machinations against the Earp faction. Neagle was therefore respected by partisans of both sides. Thus Billy Breakenridge, a Behan loyalist, could later write: "Nagle [*sic*] was very much in evidence in Tombstone in the early eighties. . . . He was a fearless officer and a good one,"[25] and Wells, Fargo operative and a staunch Earp supporter Fred Dodge would describe Neagle as a "square man [who] could not tolerate the work of Johnny Behan and there was a sure and final break between the two."[26] Wyatt Earp, who had nothing good to say about his Tombstone enemies, thought Neagle "not very shrewd" for being in the Behan camp, but grudgingly conceded that "he was honest and courageous; he did all of Behan's work that needed a fighting man."[27]

As an officer of the law in Cochise County Neagle arrested a number of tough and desperate characters, including his fellow deputy Frank Stilwell and bad man Pete Spence as suspects in a stagecoach robbery in September 1881.[28] In July of that year he took the ever dangerous Doc Holliday into custody on a similar charge, and in November he collared the feared gunman John Ringo, charged with robbery of a poker game.[29] In January 1882 he arrested Sherman McMaster, one of Wyatt Earp's cadre of gunfighters, at the Earp camp outside Tombstone,[30] and for discharging a pistol in the Oriental Saloon in March 1882 he collared the notorious J. J. Harlan, known throughout the frontier as "Off Wheeler," because of the extraordinary breadth of his shoulders and mulelike strength.[31] Remarkably, Neagle managed all of these arrests without once resorting to deadly force.

Neagle was out of town attending to business on October 26, 1881, when the Earp brothers and Doc Holliday fought their famous gun battle with the Clanton and McLaury boys near the OK Corral, and therefore did not witness that memorable event.

The election of Tombstone city officials was scheduled for January 3, 1882. At a meeting of the People's Independent Party on December 24, 1881, John Carr was nominated with little opposition as the party's candidate for mayor. It was a different story when it came time to nominate a man for city marshal. Eight men were in the running, including incumbent James Flynn, Deputy U.S. Marshal Leslie F. Blackburn, John L. Fonck, and Deputy Sheriff David Neagle. On the first ballot nine votes were cast for Flynn, eight for Neagle, two for Flonck, and none for Blackburn. Neagle won nomination on the third ballot, receiving seventeen votes to Flynn's thirteen. Tombstone's two newspapers split over the coming election, the *Nugget* backed the People's Independent candidates, Carr and Neagle, and the *Epitaph* threw its editorial support to Lewis Blinn for mayor and James Flynn for city marshal.

On the evening of December 28 Virgil Earp was shot and severely wounded in a shotgun ambush attack on the streets of Tombstone. Not only was this another provocative act in the developing war between the Earp and "cowboy" factions, but it precluded the election of Virgil Earp as city marshal on the Citizen's ticket.

At the election, held only a week after the attempted assassination of Virgil Earp, all the People's Independent candidates were elected, including the party's candidates for city council. Carr won an easy victory, receiving 830 votes to his opponent's 298. Neagle's election was a little tighter, but still decisive; he garnered 590 votes against 434 for Flynn and 103 for Blackburn.[32]

City Marshal Neagle, after assuming his new office, submitted to the council for approval the names of the men he wanted on his police force. All were Irishmen: James Kenny, James Coyle, Harry Solon, and Joseph Poynton. The council approved them all.[33]

Four months after assuming office as city marshal of Tombstone Neagle shot and killed a man. In the early morning hours of May 10, 1882, Officer Joe Poynton was called to a saloon in the Mexican quarter on Allen Street to quiet a group of Hispanics who, in a continuing celebration of Cinco de Mayo, had fired off weapons and created a disturbance. Poynton arrested two men and locked them up. Arraigned and fined hours later, they asked permission to seek out friends for money help. When Poynton returned to the saloon with the two, he was threatened by several celebrants led by Antonio Figueroa. The officer returned his prisoners to the jail and sought out his boss.

Marshal Neagle and Policeman Poynton, determined to disarm the crowd and arrest the troublemakers, again returned to the saloon. As they approached, Figueroa stepped out with a Henry rifle, fired, downed Poynton, and took off on foot. Neagle emptied his pistol at the fleeing assailant without effect. He ran back to his office, grabbed a Winchester rifle, and commandeered a horse from a passerby. He pursued Figueroa out of town about a half a mile, all the while shouting at him to stop. When his order was ignored, he dismounted and took aim with the rifle. His first shot missed, but the second struck Figueroa in the spine, killing him.

At a coroner's hearing, the dead man was described as forty-five years of age and "a tough customer" from Hermosillo, Sonora, Mexico. The coroner's jury found that "Figueroa died at Neagle's hands and that the marshal did it in discharge of his duty and thereby is exonerated from all blame."[34]

Poynton's injury was severe, and, while attending physicians believed his chances for recuperation were small, he eventually did recover. For two months he was nursed by the legendary Irish American entrepreneur and public benefactor Nellie Cashman, who put him up in her American Hotel. When the parsimonious city council refused to pay Poynton's medical expenses, amounting to more than $300, Dave Neagle began a campaign to raise money to cover those expenses and by mid-July had collected enough to pay off his deputy's debts.[35]

At the Democratic convention in September 1882 Neagle allowed his name to be entered as a candidate for sheriff, thereby challenging his old boss, John Behan, who sought reelection. Others contending for the post were Mike Gray, Larkin Carr, and another Behan deputy, Billy Breakenridge. When after six ballots it became clear that incumbent Behan lacked the support to gain the nomination, his name was withdrawn from contention. Neagle and Breakenridge also dropped out, and Carr finally defeated Gray for the nomination in a close vote.[36]

Infuriated by the finagling among the Democrats during the nomination process, Neagle ran for sheriff as an independent. Although he lacked the backing of either major party, he thought he had a good shot at winning the coveted office, for he was popular among the miners, especially with the copper workers at Bisbee who, according to Fred Dodge, were solidly in his camp.[37] Some of his backers claimed he was responsible for driving Wyatt Earp and his gunmen out of town. He was, they said, "a fast gun and that only [Bat] Masterson and [Johnny] Ringo might be in his class." The *Epitaph*, in opposing him, contended that "his hasty, ungovernable temper, his inclinations to harsh measures, his habit of drawing and using firearms to intimidate when unwarranted by facts, all prove him to be an unfit person to trust with . . . the office of sheriff."[38]

In the end all that Neagle's candidacy accomplished at the November 7, 1882, election was a split in the Democratic vote, allowing Jerome L. Ward, a Republican, to capture the sheriff's office. Ward received 1,096 votes to Neagle's 835. Carr finished a close third with 802 votes.[39]

Neagle did not take his defeat gracefully. As the polls were closing he attacked Milt Joyce, a county supervisor and the proprietor of the Oriental Saloon. He had considered Joyce a friend, but now accused him of secretly working to subvert his candidacy. After exchanging some hot words the two men resorted to blows. Neagle reportedly gave Joyce a thorough beating.[40]

He won the fistic battle, but lost any hope of a political career in Cochise County, Arizona. Soon thereafter he packed up his family and departed.

He spent some months of 1883 back in the Prescott area, and it was there that another child, a son, Albert, was born.[41]

By early 1884 Neagle had transferred all the way to Montana and taken a woodcutting contract to supply fuel to the Anaconda Company on Mill Creek near Butte. There he was involved in another shooting affair. On March 1 a man said to be a partner of Neagle's in the operation drew $600 in cash from the company, money intended as wages for the employees. Instead of paying off the workers, the man absconded with the money. Neagle went in pursuit, overtook the miscreant, and in a running gunfight on horseback downed the man with a well-aimed bullet. The injured man lingered near death for some time, but Neagle was exonerated of any wrongdoing at a preliminary hearing, and it is said became something of a hero around the woodcutters' camp for saving the workers' wages.[42]

Neagle did some work in the sheriff's office at Anaconda, and his name was mentioned as a possible candidate for sheriff, but evidently not all in the region looked on the man and his quick gun with favor. It was rumored that there were muttered threats of a lynching if the injured man died, and some advocated running Neagle out of town.[43]

Whether or not there was substance to the stories, Neagle definitely was not chased out of town after the shooting. A full year later he was still in the Anaconda district and apparently doing quite well financially, for the *Daily Miner* of Butte of March 8, 1885, reported that he had bet $100 on a horse race there. He did leave later that year, however, and returned to San Francisco.[44]

There he became a protégé of Christopher A. Buckley, the blind political boss of the city.[45] Buckley got him several state job appointments, including assistant sergeant of arms at the winter session of the California legislature and deputy sheriff assigned to the license bureau. No doubt Buckley influenced U.S. Marshal John C. Franks in his selection of Neagle as a deputy, a move destined to thrust Neagle eventually into the national limelight.

Marshal Franks twice appointed Neagle a special deputy marshal to maintain order at the polls during hotly contested congressional elections. "Both times," Franks said, "I assigned him to a precinct notorious for the rough character of its voters, where he acquitted himself with great credit; and it was mostly due to his great coolness and firmness that for about the first time in its history no disturbance occurred at the polling precinct at either election."[46]

Neagle joined two prominent legal figures and a voluptuous fiery female as leading players in a melodrama that grabbed the attention of the American public, and his performance in that drama eventually led to an important U.S. Supreme Court ruling that carries his name to this day.

The feminine lead in the piece was Sarah Althea Hill, a formidable woman of fashionable buxom physique who, after an apprenticeship in male enticement at a San Francisco bagnio, became the mistress of Senator William Sharon of Nevada, a widower worth millions. For a time Sarah, set up in style in a suite of hotel rooms and with a monthly allowance of $500 provided by her lover, lived the grand life. But when Sharon tired of her and turned off the financial spigots, Sarah cried foul. Claiming she had a document proving she and the senator had been legally married, she charged Sharon with flagrant adultery, and sued for divorce and a large alimony settlement.

The lawyer representing her in this action (and sharing her bed) was one of the most colorful figures in California history and another leading actor in the unfolding story. David S. Terry, born in Kentucky in 1823, fought under Sam Houston at the age of thirteen, was an early Texas Ranger, served as a lieutenant in the Mexican War, and in 1849 joined the gold rush to California, where he became a leader of the vigilance committees of 1852 and 1856. He served as chief justice of the California Supreme Court, but resigned in 1859 to fight a duel over the issue of slavery with U.S. Senator David Broderick, whom he killed. Indicted for murder, he was acquitted on the ground that killing a man in a duel was not murder. A handsome man of impressive bearing, he stood six feet three inches tall, weighed 250 pounds, and was notorious for his prodigious physical strength and explosive temper. He was believed to always have on his person a wicked-looking bowie knife. He used that knife to stab a man in the lobby of the Mark Hopkins Hotel and was nearly lynched by the vigilantes. Adamantly proslavery, he went back east to fight for the Confederate cause in the Civil War and, as the commander of a brigade, was one of the last to surrender. Returning to California after the war, he practiced law for the next twenty years and was recognized as one of the foremost legal figures in the state. As he fought Sarah's case against a battery of lawyers employed by Sharon, Terry confirmed his commitment to his client by marrying her in 1886.

The California Superior Court had granted Sarah a divorce decree and a monthly alimony in the amount of $2,500 in 1885, but Sharon's lawyers, denying that a legal marriage had ever been performed, appealed the ruling. They brought suit in U.S. District Court to have the purported Sharon marriage document thrown out as a forgery, thereby nullifying the Sharon marriage and the subsequent divorce. On November 15, 1885, Sharon died, with both state and federal cases still unresolved.

The federal case was referred to a master, and his hearings were disrupted constantly by Sarah, who often appeared flashing a pistol and mouthing threats. The master appealed to Stephen J. Field, justice of the U.S. Supreme Court, who directed U.S. Marshal J. C. Franks to control the woman. This action brought onto the stage the last two major players in the drama, Justice Field and Deputy U.S. Marshal David Neagle.

Stephen Field, another veteran of the California gold rush of 1849, had taken Terry's place on the bench of the California Supreme Court when Terry had resigned to duel Broderick. Field and Terry had always been political adversaries, but the Sarah Althea Hill case would bring them to deadly confrontation.

On January 31, 1888, the California Supreme Court affirmed the lower court ruling that granted Sarah a divorce, although the court reduced the amount of alimony. Lawyers representing the Sharon family responded by pushing hard for a favorable decision in federal court on the fraudulent marriage issue.

Anticipating a violent reaction from Sarah and Terry at a scheduled hearing in federal court in San Francisco, Judge Lorenzo Sawyer cautioned Marshal Franks about maintaining order. Franks assured the judge that a number of federal deputies and San Francisco police officers would be stationed throughout the courtroom, and decorum would be preserved. One of those peacekeepers was Deputy Marshal David Neagle, the last key performer in the developing tragedy.[47]

Well aware of the Terry couple's reputation for disruptive behavior in courtrooms, Neagle was on hand when Judge Sawyer convened his court on September 3, 1888. Neagle had no official status, but entered and took a seat as an interested spectator.

When midway in the proceedings it became apparent to Sarah that the ruling of the court would not be in her favor, she stood up, berated the justices in shrill language, and fumbled in a satchel she carried, a satchel later found to contain an English bulldog pistol with six loaded chambers.[48] Officers pounced on her and dragged her screaming from the room. In a rage David Terry "struck Franks a terrible blow on the neck with his fist which sent the marshal rolling across the floor."[49] Bailiffs and deputy marshals converged on Terry and shoved him into a chair.

By this time Neagle had joined the action. As he later testified, he grabbed Terry and assisted in holding him down. When he was finally allowed to stand up, Terry slid a hand inside his vest, pulled out a knife, and raised it over his head. Neagle said he heard him repeatedly threaten to "carve his way" out of there. The officers seized him again, and a deputy marshal named Taggart "held a six-shooter right to his temple and told him to drop the knife." With his right hand Neagle grabbed the knife by the blade and with his left bent Terry's fingers until Terry released his grip on the handle.[50]

Terry was at last quieted, but his wife still showed fight. Some time later Franks entered a room where the couple was being held under guard, and Sarah immediately "made a violent attack on him and beat him about the face and head" before deputies once again subdued her.[51]

The Terrys, initially jailed for contempt of court, were later indicted and jailed on charges of threatening and assaulting the U.S. marshal and several of his deputies. An additional charge of assault with a deadly weapon was brought against Terry. He received a sentence of six months in jail, and Sarah got thirty days.[52] One newspaper editor reminded Terry "that the days when a man can run a court of justice with a bowie knife in each boot, a stiletto down the back of his neck, a derringer in each vest pocket, a Texas dragoon six-shooter in each sleeve, and a Fort Sumter mortar in the pleats of his shirt have gone by."[53]

This type of ridicule troubled Terry not at all, and even as he served his jail time he continued to heap vituperation on his enemies, real and perceived, with special attention given to Justice Stephen J. Field. Sarah also took every opportunity to vilify the judge.

Supreme Court justices at this time followed a circuit, and Justice Field was scheduled to return to California from Washington in July 1889. Federal officials were still apprehensive that the Terrys would again attack the judge, and U.S. Attorney General W. H. Miller on May 27 sent Marshal Franks written authorization to employ a special deputy at $5 a day to serve as a bodyguard for Field. Franks selected Dave Neagle, and on June 17, 1889, Neagle was sworn in as deputy marshal.[54]

Special Deputy Marshal Neagle met the westbound train of Justice Field and his wife at Reno, Nevada, and rode with them to San Francisco. Then, on August 8, he accompanied Field on his trip south to hold court at Los Angeles. Five days later, on August 13, the judge and his bodyguard boarded a Pullman car for San Francisco, where David and Sarah were to appear in federal court the next morning to answer the charge of criminal contempt still outstanding against them.

Aware that the Terrys lived in Fresno and the train would stop there during the night, Neagle asked the porter to rouse him before the Fresno stop. He was therefore awake and watchful at three o'clock on the morning of August 14 when David and Sarah came aboard. He noticed that the couple had no luggage, but he did recognize the satchel Sarah carried as the same one in which she had secreted a pistol at the tumultuous court hearing a year earlier.

Concerned about the safety of his judicial charge when he and the Terrys came face to face at Lathrop, where there would be a thirty-minute stop for breakfast, Neagle had the train conductor dispatch telegrams ahead from Merced, the next stop. One warned the constable at Lathrop to be on hand at the depot and prepared for trouble; the other requested the sheriff of San Joaquin County "to secure assistance for Neagle, should it be required."[55]

When Justice Field arose in the morning shortly before the 7:30 arrival at Lathrop, Neagle told him of the proximity of the Terrys and urged him to take his breakfast in the dining car. But Field refused, saying that would be an indication of cowardice. Together they entered the depot dining room and took seats at a table near the center of the room.

Not long afterward the Terrys came in, stopped near the door, and surveyed the room. When they spotted Field, Sarah left hurriedly. Neagle, his hand on the handle of his six-shooter,[56] watched as Dave Terry strode directly up to the justice's table. For a moment the big man, with glaring eyes, paced menacingly back and forth behind Field's chair. Suddenly his hand shot out, and he struck Field twice, once in the face and again in the back of the head.

Justice Field later testified under oath to what happened then: "Coming so immediately together, the two blows seemed like one assault. Of course, I was for a moment dazed by the blows. I turned my head round, and I saw that great form of Terry's with his arm raised, and his fists clenched to strike me. I felt that a terrific blow was coming, and his arm was descending in a curved way, as though to strike the side of my temple, when I heard Neagle cry out, 'Stop! Stop! I am an officer.' "[57]

Revolver in hand, Neagle leaped to his feet, as Terry made a move that Neagle took to be an effort to draw that famous bowie knife. Without hesitation Neagle fired two shots in quick succession. One bullet struck the big man in the chest, and the other hit him in the head; either would have been fatal.[58]

The sounds of the shots were still reverberating in the room when Sarah, clutching her satchel, appeared in the doorway. Seeing her dying husband stretched out on the floor, she screamed, ripped open her satchel, and pulled out a large revolver. Before she could turn it on Field or Neagle, the dining room manager and bystanders grabbed her and tore the weapon from her hand. She then broke free, ran to her husband, and threw herself on his body. Even as she wailed that her "darling," her "sweetheart," had been murdered, she was, lawyers for Neagle would later claim, furtively secreting Terry's bowie knife in her bodice.[59]

As shocked bystanders crowded around, she pointed an accusing finger at Field and screamed, "Why don't they hang the man? The cowardly murderer! He was too cowardly to be given a trial so he hired an assassin! They shot him down like a dog in the road." The distraught woman, plainly hysterical, called for an immediate lynching. "If my husband had killed Justice Field, the crowd would have lynched him! Will you not help me punish the murderers of my husband?"[60]

As Terry's body was carried to a barbershop next to the railroad dining room, Neagle hurried Justice Field back to the train. A number of Terry's admirers attempted to block his way, and Neagle had to brandish his pistol to make his way through the crowd.[61] A few moments later Sarah also boarded the train and tried to force her way into the car where Neagle was ministering to the bruise on Field's face. "Keep her out," Neagle shouted, "or I'll kill her too!"[62]

Sheriff R. B. Purvis of Stanislaus County was also a passenger on the train. Over the vigorous protests of Justice Field, he disarmed Neagle and at Tracy, the next stop, placed him under arrest and turned him over to deputies, who escorted him in shackles over back roads to Stockton, where he was locked up in the local jail.

Meanwhile, Sarah enlisted the aid of San Joaquin County Sheriff Thomas Cunningham, a longtime friend of her husband's, and attempted to have Justice Field arrested in San Francisco on a charge of murder. Cunningham wired Oakland, and a detective from that city met the train when it arrived, but Marshal Franks, forewarned, also met the train and threatened to arrest the detective if he harassed the judge, and the detective backed off.[63]

At Stockton, Neagle, taken before a justice of the peace and charged with murder, was having some perilous moments. He was held without bail until a hearing scheduled for August 21. That meant he would remain in the dismal confines of the county jail an entire week while an unruly mob of Terry supporters milled in the streets, clamoring for a necktie party.[64]

But his friends in San Francisco were not unmindful of his predicament. Field's colleague, Judge Sawyer, had a writ of habeas corpus issued, and on Friday, August 16, Marshal Franks, accompanied by another deputy and a lawyer, entrained for Stockton. There he served Sheriff Cunningham with the writ, which directed him to release Neagle in the marshal's charge forthwith. Moving before dawn the next morning to avoid possible interference by Terry supporters, Franks secretly removed Neagle from the jail and, together with his deputy and attorney, escorted him to the depot, where a special train

Newspaper artist's depiction of Dave Neagle. From the author's collection.

waited. The train passed through Lathrop, the scene of the shooting, and arrived in San Francisco. There Neagle was again locked up in a jail cell to await a Tuesday hearing on the habeas corpus case, but free, at least, of fear of a lynch mob.[65]

Whether that fear had a basis in reality was discussed in the press. The editor of the *Salt Lake Tribune* editorialized that he was "heartedly glad" that Neagle had been taken to San Francisco, for if he had met violence in Stockton it "would have been an eternal disgrace to that city and to the State of California." The accounts by special reporters, he believed, could not be relied upon, for in their competition with each other some had drawn upon their imaginations for their accounts. "But," he acknowledged, "there is a desperate, ungovernable woman there, and she has a brother at her side. Stockton was long the home of Judge Terry, and he had many personal and partisan friends, and, moreover, a son or two, and so long as Nagle [*sic*] remained in Stockton it was possible that a single spark dropped at the right moment, might have exploded a magazine."[66]

Interviewed by reporters at the jail, Neagle said that he had been ever mindful that it was his responsibility to protect the life of Justice Field, adding, "I would have looked nice escorting a dead judge of the Supreme Court back to San Francisco."[67] To suggestions that he could have used less than lethal force to control Terry, he emphasized the huge difference in size and strength between the giant and himself. "If I'd got to close quarters with him," he reminded the newsmen, "he could bend me in two." Having witnessed Terry's violent knife-brandishing behavior in a federal courtroom, when it took six men with pistols to bring him under control, Neagle was convinced the man was intent on killing Field. "If I had hesitated, there would have been a different end to the affair. I'm sorry for the old man. But it was my duty and I had to do it."[68]

To other reporters Neagle said that he had never before seen such a demoniacal expression on a man's face in his life. "It meant murder and I knew it in a moment. . . . I got there first, that's all. . . . What chance would I have had against him, a man who weighed 240 pounds while I weigh only about 145? . . . Suppose Justice Field had been killed or seriously injured, what would have become of me? I would have been compelled to go to Africa or some other country; but I

Another newspaper artist captured Dave Neagle's pugnacious nature in this drawing. From the author's collection.

believe that I would have turned the pistol to my own head and blown my brains out."[69]

A reporter for the *San Francisco Examiner* even paid a visit to Bertha Neagle to obtain an interview. He found her in the Neagles' "cozy little flat on McAllister street, surrounded by the comforts of a refined home, [and] busily engaged in writing a letter to her husband in prison. . . . Two children brighten the home — Winnie, a tall, dark, winsome child of fourteen years, and Albert, a fair-haired little chap of seven." Bertha staunchly defended her husband, saying she was confident he would be cleared of any wrongdoing, for she knew him "to be cool-headed and a man who never acts on the impulse of the moment and one who is a quick thinker and usually right." She denied that he was a gunfighter who had downed a man in Arizona and another in Montana, saying that she had been with him all the time and that there was absolutely no truth to the reports.[70]

News of the shooting created sensational headlines in newspapers across the nation, for most of the participants in the affair were already well known to the public. William Sharon had been one of the nation's wealthiest men, and the sordid story of Sarah's legal battle to get her hands on his millions had already made her name familiar in American households. Terry had been extolled and vilified in press accounts since the day he killed David Broderick thirty years earlier. Stephen Field, as a justice on the U.S. Supreme Court, was one of the most important men in the country. Only David Neagle, the man who had snuffed out Terry's life in defense of Field, was a nonentity, but that, too, would change when the story broke. A dispatch that went out over the news wires from San Francisco the day of the shooting introduced him: "David Nagle, who killed Terry, is well known here. He lived in Arizona about ten years ago, and was at one time chief of police at Tombstone. He had the reputation there of being a man of undisputed courage, and he once killed a Mexican desperado who resisted arrest. He was appointed a deputy marshal here a year ago."[71]

Newspaper comments regarding David Terry were remarkably uncomplimentary. The editor of the *Evening Gazette* of Reno, Nevada, called him "one of the most unpopular men in California [who] seems to have had a penchant for making himself generally disagreeable."[72]

E. L. Godkin in the *Nation* declared that "somebody ought to have killed Terry a quarter of a century ago."[73]

On August 16 the *Chicago Chronicle* reported that in that city the feeling was "unanimous" that Terry had received his just deserts. "Gentlemen familiar with Pacific Coast matters," it said, "expressed the opinion that Terry only got what he deserved." The *Chronicle* went on to reprint some of the disparaging comments about Terry appearing on the editorial pages throughout the country.

Neagle was indicted for the murder of Judge Terry in the California courts, but on August 22 Judge Sawyer released him on $5,000 bail pending a hearing on the writ of habeas corpus scheduled for September 3 before Judges Sawyer and Sabin. On that date James T. Carey, the U.S. attorney in San Francisco, flanked by seven of the leading lawyers of the city specially recruited by Justice Field, appeared in Neagle's defense. The argument they presented was uncomplicated and direct.

An officer of the United States, charged with a particular duty — that is, protecting the life of a justice of the U.S. Supreme Court — could not be imprisoned by state authorities for an act committed in the performance of that duty. Arrested, he should be "brought before the tribunals of the nation of which he is an officer, and the fact there inquired into. And if it be found that the act complained of was in the performance of his duties, he could not be tried and punished by the State."[74]

California Attorney General G. A. Johnson, assisted by Avery C. White, district attorney of San Joaquin County, represented the interest of the state. Their argument was equally straightforward: clearly a homicide had been committed in the state, and only the officers and courts of the state had authority to try and punish the malefactor.

When called to the stand to testify, U.S. Marshal John G. Franks denied the allegation in certain newspapers that Neagle was a "killer" of the border-ruffian type. He was, rather, "a peaceable, law-abiding man, but of much courage, which had been proven on several occasions," and that was why he had been chosen to protect Field from assault. He had warned Neagle that Terry was likely to assault Field, and if he did, Neagle would have to act quickly. He had advised his deputy to take no chances and to protect Field at all hazards.

Justice Field testified that in his opinion if Neagle had not shot Terry when he did, he (Field) "would have been dead within five seconds."

Dave Neagle took the stand and said that Terry slapped Field twice, first with the right hand, and then the left. Neagle said he leaped to his feet, threw out his right hand to keep Terry off, and shouted, "Stop that, I am a United States officer." Terry then turned his attention to him and raised his right arm as of to deliver another blow. "He looked like an infuriated beast. His clenched fist immediately sought his bosom. Believing my life in danger, I immediately drew my pistol, and . . . fired two shots in quick succession. Terry fell to the floor. I believe that Terry would have cut me to pieces and perhaps Justice Field if I had not acted promptly."[75]

Other witnesses also testified to the hatred Judge Terry and his wife held for both Justice Field and Judge Sawyer, one of the men sitting in judgment at this very hearing. Judge Van Dyke of Los Angeles, as a passenger on a train back in August 1888, had witnessed an act of provocation of Judge Sawyer by Sarah. An Oakland newsman testified that Sarah once told him she would probably kill Judge Field some day.[76]

The advocates for the state introduced witnesses, but they were plainly outgunned by the legal team arrayed against them and additionally had to argue their case before two judges known to be closely allied with Justice Field, one of whom had been threatened by Terry and his wife. Under those circumstances, they could not have been surprised by the ruling of the judges, which, in effect, gave the blessing of a federal court to Neagle's deed.

Amid much backslapping and congratulatory shouts from his friends in the courtroom, Neagle, still under $5,000 bond, was released on his own recognizance, pending an appeal by the California lawyers to the U.S. Supreme Court.[77]

He was then hustled down the hall to the offices of Justice Field, who, in full anticipation of the favorable ruling, had a gold watch and chain, already inscribed, as a presentation gift for the deputy marshal. The inscription read: "Stephen J. Field to David Neagle, as a token of appreciation of his courage and fidelity to duty under circumstances of great peril at Lathrop, Cal. on the fourteenth day of August, 1889."[78]

The appeal to the Supreme Court of the lower court decision by the state of California has been enshrined in the history of American jurisprudence as *In re Neagle*, an important states' rights versus federal government case. On March 4 and 5, 1890, justices of the Supreme Court, absent Stephen Field, who had recused himself, heard the respective arguments.[79] California Attorney General G. A. Johnson spoke for that state. U.S. Attorney General W. H. H. Miller, assisted by Joseph H. Choate, "probably the leading advocate of his time," represented the federal government.[80] After five weeks of deliberation, the court rendered its decision on April 14, 1890, with Justice Samuel F. Miller delivering the majority opinion, upholding Judge Sawyer's original ruling and sustaining the position of the federal government. There were two dissents.[81]

When Justice Miller read the words, "in taking the life of Terry [Neagle] was acting under the authority of the law of the United States, and was justified in so doing, and that he was not liable to answer in the courts of California on account of his part in that transaction,"[82] he removed the ominous cloud that had hung over Neagle's head since that day eight months earlier when he pumped two bullets into David Terry at Lathrop.

After his final clearing in the Terry shooting Neagle remained in the San Francisco area for the rest of his life. During the 1890s he was employed as bodyguard for Henry E. Huntington, the railroad mogul, and while working in that capacity in 1896 he became the subject of newspaper headlines again when he got involved in an ugly dispute with a San Francisco newspaper editor.

In early August 1896 a man named A. J. Collins, a former employee of the Southern Pacific who held a grievance against the company for real or perceived ill usage, approached Huntington outside the railroad offices. Bodyguard Neagle, who recognized Collins from previous problems with him, quickly stepped between the two men and, according to at least one witness, "brutally banged Collins' head against a brick wall."[83]

James H. Barry, an editor of the *San Francisco Star* who harbored a long-standing animosity toward Huntington and the Southern Pacific Railroad, pounced on the incident, which he saw as another example of the high-handed and arrogant tactics of the man and his company. In an editorial Barry viciously attacked Huntington's man,

David Neagle. He called him an "infernal miscreant" who had murdered Judge Terry and "should long since have dangled from the gallows." Neagle was a "hired villain" of the Southern Pacific where "such wretches belong if they must be outside of a jail or gallows." When Collins spoke "quietly' to Huntington, "Neagle grabbed him by the throat, threw him off the sidewalk, and threatened to kill him if he bothered railroad people again. Neagle is not, on general principles, a safe man to be at large, nor is Huntington as long as he keeps such a bulldog around him. . . . Neagle is a dangerous character who should be shot dead by any man whom he approaches."[84]

Encountering Barry later that day on the street, Neagle demanded to know if he was the author of the piece. When Barry replied that he was, Neagle, according to several newspaper reports, spat in his face. Barry responded with a wild swing. Neagle stepped back to avoid the blow, and his hand streaked to his hip pocket. "Fill your hand!" he snapped. Barry protested that he was unarmed as bystanders jumped in and led the two away before the confrontation escalated further.[85]

Barry, in a somewhat different version of this confrontation, said that Neagle rushed at him and attempted to spit in his face. "Then he drew a pistol from his left hip and twirled it by his side. He is a left-handed coward. . . . He was twirling his pistol like a cowboy." Barry said he refused to be intimidated and boldly challenged Neagle: "I know that you have threatened to kill me. Now, do it." Bystanders then intervened to prevent any further action.[86]

The story dispatched from San Francisco on the wire services received particular attention in Arizona, where Neagle was remembered from his Tombstone days. The *Arizona Republican* of Phoenix reprinted editor Barry's diatribe against Neagle and a rehash of the Terry shooting that had appeared in the *San Francisco Examiner*. The latter paper characterized Neagle as having "a reputation throughout the Pacific coast as a 'gun fighter.' "[87]

The dispatch of August 7 denied a report that Barry's friends were organizing a vigilance committee to force Neagle out of town. "There is and has been for a long time a strong feeling adverse to Neagle, and it reached a point of extreme bitterness as soon as his attack on Barry became generally known [but] there has no effort been made towards an organization of any kind with a view to ridding the town of his presence. The first reports of his assault on Barry were colored considerably by eye witnesses of the affair. There is no doubt, though, that Neagle sought an excuse to kill Mr. Barry."[88]

On August 7, almost a week after the altercation with Collins, a warrant was issued for Neagle's arrest on a charge of assault. Neagle and his supporters immediately accused Barry of being behind this. Neagle was quoted in the papers as saying he would keep the peace, but would "not allow a wanton attack upon him to pass unnoticed."[89]

At a hearing into the assault charge held on August 12 Neagle appeared in police court without counsel, entered a guilty plea, and waived a jury trial. A man named W. O. Cubery testified to seeing him throw Collins against a brick wall. When Prosecuting Attorney Reed said Neagle was a "bouncer for the railroad" and little more than a hired ruffian, the defendant leaped to his feet and advanced toward him, shouting, "I am not a hired ruffian!" Judge Low, fearful that a row was about to break out, quickly adjourned court until the next day and admonished Neagle to have an attorney with him at his next appearance.[90]

Neagle appeared the following day, accompanied by an attorney, and again had to be restrained when in his testimony Collins referred to him as "a low-down, contemptible vile coward." Judge Low accepted Neagle's guilty plea and fined him $50.[91]

The *San Francisco Chronicle*, covering the Neagle-Collins-Barry imbroglio in its issue of August 6, 1896, inserted a line that Neagle was inclined to "avoid the Earp boys when they visit San Francisco," a gratuitous and dubious assertion. Wyatt Earp, a prominent resident of the city at the time, was being interviewed for a series of articles that ran over a three-week period in the *Examiner* during the very month Neagle's problems were being publicized in the press.[92] No evidence has surfaced that there was ever any difficulty between Wyatt Earp and Dave Neagle, two veteran fighting men of the turbulent Tombstone period.

After his dramatic defense of the life of Justice Field, Neagle was in demand as a bodyguard for high officials. The Southern Pacific Railroad employed him for several years as a bodyguard and gunman. In 1899 his old friend Senator William Stewart hired him as a bodyguard during his campaign for reelection in Nevada.[93] In 1907 Patrick Calhoun, president of the United Railroad, hired him for personal protection, and he also found work as a special investigator and personal bodyguard for prominent criminal lawyer Earl Rogers. During these years he was listed in San Francisco city directories as a "railroad man." But despite these ventures into security employment, his interest in mining activity never lagged. By 1898 he was describing himself as a "miner." As late as 1912, when he was sixty-five years old, he held a job as mine superintendent in Tuolumne County, California.[94]

Neagle and his wife, Bertha, lived in San Francisco until about 1910 when they moved across the bay to Oakland. Enumerated in the U.S. Census that year, the sixty-two-year-old Neagle gave his occupation as gold miner. Daughter Winifred had married a man named August Halter. Twenty-seven-year-old son Albert, an electrician with the telephone company, continued to live with his parents. A decade later Albert told the census-taker he was working as a "motion picture operator," while his father, now seventy-three, insisted that his occupation was still "mining."[95]

David Neagle died in his home at Oakland on November 28, 1925. He was seventy-eight years old.[96]

# — 6 —

## BILLY BROOKS
### 1849–1874

*Bill has sand enough to beat the hour-glass that tried to run him out.*
*— Wichita Eagle, June 14, 1872*

"There are those who say that William Brooks could have been the greatest and most efficient lawman the West had ever seen before he himself went bad," reported the author of a recent encyclopedia of crime in the United States.[1]

Those who knew him might have laughed at the suggestion that Brooks was a great and efficient lawman, even in the early days of his career, but all would have agreed that he certainly went bad. They would also have agreed that he was a gunfighter of top-notch caliber. Buffalo hunter Emanuel Dubbs, later the first judge of Wheeler County, Texas, and one who claimed to have seen Brooks in action, wrote that the man was "wonderfully quick with a gun. He carried two, one on each hip (as did nearly everyone else), and in the flash of an eye he could draw one in each hand and fire."[2]

The life of Brooks was short and violent — he only lived to the age of twenty-five — but somehow he struck people as being older and larger than he actually was. A minister's wife who knew him in Caldwell a few months before he died described him some nine years later as "doubtless a bad man. He was very large and about thirty years of age."[3]

Kansas historian Floyd B. Streeter, after interviewing Kansas pioneers who had known Brooks, described him as "a handsome, stout-built fellow, five feet, eight inches tall, about forty years of age, [who] had a large head of hair that reached to his shoulders."[4]

Men with fearsome reputations as killers often were remembered as older men of large stature, when in fact many were youthful in years, although perhaps prematurely aged by frontier experience, and on the smallish side. The only photograph we have of Billy Brooks shows a man of not unusual size, rather slender, with normal-length hair. If it were not for his prominently displayed white-handled six-shooter and gun belt, he might, in his baggy pants, unbuttoned vest, and ridiculous hat, look more like a rodeo clown than a dangerous gunfighter.

Born in Ohio in 1849, the eldest son of blacksmith Edmund Brooks and his wife, Cynthia,[5] William Brooks as a teenager found his way to the plains of Kansas. There he joined the great buffalo hunt then getting under way, and demonstrated a skill with weapons that eventually earned him the appellation "Buffalo Bill."[6]

By 1870, when he reached the age of twenty-one, he took employment with the Southwestern Stage Company as a driver of coaches between El Dorado and Wichita. It was a tough, demanding job, and Billy Brooks soon gained the respect of his employers and the traveling public for his courage, stamina, and dogged dedication to duty. A story demonstrating his virtues made the rounds. After a torrential storm Brooks and his stagecoach came on swollen Chisholm Creek, surging out of its banks. Most drivers would have turned back, but Brooks drove his mule team forward and successfully carried the mail across the flood.[7]

When the Atchison, Topeka & Santa Fe (AT&SF) Railroad reached Newton in July 1871 the El Dorado to Wichita stage line was discontinued, and Brooks took on a new run, from Wichita to the burgeoning town of Newton. Like most end-of-track towns of the American West, Newton attracted the flotsam of the frontier: thugs and saloon loafers, gamblers, and whores, the entire roster of border riff-raff. And with them, assuredly, came wanton violence. As residents of the closest railroad shipping point in Kansas for Texas cattlemen, Newtonians braced themselves in the coming 1872 season for another invasion, hordes of trail-tough Texas cowboys. A hard-bitten, no-nonsense lawman was needed to ride herd on this volatile mixture, and young Billy Brooks was tapped for the chore.

Billy Brooks wears a comical-appearing hat, but his big pearl-handled pistol looks fearsome in this photograph. Courtesy of the Boot Hill Museum, Dodge City, Kansas.

In February 1872 residents of Newton organized their community as a third-class city and at elections two months later elected James H. "Pop" Anderson mayor. On April 1 Anderson appointed Billy Brooks the town's first city marshal at the munificent salary of $75 a month. The reputation of the erstwhile buffalo hunter and stagecoach driver for fearlessness and proficiency with weaponry no doubt had much to do with his selection; rumors were rampant that Brooks had already gunned down bad men in other rough railroad towns.[8]

A little over two months after pinning on the city marshal's badge in Newton Billy Brooks had an opportunity to display the bulldog tenacity and fighting spirit for which he was noted. On Sunday night, June 9, 1872, a bunch of Texans, fresh from the trail, took over a Newton saloon and dance hall and "corralled" the proprietor, Edward T. ("Red") Beard, "with their six-shooters."[9] Beard was a mighty tough hombre, as he would often prove before his sudden demise at the hands of saloon competitor "Rowdy Joe" Lowe in a celebrated gunfight at West Wichita a year later, but on this occasion he was unable to control the obstreperous Texans. He sent for Marshal Brooks.[10]

Hurrying to the scene, Brooks managed to talk two of the cowboy leaders into leaving the establishment. They mounted up, and appeared to be leaving when suddenly one of them pulled a gun and fired at the officer, hitting him in the shoulder. Both then put spurs to their ponies and rode hard for their outlying camp. With a bullet lodged next to his collarbone, Brooks swung into the saddle and tore off in pursuit. In the running fight that ensued he was hit twice more. A Wichita paper reported that he "continued his pursuit for ten miles before he returned to have his wounds dressed. One shot passed through his right breast and the other two were in his limbs."[11]

None of the wounds were life-threatening, and the next day Brooks swore out "John Doe" and "Richard Roe" complaints against the two drovers, who had been identified as James Hunt and Joe Miller. Harvey County Sheriff W. B. Chamberlain arrested Hunt, but Miller was not to be found. After a hearing in which Brooks, Beard, and several other witnesses testified, a magistrate bound Hunt over to the district court and ordered him jailed at Emporia.[12]

Perhaps in need of a rest to recuperate from his wounds, Billy Brooks resigned as Newton city marshal on June 17, 1872, and accepted payment of $110 to cover his salary for the month of May and partial June.[13]

From Newton, Brooks drifted on to Ellsworth, where recovery from his injuries did not prevent him from taking on a short stint as policeman. On August 7, 1872, the Ellsworth city council authorized payment of $17.50 to Brooks for his services.[14]

By October he had settled in at the latest terminus of the AT&SF Railroad, a little burg soon to become famous as Dodge City, "the Beautiful Bibulous Babylon of the Frontier," as it was famously termed by the editor of the *Kinsley Graphic*.[15] It was there that many of the most celebrated gunfighters of the West — Wyatt Earp, the Masterson brothers, John H. ("Doc") Holliday, Ben Thompson, Luke Short, Bill Tilghman, David ("Mysterious Dave") Mather, Clay Allison — strode the streets in the late 1870s and early 1880s when Dodge City became known throughout the West as the "Cowboy Capital." According to popular belief, during this period, when wild Texas herders off the longhorn trail attempted to hurrah the town and tough lawmen struggled to hold them in check, gunfights became common occurrences and Dodge gained its notoriety as the wickedest town in America. But Dodge's well-deserved reputation for violence predated its cattle town period. The town's unsavory reputation as a scene of wanton bloodletting was actually established in the first year of its existence, long before it became a terminus of the Western Cattle Trail. Billy Brooks would be a major figure in creating that reputation.

On September 5, 1872, a month before Brooks transferred there, the AT&SF Railroad in its westward development reached a rude outpost called "Buffalo City." The town that sprang up there soon became an outfitting and marketing center for the hide hunters carrying on the great buffalo slaughter then in progress on the plains of western Kansas. It also became a vice center, providing whiskey, wagering, and whores for carousing buffalo hunters, area cowboys, and soldiers from nearby Fort Dodge. Visiting the new town only two days after the arrival of the railroad, a correspondent described it in a letter to a Leavenworth newspaper: "Saturday evening [September 7] we reached Dodge, or Buffalo City, as it is called. . . . The 'city' consists of about a dozen frame houses and about two dozen tents, beside a few adobe houses. The town contains several stores, a gunsmith's establishment, and a barber shop. Nearly every building has out a sign in large letters: 'Saloon.' "[16]

The town expanded rapidly and soon could boast of mercantile establishments, a doctor's office, a drugstore, a gunsmith's shop, and, of course, its inevitable cluster of saloons and dance halls. There were few women, and most of those present were denizens of the dance halls.

An exception was Mrs. A. J. Anthony, the wife of one of the town's early businessmen, who, on arriving, looked in vain for a female face until she was finally introduced to the landlady of the Dodge House. She sat down to breakfast with "a great crowd of long haired hunters" clad in buckskin suits and wearing pistols. The revolver, she said, was a "strong factor in all departments of social life, differences and disputes often ending in violence, as Boot Hill could testify. . . . Every few days we used to hear of some poor soul gone to his account from sudden death."[17]

Living with Billy Brooks at Buffalo City was one of the dance hall damsels, a twenty-one-year-old named Matilda, described as "small in stature, with pale and delicate features, large bright eyes and short curly hair."[18] She took his name and passed as his wife, although it is unlikely there ever was a formal marriage. Whether she came with him from Ellsworth is not known, but "Matilda Brooks" was enumerated with "W. Brooks" when an organizational census was taken of the residents of the town on January 11, 1873.[19]

In early Dodge City the propensity for violent behavior that characterized Brooks's short career clearly became evident. It was there that he lost the appellation "Buffalo Bill" and came to be called "Bully Billy." He turned to gambling as a profession and appears to have formed a partnership with a well-known saloon man and gambler named Matt Sullivan, who conducted a game in the Kelley and Hunt dance hall.

In November there was a violent outbreak in the establishment when some Texas cowhands tangled with Sullivan and his partner, identified only as "Billy" in the newspaper reports, but is believed to be Billy Brooks.

The *Newton Kansan* gave the story only a single line: "There was a man shot at a dance house in Dodge City a few nights ago."[20] The casualty list in the *Leavenworth Daily Commercial* was increased to three, warranting thusly two lines of copy: "Dodge City is winning the laurels from Newton. Three men were shot at a dance house there the other night and thrown into the street, while the dance went merrily on."[21]

The *Kansas City Times* provided more details under the headline: "A SHOOTING AFFAIR OF A DESPERATE CHARACTER." The trouble developed, it seemed, on November 14 when one of the Texans lost a large wager in a game presided over by Matt Sullivan and "Billy." The angry cowboy charged the gamblers with cheating, and "grabbed the entire wealth of the concern to appropriate it." There was immediate chaos. Whipping out a six-shooter, Sullivan struck the man "above the left temple, fracturing the skull and penetrating the temporal lobe of the brain with the hammer of the revolver, inflicting a mortal wound." Another herder leveled a revolver at Sullivan's back, but Billy "shot him dead, the ball entering the cheekbone and coming out the base of the brain." Sullivan turned his pistol on a third cowboy, shooting him "through the neck, the ball just grazing the jugular vein." Two of the Texas cowboys were dead, according to this report, while the third, although dangerously wounded, was expected to live. He departed by train for Topeka the next day to seek medical attention.[22]

Commenting on the affair a few days later, the paper said, "three men were shot and thrown out into the frost [at Dodge, where] they make no trouble about killing a few men at a dance house fandango."[23]

A man named Knarf, who claimed to have been an eyewitness to the affair, took issue with the slim account in the *Topeka Daily Commonwealth* and in a letter to that paper attempted a correction. When the herders behaved in a "high hand" manner and bragged that they had come to take the town, he said, Sullivan "seized the leader of the party by the collar and struck him over the head with a revolver, sending him to grass. At this, one of the Texans drew a revolver to shoot Sullivan, when another citizen, who had his pistol ready, shot him through the back of the neck. . . . A third one then fired at the party, when Sullivan shot at him, the ball striking him in the jaw and passed out the back of his head." Knarf expressed no sympathy for any of the cowboys, saying they "got no more than they deserved." He did insist, however, that the wounded men were not cruelly thrown out into the cold, as had been reported. Someone brought a doctor, who dressed the wounds. Later citizens helped carry the man pistol-whipped by Sullivan to his room in the town's only hotel, the Essington House (later the Dodge House), while the other two were removed to Fort Dodge and given over to the care of the post surgeon. At the writing all were still alive, as far as Knarf knew.[24]

A young man named Henry H. Raymond arrived on the train from his home in Sedgwick, Kansas, early on the morning of November 16, 1872, little more than twenty-four hours after the shooting fracas in the Kelley and Hunt dance hall. Years later he could recall vividly his first experience: "Daylight was just breaking. I saw a light in a window across the street, so we entered the place. Some persons were around a table, engaged in a game of cards with piles of poker chips, also currency. They apparently had been gambling the whole night. The man sitting with his back to the door as I entered wore two big revolvers, whose ends showed beside the stool on which he was sitting. I learned afterwards that he was Bill Brooks, a gambler and all around crook."[25]

Other early residents of Dodge City remembered Billy Brooks well. Emanuel Dubbs counted Brooks "among the many lawless characters who in the very beginning drifted into town" and said that "in a few weeks he had established a reputation as a killer. . . . In less than a month he had killed or wounded fifteen men."[26]

Western writer William MacLeod Raine, who knew Dubbs in his later years, said he couldn't "quite swallow that 'fifteen.' Still, [Brooks] had a man for breakfast now and then and on one occasion four."[27]

Dubbs described the shooting of the four. One night in the winter of 1872–73 he heard shooting and saw four men crossing to the south side of the railroad tracks where a dance hall "was in full blast of activity, as this was the nightly resort of such characters as Billy Brooks and lewd women." Joined by Fred Singer, another buffalo hunter, who told him the four were gunning for Brooks, Dubbs followed the men and, as they entered the dance hall, shouted a warning. "They fired several shots back at us, which we returned. Then from the door of the dance hall came such a fusillade of shots from the revolvers in the hands of Brooks, who stood in bold relief in the light of the door, that it appeared to me as if a whole company had fired at the same time." When the smoke cleared two of the four lay dead, and the others were dying. Brooks sustained a slight wound in the shoulder, and one of the dance hall girls was seriously wounded by a stray shot. Dubbs later learned that the men were four brothers from Hays City out to avenge a fifth brother killed by Brooks. He said there was no investigation of the Dodge City shooting as the brothers "got what the people thought they deserved."[28]

No other Dodge City pioneer mentions this dramatic shooting affair, and contemporary newspapers are strangely silent about it. As Brooks researcher Gary L. Roberts has noted: "While the lack of a newspaper citation fails to prove that the incident did not occur, it would be folly to conclude that it did happen on the basis of a single, unsubstantiated account by an old timer with a reputation for telling windies."[29]

The Dubbs account should not be entirely disparaged, however. Dodge City had no newspaper at the time, and reports of violence within the new town reaching other papers in the state were fragmentary and often incorrect. On at least three occasions newspapers reported erroneously that Billy Brooks had been killed in Dodge.[30] The *Wichita Beacon*, for instance, told its readers in February 1873 that "Bill Brooks, who used to swing the longest lash and make the best time on the old stage line between Newton and here, died with his boots on at Dodge City Sunday night. He was shot dead. Billy of late lived at the revolver's mouth, and has finally died there. He was clever and brave but merciless to a foe." Calling Brooks "the intrepid marshal of Dodge City," the paper noted that "one by one the leaves are falling."[31]

The following week the editor of the *Beacon*, somewhat abashedly, had to admit his error and print a retraction. "We have written in a brief run of four months, two obituary notices of Bill Brooks; he invariably lives to make us out a liar. We quit now for fear he will ride down our way and make an obituary notice of us, some of these lovely mornings. Twice we have been misinformed by our friends here; the next time they want an obituary for him they must show cause why."[32]

The editor's reference to Brooks as "marshal" in his original item was also misleading. Dodge was not incorporated as a city of the third class until November 1875 and did not elect officers until December of that year. As J. B. Edwards, who was in Dodge those first few months, stated emphatically: "There was no law, no organized law, in existence during the period I was there. We needed officers of the law bad enough, God knows! But some way, or somehow, only those died with their boots on who could well be spared. I helped bury a few of the first ones killed there on Boot Hill."[33]

When violence erupted in newly formed towns on the frontier, concerned businessmen, who had a vested interest in the growth and success of the infant community, often hired gunmen of demonstrated ability as peacekeepers to ride herd on troublemakers. These fellows were called "marshals," but were in fact privately employed security guards. Dodge City followed this pattern, and in those early months Jack Bridges, who, as a deputy U.S. marshal, was the only legally authorized law enforcement officer in town, took employment as "marshal" at Dodge. Billy Brooks was hired as his assistant.

Two days before Christmas, 1872, Brooks engaged in a gunfight and shot a man. The meager report in the *Wichita Eagle* said only that a "shooting affray occurred at Dodge City on Monday night of last week [December 23], between 'Bully' Brooks, ex-marshal of Newton, and Mr. Brown, yardmaster at the former place, which resulted in the death of Brown. Three shots were fired by each party. Brown's first shot wounded Brooks, whose third shot killed Brown and wounded one of his assailants. Brooks is a dangerous character, and has before, in desperate encounters, killed his man."[34]

Robert M. Wright, an early businessman of Dodge, remembered the encounter differently in his history of Dodge City published in 1913. He said that Brooks, while "acting assistant marshal," shot "Browney, the yard-master," in a dispute over a woman remembered only as "Captain Drew."[35] The bullet from Brooks's gun struck Brown in the back of the head, and, said Wright, "one could plainly see the brains and bloody matter oozing out of the wound, until it mattered over. . . . The ball entered one side of his head and came out the other, just breaking one of the brain or cell pans at the back of the head, and this only was broken." Incredibly, Brown survived this terrible wound and "was back at his old job in a few months."[36]

And then, less than a week later, Matt Sullivan, Brooks's gambling partner in the Kelley and Hunt dive, was assassinated. According to the account in a Topeka paper, on Saturday, December 28, 1872, someone fired through a window of the saloon, hitting Sullivan and killing him almost instantly. "It is supposed," ran the story, "that the unknown assassin was a character in those parts called Bully Brooks, but nothing definite is known concerning the affair, or what led to it."[37] That Sullivan's erstwhile partner was immediately suspected of the murder suggests two things: that the two gamblers had earlier quarreled and dissolved their partnership, and that Brooks's reputation as a killer had reached new heights in Dodge.

The murder of Matt Sullivan became just another of the many unresolved homicides that took place in Dodge City during its first year. Exactly how many people died violently in those early months can never be determined with certainty. Those men present during those turbulent times are not in agreement. George M. Hoover, who had a liquor store and saloon in Dodge from its inception, remembered there were "no less than fifteen men killed in Dodge City during the winter of 1872 and spring of 1873, all buried on Boot Hill."[38] Robert M. Wright, another town founder, wrote that "these shooting scrapes, the first year, ended in the death of twenty-five, and perhaps more than double that number wounded."[39] Estimates by historians of the period range from nine "with another three as possibles,"[40] to seventeen, "according to various area newspaper accounts,"[41] to "between 25 and 35."[42]

In his book *Hard Knocks*, Harry ("Sam") Young, who spent some time in Dodge that first year, related a story illustrative of the arrogant bravado Billy Brooks was displaying at the time.

While riding a construction train from Dodge to Sargent, Brooks was asked for his fare by a conductor. Drawing his six-shooter, Brooks growled, "I travel on this." The conductor said nothing, but after collecting his fares went forward to the locomotive, got his shotgun, and had the engineer slow down. He dropped off the engine and jumped back on the last car, where Brooks was seated. Approaching the notorious gunman from the rear, he announced, "Brooks, the fare to Sargent is $2.75." Glancing over his shoulder, Brooks looked down the barrel of a shotgun.

Docile now, he asked whom he should pay.

The conductor told him to pay the brakeman and also hand over his six-shooter, which would be returned to him at Sargent.

Brooks meekly complied.[43]

Billy Brooks's days as cock-of-the-walk in Dodge City came to an abrupt end on March 4, 1873, when he tangled with a tough buffalo hunter named Kirk Jordan. He barely avoided cashing in his chips and giving the chagrined editor of the *Wichita Beacon* an opportunity to publish a factual obituary of his demise. He survived the encounter, but his craven behavior assured his demise in Dodge City.

It is not clear what precipitated the trouble between Brooks and Jordan. Some later writers have advanced the theory that the men were at odds over the affections of Lizzie Palmer, madam of a Dodge City brothel, or one of her girls,[44] but Henry Raymond, the only contemporary to comment on the reason for the clash, believed Jordan was seeking revenge for the killing of one of his friends by Brooks.[45]

In any event, Jordan, gunning for Brooks, rode into Dodge that day in March with his Sharps .50-caliber buffalo rifle in the crook of his arm. He set up his post in the doorway of a saloon and waited for his quarry to appear. When Brooks came in view across the street, Jordan picked up his rifle, steadied it against the door facing, took aim, and was about to fire when someone passed between him and his target. Raymond said Jordan then raised the gun to avoid hitting the other party. Brooks, "ever on the lookout, caught the motion of that gun barrel. He suddenly threw himself to a sitting position on the ground behind two [barrels] of water, trying at the same time to draw one of his guns. Somehow the gun hung and he failed to pull it from the scabbard. Jordan fired at the barrels and the bullet lodged against the last iron hoop next to Brooks. Brooks sprang to his feet before Jordan could reload and someone helped to hide him."[46]

Josiah Wright Mooar, another buffalo hunter who was in town that day, recalled that Jordan "throwed one of these Big 50 guns down on Brooks; Brooks jumped behind the water barrel and Jordan let drive. The bullet . . . went through the barrel [and] lodged in the hoop but cut a hole through it so the water spouted out and ran down Brooks' neck." In the Mooar recital, Brooks's reaction to the attack was much cooler. Mooar said Jordan, thinking his single shot had killed Brooks, jumped on his horse and rode off. Brooks then stood up, fished the bullet out of the barrel, and carried it with him into a saloon.[47]

He no doubt needed a drink to celebrate his survival.

Robert Wright in his history of Dodge City described the shooting by Jordan and said the affair presaged an ignominious end to Brooks's stay in the town. Wright said he and other businessmen of the town hid Brooks under a bed in a livery stable over night, and the next day escorted him to Fort Dodge, where he caught an eastbound train. "I think," said Wright, "these lessons were enough for him, as he never came back. Good riddance for everybody."[48]

Wright's account was contradicted by a diary kept by Henry Raymond. It established March 4 as the day of the shooting with a terse entry on that date: "Bill Brooks got shot at with needle gun[,] the ball passing through two barrels of water[,] lodging in outside iron hoop. Jerdon [*sic*] shot at him." The next day's entry indicated the two combatants had reached some sort of peace agreement: "Saw Brooks and Jerdon compromise today."[49]

Elaborating on that point later, Raymond said that "Jordan left town but it was certain if he & Brooks should meet one of the two would die. Certain ones of the town wanted to avoid a killing and held councils with both of them."[50] The next day Jordan rode into town unarmed. Reining in at the hitching rack where Raymond was standing, he said, "Boys, you've got me into it!" Brooks walked up just then, and Raymond noted he wore a white starched shirt and carried no gun. "I never saw him thus before." Approaching Jordan with a broad smile, Brooks offered his hand. Jordan shook his hand, but no friendly smile crossed his face. "Jordan says, 'What you've got to say we don't need to say to this crowd. Let's go inside!' "[51]

And so Brooks and Jordan resolved their differences, whatever they were, without further trouble. The incident precipitated another rumor across the state that Brooks had been killed. The editor of the *Wichita Eagle*, wary of repeating the errors of his competitor at the *Beacon*, assured his readers that "Billy Brooks, the whilom stage driver, is not dead, as was reported, but is on duty at Dodge."

Brooks would not remain on duty long in Dodge, however, for his less than heroic performance that day in March 1873 spelled the end of his effectiveness as a fearsome, gun-packing keeper of the peace in the town. He was soon off to other venues, leaving as his legacy the memory of one of the most dangerous killers in the most violent period in the history of one of the most violent towns in western frontier history. With the dearth of governmental criminal records and newspaper reports and the confusing and contradictory accounts of old-timers, it is impossible to determine exactly the contribution of

Bill Brooks to that sanguinary history, but Merritt Beeson, son of Dodge City pioneer Chalkley Beeson and a careful chronicler of the town's history, concluded that Brooks shot five men while in Dodge, but could not confirm that all of them died.[52]

One of the ongoing myths about the career of Billy Brooks is that he turned up in Butte, Montana, and engaged in a shootout with Morgan Earp, the younger brother of the more famous Wyatt. This story can be credited to Stuart Lake, who, in his hugely successful biography of Wyatt Earp, wrote that Morgan was hired as marshal at Butte, a job coveted by Brooks, "that remarkably expert gunman who had preceded Wyatt as marshal at Dodge." According to Lake, "Billy resented Morg's appointment, and advertised that he would gun the new officer at first opportunity." Learning of the threats, Morgan sent word to Brooks that he would shoot him on sight. The two met in the street, and "two shots roared as one. Morg was hit in the shoulder, but he put Billy Brooks out of business with a slug that struck the killer full in the stomach."[53]

The story is a canard, as more recent Earp research has shown. Morgan Earp did serve as a policeman in Butte from December 16, 1879, to March 10, 1880, but this was long after the death of Billy Brooks.[54]

Actually, following his departure from Dodge, Brooks remained in western Kansas and returned to the buffalo hunt. He moved into a cabin on Kiowa Creek in desolate Comanche County, near the Indian Territory line. The cabin was stoutly constructed, with rifle ports on all sides to repel attacks from hostile Indians.

That hostility of the reservation Indians, increasing rapidly during this period, would culminate a few months later in the Red River War. The Indian way of life was threatened on two fronts: the systematic slaughter of the buffalo herds, on which the Indians relied for their sustenance, and the loss to white thieves of thousands of horses, the primary source of an Indian's accumulated wealth.

Billy Brooks participated in both of these attacks: he slaughtered buffalo, and he stole Indian ponies.

He was joined in his thievery by other buffalo hunters, including Bat Masterson and Bill Tilghman, both of whom would later be extolled as frontier heroes and legendary lawmen. For a time during these crucial months Tilghman teamed up with William "Hurricane Bill" Martin, one of the most successful and notorious horse thieves in southern Kansas, Indian Territory, and northern Texas.[55]

W. B. ("Bat") Masterson and a pal, after stealing some horses from the Cheyenne, found themselves being hotly pursued by a party of braves, and made tracks for Brooks's fortified cabin where, Masterson later said, "we knew that we could stand off a thousand redskins and that Bill would help us."[56] Masterson identified his companion in this escape only as "Jordan," but he was probably Kirk Jordan, the man who had tried his best to kill Brooks in Dodge, and the fact that Brooks welcomed him into his cabin is further evidence that the two adversaries patched up their differences after the gunplay.[57]

Masterson evidently eschewed horse stealing after his narrow brush with the enraged Cheyenne and concentrated on buffalo hunting. A few months later he gained his first fame as the youngest of a little band of heroic hidemen who turned back repeated assaults by Indian tribesmen at the Battle of Adobe Walls in the Texas panhandle, the onset of the Red River War. As for Tilghman, he lost all taste for horse thievery when his brother Dick and several others were killed by a posse and Bill himself barely escaped with his life.[58]

By early 1874 a pattern of criminality had developed in the region. White thieves stole horses from the Indians, who retaliated by stealing stock, both horses and cattle, from white settlers. This gave the white outlaws the opportunity to disguise themselves as Indians and steal from the settlers also. Organized gangs headed by veteran outlaws "Hurricane Bill" Martin, Charles ("Doc") McBride, Wellington ("Bill") Henderson, and others were active on the Chisholm Trail all the way from Fort Griffin in north Texas, through the Indian Nations, to Wichita, Kansas. Many of their followers worked on small cattle ranches or held jobs at stage stations or roadhouses along that route.

That spring Billy Brooks and Matilda, his "wife," moved into a dugout near Caldwell, a little town situated on the trail. The Southwestern Stage Company was headquartered at Caldwell, and Brooks went to work for the company. Two other Caldwell residents, livery stable owner Judson H. ("Judd") Calkins and L. Ben Hasbrouck, a young attorney, were also employed by the stage company. Both would play prominent roles in the final chapter of the Billy Brooks story.

In June Southwestern Stage Company employees received the distressing news that Vail & Company, another stagecoach operation, had underbid Southwestern for the lucrative Caldwell to Fort Sill mail contract. This spelled disaster for Southwestern, for without that mail contract it was unlikely the company could maintain its passenger service, and it would have to close down its operations in that area.

A group of men with financial interest in keeping Southwestern in business met in Caldwell to develop a plan to thwart the Vail & Company enterprise. Prominent among the group were Billy Brooks; liveryman Judd Calkins; lawyer L. B. Hasbrouck; A. C. McLean, a Caldwell saloonkeeper of shady reputation;[59] and Hurricane Bill Martin and "One-Armed Charlie" Smith, two of the region's most notorious desperadoes. There were about nine others.[60] The plan, reportedly devised by Brooks, seemed simple enough. To prevent Vail from fulfilling its contract and driving Southwestern into bankruptcy, the company's horse and mule stock would be systematically stolen and the thefts blamed on the increasingly restive Indians.

By late June the conspiracy was in full operation. When four mules and a horse mysteriously disappeared from Judd Calkins's stable, the *Sumner County Press* reported that "the mules belonged to Vail & Co. and had just been sent down to stock the mail line between Caldwell and Fort Sill. This is another of a series of thefts perpetrated by an organized band of outlaws who have so far escaped detection themselves and who have succeeded in so effectively concealing the stock that no trace of them is left behind to guide pursuit."[61]

A Caldwell correspondent for the *Topeka Daily Commonwealth* reported a few days later: "The country around here is full of horse-thieves, the town of Caldwell and the timber of Bluff Creek being a sort of refuge for them. . . . Bully Brooks, formerly of Dodge City, and a number of ruffians of that kidney, have been driven in from the Territory by fear of Indians, and are hanging around the cavalry and militia, casting wistful eyes at the horses."[62]

The "fear of Indians" mentioned was very real, for the campaign by Brooks and company against Vail & Company coincided exactly with the outbreak of hostilities by reservation Indians, culminating within a few months in the Red River War. Honest frontiersmen, heavily armed, holed up at stage stations and drove off both Indians and outlaws. Two members of the Brooks conspiracy, William Watkins and Jasper Marion, seeking refuge, were repulsed at Kingfisher Station. Retreating to Caldwell, they encountered a Cheyenne war party, and in a running fight Watkins was killed and Marion had his horse shot from under him. Hurricane Bill Martin and Bill Tilghman later narrowly escaped from the same party of Indians.[63]

By July the citizens of Sumner County, Kansas, doubly threatened by marauding Indians and larcenous outlaws, began to take protective measures. They could do little about the Indians, but they could move against the horse thieves, who were taking advantage of the Indian scare to run off valuable stock. On Monday, July 27, Justice of the Peace James A. Dillar of Wellington, the county seat, issued warrants for the arrest of those believed to be leaders of the outlaw gang. Named were Billy Brooks, L. B. Hasbrouck, Judd Calkins, and A. C. McLean. Sumner County Sheriff John G. Davis, armed with the warrants, started that day for Caldwell.

"Some of the parties for whom the warrants had been issued were known to be desperate characters, who were constantly on the look out, and who were always well armed," said the *Sumner County Press*. "Understanding this fact, the sheriff summoned to his assistance several of the citizens of Wellington with whom he left for Caldwell."[64]

In addition to Sheriff Davis and his posse, bands of vigilantes were soon in the field searching for those named in the warrants and also for One-Armed Charlie Smith and Dave Terrill, both believed to be prominent members of the outlaw gang.[65]

One by one the suspects were hunted down. Hasbrouck was taken in a cornfield outside Caldwell, McLean at his home, and Terrill in the home of a friend three miles out of town. Smith fled south into Indian Territory, but was captured the next day after a chase of twenty-five miles.[66]

Billy Brooks was the only one to resist arrest. Sheriff Davis and his posse cornered him in his dugout, where he was holed up with his wife.[67] According to Mrs. J. B. Rideout, the wife of a minister, who evidently got the story from Matilda, the following colloquy ensued:

> Davis: Come out and give yourself up like a man.
> Brooks: You will never take me alive.
> Davis: If you give yourself up, I will defend you from the mob and you shall have a fair trial.

Brooks: I should never get to Wellington alive.

Davis: I have control of my men, and if you will give yourself up, I pledge my word you shall have a fair trial.

Brooks: I know the mob will hang me, and I will not give myself up alive. If you take me, you will take a dead man; but I will sell my life as dearly as possible.

Davis: I will give you ten minutes to send your wife out of the dugout.

Brooks: My wife will assist me; so proceed as you like.

Davis: Send your wife out and we will let her depart in peace. I do not wish to fight a woman.

Brooks: My wife will not leave; she is a better warrior than you or any of the men you have in your crowd.

Davis: You're foolish to lose your own life and endanger the life of your wife rather than defend yourself before an honorable court, with the probability of being set at liberty.

Brooks: I am not afraid of an honorable court, but I understand mob-law too well to expect any such thing as that should I give myself up as a prisoner to-day; so I shall not throw myself into the hands of a mob. But I do not object to dying here. I have the advantage and will sell my life as dearly as possible.

Davis: I have two hundred men and it will not take long to bring you out.

Brooks: I know that, but you will exchange a good many lives for mine. I am all ready; so go right ahead without any more talk.[68]

Matilda is said to have urged Brooks to resist: "She had great confidence in herself, as well as in her husband, and she doubtless thought that within the fort they could cope with the whole crowd. . . . She said in a low but unfaltering tone, 'Will, be firm. I will stand by you to the last. We will either conquer or die together.' As she said this she lifted a revolver in one hand and held a knife in the other, firmly grasped; nor did her slender hands tremble."[69]

The siege went on for several hours, but finally a posseman named John Kirk, whom Brooks knew and trusted, was permitted to enter the dugout. On his promise of safe transport to the Caldwell jail Brooks agreed to come out if he could retain his arms. The request was granted, and Brooks emerged with his six-shooters strapped on and a Winchester in his hand. He kept the weapons until the party reached Caldwell, and there he turned them over to Sheriff Davis. The moment he did so, John Kirk, the man he had trusted, cracked him on the head with his pistol. "I'll kill you for that if I ever get out of this," Brooks grated through clenched teeth.[70]

Brooks, Hasbrouck, Calkins, Terrill, and McLean were transported to Wellington and confined in the Sumner County jail. Later Smith also found a cell there.

The *Sumner County Press*, published in Wellington, heralded the arrests in its July 30 edition. It reported that on Tuesday, July 28, Justice Dillar held a preliminary examination in his court and charged Brooks, Hasbrouck, Calkins, McLean, and Smith with "being connected to an organized gang of horse thieves" and specifically with "being principals and accessories in the wholesale theft of Vail & Co.'s mules." He found no charge against Terrill and discharged him, and allowed the release of Calkins on $500 bail. The two immediately went to the home of Dr. P. J. M. Burkett and threatened his life. Burkett, it appears, had been the key to the crackdown on the gang. After McLean had foolishly divulged to him the identity of the conspirators and their plans to destroy Vail & Company, he had given that information to the authorities. Now he went again, and reported the threats by Calkins and Terrill. New warrants were issued for the two men, but they eluded apprehension, slipping out of town under cover of darkness, headed for Wichita.

Brooks, Hasbrouck, and Smith were locked up together in the calaboose at Wellington, but McLean, whose big mouth had brought this calamity on the other gang members, was kept separate from the others, probably for his own safety, and held under guard at another location.

The editor of the *Sumner County Press* promised new revelations as County Attorney Charles Willsie and Judge John G. Woods readied the case against the suspects. "What the testimony will be we are not prepared or at liberty to state; but our readers may be prepared for startling disclosures, and the presentation of an array of evidence that will prove the existence of an organized band of horse thieves extending all along the border." The story concluded prophetically: "The end is not yet."[71]

The type for that account had barely been set when a new and even more dramatic story broke, and editor John H. Folks had to revise his entire front page before turning the edition over to his pressman with the screaming headline:

DEAD! DEAD!! DEAD!!!
The Vigilantes at Work
Three Men Hanged by the Neck Until They Are Dead.
A Fearful Retribution.
The Beginning of the End.

The story was short and to the point. The night before, at about midnight, a large body of armed men overpowered the guards at the county jail, removed the prisoners — Brooks, Hasbrouck, and Smith — took them to the Slate Creek bridge a mile out of town, and hanged all three from a limb of the same tree. Editor Folks said that, with other citizens of the town, he visited the scene early that morning "and looked for a moment on the ghastly spectacle. The bodies were hanging facing the south. Hasbrouck was on the left, Brooks in the center and Smith to the right and nearest to the tree. The distorted features of Brooks gave evidence of a horrible struggle with death. The other men looked natural and evidently died easily."[72]

Later that day officers took the bodies down and laid them out in the courthouse. Reverend Rideout and his wife were standing there when Matilda Brooks came in. They watched as the distraught woman fell to the floor beside Billy and "wept as though her heart was ready to burst with grief." She later purchased a coffin for the burial of the man she called her husband. The other two lynch victims were interred in simple wooden boxes.[73]

Evidently few in Kansas shared Matilda's grief in the passing of Billy Brooks. Newspapers in Wichita, Topeka, and even Newton, where Brooks had served as marshal, took little note of his ignominious demise.[74] Like many of his gunfighting ilk, he had straddled that dim line separating the lawman from the lawless, and when he was gone he was quickly forgotten.

# — 7 —

## PORT STOCKTON
### 1849–1881

*Two brothers who bore the names of "Port" and "Ike" Stockton . . .
made their names notorious throughout the length and breadth of
Texas and New Mexico by their daring thefts, intense violence and
utter carelessness of personal safety. They . . . knew not fear, and brutal
by nature and temperament, had developed into mere human brutes,
whose only pleasure and law was the gratification of their licentious
passions.*

— *Rocky Mountain News,* March 31, 1881

The history of violence in the American West is replete with brother-
hood connections. The nucleus of many notorious outlaw gangs were
brothers, from the Reno boys, credited with inventing train robbery
shortly after the Civil War, to the Barrow and Barker brothers of the
1930s. Western outlaw brothers included the James boys and the
Youngers, who together formed the most famous outlaw gang in
American history. The Christians, the Ketchums, the Logans, the
Kilpatricks, and the Daltons were brother combinations of widespread notoriety in later years.

Other fraternal combines could not be classed as career outlaws but
gained fame as gunfighters, among whom were the Clantons and
McLaurys of Tombstone, Arizona. Texas provided many of this class,
including Ben and Billy Thompson; the seven-brother Horrell clan;
Print, Jay, and Bob Olive; and the Mannings — Frank, James, and
"Doc" — of El Paso notoriety.

Texans Port and Ike Stockton were in the latter category. They did not rob banks or trains, but they trod that dim line between the law and outlawry and for a period in the early 1880s were both respected and praised, feared and hated, in a large section of southern Colorado and northern New Mexico.

William Porter was the elder of the Stockton brothers. "Port," as he was always called, was born in Upshur County, Texas, in October 1849. His parents, Samuel and Jane Stockton, had nine children, five girls and four boys. Samuel died sometime during the 1850s, leaving Jane to support her brood as a weaver at Sulphur Springs, Hopkins County, in east Texas.[1]

In later years there would be newspaper reports that Port, at about the age of twelve, slew a man "for calling him a liar, shooting the top of his head off."[2] The story has been repeated by modern writers, but nothing has been found to confirm its veracity.[3]

The first known incident of violence involving Porter Stockton occurred in February 1871 when he tangled with a man in Erath County, Texas. Two months later a grand jury indicted him on a charge of assault with intent to murder. His legal counsel managed to get continuances, and he was free on bail provided by his sureties until January 1875 when Erath County Sheriff W. G. Waller brought him in again to stand trial at the February session of district court at Stephenville.[4] Once more released on bail, Stockton skipped town and the state, leaving his sureties holding the bag. He never came to trial. Named as a fugitive from justice in a list provided all law officers in the state by the adjutant general of Texas, Stockton was described as weighing about 140 pounds, five feet eight inches in height, with light complexion, light hair, and a sandy mustache. The charge would stay open until November 14, 1887, when the Erath County district attorney dismissed it "because of the death of the defendant."[5]

A Stockton biographer has written that Port Stockton trailed cattle to the Kansas cow towns during the years 1873–76 and was active in the cow towns of Ellsworth, Wichita, and Dodge City. Lurid tales are related regarding Port's activities with the notorious Texas gunmen Ben and Billy Thompson and soon-to-become famous Wyatt Earp. At Ellsworth, we are told, a Texan cattleman goaded Port into shooting Earp, and when he refused, a cowboy "taunted him with cowardice and . . . Porter told him to draw. This was his first killing." Later at

Wichita Port did attempt to assassinate Earp, only to have the gun shot out of his hand by that consummate gunfighter. During these years, this writer relates, Stockton killed a man in Dodge City "who opposed him," and, turning to outlawry, participated in the holdup of a Walls Fargo shipment near Hays City, shooting a guard in the process. With his share of the loot he hightailed it to Fort Worth, Texas, where he married "a flaxen-haired minister's daughter" named Irma.[6]

This account is pure fiction. Port is not mentioned in any of the well-researched histories of Ellsworth, Wichita, and Dodge City, or in biographies of the Thompsons or Wyatt Earp.[7] Additionally, during the period that this was alleged to have happened, Port had been married for several years and had fathered children. In 1870 he married Emily Jane Marshall (nee Cowan), seven years his junior, in Erath County, Texas. They had three daughters, Sarah E., born in Missouri in 1872; Mary J., born in Colorado in 1875; and Carrie, born in Colorado in 1879.[8]

It is not known where these fictitious stories may have originated, unless they derived from Port Stockton's braggadocio, for he was quoted in later newspaper reports as saying that he had killed eighteen men.[9]

As early as 1873, the very time when he was reportedly trailing cattle from Texas to Kansas and consorting with the gunmen of the Kansas cow towns, Port was known to be in the Ute Park area of Colfax County, New Mexico Territory. There in 1867 Thomas Stockton, a cousin, had constructed the Clifton House, an impressive building six miles south of Raton, which served as headquarters for his ranching operation. During the 1870s the place was leased to the Barlow-Sanderson Stage Line and became popularly known as "Red River Stage Station."[10]

The *Santa Fe New Mexican* of April 16, 1873, copied an item from the *Cimarron News* reporting that a charge of murder had been brought against a man named Stockton, but an indictment had to wait until the action of the next grand jury. The Stockton mentioned was undoubtedly Port, as Cimarron was one of his favorite hangouts in this and later years. No additional details of the case have been uncovered, and evidently the grand jury failed to hand down an indictment.

Porter Stockton and wife, Emily Jane, photographed in Durango, Colorado. Courtesy of Pam S. Birmingham and James S. Peters.

Late in 1873 Port was in Trinidad, a town in southern Colorado near the New Mexico line and just north of Raton Pass. On December 23 a rough character named Colbert, said to be "a half-breed Cherokee Indian who went by the name of 'Chunk,' "[11] got an early start on the Christmas celebration. Loading up on tanglefoot whiskey, he rampaged through town, shooting promiscuously. Colbert was a dangerous desperado who bragged that he had killed six men.[12] That day he killed his seventh,[13] a man named Walter Waller (or Walton Walled), who happened to be a friend of Port Stockton's, and hightailed it out of Trinidad, taking the road south through Raton Pass into New Mexico Territory. Stockton, at the head of a posse, immediately went in pursuit.[14]

The only way through Raton Pass was a toll road, owned and operated by a famous mountain man, Richens Lacy ("Dick") Wootten, who had overseen its construction in 1865 and maintained a stage station and roadhouse along its route.

As Wootten later recalled, when Stockton reached this station he came in "with a cocked six shooter in each hand." Wootten asked him what he wanted, and Stockton replied: "You know what I want, I'm looking for that dirty son-of-a . . . , Chunk." Wootten told him Chunk had left and asked him to put his pistols away, "reminding him that it was not a very genteel performance to come bursting into a public house, flourishing a couple of guns and frightening people until their hair stood on end." Stockton and the men who came with him then left. The next day Wootten heard that they had gunned down an innocent man whom they had mistaken for Chunk.[15]

No details are available regarding the reported killing of "an innocent man" by the posse, but it is known that Chunk Colbert did not long survive. Only two weeks later, on January 7, 1874, at Thomas Stockton's Clifton House the notorious gunfighter Clay Allison sat down to a meal across the table from Colbert. When the meal was finished, Allison blasted his eating companion with a six-shooter. The killing, some said, was performed as a favor for Port Stockton.[16]

Two years later, on January 1, 1876, at Cimarron, Port Stockton shot and killed a man named Antonio Arcibia, said to be a part-time deputy of Colfax County Sheriff Isaiah Rinehart.[17] There are several accounts of the cause of the shooting. One alleged that Stockton shot the man because his snoring annoyed him.[18] According to another story Port shot Arcibia when the man accused him of making improper advances toward his wife. Brother Ike would later claim that Arcibia was a horse thief, and Port killed him in self-defense.[19]

The following March a Taos grand jury brought in a murder indictment, charging that Port Stockton "with a certain pistol" did shoot Arcibia "in the left breast, a little below the left pap," the bullet penetrating "to the depth of six inches," from the effects of which the victim "instantly died."[20]

After the shooting Port had skedaddled across the convenient Colorado border to Trinidad, and notices went out to officers there to be on the watch for him. On August 20 Sheriff Casimero Barela at Trinidad wired acting New Mexico governor W. G. Ritch at Santa Fe that he had apprehended Stockton and was holding him for necessary requisition papers. The following day Sheriff Rinehart reaffirmed the request by telegram to the governor's office. Ritch ordered the requisition issued on August 28.[21]

In early September Colfax County officers conveyed Stockton from Trinidad to Cimarron and billed New Mexico for expenses amounting to $135.65. The governor's office approved the bill on September 16, but that same day Port Stockton, with the assistance his brother Ike, escaped from the stone jail in Cimarron.[22]

A Denver newspaper in a lengthy story on the Stocktons five years later gave details of that jailbreak. According to this account, Ike approached the jailor, a man named McMahon, and requested an interview with Port "as he had something of importance to communicate to his brother." When he was granted admittance to the cell, Ike "conversed earnestly" with Port, while McMahon watched closely to be sure Ike did not pass "any jail-breaking instrument or shooting irons to his brother." After a short conference Ike signaled the guard he was ready to leave, but when McMahon swung open the cell door Ike suddenly "gripped him fiercely by the throat, and flung him against the wall." Port leaped from the cell and helped his brother subdue the jailor. They bound his hands and feet with bed clothing, tied him to the bed, locked him in the cell, and departed. The escape was not discovered for hours, too late for immediate pursuit.[23]

Later writers have asserted that a month later Port killed another Hispanic male, a man named Juan Gonzolez, in Cimarron,[24] but these reports seem to be based on nothing but a confusion with the Arcibia murder. Another story circulated that Port in December 1876 killed a man in Trinidad, and was arrested and jailed, but again made his escape with the complicity of Ike.[25] However, no contemporary record of this incident has been found.

After the shooting of Arcibia in Cimarron, Port Stockton kept clear of Colfax County for the next three years, and his activities during that time are unknown. He surfaced again in the summer of 1879 in the fresh new town of Otero, an end-of-track town on the Santa Fe Railroad, then building into New Mexico. The town, a few miles south of Raton, sprang up almost overnight and at its height claimed a population of three thousand.[26] Many peripatetic members of the sporting crowd flocked into this latest hell-on-wheels community. John H. ("Doc") Holliday and William ("Hurricane Bill") Martin, both veterans of Fort Griffin, Dodge City, and other uproarious frontier communities, were on hand. Like many fast-blossoming railroad towns, Otero was short-lived and quickly disappeared, but in the summer of 1879 it followed the usual pattern of end-of-track camps and erupted in violence. Doc Holliday, no stranger to violent encounters, seems to have avoided sanguinary conflict while in Otero, but Hurricane Bill and other less-known characters, Bill Withers and Harry Bassett, were destined to play important roles in Port's adventures there.

Hurricane Bill Martin, long known as one of the most notorious horse thieves operating out of the Indian Nation, Kansas, and the northern counties of Texas, somehow managed to get himself appointed city marshal at Otero. In the June 5 issue of the *Otero Optic*, the editors, W. J. ("Jap") Turpen and R. A. ("Russ") Kistler, described the town's new lawman as "an individual, taller than the majority of men, wearing a large revolver strapped in sight, and more than ordinary determined expression of countenance." They applauded him and the job he was doing as marshal of Otero. With his reputation at stake, they said, "he is interested in keeping order, and is equally as active in keeping the peace as he ever was successful in breaking it."

Brothers William and Ed Withers also had a past history of swiping ropes with horses tied to the other end. In 1877 federal officers arrested them in Kansas for the theft of fifteen or twenty horses in the Indian Nation.[27] They were closely allied with Hurricane Bill in

Otero and in all likelihood were former members of his gang who had followed him west to New Mexico. In Otero, they kept a livery stable and ran some cattle on nearby ranges.

Harry Bassett, a deputy of Colfax County Sheriff Pete Burleson, was stationed at Otero. Details are lacking, but apparently the two lawmen in town, Deputy Sheriff Bassett and City Marshal Martin, both had incurred the wrath of Port Stockton, who was running cattle on ranges near Otero. Stockton and other cowboys delighted in hurrahing the infant town, galloping their horses through the streets, shooting off their pistols, and scattering the residents. When the officers admonished him for his antics, Port defied them. In June Hurricane Bill finally arrested him and hauled him into a justice of the peace court, where he was fined.[28]

A few days later, on June 11, someone ambushed one of the Withers brothers on an Otero street and shot him dead. Sam Baldwin, a veteran cattleman who was in the town at the time, said the victim was Ed and his killer was Port. "Hurricane Bill's great friend and sponsor was Ed Withers [who] used to be a bad man down there in the Panhandle of Texas," recalled Baldwin. Withers ran a livery stable in Otero. "Somebody went down there and told him that Hurricane Bill was getting in trouble with the cowboys. He fixed up his six-shooter and comes up there himself, comes near where [John] Madden had a saloon there, and just as he got up there Porter Shagden [sic] happened to be there and saw Ed Withers and killed him. The town went wild over it. The cowboys got to pouring around and Hurricane Bill ran down to the livery stable and hid in the hay."[29]

Although many in Otero agreed with Baldwin that Stockton was the murderer of Withers, there was insufficient evidence to convince a grand jury, and it refused to indict him for the crime.[30]

Stockton was suspected of another killing in Otero a few months later. On November 26, 1879, Colfax County Deputy Sheriff Marion Littrell, accompanied by Will South and Zeneas Curtis, arrived in town with warrants for the arrest of several men. They met with Harry Bassett, the local deputy, and found him uncooperative, probably because he previously had difficulties with Curtis and resented his presence there. Harsh words were exchanged and guns drawn. Bassett shot Curtis, wounding him in the side. Someone then fired a rifle.

The bullet struck Bassett in the chest and passed through his lungs, inflicting a fatal wound. Many in Otero believed Port Stockton, observing the argument between the officers and the resulting gunplay, took the opportunity to dispatch Bassett, whom he believed had testified against him at the inquiry into the Withers murder.[31]

Stockton was not indicted for this killing either, but things had gotten warm for him in Colfax County again, and he decided not to press his luck there too far. In early 1880 he rounded up his few head of cattle and, with wife, Emily Jane, and three young daughters, headed for the Four Corners country, where New Mexico, Colorado, Utah, and Arizona meet. There he joined his brother Ike near Animas City, La Plata County, Colorado, just across the border from Rio Arriba County, New Mexico.

Another Stockton brother, Samuel, six years younger than Porter and four years younger than Ike, apparently had acquired their propensity for violence. In April 1880, about the same time Port and Ike were getting back together, Sam Stockton showed up in New Mexico. Wanted in Texas for the murder of a Texas Ranger, Sam Stockton was using the alias "West Brown" when he got into a gunfight at the Jim Greathouse ranch near Las Vegas. Texas cattlemen and lawmen had tracked stolen horses to the ranch, and Stockton, who was working with the notorious Greathouse, began shooting at them and was wounded in the return fire.

Arrested and taken to Las Vegas, Sam Stockton was "sent back to Texas without benefit of preliminary hearing or evasion of extradition," but he broke jail in Decatur and fled to Colorado, where his outlaw career ended abruptly at the end of a vigilante rope.[32]

By the spring of 1880 Porter Stockton was walking the streets of Animas City, sporting the badge of city marshal.[33] Although some who were acquainted with his disreputable history might have been surprised at this turn of events, it was not unusual for officials of frontier towns to hire as enforcers of the law men with shady backgrounds but demonstrated weapons ability and the grit to use them. The employment of the notorious Hurricane Bill Martin as town marshal of Otero was a recent example.

Animas City was a small community in the valley of the Animas River, about two miles north of the town of Durango. In a letter to the editor of the *Ouray Times* written about the time Port arrived there, someone identified only as "C" said that Animas City had only about two hundred residents, "about half of which are miners, gamblers and cowboys."[34]

As one newspaper put it, once Porter Stockton pinned on a badge, he became "extremely free with his pistol since he had a little authority."[35]

In July 1880 he unlimbered that pistol and shot a visitor identified only as "Captain Hart of Montezuma Valley," whom he said disobeyed his order to turn over his guns on entering town. One newspaper reported that "several shots were exchanged between the parties" before a bullet from Stockton's gun hit Hart in the cheek and came out under his nose, inflicting a painful and facially disfiguring but nonlethal wound.[36] The newspapers seemed to agree that Stockton's actions were in the performance of his duties and fully justified,[37] but George Coe, a veteran of the recent Lincoln County War who had also relocated in the area, said the shooting resulted "from a little gambling scrape."[38] Some Animas City old-timers always contended that "Hart and Stockton had trouble in New Mexico and Stockton simply brought it to a head when he thought the law was on his side."[39]

Port's victim in this gunplay, identified as "Caphart" in some accounts,[40] was probably D. F. Hart, age forty-eight, who farmed a piece of property near Farmington, New Mexico, where he lived with his wife and three children.[41] The incident may well have been one of the opening clashes in a war about to develop between the Stockton brothers and a group of adversaries soon to become known as "the Farmington mob."

A year later, after that war had broken wide open, a Santa Fe paper described the Hart shooting in a manner decidedly unfavorable to Port Stockton. In a deliberate, cold-blooded murder attempt, said the paper, Port had

> walked up to his man and holding his pistol within two feet of his head, fired. A backward movement of Caphart's head saved his life perhaps, because it caused the ball to pass into his mouth at one side and out of the other, carrying away with it one of his side teeth. The assaulted man went for his pistol and Port turned and ran like a quarter horse. Caphart fired and missed, after which he spat something out on the ground, saying, "I caught this darn ball in my mouth, anybody that wants it can

have it." While Caphart walked carelessly off a looker-on went in search of the ball and found the tooth on the ground. Port had picked the wrong man that time and when he found it out he did the wise thing and left.[42]

It wasn't long before Port's pistol spoke again. On September 16, while under the influence of alcohol, he wandered into a barbershop and demanded a shave. Assisting proprietor Phil Weber in his tonsorial services was a dark-skinned man, said to be a Maori from New Zealand or Australia, whose name has been reported variously in contemporary papers as J. W. Allen and Thomas Smith. Accounts also disagree as to what triggered an ensuing ruckus. Port is said to have been enraged when the black barber nicked him with his razor.[43] Another version had it that Stockton would not permit the Maori to shave him, saying that the "black son of a bitch could not lay a razor on his face." He then jerked out his pistol and struck the inoffensive fellow over the head with it.[44]

However the altercation started, the poor barber was soon running down the street, pursued by Stockton, who fired a shot. The bullet glanced off the man's head, inflicting a minor wound and knocking him to the ground. Stockton ran up and again beat the barber unmercifully over the head with his pistol. A newspaper called the entire affair "a dastardly act."[45]

Animas City mayor Eugene Englin deputized several men,[46] including the town blacksmith, Charles Naeglin, to help him arrest Stockton. They took him into custody without trouble, but it seems the mayor and his deputies were more interested in arranging a quick riddance for their troublesome city marshal than they were in prosecuting him. First, they allowed him to keep his weapon,[47] and then they permitted him to return to his own house and enter, unattended, to confer with his wife. While Mayor Englin himself stood guard at the door, Stockton climbed out a back window, appropriated a convenient horse from the Myers and West livery stable, and galloped out of town, thus writing "finis" to his job as city marshal of Animas City. City officials formed a posse and made a desultory effort to pursue the runaway gunman, but were unsuccessful — to the surprise of no one.[48]

As was his wont when he got in trouble in one state or territory, Port hightailed to the neighboring jurisdiction. He rode to Bloomfield, San Juan County, New Mexico, just east of Farmington and some fifty miles south of Animas City, where, amazingly, he talked himself into another city marshal post. But when word reached the town of Port's six-gun promiscuity in Animas City his services were quickly terminated. Said a newspaper: "People of Bloomfield now feel that their recently hired marshal, Porter Stockton, can not be trusted with a gun and have given him his dismissal notice."[49]

Stockton then acquired some land near Bloomfield, ran his small herd of cattle onto it, and moved his wife, Emily Jane, and daughters — Sarah, eight, Mary, five, and one-year-old Carrie — into a small house there. There were reports that he obtained the property illegally and perhaps with violence. According to one account, he jumped the ranch of a widow;[50] another had it that he mortally wounded a man employed by the woman.[51] Charles Naeglin, who had helped arrest Port back in Animas City, recalled that Stockton jumped the homestead of a settler who was off filing a claim for the land, and killed the man when he returned.[52] No contemporary record has been found to confirm any of these allegations.

By September 1880 the Port Stockton family was settled in a cabin on a small ranch near the town of Bloomfield. That town and the surrounding countryside were at the time in a state of turmoil. A little over a month earlier, a resident of the area, identifying himself only as "X. I. X.," wrote a letter to the editor of the *Dolores News* of Rico, Colorado, saying that "a dismal gloom" was hanging over that section of the country. "A lawless mob" operating there was "driving civil laws and law-abiding citizens from the valley," he claimed. "A man's life here," he said, "is not worth much that does not belong to the mob."[53]

A resident of Animas City in a letter of complaint to New Mexico territorial governor Lew Wallace recounted some the "atrocious offenses" committed by this "mob." A man accused of stealing, he said, had been tried before "a bogus court," was pronounced guilty, and later was "found hung by the neck." Free speech was suppressed, and when a man named Crouch and a Mrs. Adams violated this edict, they were ordered out of the county "under pain of death." A constable, executing a court order, confiscated a span of mules to satisfy a $40 debt, only to have two members of the mob, O. H. Hanson and Frank Myers, take the mules from him by force of arms. Arrested and taken before the judge, a man named Walford,[54] Hanson and Myers were liberated by their mob friends, and Judge Walford had to leave town "under penalty of death." In June 1880 Mrs. Hubbard, "an estimable lady," received a notice: "Mrs. Hubbard. The law-abiding citizens have been watching you. You have prostituted yourself with old Walford and others. You are ordered to leave under penalty of rope, tar and feathers." The author of the letter, C. H. McHenry, in October 1880 got into difficulty himself and was threatened by members of the mob when he participated in a caucus nominating for office candidates opposing mob law.[55]

Members of the "mob" were some eighty cattlemen and their chief employees ranging herds in San Juan and Rio Arriba counties of northern New Mexico. They had organized as the Farmington Stockman's Protective Association. Prominent in the organization were Frank Simmons, often named as the leader; Alfred U. Graves, foreman of the large Thompson and Lacy spread; Tom Nance of the Two Cross Ranch; Francis M. Hamblet and his sons, Lee and John; George Lockhart; Aaron N. Barker; John Cox; Frank Myers; and the many interrelated Coe boys: Lewis ("Lew"), George Washington ("Wash"), Ben Franklin ("Frank"), and Jasper ("Jap"). Others who rode along on some of the mob's raids were James and Cal Razor, Fred and James Tully, George Thompson, Ed Thomas, John Brown, Ed Ray, Al Dustin, Henry Hanson, Burr Milleson, and Al Strumpf.[56]

This organization, representing the interests of the large ranches, was said to have driven several farmers and smaller ranchers out of the country and killed a few who resisted. Newspapers across the border in Colorado railed against these highhanded tactics. Recognizing the influence of the Coes, the *Dolores News* of Rico referred to the group as the "Lincoln County mob," and the *Durango Record* called the Farmington association the "Coe Consolidation."[57]

Members of the organization in turn charged that rustlers operating out of Colorado were stealing cattle in the Farmington area, butchering the cows, and selling the beef to the army at Fort Lewis, near Durango. They named the Stockton brothers, Port and Ike, as leaders of the gang.

Shortly after Port Stockton moved into the area, cowboys employed by the Pierson Brothers, a New Mexican cattle outfit, drove a herd of Pierson cattle onto a range near Durango, Colorado. The owners wanted to hold the herd a few days before selling it and offered their riders a bonus of $10 or $15 if they would stay on, but several waddies, including Erastus Thompson and Ben Quick, were anxious to get home and declined the offer. A group of Colorado cowboys, led by the Stockton brothers, stepped in, accepted the offer, and took charge of the stock. When the cattle were finally sold, it appeared that the herd had diminished in size considerably during the time the Colorado cowboys had controlled it. This precipitated an all-out gun battle.[58]

Learning that the Stockton brothers and their pals were spending their ill-gotten proceeds in the saloons lining Railroad Street in Durango, the Farmington cowmen rode into town, corralled their horses, took up firing positions on a hill overlooking the town, and sent word that they had their enemies surrounded.

The Stocktons and their followers burst from the saloons, guns blazing. Although the battle lasted more than an hour, when the combatants' ammunition was exhausted and the smoke cleared, there were only minor casualties on either side.[59]

There followed a period of relative quiet for several months. Ike Stockton took advantage of the lull to return to Texas in November on a cattle-buying trip. He was gone, therefore, when violence erupted again on Christmas Eve, 1880, at two separate locations.

That night in Durango's Marnhal Saloon Bert Wilkinson, a stalwart Stockton fighting man, shot and killed a gunman remembered only as "Comanche Bill."[60] As the story was reported in the press, the difficulty grew out of a dispute over a poker game played over a year earlier, but it is much more likely this was a confrontation between combatants of the two warring factions.

On the same night a Christmas celebration dance was held at the home of Frank M. Hamblet, near Bloomfield. The Hamblets, father and sons, were charter members of the Farmington Stockmen's Protective Association, and most of their guests were also allied with the organization. Conspicuous by their absence were the Hamblets' close neighbors the Porter Stockmans, who had not been invited.

At the height of the festivities several of Port's friends showed up, including Dyson Eskridge and Jim Garrett, men of fighting repute. Also with them was Oscar Puett, a young man who was not considered dangerous, but only a kind of camp follower.[61] Obviously

Porter Stockton (*standing*, *right*) and three unidentified cronies in Durango, Colorado. Courtesy of Pam S. Birmingham and James S. Peters.

under the influence of alcohol, these fellows attempted to crash the party, but were rebuffed by several of the guests, including a cowboy named George Brown. A shooting broke out in which Brown and Oscar Puett were killed and Eskridge wounded. According to one newspaper account Brown "attempted to draw his pistol to shoot Eskridge," but Dyson was "too quick for him [and] fired and killed Brown."[62] Jasper Coe, who was probably a guest at the dance and a witness to the shooting, said in a letter to a Colorado paper that "after Brown was shot he killed Puett and wounded Eskridge," but he did not identify the killer of Brown.[63]

Eskridge and Garrett fled. Said the *Durango Record*: "The community [residents] are greatly outraged and seventeen of the best citizens are out in pursuit of the murderers and a thousand dollar reward is offered for them, dead or alive. If caught, short work will be made of them."[64] The "best citizens," all members or supporters of the Farmington Stockmen's Protective Association, reportedly "ransacked the house of Eskridge and Garrett—stole and destroyed all valuables, burnt the house, stole or forcibly took their riding stock, killed their cattle, and appropriated them to their own use."[65]

Less than two weeks after the Christmas Eve shootings, on January 4, 1881, a party of these vengeance seekers rode up to the cabin occupied by Port and Emily Jane Stockton. Newspapers at the time reported that the party was large, consisting of eighteen "unknown" riders,"[66] but Ike Stockton, in an interview a few months later, repeating information he had gotten from his sister-in-law, Emily Jane, said there were only seven. These have been identified by other sources as Alf Graves, Aaron Barker, Tom Nance, Frank Coe, Burr Milleson, George Lockhart, and Al Dustin.[67]

Ike said two of the men, Graves and Barker, approached the cabin while the other five rode off a ways. Port, who had been cleaning his pipe when he heard the horsemen, came to the door with his "pipe in one hand and a straw in the other," completely unaware of the evil intentions of his visitors. Graves and Barker engaged Port in an apparently friendly and neighborly conversation for about ten minutes.

While Port's back was turned, Ike went on, the other five men went down the road a short distance, dismounted, pulled their rifles from the scabbards, and took aim at him. When one of them yelled: "Throw up your hands!" Port turned. Immediately Graves and Barker drew their revolvers and fired. One bullet struck Port in the breast, the other in the neck. Still clutching his pipe in one hand, the straw in the other, he toppled over. Some of the five riflemen also fired, said Ike, but Port was already finished, dead when he hit the ground.

Hearing the shooting, Emily Jane ran from the kitchen, grabbing Port's Winchester rifle on her way to the yard. When she appeared, gun in hand, one of the men, identified as Lockhart by Ike, shouted: "Shoot the damned bitch!" Two men fired. A ball smashed into the Winchester rifle. The other struck the woman in the hand and penetrated her side. She fell beside her husband.

"The ruffians," said Ike, "departed, leaving her for dead. They had not pity or care for the three innocent terror-stricken children in the house. These they left alone with their, as they supposed, dead parents."[68]

Accounts of the Porter Stockton killing originating with members of the Farmington crowd differed greatly, of course. In a letter to a Colorado Springs paper written on March 18, 1881, Jasper Coe said that a party of men searching for Dyson Eskridge and Jim Garrett came on Port Stockton, whom he characterized as a "notorious cow thief and murderer who boasted of having killed eighteen men in his time. He had stolen cattle here and had threatened the lives of some of our best citizens." Stockton, said Coe, "hailed one of the party and commenced a row, thinking perhaps the rest of the party would go on, but the boys tumbled to his game, threw down their guns and shot him dead. His wife came on the scene with gun in hand but it was shot from her before any damage was done, she being slightly hurt."[69]

And George Lockhart, named as a participant in the Port Stockton killing, wrote a letter to a Durango newspaper in which he appeared to justify that killing as an act of community improvement. "It seems almost absurd to touch on that affair," he said, "as you must know what an unprincipled fellow [Port Stockton] was, leaving Animas City as he did for knocking a poor unoffending and unarmed negro in the head with a pistol, and no sooner did he get here, but he must do the same thing to a white man. He, too, was caught stealing stock and selling both meat and hides, and even had the impudence to offer to give a bill of sale for the hides. You, of course, are aware how matters were settled with him."[70]

Other accounts, originating with the Farmington warriors or their supporters, related how "Stockton and his wife both came to the door armed with rifles. Both sides opened fire and Stockton fell pierced with eighteen bullets. His wife, who had fired one shot, was struck in the abdomen by a splinter from the stock of her rifle, which had received a bullet."[71]

Several months later another, completely inaccurate, account of Port's demise went out on the wire services and was reprinted in newspapers throughout the country. Port, it said, "entered a saloon, and, as usual, invited everybody to take a drink, the penalty being death in case of refusal. A ranchman not complying, Port drew a revolver, but was immediately shot and killed."[72]

When Ike Stockton heard of his brother's death he hurried back to the San Juan country. Concerned for Port's family, he took them into his own home, where he and his wife, Amanda, cared for their wounded sister-in-law. Emily Jane's injuries were severe, and she was not expected to live. There were even newspaper reports that she had died from her wounds.[73] Emily Jane survived, but remained a cripple the rest of her life.[74]

Port's family and his brother no doubt grieved over his death, but few others in the San Juan country joined them in mourning.

Charles Naeglin admitted fearing the man who had publicly threatened to kill him and Mayor Englin of Animas City on sight and said he was relieved to learn that he had been killed. "That was a tough fellow and I was glad he was out of the way."[75]

Even Charles B. Jones, editor of the *Dolores News* of Rico and a staunch supporter of the Stockton-Eskridge combine in its war with the Farmington faction, could find little to criticize in the elimination of Porter Stockton. The man was, said Jones, "well and unfavorably known throughout southern Colorado and northern New Mexico. . . . He lays claim to having killed 12 men, and he had made threats against the lives of several citizens, it was thought best to give him to the angels, who now minister to his wants."[76]

The editor of a Durango paper agreed, saying that the well-known Porter Stockton "has been a terror to the community wherever he has lived and lays claim to the killing of nineteen men, which is a fair average for a man of his years — about 30. . . . The immediate cause of the visitation on him and his household was the threats he had lately made against the lives of half a dozen of the community. As he never went back on his word in that respect, it was deemed by the gentlemen interested that he had better receive a quietus. Therefore the expedition."[77]

Another New Mexico paper said that Port had acquired "an unenviable reputation," claiming a personal death toll boast of eighteen, an exaggerated boast perhaps, but "at any rate he has been the means of putting quite a number of men under the sod. . . . For the past year or more Stockton has been stealing cattle in the Lower Arkansas country and it is very gratifying to write the obituary of such a desperado. He died with his boots on."[78]

Interestingly, William Porter Stockton's death is listed as a "lynching" in a recently published chronicle of New Mexico's extralegal executions.[79]

The killing of Port Stockton took the escalating conflict between the Farmington Stockman's Protective Association of New Mexico and the Stockton-Eskridge combine of Colorado to a new level of violence, as it precipitated what one writer has called "the private war of Ike Stockton."[79]

# — 8 —

## IKE STOCKTON
### 1851–1881

*Ike Stockton claims to have killed six men in the San Juan country and hopes to kill more in Rio Arriba county. The number of his brother's victims is estimated at fourteen.*

—*Arizona Weekly Star*, April 21, 1881

Isaac T. ("Ike") Stockton was born in Upshur County, Texas, on Leap Year Day, February 29, 1852, two years after his brother Port.[1] Less impetuous and prone to violence than his volatile older sibling, Ike evidently had no trouble with the law during the early years in Texas.

While living in Erath County in the 1870s, the brothers married. Amanda Ellen Robinson, Ike's bride, was a half-sister of Emily Jane Marshall, Port's wife.[2] Like Emily, she was seven years younger than her husband. She and Ike had two children, Delilah, born in 1875, and Guy, born in 1879.[3]

Ike was with Port at Colfax County, New Mexico, in the mid-1870s, where he reportedly helped his trouble-prone brother escape from hoosegows on one, or perhaps two, occasions. He next appeared in the turbulent town of Lincoln, where the bloody Lincoln County War was about to erupt. Ike kept a saloon in Lincoln, and it is said Port joined him there to help in the operation.[4]

One chronicler reported that Port kept the saloon while Ike rode with the Billy the Kid gang. During this period, he wrote, the Stockton brothers "killed at least three men and pistol-whipped numerous others."[5] This is an assertion no other Lincoln County War historian has accepted.

Most histories of the conflict mention Ike briefly and Port not at all. Ike did witness the controversial shooting of Sheriff William Brady and his deputy, George Hindman, on the streets of Lincoln on April 1, 1878, when William ("Billy the Kid") Bonney and his cohorts, firing from ambush, cut down Brady and Hindman. Brady expired almost instantly. When the mortally wounded deputy called plaintively for water, Ike ran from his saloon to the nearby Rio Bonito, filled his hat with water, and carried it back to the dying man. This act of compassion was done at some personal risk, for there was more shooting and, even as Stockton was helping Hindman, another bullet struck the deputy, killing him.[6]

This seems to have been the only part that either Stockton brother played in the turbulent Lincoln County War. Governor Lew Wallace drew up an extensive list of those who were wanted by law enforcement for participation in the conflict, and the names of the Stockton brothers do not appear.

Following the tumultuous years in Lincoln County, Ike returned to northern New Mexico Territory and the lush grasslands near the Raton Pass and the Colorado border, where he reportedly signed on as a cowboy with the large Thompson and Lacy cattle company in that district.[7]

Later on he followed the Coe clan — the interrelated men, Lewis, George, Frank, and Jasper, and their families — to the Four Corners country, where Colorado, New Mexico, Arizona, and Utah meet. The Coe boys, particularly George and Frank, had been active participants in the Lincoln County violence, and when Governor Wallace and the U.S. military cracked down on the combatants, thought it wise to move on to other climes. Ike had been friendly with George and Frank back in Lincoln, and when he moved to the northwestern corner of New Mexico Territory, he and his family lived for a time in the Coes' home.[8] By late 1879, with a small ranch and a residence of his own, he was well established at Animas City, La Plata County, Colorado, just north of Durango.

Shortly after Port and his family arrived in the district with a small herd of cattle, local ranchers noticed decreases in their stock. The Stockton brothers became immediate rustling suspects. The cattlemen, who ranged their herds in New Mexico, were officially organized as the Farmington Stockman's Protective Association, but since the Coe boys formed an important faction within the group, Colorado newspapers often referred to them as the "Lincoln County mob" or the "Coe Consolidation."[9]

Ike, who previously had been on the best of terms with the Coe boys, now became their bitter enemy. He recruited a coterie of fighting cowhands from Colorado headed by the Eskridge brothers, Harg and Dyson. The Stockton-Eskridge gang, as the New Mexicans began to call the group, included Dyson Eskridge's brother-in-law James W. Garrett, Bert Wilkinson, Charles Allison, Lark Reynolds, Tom Radigan, "Texas Bill" Hunter, and Wilson Hughes.[10]

A pitched battle fought on the outskirts of Durango was the opening clash in a conflict that would go on for two years, involve the governors and newspapers of Colorado and New Mexico in factional controversy, make headlines across the nation, and take a number of lives, including both Stockton brothers (see chapter 7).

Ike, of course, was infuriated by the killing of his brother, and even as he took his wounded sister-in-law and her children into his home and cared for them, he planned revenge. As one wire dispatch reported: "Ike Stockton, the leader of the Rio Arriba county desperadoes, says he may be killed in the attempt to avenge his brother's death, but that he has other brothers who will then take up the fight."[11]

Emboldened by the elimination of Porter, an acknowledged gunman and killer, the Stockton enemies appeared to have no fear of Ike, who, despite provocative prose to the contrary, had never been known to kill anyone. According to the *Dolores News* of Rico, Colorado, a pro-Stockton journal, on January 16, 1882, two weeks after Port's death, three members of the Farmington "mob" perpetrated another outrage. With drawn revolvers they accosted an inoffensive one-armed man named Seth Welfoot and escorted him to Farmington, where at a mock trial a kangaroo jury found him guilty of publicly condemning the gunmen who shot Port's wife. He was ordered to leave the country within ten days or be shot on sight. *News* editor Charles B. Jones suggested that the act was pulled off so the cattlemen could buy up Welfoot's property cheaply.[12]

Not intimidated, Welfoot remained on his property, and the Farmington bunch did not carry out their threats.

When the month of February 1881 passed quietly, with no further incident, the editor of the *Santa Fe New Mexican* was prompted to note that excitement over the recent killings had subsided. Although "a brother of Port Stockton" and several others "have threatened to invade Farmington and avenge the deaths of [Oscar Puett, killed earlier] and Stockton . . . , they have not done so yet and probably will not. In order to meet the danger the citizens [have] formed a vigilance committee."[13]

But the fragile peace would be shattered in March. On the day the Santa Fe paper appeared, Ike Stockton and a party of six herders were camped on the La Plata River, in the realm of their enemy. When Tom Nance and Aaron Barker, two of the Farmington leaders who had participated in the killing of Port Stockton, appeared, guns roared. One of Ike's riders, Tom Radigan, was hit in the leg, and Barker was shot dead. Nance escaped in a hail of gunfire.[14]

Of course members of the feuding sides gave contradictory accounts of the action. Some time later Ike gave his version to a reporter for a Denver newspaper. He said that when he saw a rider approach the camp, he raised his rifle, "as behooves one in that country," and Barker, the horseman, immediately "drew his revolver and fired, hitting Tommy Radigan in the leg. Then firing became general and Barker and his horse were both killed. [Nance] drew his revolver when Barker fired. He shot and retreated. We chased him seven or eight miles but he made his escape." Returning to camp, Stockton's crew took Radigan to Fort Lewis for treatment.[15]

In a letter to a newspaper, Jasper Coe, who was not present but must have gotten his information from Tom Nance, contended that "the gorillas," as he termed Ike Stockton's party, ambushed the two Farmington men. After killing Barker and his horse, they stripped their victim of his money, saddle, bridle, and arms. Radigan was shot in the leg, he said, during the chase after Nance.[16] George Lockhart, a Coe cohort, repeated this line and accused the Stockton riders of rustling stock.[17]

The Colorado newspapers, as usual, readily accepted the Stockton version.

The *La Plata Miner* of Silverton reprinted a story from the pages of the *Durango Southwest*, which accused the Farmington group of beginning the fireworks and seemed to laud the Stockton party for its quick lethal response. More violence was predicted for the future. It said Stockton and his followers, numbering about thirty-five men, were resolved to round up their cattle in that country "if they have to kill all the thieves down there to do it. We take great pleasure in awaiting obituary notices."[18]

March 1881, having opened with the bloody confrontation between two of the Farmington men and the Stockton bunch, continued as a month of violence and contention in the San Juan country.

On March 17 Ike Stockton's cohort, Charley Allison, got into a scrape in Larsh's Dance Hall, a Durango deadfall. Using his pistol as a bludgeon, he clubbed a man named Andy Guinan over the head before shooting him. Guinan received a bullet wound through his wrist, and Allison was shot in the left thigh. Witness reports were confusing and conflicting, but it appeared Allison, in an advanced state of intoxication, was struck with his own bullet after it passed through Guinan's wrist.[19]

The outbreak of violence spawned unconfirmed reports of more bloodshed. When a former resident of Rico named W. H. Sockrider disappeared, a rumor spread that he had been murdered for his money and stock by the Farmington "mob." While so far only rumor, opined editor Jones of the *Dolores News*, "it is in such perfect accord with the doings of this miserable outfit of cutthroats and thieves" from Farmington.[20]

On March 18 Jasper Coe was prompted by the rush of events to pen a long letter to the editor of the *Daily Gazette* of Colorado Springs, defending the Farmington cattlemen.[21] As published, the piece was headlined "A Reign of Terror."[22]

"This valley was quiet and prosperous until about one year ago, the people being mostly poor but industrious, and for reasons better known elsewhere there has never been any law or legal officers established here," Coe began. This all changed with the arrival of the Stockton-Eskridge gang. "Low browed cutthroats [bent on] murder, pillage and plunder," they numbered about thirteen. These he compared to the peaceable farmers and stockmen of the Farmington district, about eighty in all, who had labored hard for their homes and families. He concluded with an ardent defense of his clan, the Coes, who, he said, had led the resistance against cow thieves and had been unjustly castigated in the press as leaders of a vicious mob.[23]

Jasper's arguments were refuted a few days later by C. H. McHenry of Animas City, Colorado, a staunch supporter of the Stockton faction, in a letter to New Mexico Governor Lew Wallace. McHenry enumerated the alleged crimes of the Farmington "mob" and reminded the governor that three Coe family members had been "some of the principal men in the late Lincoln and Colfax County troubles."[24]

In April a grand jury at Tierra Amarilla, New Mexico, after hearing testimony regarding the shootings on the La Plata River, brought in indictments for murder, assault with intent to murder, and horse stealing against Ike Stockton, Harg Eskridge, Charley Allison, Jim Garrett, Tom Radigan, Lark Reynolds, Wilson Hughes, and three John Does. Soon thereafter Governor Wallace issued reward notices, offering $500 for the capture and delivery of Stockton and $250 each for Allison, Eskridge, Garrett, Radigan, Reynolds, Hughes, and Bill ("Tex") Hunter.[25]

Association with known outlaws, especially Charley Allison, undoubtedly a loose cannon, had caused Ike Stockton uneasiness for some time. As he told a reporter for a Denver paper some months later, organizing a band of fighting men was no easy task. "I tried to get good men to go with me," he said, "but several bad men, like Allison, slipped in. In a new country like this it is hard to find a crowd . . . without getting some poor material."[26]

Finally Ike told Allison and a few others to go their own way, and the band split up. Leaving with Allison were "Little Tommy" Seeley, Lewis Perkins, and Henry Watts, and other recruits joined this bunch later.

Allison then led his followers on a criminal rampage, robbing stores and stagecoaches. Run down and captured, they were tried, convicted, and sentenced to long prison terms.[27]

In his Rico journal Charles Jones took umbrage when the editor of the *Conejos County Times* appeared to equate Stockton and his followers with the Allison outlaw gang. He was angered by the rather mild comment that "since the Stockton gang and the Allison gang of robbers have been gathered in, it would appear that southern Colorado is an unhealthy location for such gentry."[28] Always quick to defend Stockton and his cronies, Jones responded ferociously, calling his journalistic counterpart from Conejos County a "poor, idiotic, stupid fool." The remark was "absurd," he said, a "little bit of ignorant and cowardly abuse."[29]

Despite the absence of Charley Allison and his cohorts from the scene of battle in the San Juan, the violence continued in that sector throughout the month of April.

In Durango on April 10 Henry Read Moorman shot James K. Polk-Prindle in the abdomen, fatally wounding him, and put a bullet through Perry Steffey's wrist. Several onlookers, including Stockton stalwart Jim Garrett, collared Moorman, and he was locked up, but later the Durango Committee of Safety, a vigilante organization, took him from the jail and hanged him from a tree.[30]

Learning that Ike Stockton, the Eskridge brothers, Garrett, and several others of that crowd had taken up residence in Durango, the Farmington bunch decided to mount an offensive against their enemies. About thirty of them rode into Durango just as the Moorman lynching was in progress. Seeing that this was an inappropriate time to begin hostilities, they continued on to Animas City, where they found Sheriff Luke Hunter and pressed him to arrest the members of the Stockton-Eskridge party and turn them over to them. The sheriff said he could not do that without the proper requisitions from the New Mexico governor.[31]

Displeased with this response, the Farmington party returned to Durango, where about noon the next day, April 11, they had a long-range gunfight with the Stocktons on a mesa east of town. An estimated fifty to one hundred shots were fired, but two noncombatant spectators were the only reported casualties.

The *Dolores News* quoted the *Durango Record*, which condemned the Farmington people for making the grave mistake of attacking this town, firing near women and children, and endangering the lives of people who had no part in their quarrels. "There is a legal way of making arrests," the paper said, "and the people of Durango will not permit men to come into this town to take them in any other way, especially a band of men who have shown the reckless disposition manifested by this party. There are a thousand armed men in Durango ready to repel any forcible invasion of this place. If there are men here who have been guilty of crimes in New Mexico, let the authorities move in the matter, and not an irresponsible body."[32]

On April 12 Sheriff Hunter acted. He ordered out the Animas City militia and set up camp on the outskirts of Durango. A newspaper correspondent from Ouray, Colorado, covered the events in the embattled town. He said a report was circulating that the Coe party had been seen with a wounded man and a pack animal carrying a dead body. The manager of the Coliseum had closed it down for two weeks, waiting for peace to be restored. "It seems," he said, "all the murderers and outlaws make it a point to commit their hellish deeds at his place."[33]

By April 1881 the violence in the San Juan had caught the attention of the nation's press, and dispatches largely emanating from anti-Stockton sources began to appear in newspapers around the country. Early that month a paper in Reno, Nevada, reported that "the whole section of country around Rio Arabia [sic], New Mexico, is in a state of nervous excitement and terror. The cause of the terror is Ike Stockton and his gang, who with his brother 'Port,' have for years been depredating through New Mexico and Texas, murdering, stealing, etc."[34]

An editor in Atchison, Kansas, repeated these charges, adding, "It will afford us much pleasure to record the early demise of Ike Stockton [who] is too reckless with his pistol," and among his other crimes "has no respect for newspaper men."[35]

And a paper in faraway Pennsylvania reported that "Stockton's gang of desperadoes are ruling Rio Arriba county, with terror, robbery and murder."[36]

Late in March the leaders of the Farmington Stockman's Protective Association, "eight of the 'best citizens of Rio Arriba County,'" had petitioned Governor Wallace in Santa Fe "to take prompt action against the desperadoes who disgrace the territory." Wallace responded by issuing his reward notices for the capture of Stockton and seven of his followers. When threats of violence began to escalate in April he ordered Adjutant General Max Frost to go to the scene of the trouble with sixty stands of rifles and ten thousand rounds of ammunition, and there organize two infantry companies to act as a sheriff's posse.[37]

*Dolores News* editor Jones dutifully reported these moves, but, still in sympathy with Stockton and his followers, expressed disagreement in his edition of April 9. The paper, he said, "is not inclined to believe that the above petitioners are the best citizens, but *vice versa*. Among the men called robbers there are (to our knowledge) several honor-able gentlemen, belonging to a higher sphere than the worthy (?) petitioners."

When Adjutant General Frost arrived in Rio Arriba County, how-ever, he reported back to Governor Wallace that the state of affairs appeared to be much as the petitioners had stated. It seemed to Frost that many in that county feared Stockton and were afraid to talk. He repeated a rumor that Stockton had bragged of having killed six men and expected to kill more. "Ike's six added to Port's fourteen make quite a showing for two brothers," Frost mused.[38]

On April 15 the *Daily Gazette* of Colorado Springs carried two dispatches from the front. The first, datelined Santa Fe, April 13, quoted Frost's latest report to Governor Wallace. The band of des-peradoes still held their own, Frost said, for he had been unable to organize a citizen company to attack the Stockton gang. If necessary Governor Wallace indicated he would declare the country in a state of insurrection, and call on the United States troops for aid.[39]

The second, headed "Durango Deviltry" and datelined Denver, April 14, reported that the Stockton gang was "still deprecating" and that Durango was "in a state of excitement bordering on anarchy." The desperadoes were "sending raiding parties toward Farming-ton . . . for the purpose of stealing cattle and killing cowboys." A few days earlier they had driven thirty-five head of stolen cattle into Durango. The *Denver Republican* reported that "citizens dare not write an impartial account of the state of affairs to anyone outside for fear of being shot," and "a Denver newspaper man who was suspected of having written a letter to a paper was stopped on the street at the muzzle of a revolver by Ike Stockton, but, fortunately, was allowed to go unharmed."[40]

The April 16 edition of the *Santa Fe New Mexican* also reported that the Stockton gang had stolen fifteen horses from the ranch of Isaac W. ("Tom") Lacy and were daily driving rustled cattle to Durango and selling them to butchers. It quoted J. H. Cox of Farmington as saying that Stockton gang members had informed him they "intended to kill Alf Graves, John Cox, the three Coe brothers and several others before they would stop."

Among the press outlets of Colorado and New Mexico, the *Du-rango Record* and the *Dolores News* of Rico stood almost alone in defense of the Stockton-Eskridge forces. The editors of both papers recognized that much of the discord between the residents of the state of Colorado and the territory of New Mexico over the issue was the result of natural regional partisanship, and bitterly resented attacks on the Stocktons by other Colorado newspapers. When the *Rocky Mountain News* of Denver published a letter, purportedly written by someone in Durango, castigating the Stockton gang and entitled "A Reign of Terror," the *Record* struck back in an editorial headed "Refutation of a Slander Upon Some of Durango's Citizens," which the *Dolores News* reprinted in full.

The author of the letter, said the *Record*, claimed to be from Durango, but exhibited no knowledge of the town or its history. Incidents narrated were so far from the truth as to be unrecognizable by locals. Typical was a distorted account of Port Stockton's killing, "a version never before heard in Durango." The editor of the *Record* went on to clarify the history from the Colorado point of view.

The problem developed, he said, when the big cattlemen of the Farmington country mounted a campaign to drive out the farmers and small ranchers who were fencing the country and breaking up the open range required by the large cattlemen for their huge herds. They enlisted a group of fighting men that came to be called the "Coe party" to execute these designs. The Coes began a program of intimidation that led to the Seth Welfoot affair, the murder of Port Stockton and the wounding of his wife, and the flight of many Farmington residents across the border to Colorado, including the newly elected representative to the New Mexico territorial legislature. Resistance to these high-handed tactics came in the form of the Stockton-Eskridge combine, fighting men of equal caliber.[41]

Editor Jones of the *Dolores News* chimed in with his own views. There was talk, he said, that the Farmington faction was endeavoring to get a requisition from the New Mexico governor for the arrest of the Stockton party in Colorado. In the event such a requisition were to be issued, he implored Colorado Governor Pitkin to reject it and not deliver the men into "the unmerciful hands of lawless New Mexico," for they would be murdered as soon as they crossed the border. If the requisition was approved, he suggested that during the trial of the Stocktons either in New Mexico or Colorado, they be protected by a company of Colorado militia.[42]

Actually, the residents of Durango were deeply divided over the issue. The vigilante organization styling itself the Durango Committee of Safety contained several prominent leaders who favored the Farmington position and were vociferous in protesting the Stockton gang's presence in town. They held a public meeting on the afternoon of April 11, after the gunfight on the mesa outside town, and demanded the removal of the Stocktons, by force if necessary.

In retaliation, a group called "Friends of the Eskridge-Stockton party" held its own meeting that evening. Conducted by lamplight in front of Myers and West's Livery Stable, the members denounced the proceedings of the Committee of Safety. Declaring that they were "just as good law-abiding citizens as those who called or attended the meeting of the afternoon." The resolution read: "Resolved: That we, the law-abiding citizens of La Plata county, believing the Eskridge party to be good, law-abiding citizens, and as yet have violated no law in this county. Pledge ourselves to protect said party against any violence of Safety committee or any set of persons not acting in accordance with law and order."[43]

Adjutant General Max Frost, meanwhile, was busy organizing a militia unit called the San Juan Guards as a *posse comitatus* to preserve the peace under the authority of Rio Arriba County Deputy Sheriffs Moses Blancett and Will Shard. He gave leadership positions in the Guards to Farmington faction members, appointing H. C. Coe as first lieutenant, Alfred T. Strumpf as second lieutenant, and George Lockhart as sergeant. He presented Deputy Sheriffs Blancett and Shard with warrants for murder to be served on Ike Stockton, James Garrett, Harg Eskridge, and six others if any of them crossed the border into New Mexico. Armed guardsmen were stationed at the approaches to the Animas Valley to prevent any marauders or rustlers from entering the valley from Colorado. Lieutenant Strumpf led a squad of ten men to the La Plata River country searching for Ike Stockton. A force of twenty-one marched to Canyon Largo with orders to arrest anyone seeking to enter New Mexico Territory from Colorado who did not have legitimate business there.

Frost also made temporary appointments in an effort to establish a badly needed legal system. William P. Haines, the postmaster at Bloomfield who had held up the election results the previous fall, was appointed justice of the peace for Precinct 19, with P. F. Salmon as constable. G. W. Markley was named justice of the peace for Precinct 20, and Boyd Vaughn constable.[44]

The *Santa Fe New Mexican* announced these moves and added: "It is believed that Stockton and his gang will leave town before they can be arrested. It is said that they will make one more raid to kill the Coe brothers before heading out for Texas or Utah. They also want to kill Thomas Nance and anyone who had anything to do with the killing of Port Stockton."[45]

The editors of the *Santa Fe New Mexican* were stridently antagonistic to the Colorado faction in the dispute. The Ike Stockton gang of "desperadoes" found its support, they charged, among saloon men, gamblers, and others in the "fast life" of Durango. This group outnumbered the honest businessmen, who feared them. "The town is in the control of the Stockton gang who raid far and wide. Cattle are killed and sold openly in town. Ike Stockton [is] well supplied with funds which he uses freely in fitting out men who wish to join him."[46]

But on the very day the *New Mexican* published this screed, asserting that the Ike Stockton gang was in complete control of Durango, newspapers across the nation announced that the Stockton gang had fled Durango and were believed to have left the state to avoid arrest on a requisition from the governor of New Mexico.[47]

As was his habit, editor Jones of the *Dolores News* rose to the defense of the Stockton-Eskridge bunch and chastised the New Mexicans. He said he had information from several sources that the Farmington "mob" was divided, and two elements were fighting among themselves. He expressed satisfaction with that, as it indicated there were men in Rio Arriba County who refused to be identified with "the miserable mob so long a terror to the country." Harmony in that sector was broken, he believed, by Max Frost's organization of the San Juan Guards and his exclusion of several of the leaders, including Frank Simmons, "the self-styled 'Captain' of the old mob."[48]

The New Mexico and Colorado press, most notably the *Denver Republican* and *Santa Fe New Mexican*, were filled, he said, with false reports in which Stockton and Eskridge were called the "Durango Desperadoes" and portrayed as outlaws. After reviewing the events of the past months he could find no action in which Stockton, Eskridge, and company had "not been in the right, absolutely and entirely." In every respect they had been gentlemanly and law-abiding, with the possible exception of the shooting incident on the La Plata River, for which indictments had been brought against them. And a hearing in a fair court of law would show, he was certain, that even in that case their actions were completely justified. But they had resisted arrest, knowing that if they gave up their arms and submitted to their enemies, "it would be certain death to all of the Stockton party . . . as they would have been shot or hung within a few miles of the scene of their arrest."[49]

The *Santa Fe New Mexican* reported that there was decided dissension in the ranks of the Stockton-Eskridge forces. Charley Allison had taken his leave, together with a few other outlaws of his ilk, but some malcontents remained, including a young tough named "Kid" Cherry, reputed to have several notches on his gun. Outside Armago he quarreled with his boss, Dyson Eskridge, and Eskridge proceeded to plant a bullet in his back. Leaving Cherry in the road to die, Eskridge rode off to Durango. Later he returned with Ike Stockton and Jim Garrett to oversee the burial of the man he had killed. Since the demise of a desperado like Cherry went unlamented, remarked the paper, there was no talk of prosecution or lynching.[50]

About this time the energetic and oft-quoted Durango correspondent for the *Ouray Times* had the opportunity to interview Ike Stockton and Dyson Eskridge. Although it was "generally conceded that [Stockton was] a desperate man when aroused," the newsman "found him to be peaceable and quiet, never talking of his troubles unless closely questioned," and then quite guarded in his remarks. "He has no ruffian style," said the newsman.

> You would not notice anything wild about him, only his restless eyes which seem to be continually glancing here and there. He is a little smaller than the medium size of men, walks briskly, slightly stooped. Dresses well — wears a white shirt, black suit, stiff hat, and a neatly fitting boot. Dark hair, cut short, is dark complexioned, sharp features, slight beard, eyes small and piercing. He has a clear, feminine ringing voice, and when talking is quite sociable and entertaining. I have studied him closely and see nothing which would indicate a desperate character.

He found Eskridge to be quite different. "A tall, raw-boned young man, dark complexioned, with a fine black mustache, heavy jaw bone and large, prominent chin," he was tight-lipped, spoke only when spoken to, and seldom laughed. "The crack shot of the gang," he was ever on the alert. The newsman considered him the most "cold-blooded and naturally desperate" member of the outfit, "but it was clear he did not command the respect afforded Stockton."

He had been guilty of several bullying acts and gun plays in recent months. In Animas City he had severely beaten a man who had simply made favorable comments about the Coe party. While traveling in a hack to Durango with Eskridge the reporter had personally witnessed the man's "quick temper and penchant for violence."

When a wagon momentarily blocked the roadway, Eskridge pulled his pistol and would have shot the teamster but for the intervention of a Durango deputy city marshal who was also a passenger. On arrival in Durango, the hack pulled up at a saloon, and Eskridge ordered drinks all around. "While waiting for the drinks he sat in the hack and fired one shot at a man who was going across the street, just to see how near he could come." The other passengers, including the law-man, laughed, but the target of Eskridge's marksmanship did not appreciate the joke. Later, when a Durango resident expressed some pro-Coe sympathies, Eskridge "made the fellow dance, shooting be-tween his legs and cursing him." No effort was made to arrest the desperado for these criminal acts.[51]

In mid-May folks throughout the Farmington-Durango region were shocked to learn that one of the most important men in the dis-trict had been shot to death. Isaac W. ("Tom") Lacy, partner of wealthy Trinidad entrepreneur George W. Thompson and overseer of their large, jointly owned ranch in the San Juan district, was gunned down on May 12 by "Big Dan" Howland, a man with an unsavory reputation as rustler and murderer who had been hired by Lacy as a detective to determine who was stealing horses and cattle from the ranch. A twenty-man posse rode in pursuit of the killer, but lost his trail and returned empty-handed. Lacy's widow offered a reward of $2,000 for his capture, but "Big Dan" had disappeared.

Tom Nance of the Farmington crowd was present at the shooting, and many Coloradoans, including editor Jones of the *Dolores News*, believed he was implicated in the crime. Jones thought it significant that Tom Lacy was related to Ike Stockton by marriage and that the two men had been friends and business associates for many years.[52]

"Big Dan," he said, "was "a murderer at heart and could not but obey the instincts of a depraved nature," who bragged that he was a cousin of the notorious Dave Rudabaugh, lieutenant in the gang of the infamous outlaw Billy the Kid. "It is no disgrace to a man to be a relative of a notorious criminal," Jones remarked, "but to be proud of the fact is a deep disgrace."[53]

The violence continued. A few days later Harg Eskridge fatally shot a young desperado and gang hanger-on named Jim ("Kid") White, after receiving a tip that White was out to kill him for the reward money on his head. White's death elicited no sympathy from editor Jones, who wrote in his paper that "White has paid the penalty of his loud mouthed bravado." He said the young man was worse than a murderer, having undertaken the killing of Eskridge for money and then foolish enough to brag about it to others. "This last crowning piece of folly and crime leaves him with comparatively none to regret his death."[54]

Not only were there few, if any, to mourn the death of Kid White, there were apparently no officers of the law to care about his passing either. In the next issue of his paper Jones of the *Dolores News* reported that Ike Stockton, Harg Eskridge, and Lark Reynolds had ridden into Rico accompanied by a man calling himself "M. C. Cook," an old Texas crony of Stockton's, where they were warmly welcomed by many friends. After a few days in town, cutting up old touches with those friends, the four men went up on Expectation Mountain to work on the Lookout silver mine, owned jointly by Stockton, Eskridge, and Burt Wilkinson. The Lookout, said the *News*, was "a splendid piece of property" that had assayed out the previous season in high-grade silver. Editor Jones noted that they did "not appear to be reckless, desperate characters, but behaved themselves like gentlemen, as those who are acquainted with them know them to be." He wished them luck in their mining enterprise.[55]

While Stockton and his friends were in Rico two almost identical letters were written and directed to the governors of New Mexico and Colorado. They were signed by Ike Stockton and Harg Eskridge, but Rico newspaper editor Charles Jones was the author of both.

In the letters the two claimed they were "respectable, law-abiding citizens [who] had not violated any law of the United States, Colorado, or New Mexico." Requisitions for their arrest had been ob-

tained by "misrepresentation and perjury" of members of an organized band sworn to kill them. "Should we deliver ourselves into their
midst or allow ourselves to be taken into or through that portion of
the country infested by them, without sufficient protection, we would
be in great danger of being assassinated." They said they were not
only willing but anxious to have a fair and impartial trial for all offenses charged against them if protection was provided guaranteeing
their safety to and from the courtroom and during the trial.[56]

Down in Santa Fe, the editor of the *New Mexican*, no friend of the
Colorado fugitives, remarked that even if it were true that Stockton
wanted to call it quits, "the people had no confidence in the word of
Ike Stockton."[57]

Passing with little notice, another occurrence took place that
month of May that would ultimately have a profound effect upon the
future of Ike Stockton and his followers. At Silverton, a bustling
mining town some twenty miles northeast of Rico, a young man
named Clayton Ogsbury was installed as city marshal. Ogsbury, who
had kept a liquor establishment in Silverton in its earliest days and had
also engaged in mining, was personable and popular, and his appointment was welcomed warmly by the local folk.[58] Within two weeks of
pinning on the badge Ogsbury rewarded their trust in him by nab-
bing a man named Belcher, who was suspected of robbing a man of
more than $4,000 in cash and certificates of deposit.[59] But only three
months later Marshal Clayton Ogsbury would be shot dead, and the
Stockton gang would be the center of a storm of outrage.

In the meantime the *Dolores News* of Rico continued its editorial
defense of the Stockton-Eskridge faction in its ongoing conflict with
the Farmington combine.

At the spring roundup Dow Eskridge, the older brother of Dyson
and Harg, had attempted to gather cattle he had been ranging in Rio
Arriba County and was prevented from doing so by members of the
Farmington Stockmen's Protective Association, who told him that
"Colorado stockmen would not be allowed to drive any of their stock
from New Mexico, unless Ike Stockton is arrested and held subject to
their orders." Said the *Dolores News*: "The Farmington mob has in an
unguarded moment thrown off the garb of injured innocence enough
to once more disclose the cloven hoof. By what right a band of men
can hold the stock belonging to other men, pending the arrest of

IKE STOCKTON, THE SOUTHERN COLORADO AND NEW MEXICO OUTLAW AND DESPERADO — A REWARD OF $2000 FOR HIS CAPTURE.

The *Illustrated Police Gazette* featured Ike Stockton as a wanted criminal. Courtesy of Fred Nolan.

a man, even though he should be a criminal, is past our comprehension. They fear that Ike Stockton will revenge himself for their wrongs on him and they are wonderfully eager to have an opportunity to murder him."

The paper went on to say it was "a dead moral certainty" that the Farmington cattlemen were harboring "Big Dan" Howland, the slayer of Tom Lacy. Howland, said the paper, was hiding out at Farmington. "People are beginning to realize that Farmington is headquarters for a set of thieves and murderers who have compelled all decent citizens to leave. Their attacks by misrepresentation on the Eskridge boys and Ike Stockton are positive proof of a conspiracy to get those men into their hands for the purpose of murdering them, as they have always murdered their enemies before."[60]

In June 1881 the attention of southwestern Colorado residents was temporarily diverted from the Farmington-Stockton conflict. When the bodies of three men were found robbed and murdered, the outrage was blamed on a band of renegade Indians.[61] Twenty-five volunteers from the Rico, Durango, and Montezuma districts, including Ike Stockton and Harg Eskridge, enlisted to hunt down the culprits. For two weeks they tracked the Indians, finally locating them about twenty miles west of Moab, Utah. With the terrain favoring them, the Indians soundly defeated their pursuers, killing seven and wounding several others, including Harg Eskridge, who received a severe leg injury. Early newspaper dispatches incorrectly reported both Stockton and Eskridge were killed.[62] How many Indians died or were wounded in the fight is not known, but a newspaper later credited Harg Eskridge with killing nine himself.[63] Both Eskridge and Stockton were praised later for their part in the fight. One newspaper said that, even after he was wounded, "Harg continued to fight like a tiger. He was certainly no quitter."[64] Others lauded Ike for his tenacity during the long pursuit and deadly battle.

Even as Ike Stockton was off fighting Indians he was being attacked in the press, especially in the pages of the *Santa Fe New Mexican*. Charles Jones of the *Dolores News*, however, ever ready to support Stockton in his editorial columns, offered his defense under the head "Malicious Persecution" in his issue of June 18, 1881. He found it "incomprehensible" that the *New Mexican*, which he called "the official paper of the territory of New Mexico," should consistently support "murderers and cattle thieves," while attacking Ike Stockton at every turn with "false and atrociously malignant" stories "forced upon a nauseated and long-suffering public." While his paper had been accused of being the "organ of the Stockton-Eskridge party," Jones said he appreciated the opportunity "to rectify some of the malicious lies which have been circulated about them."[65]

In mid-July friends of Harg Eskridge brought him back to Rico, where surgeons operated on his leg and foot. His brother Dyson, Ike Stockton, and Marion C. Cook were there to lend support to their pal who was going through an extremely painful period. Harg would be crippled by the leg injury for many months to come.[66]

Meanwhile little had changed with regard to the conflict between the Farmington cattlemen and the Colorado-based Stockton gang. Governor Pitkin of Colorado, apparently unconvinced that the safety of the Stocktons could be assured if they were turned over to the New Mexico authorities, had not issued the requested requisitions. Adjutant General Frost had returned to Santa Fe and the San Juan Guards had disbanded, but in August the fear of a raid across the border into Rio Arriba County still occupied the minds of the Farmington men. And the war of words between the New Mexico and Colorado papers went on.

In its edition of August 7 the *Santa Fe New Mexican* said that while the Stockton gang was poised for a raid on Rio Arriba County from Durango, Governor Pitkin's failure to respond to the requisition of Governor Wallace was inexplicable. The paper again excoriated the Stockton-Eskridge combine as "a set of desperadoes who do not scruple to commit any crime, and at the same time pay no regard to law, but rather control the agents and officers by intimidation."[67] The inference was that the Colorado governor had been so intimidated.

Responding to what it called "an uncalled-for slur on our governor" the *Dolores News* said the *New Mexican* should find better matters of interest for its readers than "such absurd trash." In an obvious jab at the Coes, the paper said Governor Pitkin was correct in not honoring requisitions for peaceable Colorado citizens obtained by the perjury of men who fled other New Mexico counties to escape the clutches of the law.[68]

In another edition the *Dolores News* observed that the *New Mexican* was "unnecessarily alarmed" over reports that Ike Stockton was organizing a large party for a big raid into Rio Arriba County. Although some alarmists were calling upon Acting Governor W. G. Ritch to prepare to defend the border, editor Jones said Ritch would be better advised "to turn his militia loose on the Apaches," for the border was entirely safe. "Law and order prevails in southwestern Colorado, and there is not a particle of danger of a raid into New Mexico from that quarter."[69]

During this period of newspaper jousting a reporter for the *Denver Republican* interviewed Ike Stockton in Durango's Inter Ocean Hotel where Ike was staying, and the central figure in the continuing controversy had his opportunity to present his side of the story.

The newspaperman described his subject as "a pleasant faced, mild-mannered gentleman." Only twenty-nine years of age, he looked five or six years older. Standing five feet four inches in height, he was compactly built, weighing 164 pounds. He sported a neat goatee and mustache, and had grayish blue eyes. "The face was a mild one, and rather attractive. There certainly was nothing repulsive or brutal about it." Neatly dressed, Stockton wore plain round gold studs in his shirt and a silver chain draped across his vest to a silver watch in a vest pocket. "He was," said the man from Denver, "an innocent-looking man and totally unarmed."

Stockton was aggrieved, he said, because "the press of the country had branded him a murderer, thief and outlaw, and a desperado of the worst type." Looking intently at the reporter, Stockton said, "You have come down here into my house; you will mingle with the best people here; all I ask is that you inquire fully into my character and into my conduct since here, and publish what you find without prejudice."

Stockton told of his early life in Texas where, he said, he "took part in several scrimmages against the Comanches." He came to the Lower Animas country in 1879, raised cattle, and lived at peace with his neighbors until his brother was killed the previous January. Port, he admitted, was "a wild man" who had killed a horse thief in self-defense back in Colfax County and had been "in many scrapes," but Ike denied the reports that his brother was the bloodthirsty slayer of many men as depicted in the press.

It was the gunning down of Port and his wife, a "diabolical act," and the failure of officers of the law to bring the killers to justice, Ike said, that caused him "to vow vengeance."

Despite all the nonsense that had been written about him, Stockton declared, he was not a thief or a murderer. He said he had never killed anyone except Indians, and then in warfare. He had never stolen cattle or sold a pound of beef. There were thieves who did steal under the cover of the feud, but he and his followers, he said, had nothing to do with them.

Stockton gave his account of the gunfight at his camp on the La Plata in which Barker was killed and Radigan wounded, the scrap that had caused a reward to be issued for his arrest.

He also told of the fight with the Farmington men on the mesa above Durango. When the townsmen learned that the New Mexico force was on its way to engage the Stocktons, Ike said, "One of the marshals came to me and said: 'For God's sake, have no fighting here among the women and children.' We did go out and met them on the mesa. I can't say who did the first firing. They were shooting at me and I returned the compliment. There were probably two hundred shots fired. None of our party was seriously hurt. It was a running fight, and we didn't follow them. We were simply defending ourselves."

Stockton went on:

In what is called the Farmington gang there are some good men, men against whom I had nothing in the world.

I met some of them today and had dinner with them. Among them was the sheriff's brother, the sheriff's wife and others equally important. They have no [ill] feeling against me nor I against them. They want to compromise matters and we will effect a compromise. Myself and some Farmington men will meet soon. While I am ready to compromise with these men, I can never compromise with the men who shot my brother. I mean that those men will be tried by the courts, and I will not rest until they are tried and punished. The Farmington gang is headed by Lou Coe, a cattle man. Others of the party are Alf Graves, Thomas Naines [Nance], George Lockhart, Aaron Barker, George Fox, George Lynch, Jack Lynch, Frank and Jap Coe (brothers to Lou), Lee Hamblet and brother, and Dan Howland alias Big Dan, who shot Lacy.

He admitted that although Charley Allison "came here with good letters and we believed him to be a square man," it had been a mistake to accept him and his outlaw pals into the band. "The whole party," he said, "was so disgusted with him that all declared they would never go out again if he went along. On our return he shot himself in attempting to shoot another man. When he got well he started on his own hook, and got himself where he belongs."

The *Republic* reporter concluded by saying that in Durango public sympathy was entirely with Stockton, who the people regarded as a quiet, peaceable, and enterprising citizen. He maintained a comfortable home at Animas City, a few miles from Durango, where his "fair faced and pleasant young wife" and two children resided, as well as his brother's widow and orphans whom he had taken in. He was, the reporter believed, "anything but a ruffian."[70]

Less than two weeks after this interview appeared, a shooting incident in Silverton, Colorado, started a chain of events that completely altered the direction of the San Juan Valley War. About August 22 Bert Wilkinson, Jim Catron, and a mulatto named Thomas, known variously as "Black Kid" and "Copper-Colored Kid," all known members of the Stockton outfit, held up a saloon and spent that night and the following day on a spree in Durango. Catron got too rowdy and was arrested, but Wilkinson and Thomas soon broke him out of the flimsy calaboose. Catron disappeared, probably to sleep off his toot. Wilkinson and Thomas, joined by Dyson Eskridge, rode off to Silverton, forty miles north, in neighboring San Juan County.[71]

Clayton Ogsbury, the young city marshal at Silverton, soon became aware of the presence of the three in his town. He also was alerted that Sheriff Luke Hunter of La Plata County was on his way north with warrants for the arrest of Wilkinson and Thomas for the saloon holdup. By ten o'clock on the night of the 24th there was no sign of Hunter and his warrants, so Marshal Ogsbury retired to his room behind Johnnie Goode's saloon and went to sleep. Shortly before midnight Sheriff Hunter rode in. He woke up Ogsbury, and together with a man named C. W. Hodges, they went looking for the carousing cowboys.

They found them at the Diamond Saloon. As they were about to enter the saloon Ogsbury discerned a figure standing outside in the shadows. Peering into the darkness, he recognized the man as

Wilkinson, but before he had a chance to speak or reach for his revolver, Wilkinson drew his gun and fired, striking the marshal a mortal blow. With a groan Ogsbury fell face downward. Hodges, with bullets "whistling by him on every side," rushed to his side, but saw that he could do the fallen officer no good, and fled across the street. He later estimated that about twelve shots were fired.[72] When the shooting stopped Hodges went over and found Ogsbury gasping his last breath.[73]

Not taking the time to get their horses quartered in the Carlisle Livery Stable, Wilkinson, Eskridge, and Thomas fled on foot. Someone rang the fire bell, and soon parties of horsemen were organized and started out in every direction. "Black Kid" Thomas was discovered hiding behind the Grand Central Hotel and taken without resistance. "We think his court martial will be a brief and summary one," said the Silverton paper. "It is earnestly hoped that the lawless band, who have in cold blood shot down one of our best beloved and respected citizens, may be captured and then the people of this camp will attend to the balance."[74]

The paper announced that the San Juan County commissioners had offered a $1,500 reward for the arrest of either Eskridge or Wilkinson, but in a later issue it reported that rewards totaling $4,000 had been posted for the two fugitives. Also commented upon was the strange behavior of La Plata County Sheriff Luke Hunter, who reportedly rejected Ogsbury's suggestion that they get more reinforcements before attempting the arrests, and then, when the shooting commenced, seemed to have disappeared. "The people do not accuse Hunter of being Ogsbury's murderer directly," said the *Herald*, "but they do claim that the murder is indirectly traceable to criminal carelessness and foolhardiness on the part of the sheriff of La Plata."[75]

Thomas was quickly captured and held overnight. In the morning a vigilante party took him from his guards and hanged him. The *San Juan Herald* of Silverton said that although his bullets had not killed Ogsbury, Thomas had fired four shots into the saloon. There was said to be a $1,200 reward outstanding for the "Copper-Colored Kid" in Texas, and those who lynched him, the editor believed, "did the state, county and town a favor."[76]

The anger of the Silverton residents over the murder of their popular city marshal extended beyond Wilkinson to Eskridge, and the talk on the streets was that they "would hang anybody who bore the name of Eskridge."[77] The *Ouray Times* said Dyson Eskridge was "a desperate man, bloodthirsty, and knows no law. Hanging is too good for him."[78]

A few days later newspapers throughout Colorado were carrying a truly sensational story. Bert Wilkinson, the accused murderer of Marshal Clayton Ogsbury, had been captured, and, to the consternation of all, his captors were his highly publicized gang leader, Ike Stockton, and Ike's new pal, Marion Cook.

"Ike Stockton rode into town last evening," said the *Durango Record* of September 1,

> claiming that he had captured Burt Wilkinson in the mountains, some fifteen or twenty miles north of here. [Wilkinson] was in company with Dison [*sic*] Eskridge when Stockton rode up to them. Stockton refuses to tell anyone outside his attorney, J. L. Russell, where he has his man, but simply says he has him, and when the Silverton people and San Juan county pay him the cash for delivering over his prisoner, he will give him up. He left last night for Silverton to consult with the authorities there, and in the meantime his prisoner is in safekeeping. He says that Eskridge is gone, but he does not know where.[79]

Stockton had not gone to Silverton as the paper stated, but had dispatched a man named Frank Williams to inform San Juan County Sheriff George Thornilly of the capture and to inquire about procedure for payment of the rewards. Stockton returned to where Cook was holding Wilkinson. Later, under cover of darkness, they brought their prisoner into Animas City and held him in a hotel there.

Denver's *Rocky Mountain News* provided other details. Wilkinson, it said, was captured in the Needle Mountains by Stockton "after a hard chase" at about four o'clock the previous afternoon. Dyson Eskridge was also arrested by his brother Harg, "but a successful effort has been made to show his innocence of any participation in the crime." Wilkinson was taken to Silverton on September 1 and held under heavy guard, but "it was generally felt that he would be lynched by the enraged populace."[80]

Wilkinson was described as twenty-three years of age, five feet eleven inches in height, weighing 170 pounds, "a pretty good chunk of a man." The large reward offered for him, dead or alive, had brought many bounty hunters into the area, among them Captain C. A. Hawley, a renowned sleuth of the Rocky Mountain Detective Agency, headquartered in Denver, who, after the murder of Ogsbury, an agency operative, went to Durango in disguise to hunt down his killers.[81] "The detective association was very anxious to effect the capture as Ogsbury had been a popular and valued member of the force."[82]

With the capture of Ogsbury's killer the depiction of Ike Stockton in much of the press abruptly changed. Where he had once been characterized as "a murderer, thief and outlaw, and a desperado of the worst type," it was now suggested that the residents of Durango had never really considered him a bad man. He was, said the Denver paper, more "a victim of circumstances than anything else." He had led "a kind of outlaw life, and it is thought the capture of Wilkinson may have been a move on his part to regain the good graces of respectable people and facilitate his return to civilized society. There is no doubt but that the capture of the murderer of Ogsbury, for it is now known that Wilkinson did all the shooting and that Eskridge is not held accountable, will result in making Stockton one of the most popular men in this section."[83]

The *Durango Southwest* had the most complete account. It said that after the Ogsbury murder in Silverton, Sheriff Luke Hunter had deputized Ike Stockton to hunt down and arrest the killer. Stockton enlisted the aid of M. C. Cook, who had been appointed a deputy marshal of Durango, and on Saturday, August 27, the two left Durango and searched for three days. On Tuesday morning they spotted him on the mesa west of the Animas River and northeast of Animas City, and trailed him to his camp. Wilkinson was alone; Dyson Eskridge was not there. "Ike Stockton got the drop on him with his rifle, and told him to 'throw up.' Wilkinson turned pale and was dumb founded, and did not speak for a few seconds, and held up his hands but not very high. His eyes wandered around as tho' in search of a weapon, until Stockton ordered him to hold his hands up high, when he [made] the remark, 'Ike, you've got the drop on me. I wish you had shot me instead of taking me.' "[84]

Cook manacled Wilkinson and helped him on his horse. He kept the prisoner under guard while Stockton rode to Durango to inform Sheriff Hunter of the capture and send Frank Williams on his mission to Silverton. Wednesday night he and Cook brought Wilkinson to Animas City and held him in Keith's City Hotel, where he remained under heavy guard to protect him from anticipated vigilante action.

A representative of the *Durango Southwest*, calling on Wilkinson in the hotel, found him stretched out on a cot, smoking a meerschaum pipe and reading a newspaper. The reporter described the prisoner as "well built, of light complexion, blue eyes, and . . . dressed in dark trousers, blue shirt, with a cartridge belt strapped around his waist. His shoes were somewhat worn, and through the holes it could be seen that he wore no socks." Asked for a statement, Wilkinson simply replied that all he wanted was a fair trial.

After the reporter's assurance that he was not there for the purpose of satisfying idle curiosity, but would appreciate any comments that might throw light on the case, Wilkinson opened up a bit. The lynching of "the Kid" particularly bothered him. He called it "foul murder." He said he would not make any statement incriminating himself or others, but his remarks indicated he considered himself responsible entirely for Ogsbury's killing. His greatest fear, it seemed, was a lynching by the Silverton people. "His fears are well grounded," noted the reporter, for "the fate of the Kid is probably but a precursor of his own."[85]

The *Durango Record* of September 2 said that Wilkinson was "still in Animas City, in Stockton's custody, and likely to remain there until the sheriff of San Juan county comes down with the wampum and pays Stockton for his man. Not a man has as yet come down from Silverton to confer with Stockton with reference to the matter." The paper's editor also went to Animas City to interview Wilkinson, but arrived just as his guards, "all armed to the teeth," were taking him away, presumably to be turned over to authorities from Silverton at a secret rendezvous. After completing reward arrangements with Stockton, he said, the Silverton people would start back with the prisoner, but the newsman thought it questionable that Wilkinson would ever reach Silverton alive.[86]

The Colorado papers seemed unanimous about the slimness of Wilkinson's prospects for survival in Silverton. Said the *Daily Gazette* of Colorado Springs: "There is a strong feeling in favor of lynching Wilkinson."[87]

The editorial comments proved to be well founded. On Saturday, September 3, Ike Stockton, M. C. Cook, Mayor Fox of Animas City, and John Hull conveyed Bert Wilkinson some thirty miles to a point about ten miles from Silverton, where they met Sheriff Thornilly of San Juan County and a posse of twelve men. After turning over the reward money, said to be $2,500, to Stockton, Sheriff Thornilly took charge of the prisoner, escorted him to Silverton, and placed him in jail. Flora Pyle, Wilkinson's sister, was there and, well aware of the lynching talk, implored all who would listen to help her get a fair trial for her brother. But, said the *La Plata Miner*, she was informed by everyone, including the town and county law officers, that "the moment the fatal bullet entered Ogsbury's body, the fate of his murderers were sealed in case they should ever be brought to Silverton. Being informed that her brother would be hung whether she were present or not, she deemed it best to leave town and did so on Sunday. Her presence in Silverton is all that saved Bert's life through Saturday night. She was kindly informed by the sheriff that her brother's body would be sent to her."[88]

Shortly after nine o'clock Sunday, September 4, a party of masked men entered the Silverton jail, overpowered the guards, and took out Bert Wilkinson and hanged him. The *La Plata Miner* observed that he exhibited "the grandest bravery ever shown by any man in the face of death, [having] made up his mind that he had to give up his life as a penalty for the crime he had committed."[89]

Newspapers generally applauded the lynching. Typical was the comment of the *San Juan Herald* editor: "Silverton does nothing by halves—now for Eskridge." He reported a rumor in Silverton that La Plata County Sheriff Luke Hunter had resigned his position and, amazingly, that the hero of the hour, Ike Stockton, would be appointed to the vacancy.[90] Only part of that rumor was correct; Hunter did resign, but Barney Watson became the new sheriff, not Ike Stockton.[91]

The *Dolores News*, of course, gave extensive coverage of the Ogsbury murder in Silverton, Stockton's capture of Wilkinson, and the subsequent lynching, quoting liberally from other papers. Editor Charles Jones, whose comments had been most favorable to Ike Stockton, the Eskridge boys, and their followers during the many months of the San Juan Valley War, was deeply affected by the recent events. Clayton

Ogsbury had been a personal friend, and he shared the sorrow and shock of the Silverton folks in his sudden death. But Jones said he had also liked and admired another young man, Bert Wilkinson, not yet twenty years old. "We knew Wilkinson when he was nothing but a great, simple, overgrown boy, generous and good of heart, and even at the time of his death his career of crime had been of very short duration," Jones noted.[92]

And now Wilkinson had gunned down Ogsbury and been hanged for the crime—the lives of two fine young men snuffed out unnecessarily.

Charles Jones had an epiphany, but it was triggered not so much by the two violent deaths as it was by the actions of the men Wilkinson rode with, particularly Ike Stockton, the leader Jones had so long championed. In a remarkable editorial Jones said that Wilkinson had been misled by "evil associations," and while his crime could not be excused, the man who captured him possessed "a blacker heart" than Wilkinson, and that man was Ike Stockton.

Jones admitted that readers might by amazed at such a statement coming from one who had championed Stockton and his friends when they had been condemned on all sides. Defending the Stocktons had cost him money and friends, Jones said, but, believing them to be honest men, fighting against notorious outlaws and cattle thieves, he had stood by them through thick and thin. Recently, however, he had learned some facts of Stockton's inglorious past, but the man's treachery in dealing with his longtime friend and compatriot, Bert Wilkinson, had opened his eyes.

As evidence of Stockton's duplicity, Jones printed a statement by Flora Pyle, Wilkinson's sister. She said that Ike Stockton had arrived at her home at Castle Rock Springs the evening of Sunday, August 28, saying that a search party was on its way from Silverton and that he had come to warn the boys if they showed up. Later that night, when Ike was asleep in one of the outbuildings, her brother Bert and Dyson Eskridge staggered in. They were in bad shape—tattered and hungry—and Dyson was barefooted. When she informed them of Ike's presence, they seemed "overjoyed and expressed a desire to see him immediately." Ike was sent for, and when he came to the house, she said, "his teeth were chattering, he was trembling," and he remarked about the cold, "to hide the true cause of his nervousness, which was that his conscience smote him for the treachery he was practicing toward his friend, whom he intended to deliver up to be hung for money's sake."

Flora Pyle admitted that to aid the fugitives in their escape she provided horses and provisions to last them four or five days. "If it be criminal, I would not regret it, for Bert was my brother, and Dison [*sic*] his sworn friend. Had I not done as I did, I would feel that I were inhuman."

Stockton, she said, while eating a hearty breakfast, talked largely about his own problems. "He had a great deal to say about his living in dread of the law and said many of his friends had advised him to leave this country and change his name." What happened after he left with Wilkinson and Eskridge she was told by Bert after his capture.

The three met Marion Cook at an agreed-on rendezvous, and Stockton rode off with Eskridge, leaving Wilkinson in the care of Cook. Stockton returned alone at three o'clock that afternoon, saying that they were to meet Dyson and Harg Eskridge with fresh horses some five miles away. Then, as the sister related the story: "Bert got up to cinch his saddle and left his pistol on a blanket on which he had been lying; the horse was five or six yards from him and as he started for him Stockton jumped in between him and his pistol and told him to throw up his hands; Bert did so, laughing, thinking it was a joke, but seeing Stockton's face the truth commenced to dawn on him and he said, 'Ike, do you mean it?' to which Stockton replied, 'Yes, I do mean it — money is what makes men in this country.' Bert said: 'You've got the drop on me, Ike, but I'd rather you'd kill me.' "

Charles Jones added that he had known Flora Pyle for many years and assured his readers that her account of the capture was accurate and other differing reports were false. Her brother, he said, was simply "a misguided boy, encouraged in his misdeeds by Stockton and his companions . . . the treachery of Stockton in delivering up his comrade to be hung for a monied consideration solely, is an action which had caused the loss of all the friends he had. The capture of Wilkinson by any other agency would have been a thing to be greatly rejoiced at — as it is, the capturer is more scorned that the captured. The result is a good thing, but the means are detestable."

To illustrate Stockton's "inordinate greed" for money, the editor related the story of Tom Radigan, who had been wounded in the fight with Tom Nance and Aaron Barker in which Barker was killed and Radigan wounded. Stockton took Radigan to Fort Lewis and turned him over to the doctors there, but returned to visit him only once, even after the young man's leg was amputated. Radigan "lay there for two months, [ignored] by the men for whose sake he lost his leg. . . . He stayed there suffering all that time with no care other than that of utter strangers. . . . There is generosity for you!" Jones charged that when rewards were offered for Stockton's followers, including Radigan, "as manly a boy and as much a gentleman as breathes," Stockton conspired to have the crippled young man arrested and turned over to the tender mercies of the Farmington crowd in order to collect the reward for him and gain leniency for his own crimes.[93]

Jones believed that the only reason Stockton did not betray Dyson Eskridge and turn him over to the lynch mob with Wilkinson was his fear that Dyson's brother Harg would hunt him down and kill him.[94]

Editor Jones of the *Dolores News* was not alone in his denunciation of Ike Stockton. Other Colorado newspapers expressed disgust at his action. In a story headlined "STOCKTON'S TREACHERY" a Colorado Springs paper quoted the *Denver Republican*: "In delivering up to justice the murderer, Bert Wilkinson, Ike Stockton rendered society a good service, but the motive that actuated him was base. Wilkinson was his friend, a member of his fighting faction, he captured him by the betrayal of his friendship, and did it for $2500. Stockton's own story shows this, and must lower him in the estimation of those who have clung to him through so many months of abuse. We mistake the temper of the people if Durango will not become too warm for Stockton."[95]

The *Republican* editor did not mistake the temper of the people, and his concluding comment was prophetic. Only ten days after that item appeared, the town of Durango became exceedingly "warm" for Ike Stockton.

About noon on Monday, September 26, he and his pal Marion Cook drove a wagon into Durango from Animas City. They stopped at the corner of First and H streets, and Stockton got out and walked off, leaving Cook at the wagon. Watching them keenly were the newly appointed sheriff, Barney Watson, and his chief deputy, James J. Sullivan. Watson had in his possession a requisition from the governor of

New Mexico for the arrest of Stockton in the matter of the Aaron Barker shooting, and another from the governor of Texas for the arrest of Cook, who was wanted under his real name, M. H. ("Bud") Galbreath, in that state. In anticipation of the appearance of the two fugitives in Durango, Watson had specially commissioned several deputies and told them to stay alert and be ready to come to his assistance when called upon.

Sheriff Watson and Sullivan first approached the wagon from the rear, one on each side. Catching Cook by surprise, they covered him with six-shooters and ordered him to throw up his hands, which he did with alacrity. They then handcuffed him and, turning him over to special deputy Jack Wilson and others, set out after Stockton.

They caught up with him farther down H Street near the Brunswick billiard hall. But when Sullivan put his hand on Stockton's shoulder and told him he was under arrest, Ike jumped into the doorway of a building and tried to pull his pistol. Watson and Sullivan fired almost simultaneously. Both bullets struck Stockton in the leg. One smashed into his thigh, inches below the hip joint, breaking the bone, and the other hit lower down. With his leg knocked violently out from under him, Stockton tumbled to the ground and was quickly disarmed.

Watson and his deputies took both prisoners by wagon to the smelter across the river, a safer location, they thought, than the jail.[96] On the way Stockton suffered greatly from the pain of his wounds and was given whiskey to keep him from fainting. At the smelter a heavy guard kept watch over the prisoners while Stockton received medical attention. In all, seven doctors worked on his shattered leg, but that night gave up hope of saving it and amputated the limb.[97] Several hours later, at 2:30 in the morning of September 27, with his wife, Amanda Ellen, and his children, Delilah and Guy, at his side, Stockton died from shock and loss of blood.[98]

"The poor wife and her two children were present at the deathbed," said the *Daily Gazette* of Colorado Springs. "The oldest child is a lovely little girl, about four or five years of age [she was six], and her cries of grief were heart-rending. The second child, it seems, is a boy, and not two years old, so of course was unconscious of what was passing. His death undoubtedly seems very hard to the stricken ones, but when one remembers how much worse it might have been, it is doubtless a mercy. There will now always be a shadow of doubt as to the guilt of the father and husband and the disgrace attendant upon what might have been, will be spared his survivors."[99]

This was a strange comment for a newspaper that never seemed to recognize "a shadow of a doubt" as to the guilt of Ike Stockton during the previous year when it reported unequivocally every criminal allegation against the man.

The remains of Isaac ("Ike") Stockton, interred in a $100 casket, were laid to rest in the Animas City Cemetery on the afternoon of September 28. Said editor Jones of the *Dolores News*: "This ends the career of a man who has no doubt perpetrated many misdeeds. It is not the policy of the *News* to abuse any dead man. We gave our opinion of Stockton three weeks ago in very plain language. So soon as we found that we were supporting the wrong kind of a man we said so publicly and concluded to have nothing more to do with him one way or the other. He is dead, he deserved his fate. That ends it."[100]

# — 9 —

## JIM McINTIRE
1854–ca. 1916

*He doesn't look like a bully or desperado, although he does look as if he would be a bad customer if he were aroused.*
—*Albuquerque Evening Democrat*, June 8, 1885

Jim McIntire was one of the very few Old West gunfighters who left an account of his life and adventures in his own words. His autobiography, *Early Days in Texas: A Trip to Hell and Heaven*, published in 1902, never caught on with the public, probably because of a wildly imaginative concluding chapter describing his recollections of a journey to hell and heaven while in the throes of smallpox-induced fever. The book sold few copies and, because of its rarity, is today a highly prized item in the library of any western history collector.[1]

Some early writers of gunfighter lore recognized McIntire's contribution to that history and made passing mention of him. Charles A. Siringo, cowboy, Pinkerton detective, and prolific chronicler of his own adventures, wrote in 1927 that he was well acquainted with McIntire, whom he termed "a badman cowboy of the old school [who] had shot and killed several men." He was, said Siringo, "of a nervous disposition. When angry, his slender frame shook like a leaf and his black eyes sparkled with rage."[2] In 1934 Eugene Cunningham, seminal writer in the gunfighter field, called McIntire "a very well known Panhandle gunman, a killer of very nervous trigger fingers."[3] And in 1951 J. Marvin Hunter and Noah H. Rose in their *Album of Western*

*Gunfighters* described McIntire as "a noted Texas Panhandle gunman and killer."[4]

In a tumultuous life on the frontier McIntire pursued many occupations. He punched cattle, hunted buffalo, herded sheep, kept saloons, wore the lawman's badge, hired out his gun, and gambled professionally.

Born in Brown County, Ohio, in 1854, the second of three sons parented by Scottish-born James W. and Grace McColgin McIntire, he was christened Isaac, but at an early age adopted "James," or "Jim," his father's name, by which he was known throughout his life. He was only nine when his mother died. His father soon remarried and relocated his family at Ironton, an Ohio River town in Lawrence County, Ohio, where he opened a grocery store.[5]

Young Jim began work at an early age, first as a telegraph operator and then as an employee in a rolling mill. But lusting for adventure and new experiences, he ran off at the age of sixteen to manage a minstrel show. He worked on Ohio River steamboats and traveled the Ohio canals with the tough boatmen who were notorious for their brawling in canal-side saloons. It was all good experience for the rough life McIntire was destined to lead in the West.[6]

Like many young lads of the time, Jim McIntire and his pal Lyman ("Cash") Denny, having devoured cheap paperback novels depicting adventurous cowboy life on the frontiers of Texas, decided in 1873 to head west and share in that excitement. They went down the Ohio and Mississippi rivers to Louisiana, then up the Red River to Shreveport. There they joined a westbound wagon train and walked two hundred miles to Dallas, Texas. Going on, they spent a night at the Fort Worth home of Edward S. Terrill, the town's first settler and current city marshal.[7]

At Weatherford, thirty miles farther on, they had a fortuitous meeting with cattleman James C. Loving. Having recently moved a herd into Big Lost Valley in Jack County, Loving was badly in need of new range hands and was willing to take on two young greenhorns from Ohio.

It became clear to McIntire on his arrival at the ranch why cowhands were in short supply in that district. Indians from reservations across the Red River were making frequent raids on the cow and horse herds in the northern counties of Texas. In addition to learning the skills of the cowboy, he was expected to become a Jack County "min-uteman," and to defend to the death his employer's property from thievery by marauding Indians. That might have discouraged some potential ranch hands, but it suited the adventure-seeking nineteen-year-old from Ohio just fine.

On July 10, 1874, a party of Comanche attacked the Loving ranch, and McIntire got his first opportunity to fight Indians. In a pitched battle the raiders killed ranch hand John Heath before other de-fenders drove them off.[8]

Major John B. Jones, in command of the newly formed Frontier Battalion of the Texas Rangers, arrived with a company and enlisted McIntire and other Loving cowboys as "Special Rangers" to do battle with the Indians. Only days after the Loving ranch fight the Rangers clashed with a large party of Kiowa led by Lone Wolf in a vicious battle long remembered in north Texas as the Lost Valley Fight.

Several Rangers were wounded or killed in the fight, including one who was chopped to pieces and his flesh eaten by the Indians in full view of his comrades. Described in graphic detail by McIntire in his book, the sight was admittedly largely responsible for engendering in the Rangers, including McIntire, an extreme hatred of Indians.[9]

As an example of the savage revenge the Rangers exacted later, McIntire told how he and some Ranger scouts ambushed a Coman-che party that included a woman. Since "a squaw horsethief wasn't considered any better than a buck horsethief," they killed them all. "We proceeded to skin them. I skinned the squaw, taking only the skin from the body proper, leaving the arms, neck, and legs. We tanned these Indian hides afterwards, and I made a purse out of the squaw's belly. The boys made quirts (a kind of braided riding-whip) out of the bucks' hides."[10]

Twenty-one years old in 1875, McIntire was already a leather-tough, hardened frontiersman. With a few back-wage dollars in his pocket, he felt ready to leave the Loving employ and strike out on his own. The great buffalo hunt was then in progress on the plains of Texas, and he decided to join. Outfitting at Jacksboro, he scouted out the town's saloons, employed four drifters as skinners, and rode out to set up camp on the Big Washita River. He soon learned that three of his hires were worthless. One, still not fully recovered from a load of birdshot in his back, a memento of a run-in with Jacksboro

Jim McIntire. Courtesy of the Western History Collections, University of Oklahoma, Norman.

City Marshal William C. ("Big Bill") Gilson,[11] was sickly and unable to work. Two others showed more interest in stealing horses from neighboring hunters than skinning buffalo hides. He fired all three. The able-bodied men "became ugly," McIntire said, so he "started out by knocking one down with a gun, and had to almost kill the other before they realized [who] was running the camp."[12]

A few days later a wounded buffalo gored the sole remaining skinner, Charley Buckley, ripping out his genitals. McIntire carried Buckley half a mile to their camp and treated him with a makeshift salve composed of buffalo bone marrow, rosin, and alum. Sedating him somewhat with hot whiskey toddies, McIntire sewed up the wound with a big buckskin needle and silk thread from an undershirt. Amazingly, Buckley survived this ordeal and within two weeks was skinning the hides from all the buffalo McIntire could down.[13]

McIntire claimed his buffalo hunting enterprise was profitable even with only one skinner, but, well aware that two men isolated on the plains were vulnerable to Indian attack, he returned to Jacksboro and sold his outfit, hides, and buffalo tongues.

Still thirsting for adventure, McIntire went back to Big Lost Valley and joined Company B of the Texas Rangers, commanded by Lieutenant G. R. Hamilton. Over the next two years, 1876–78, he served in the company under the successive commands of Lieutenants Hamilton and George W. Campbell and Captain Junius ("June") Peak.

One of McIntire's Company B comrades was Milton J. Yarberry, a gun-handy Arkansan reputed to have killed a couple of men at Fort Smith and Texarkana before joining the Rangers. Yarberry would go on to six-shooter notoriety in New Mexico. After gunning down two men in Albuquerque, he would, as a newspaper put it, be "jerked to Jesus" at the end of a hangman's rope.[14]

A closer Ranger friend was his "chum and bunk-mate," Newton F. Locke.[15] McIntire and Locke had met in Jacksboro and found they shared money-making ambitions. After their Ranger service they would partner in business ventures. One such opportunity presented itself in February 1877, and the two young men tried unsuccessfully to obtain discharges from the Rangers, claiming ill health. That month Lieutenant Campbell passed on the requests to Major John B. Jones, commenting that "they are both weakly and not very strongly constituted. They would like to quit as they think their health is failing."[16] Jones denied the requests, and both men, hale and hearty, continued on as Rangers for most of the next two years.

McIntire apparently demonstrated leadership ability even as a Ranger private. On March 26, 1878, Lieutenant Campbell put him in charge of a party in search of three men wanted for murder. He was unsuccessful in this effort, but shortly after the assignment was promoted to corporal. The next month he led four Rangers in a hunt for Ben Cobb, a fugitive from Montague County, and Mose Leumley, wanted for theft in Jack County. Locating Leumley in Young County, he arrested him, turned him over to the Jack County sheriff, and returned with his squad after a journey of 184 miles on horseback.[17]

Lieutenant Campbell's company at this time was operating out of a camp near Fort Griffin in Shackelford County, which had been plagued by a wave of violence. At the heart of the turmoil was former Shackelford County Sheriff John Larn and his partner, John Selman, who headed a gang of suspected cattle thieves and murderers. In June 1878 county lawmen arrested Larn and jailed him at Albany, but vigilantes stormed the jail and riddled him with bullets. Selman escaped but rumors spread that he and his followers would return to exact vengeance. On June 24 McIntire fired off an urgent telegram to Major Jones: "John Lauren [sic] was arrested yesterday by sheriff posse and shot last night by mob while in jail. Your assistance is greatly needed as Country is in terrible excitement."[18]

Selman did not return, and in the following weeks Shackelford County quieted. McIntire and other members of Company B, now under the command of Captain June Peak, turned their attention to the Sam Bass outlaw gang, which was then riding roughshod across north Texas. In this effort they were joined by practically every law enforcement officer in that part of the state. On July 21 another Ranger unit killed Bass and destroyed the gang in a famous shootout at Round Rock.

On August 31, 1878, McIntire received his discharge from the Rangers. He was now free to pursue his business ambitions with Newt Locke. The partners opened a saloon in Belknap, Young County, catering primarily to cowboys from the large Millett Brothers ranch. They were "a tough lot," according to McIntire, "as Millett Brothers would not hire a man unless he was a fighter."[19]

In his autobiography McIntire bragged about the duplicity he employed in serving his cowhand customers, saying he watered the whisky until it could hardly be recognized as liquor. He would often collect twice for a round, taking pay from a drinker at one end of the bar and again from a man at the other. "By keeping this up," he boasted, "I would have a nice little sum of money to show for my day's business."[20]

The rough and violent Millett hands may never have "tumbled" to his cheating methods, but on one occasion they did threaten to do him in. He incurred the anger of some by closing the saloon before they were ready to leave, and they vowed to return with reinforcements, kill him, and take over the place. As McIntire told the braggadocian tale, he prepared a warm reception for them. "I armed myself with a Winchester, two six-shooters, and a shotgun. . . . I jumped right out among them with two six-shooters, threatening to kill every one of them if they didn't drop their guns. They all complied when they saw I had the drop on them. . . . That was the last trouble I had with the cowboys while I was in the saloon business."[21]

Later that fall McIntire and Locke accepted an attractive offer for their saloon, sold out, and went into the sheep-herding business. They bought a flock of sheep in San Antonio, drove them toward Shackelford County, but en route were hit by a severe winter storm that killed half their flock. Salvaging what they could by skinning the dead sheep, they went back into dispensing whisky, a commodity, as McIntire remarked, "not likely to freeze up."[22]

Their saloon was located in Mobeetie, the newly created seat of Wheeler County in the Texas panhandle.[23] Perhaps to show that he intended to stay in the new town, McIntire in April 1879 ran for a seat on the Wheeler County Commission and was elected.[24]

Word reached Mobeetie from Kansas in early June 1879 that Ford County Sheriff W. B. ("Bat") Masterson was recruiting fighting men in the interest of the Atchison, Topeka & Santa Fe (AT&SF) Railroad to combat the Denver & Rio Grande in a battle over access rights to Leadville, Colorado, and its rich silver strikes. That sounded to McIntire like something he might enjoy, so he turned over management of the saloon to Locke and struck out for Dodge City. He enlisted in the Masterson fighting corps and went to Colorado, but saw little actual combat as the "Royal Gorge War" was resolved with little bloodshed.[25]

But for McIntire, the experience proved important to the direction of his later career. In Dodge City, in Colorado, and on the train traveling back and forth, he mixed with men who were not only gunfighters of note but were also expert professional gambling men. Impressed by Bat Masterson, John H. ("Doc") Holliday, Ben Thompson, and others of the breed with whom he consorted on the expedition, McIntire determined to pattern his life after their example and take up the exciting, if precarious, career as a follower of Lady Chance.[26] While employed as a lawman or hired gun in a number of Texas, New Mexico, and Oklahoma locales in the coming years, he would never venture far from the green felt tables.

Returning to Mobeetie from Dodge, he was given an opportunity to turn to outlawry on a grand scale. While camped near Tascosa he was approached by a party of heavily armed and tough-looking horsemen led by a gunman he knew in Fort Griffin as "A. L. Mont," but whose true name was probably John Longhurst.[27]

He and his riders, Longhurst said, were members of an organized gang of desperadoes almost two hundred strong under the leadership of John Selman, who planned to lead them on raids throughout eastern New Mexico and the panhandle of Texas, stealing horses and cattle and robbing banks. Invited to join this great outlaw confederation, McIntire politely declined.[28]

When he returned to Mobeetie McIntire immediately went to County Attorney Moses Wiley and signed a written statement describing what he had seen and heard.[29] Wiley forwarded the document to Major John B. Jones of the Texas Rangers with a letter saying that McIntire was "generally considered a very reliable man," but he wished his name kept secret, for if news of the affidavit leaked out, "it might cost him his life."[30]

As it happened, nothing came of the planned great outlaw confederacy. Shortly after this, Selman was stricken with "black" smallpox and almost died. His lieutenant, Long John Longhurst, did die, killed, it is said, by a man named Trujillo.[31]

McIntire soon sold his interest in the Mobeetie saloon to his partner, Locke, and, following the example of many of his comrades in the railroad war escapade, pinned on a badge while pursuing the gambling profession. As a deputy under Sheriff Henry Fleming, he spent most of his time in the deadfalls of the town, keeping the peace while at the same time engaged in gambling. He received no censure from his boss, Henry Fleming, because the sheriff had a financial interest in a Mobeetie saloon and was not a stranger to the green felt tables himself. One memorable night he won eight hundred head of cattle in a card game with a rancher.[32] A. D. "Frosty" Tombs, the county clerk, was also recognized as a professional at the tables.[33]

As a member of the sporting fraternity, McIntire regularly consorted with the female contingent of that society, a colorful coterie of dance hall floozies, brothel madams, and bawds that included Mother Lemley, Dolly Varden, Matilda Wave, and Frog Mouth Annie. In September one of the demimonde, Belle Hines, filed a ridiculous complaint against McIntire, accusing him of "using obscene language" and being "loud and vociferous in her presence."[34]

In his memoirs McIntire alleged that while keeping the peace in Mobeetie he ran two notable frontier figures, Wyatt Earp and David ("Mysterious Dave") Mather, out of town when they showed up peddling gold bricks. After exhaustive study of Earp's life in recent years, however, researchers have never substantiated this claim.[35]

Jim McIntire played a minor role in a complicated legal contretemps that shook Wheeler County in the fall of 1879. Involved in the imbroglio were local merchants and cattlemen, Wheeler County officials, federal law enforcement officers, and the U.S. Army. It all began when Deputy U.S. Marshal Walter Johnson and Edward DeNormandie of the Internal Revenue Service rode into remote Wheeler County at the head of a party of federal officers. They carried warrants charging a number of merchants and ranchers with selling tobacco and alcoholic beverages to ranch hands without a license. Making numerous arrests, they filled the guardhouse at Fort Elliott to overflowing. The officer in charge at Fort Elliott at the time was Lieutenant H. O. Flipper, the first black graduate of West Point. Fearing an aroused citizenry might react violently to the heavy-handed methods of the federal officers, Flipper loaded the prisoners into wagons in the middle of the night and struck out for Indian Territory. Judge Emanuel Dubbs issued writs of habeas corpus and, together with Sheriff Fleming and Deputy McIntire, led a posse in pursuit. Overtaking Flipper's party, Dubbs presented his writs and demanded the release of the prisoners. After a tense confrontation that almost led to bloodshed, Flipper turned over the prisoners to the county officers.[36]

The significance of this story in the McIntire chronicle is that one of the deputy U.S. marshals in the Wheeler County raid was Timothy Isaiah ("Jim") Courtright, a man with whom McIntire would be involved in the most dramatic events of his life.

John W. Poe, a man McIntire had known on the buffalo ranges and at Fort Griffin, where Poe served as a lawman, joined him as a deputy in Sheriff Fleming's office in 1879. Poe would go on to greater fame as a deputy under Sheriff Pat Garrett of Lincoln County, New Mexico, playing a major role in the hunt for and final demise of that territory's most famous outlaw, William ("Billy the Kid") Bonney.

In early 1880 McIntire and Poe got on the trail of horse thieves Tom Henry, John Dorsey, James West, and William Randall, and followed them west until they left the state. McIntire then went on to Dodge City and caught a train to Las Vegas, New Mexico, where he believed the outlaws were headed.[37]

Arriving there, he found there were actually two Las Vegas towns. One, "Old Town," inhabited mostly by Hispanics, had been an important stop on the Santa Fe Trail before the coming of the railroad. But concurrent with the arrival of the steel rails of the AT&SF in July 1879, a new town called East Las Vegas sprang up along the tracks. Like many before it, East Las Vegas was another hell-on-wheels town, a magnet for crooks and outlaws of all varieties.

The new town was, as McIntire suspected, the gang's destination, but he arrived there too late to capture his quarry. On the night of January 22, 1880, the gang got into a vicious gunfight in the Close and Patterson dance hall in East Las Vegas with Town Marshal Joe Carson and his assistant, Mysterious Dave Mather. Randall and Carson were killed and West severely wounded. Dorsey and Henry escaped but were captured two weeks later and brought back. On February 8 vigilantes strung up Henry, Dorsey, and West from a windmill in the plaza.[38] McIntire said he arrived in Las Vegas four days too late to witness the hanging.[39]

McIntire found East Las Vegas to be a wide-awake town, a gambler's mecca, and filed the information away for future reference. Returning to Texas, he spent the summer of 1880 in Tascosa, Oldham County, a new town in the western reaches of the panhandle. There he seems to have dabbled a bit in whoremongering. The U.S. census taken at Tascosa on June 3 listed his profession as "hotel keeper," with two "boarders," Effie Grant, age twenty-eight, and Belle Hindes, age forty. Both women gave their occupation as "seamstress," a common nice-nellyism for prostitute.[40]

In the fall of 1880 McIntire returned to East Las Vegas, where he continued to ply his trade at the gambling tables and accepted a position on the police force. He was there on December 27, 1880, when Sheriff Pat Garrett and two deputies removed recently captured outlaws "Billy the Kid" Bonney, Dave Rudabaugh, and Billy Wilson from the Las Vegas jail and took them to a railroad car for transport to Santa Fe. When an angry crowd surrounded the depot, detained the train, and threatened to take the prisoners from the lawmen and hang them from that notorious plaza windmill, McIntire and two of his friends stepped into the highly charged situation and backed up the lawmen until the train pulled out.[41]

Because of the town's well-deserved reputation for wildness, city officials of East Las Vegas had great difficulty in finding a replacement for Joe Carson, the deceased city marshal. Former Kansas lawman John Joshua Webb took the position for a while, but found it too rough and resigned. No new applicant stepped forward, and the town was without a city marshal for a time. Impressed by McIntire's fearlessness in the tense situation at the railroad station, the town officials offered the job to him.

McIntire remembered these as "warm times" in the new town. Warm indeed! As one town historian has written: "In East Las Vegas the nights were rare that shooting in the streets was not the custom. . . . During this period 29 murders were recorded in a 30 day period."[42]

One night was "a howling wilderness of flying lead," wrote an editor of one of the town's two newspapers. "Bullets creased the air and sharp reports defied sleep by the law abiding citizens." East Las Vegas badly needed a stalwart police force, he added, and no better could be found than McIntire and Frank Stewart, his assistant. "These two fellows are capable of holding down the town when it comes to rackets with killers."[43]

There is no record that during his tenure as an officer in East Las Vegas McIntire resorted to gunplay, but in his autobiography he freely admitted unbridled corruption was ubiquitous in the town's law enforcement and that appealed to his larcenous nature. "I threw the town wide open and allowed all kinds of gambling," he admitted. Crooked gamblers and fakirs of all sorts were permitted to operate so long as they submitted to periodic arrest and fines, which provided income for the marshal and justice of the peace. McIntire found the process "exceedingly profitable."

McIntire said he would confer with William Steele, Jr., the justice of the peace, before every trial and inform him of the size of the prisoner's bankroll, and the justice would levy a fine in that amount, less $2 for a fresh start. "Our policy was to turn over one dollar to the county and divide the balance. We were doing a land-office business and having no trouble at all."[44]

The local newspapers made little mention of McIntire's activities as city marshal of East Las Vegas, but the *Optic* did remark that he was an "efficient" officer.[45] The job may not have been as lucrative as Mc-Intire later claimed, for after only a few months he "threw it up," as he put it, to devote full time to his gambling occupation.[46]

Sometime in 1881 Jim married a seventeen-year-old French Cana-dian girl whose given name was Catherine,[47] but was called "Kittie" by her husband and almost everyone else. Little is known of her except that she remained with him as a staunch defender of his actions throughout the turbulent years that lay ahead.

By 1882 McIntire had moved on down the line of the AT&SF to Socorro, New Mexico, where he opened a saloon and gambling hall in partnership with fellow Las Vegas sporting man George Close. After a few months they moved their operation about a hundred miles southwest of Socorro to Lake Valley, a little mining town that had sprouted up near some rich new silver strikes. The raw new commu-nity lay fourteen miles from Nutt Station, the nearest railroad point, and was accessed by stagecoach.

Like all new mining camps, Lake Valley attracted many criminal types looking for the quick buck but unwilling to seek it with pick and shovel. Ore thieves and holdup men were active. The camp had no established government, so the mine owners and businessmen of the town sought someone tough and handy with a gun to protect their lives and property. Believing McIntire fit the bill, they hired him at a huge salary, bestowed on him the title of "city marshal," and got him an appointment as deputy sheriff of Sierra County. In a letter to the *Las Vegas Optic* a visitor to Lake Valley in November noted: "Jim McIntyre [*sic*], formerly an officer on the Las Vegas police force, is marshal here and draws a salary of three hundred dollars a month. He holds the reins with a steady hand."[48]

McIntire's "steady hand" alone was not enough to control the criminal element in Lake Valley. At the insistence of Albert J. Fountain, lawyer, newspaper publisher, and big investor in the area's mines, another "marshal" was hired to assist him. That man was Jim Courtright, the former city marshal of Fort Worth, Texas, whom McIntire had met three years earlier when Courtright, in his capacity as deputy U.S. marshal, had taken part in the federal flap in Wheeler County.[49] The two gunmen became close friends. In the coming months they would be associated in the most controversial and highly publicized episode of their careers.

An El Paso, Texas, newspaper noted in December 1882 that "William Young, charged with stealing ore from the Sierra Grande Mining Company, Lake Valley, was arrested by Marshal McIntyre [*sic*]. Threats were made of lynching Young, but he was protected by the militia."[50]

The militia mentioned was an organization authorized by New Mexico Territory Governor Lionel Sheldon and commanded by Major Albert J. Fountain. Commonly called the "Mesilla Scouts," the ranks of the organization were almost exclusively composed of Hispanics. Many Anglos, including McIntire, derisively referred to the outfit as the "Greaser Militia." Fountain opened an offensive against a band of ore thieves and cattle rustlers led by notorious outlaw John Kinney. Headquartered at Kinney's Cottonwood Ranch, the gang, thirty or forty strong, caroused at nearby Lake Valley and tossed down many a drink at the saloon owned by Close and McIntire.

Whether triggered by the militia's interference in the William Young arrest or his affiliation with Kinney and his followers, Jim McIntire developed a deep hatred for Major Fountain and his Mesilla Scouts. When militia members on March 22, 1883, shot to death suspected Kinney gang members Butch Hill, John Watts, and Jimmie Hughes and left their bodies lying on a road near Lake Valley as a warning to other rustlers, McIntire was outraged. The deceased, he insisted, "were respectable citizens as far as respectability went then,"

Jim McIntire (*left*) and Jim Courtright, pistols at the ready, chomp cigars. Courtesy of the Fort Worth Public Library, Special Collections, Fort Worth, Texas.

while Fountain's militia were a "murderous lot of 'Greasers,'" who, after shooting their victims, stripped and defiled the bodies. They left notices threatening anyone moving the bodies with similar treatment. "This," said McIntire, "was too much for me, and as I wasn't afraid of Fountain or his bloodthirsty band, I got two miners [and we] brought them back to town. After dressing them up nicely, we gave them decent burial."[51]

Although angered by the militia's actions, McIntire, according to a story in the *Lake Valley Herald*, prevented others from taking hasty retaliation. A meeting of protesting Lake Valley residents assembled that night "was stopped by Deputy Sheriff McEntire [*sic*], who advised the men to keep quiet and behave themselves, which they did."[52]

Although his assertion that Fountain had the governor's approval to shoot him on sight was a great prevarication by McIntire, his outspoken criticism of the militia cost him his lucrative job in Lake Valley. He moved on to Kingston, and his friend Jim Courtright went with him. The two were running a gambling game in Kingston when cattlemen John P. Casey and William C. Moore contacted them. The ranchers were in the market for some tough, straight-shooting fighting men for a particular job, "hunting down rustlers," and were willing to pay each man $10 a day for his services.[53] That sounded good to McIntire and Courtright, and they quickly signed on.

Casey and Moore, owners of cattle herds ranging on vast stretches of grassland in the remote reaches of western Socorro County, New Mexico, were in the process of negotiating sale of their American Valley Cattle Company to a group of investors headed by John A. Logan, a famed Union general in the Civil War.

Following the war, Logan had pursued a successful political career, twice being elected to the U.S. Senate. In 1884 his name would rank high on a list of Republican presidential candidates before he accepted the second spot on James G. Blaine's bid for the White House, a run that proved unsuccessful. When Casey told him at a meeting in Washington in early 1883 that he had a firm offer of $800,000 for the American Valley ranch, Logan said that he believed he and his fellow investors could top that amount, but he wanted to inspect the property personally before making any commitment. He was particularly concerned about reports of rampant rustler activity in the region and wanted assurance that this problem was being properly handled. Arrangements were made for the interested parties to meet in Albuquerque early in May 1883.[54]

The activities of rustling gangs operating in New Mexico at the time also concerned Governor Sheldon, and he had issued officer commissions in the territorial militia to both Casey and Moore with instructions to deal harshly with the rustlers. But when their efforts met with little success, the cattlemen, fearful that the stock thief problem would sour their lucrative deal, turned to the gunmen McIntire and Courtright for help. Alexander L. Morrison, U.S. marshal for New Mexico Territory, who also had a financial interest in the proposed transaction, issued deputy commissions to both men, so that they could pin on badges and give the appearance of federal law enforcement to their efforts, although no federal laws were being broken.

McIntire and Courtright probably believed at the outset that they had been hired to hunt down (and perhaps kill) rustlers, but they would soon find that their employers had another, touchier problem that needed resolution to ensure the ranch sale. Two young settlers, Alexis Grossetete and Robert Elsinger, had homesteaded on Gallo Springs, a critical water source in the American Valley, and the big ranchers wanted them out to complete their control of the entire area.

After an early May meeting of the ranch owners and prospective buyers in Albuquerque, Casey escorted Logan and his entourage to the ranch, while Moore led a large party that included McIntire and Courtright in a last-minute sweep of the country in search of rustlers. Seventeen men strong, this party spent the night of May 5 at a company line camp. The next morning Moore announced, to the surprise of many, that he wanted only five men of his selection to accompany him on an unstated mission. In addition to McIntire and Courtright, those chosen were James Casey, brother of Moore's partner; Daniel H. McAllister, former manager of the ranch; and Mueller W. Scott, who had replaced McAllister as ranch boss.

Leading his little group of riders in the direction of Gallo Spring, Moore explained that they were on the way to dispose of two "squatters." On the road they encountered two young men driving a wagon, who turned out to be Grossetete and Elsinger, the "squatters" sought. Announcing loudly that he had a warrant for their arrest, Moore jerked out his pistol, and the other riders followed his lead. Moore disarmed the pair and ordered them to unhitch the team and mount the horses bareback. After driving them up a ravine some distance from the road, he suddenly placed the muzzle of his pistol to the back of Grossetete's head and shot him dead. Elsinger made a futile attempt to escape, but a barrage of bullets from the others cut him down.

Leaving the bodies where they fell, the little party of gunmen headed back to the line camp. On the way Moore stopped and, calling the others close, said, "We need to do something to make sure no one squeals. I want you all to repeat after me: 'If I reveal anything that has transpired today, may you all kill me.'" They all took the oath and continued on.[55]

News of the brutal murders quickly reached Albuquerque. When Logan returned there his sensitive political nose smelled big trouble ahead for anyone connected with the American Valley affair, and he wasted no time shaking the dust of the violent and tumultuous territory of New Mexico from his boots and getting back to Washington. Dan McAllister, meanwhile, found himself under indictment for cattle theft and brand altering while managing the American Valley ranch. Fearful that he was to be the scapegoat for the nefarious misdeeds of the politically well-positioned John P. Casey and Bill Moore, he copped a plea and spilled the story of the double murder near Gallo Springs to a grand jury. On May 25 Moore, James Casey, Scott, McIntire, and Courtright were named in murder indictments and warrants issued for their arrest. Officers took Casey and Scott quickly into custody, but Moore, warned by a grand jury leak, fled the city and was never apprehended.[56]

Socorro County Sheriff Pete Simpson and Tony Neis, Rocky Mountain Detective Agency operative, warrants in hand, went in search of McIntire and Courtright, who had returned to the Lake Valley country. They nabbed Courtright and placed him under guard at Lake Valley while they went after McIntire at Kingston. But McIntire had learned of the indictments, and while the officers searched for him in Kingston he slipped back into Lake Valley and helped Courtright escape from confinement.[57]

The two former officers, fugitives now, made a difficult passage across the badlands of southern New Mexico and fetched up at El

Paso, where, said McIntire, they received a warm welcome from old Texas Ranger friends, "and if their friendship was measured by the number of drinks they bought, it was all anyone could ask." Although a reward of $1,000 was offered for their capture, the Rangers, according to McIntire, "would not think of attempting to arrest us or 'give us away.' While we were with them, we were as safe as we could be anywhere."[58]

That congenial sojourn with the Rangers at El Paso was an aberration, for in the months to come the Texas Rangers would make things hot for both fugitives.

Courtright's wife and children joined him at El Paso. About the middle of June the family, together with McIntire, entrained for Fort Worth, where Kittie McIntire awaited her husband. Other well-wishers greeted their arrival. Courtright had gained many friends in the community during his tenure as Fort Worth city marshal, and all seemed willing to accept the concocted story he and McIntire told of the American Valley killings. It had been necessary, they told everyone, for them to kill some "Mexican rustlers" who resisted arrest. In revenge, the villainous "Greaser Militia" was trying to get them back into New Mexico to assassinate them. The Texans, many of whom nursed a long-standing anti-Mexican bias, bought the story. And so did their newspapers. A June 21 dispatch from Fort Worth said it clearly:

An officer from New Mexico passed through the city today on his way to Austin to obtain requisition papers from Governor [John] Ireland for the arrest of J. Courtright and McIntire, who are accused of murdering two rustlers near Albuquerque. The officer says $1,000 reward is offered. It is certain that if any attempt is made to arrest Courtright here a bloody tragedy will ensue, Courtright being determined not to be arrested, and in this resolve is backed by a host of friends, who are desperate men. Courtright says he would be murdered as soon as he crossed the line. Serious trouble is expected daily. Courtright seems to have the sympathy of the community in his trouble.[59]

Before granting the requisition Governor Ireland sent his attorney general, John D. Templeton, to Fort Worth to confer with the two fugitives. They apparently were persuasive, for the governor, after hearing Templeton's report, denied the request.⁶⁰ This calmed matters for the moment.

Confident that his many friends and political connections in Fort Worth assured his safety, Courtright bought a new home and settled down to stay. McIntire went on to Wichita Falls, where he purchased an interest in a gambling house. Both men were evidently well supplied with cash at this time, due, no doubt, to the largesse of John P. Casey and William C. Moore.

Back in Albuquerque, James Casey and Mueller Scott went on trial in October 1883 for the American Valley murders. They were the only available defendants, Dan McAllister having been granted immunity for his testimony, and McIntire, Courtright, and Moore still fugitives at large. The case went to the jury on October 13, and after two days of deliberation the foreman announced that the jury was hopelessly deadlocked. A second trial, begun just two days later, produced the same result, and Casey and Scott were freed, never to be tried for the crime again.⁶¹

Failing to convict the men in custody, the New Mexico authorities turned their attention to Moore, Courtright, and McIntire, who had demonstrated their guilt, it was believed, by fleeing the territory. On October 30 Governor Sheldon authorized posting of reward notices offering $500 each for their capture.

When he received a tip that New Mexico officers had discovered his location and were closing in, McIntire departed Wichita Falls in the middle of the night, or "between two days" as he put it,⁶² and went to Shreveport, Louisiana, where Kittie joined him. They went on down to New Orleans and booked passage on a Mississippi riverboat for Cincinnati and his old stomping grounds. The river trip turned into another adventure.

On the second night out high winds and pitch darkness caused the vessel's captain to attempt a landing on shore, but the boat swung around and hit an underwater snag, tearing a hole in the bottom. The McIntires and other passengers were at supper when the accident happened, and amid great excitement all rushed out. "Luckily," said McIntire, "we were close to shore, and all got off safely, and in a few minutes she toppled over, leaving about half the deck out of water." For four days they waited, miserable and half-starved, before a passing boat took them aboard.⁶³

Undeterred by this harrowing riverboat mishap, the McIntires boarded another vessel at Cincinnati and went up the Ohio to Pittsburgh, where they explored the Monongahela and Allegheny rivers on other boats. "We visited points in West Virginia, Ohio and Kentucky, including my old home in Brown County," McIntire said. "After visiting relatives and friends for nearly a year, we returned to Texas."[64]

The gambling enterprise in Wichita Falls had proved to be a most profitable one, financing a yearlong travel vacation for the couple, and McIntire headed straight back to the town. There he opened a game in a newly constructed two-story brick saloon and gambling house called the White Elephant.[65]

Newspaper stories continued to suggest that officers and bounty hunters from New Mexico were actively in search of the fugitives in Texas,[66] but nothing of any consequence happened until October 1884, when Albuquerque City Marshal Harry Richmond, with full knowledge of the location of two of those sought — Courtright in Fort Worth and McIntire in Wichita Falls — arrived in Austin with another requisition from Governor Sheldon. He persuaded Governor Ireland to issue a state warrant for the fugitives and order the Texas Rangers to assist in the arrests. On October 16 Richmond met with Captain George C. Schmitt of Company C, Texas Rangers, in camp near Wichita Falls, and laid plans to capture both fugitives in simultaneous raids on October 18.

Richmond and two Rangers, Lieutenant Albert C. Grimes and Corporal H. S. Hays, went to Fort Worth and took Courtright into custody without incident. Grimes then wired Captain Schmitt of the capture, and he moved on McIntire.

"I was in a little side-room of the saloon carving a turkey for the free lunch," remembered McIntire, "[when] the Rangers rushed in from three doors and covered me with their guns."[67]

The following day McIntire, heavily ironed and guarded by no less than four Rangers and ten deputy sheriffs, arrived by train at Fort Worth to find the city in a state of great excitement. Hours earlier Courtright had pulled off a dramatic escape. While dining at a restaurant, he produced two six-shooters, hidden under the table by friends, and leveled them at his startled Ranger guards. Backing out of the building, he leaped astride a waiting horse and thundered out of town.[68]

As might be expected, Courtright's spectacular escape from their custody left the Texas Rangers in Fort Worth red-faced with chagrin, "all raving mad," in McIntire's words. "They swore by all that was good and holy that I wouldn't get away. When my train pulled in at the depot, there was the biggest crowd there to meet me that had ever filled that depot. Every hack was filled with officials, and I was lionized by everyone except the Rangers. . . . On the way from the depot to the jail, the Rangers covered me with drawn revolvers all the way. An immense crowd followed us, and in a few minutes the whole town gathered at the jail."[69]

The Courtright-McIntire affair transpiring in Fort Worth received extensive press coverage throughout Texas, and the highest placed officials of the state were concerned. On October 20 Adjutant General W. H. King arrived in Fort Worth to confer with the district judge, the county attorney, and the sheriff about measures being taken to maintain the peace, and Schmitt and Richmond entrained for Austin to explain their actions to Governor Ireland.

At a habeas corpus hearing held that day in Fort Worth, lawyers representing McIntire requested and were granted a continuance.[70]

Kittie McIntire arrived from Wichita Falls and moved into the Courtright home with Jim's wife and children. One newspaper quoted her as saying that if her husband was forced to return to New Mexico, she would go along but would "kill him with her own hand [before] seeing him mobbed."[71]

With the threat of mob violence uppermost in the minds of all, McIntire was kept under a heavy guard at the Tarrant County jail until his hearing on October 24. The courtroom was packed. According to one newspaper dispatch the place looked like "a military tribunal," with eight Rangers, "rifles in hand as if looking for a fight," stationed around the room.[72] The judge ruled against McIntire's habeas corpus release, and the lawyers filed an appeal. While the case dragged on in the courts, Captain Schmitt, fearful that a mob in volatile Fort Worth might attempt a raid on the jail to free his second prisoner, ordered Lieutenant Grimes to move McIntire to the lockup at Decatur, Wise County. The next night Grimes and five Rangers secretly made the prisoner transfer.

If Captain Schmitt thought he had defused any rescue attempt, he was mistaken. A nervous jailer at Decatur soon wrote him, saying rumors of a mob raid to free McIntire were rife in the town. "Send assistance or come and get your man," he demanded. Responding in the legendary Texas Ranger tradition — one riot, one Ranger — Schmitt dispatched a single Ranger to aid in guarding the prisoner.[73]

In November Schmitt wrote Adjutant General King, warning about the conditions at the Decatur lockup and recommending McIntire's transfer to Austin or San Antonio. The Decatur jail, he said, "is now overcrowded and they came near breaking out the other day." King denied the request, scrawling across the letter: "Gov. says let the prisoner remain in Decatur until further notice."[74]

Schmitt's advice should have been heeded, for within three weeks, on the night of December 11, McIntire and five other prisoners broke out of the Decatur jail.[75] In his autobiography published eighteen years later McIntire seemed quite proud of engineering the jailbreak. He penned a lengthy account, embellished by exaggeration and immodest accounts of his daring. He claimed to have outwitted five Rangers, two deputies, and a jailer and through his cleverness secured the release of all but one of the thirteen other prisoners. That one, a horse thief, had "peached" on him about an earlier escape attempt, so he left him locked up.[76]

McIntire claimed he slipped back to Fort Worth, where, with the assistance of a lawyer friend, he hid out in the local opera house.[77]

In one hard-to-believe story a Dallas newspaperman said that McIntire and Courtright met in Fort Worth. "Armed to the teeth," they took a drink with friends in a saloon, and left after each purchased a bottle of whiskey.[78]

With typical braggadocio McIntire spun yarns of how he came out of the opera house after ten days and, under the very noses of Captain Schmitt and his Rangers, moved freely about Fort Worth in disguise.[79]

Actually, it is highly unlikely that either fugitive returned to Fort Worth after escaping, and there is no evidence they saw each other again for a year, although press accounts led readers to believe otherwise. Over that year there were numerous reports of Courtright sightings at locations ranging from Missouri to Arizona. The most persistent rumor, however, had him escaping to Central America, where he hooked up again with Jim McIntire.[80]

A wild tale appearing in an April 1885 edition of a New Orleans paper related how the two had joined the army of President Justo Rufino Barrios in Guatemala, who was fighting to unite all Central America. At the head of "a large band of well known desperadoes from New Mexico and Texas" they planned to "either seize the country for themselves or to rob it extensively [and] divide the booty."[81] The editor of another New Orleans paper scoffed at the story, saying it was only one of many fables going the rounds. The fugitives were said to be "breakfasting in New Orleans, playing billiards in Dallas, Tex., drinking in Montana and Nevada, organizing an army of 100 men in Mexico and fighting with . . . the Guatemalan army."[82]

There was some basis for the Latin America reports, however. McIntire spent some time in Denison, Texas, after his escape, but, apprehensive that reward seekers were nosing around, he hurriedly pulled out for New Orleans, where he registered at the City Hotel under the name C. T. Rogers and booked passage on a ship bound for Honduras.[83]

But before he sailed, New Orleans officers, acting on an informant's tip, arrested him in the hotel dining room on April 20, 1885. As described by McIntire, that arrest created quite a scene.

After the meal in the hotel's dining room he had gone into the "toilet-rooms" and was defenseless with his pants down when "five big, stout men" pounced on him. They "twisted my arms and neck around until I thought they would break." Without buttoning his clothes, they picked him up and carried him bodily through the dining room out to a carriage waiting in the street. McIntire said his appearance in the dining room "with pants hanging down and person exposed created consternation among the lady guests at dinner, and they screamed and ran pell-mell for their rooms, knocking over tables and breaking dishes as they went."[84]

A New Orleans reporter who saw him (hopefully after he got his pants buttoned) described the suspect as "tall, beardless, hair thrown back, [with a] clear piercing eye," wearing a western-style wide-brimmed black slouch hat. Detectives obtained a warrant and searched his hotel room, where they found "a handsome silver-mounted bone-handled six-shooter pistol" and twenty-five cartridges; three tiny fine-toothed saws "for cutting iron bars, with handles so made as to be taken apart and used as knives"; a bottle of chloroform; three packs of monte cards; "a gambler's device for marking cards on the back for swindling purposes"; and a notebook containing memorandums of money he had recently won.[85]

When advised of McIntire's apprehension, Governor Sheldon wired the New Orleans authorities to hold him until receipt of a forthcoming requisition. The promised papers arrived, but McIntire remained in the parish jail for more than a month as Louisiana and New Mexico officials wrangled over which jurisdiction was responsible for the cost of returning him.

Finally, on May 30, Police Chief Zach Bachemin, assisted by Detectives T. J. Boasso and C. C. Cain, left with the prisoner for New Mexico. They took a circuitous route by way of Kansas City, avoiding Texas, as they feared a rescue attempt there by his friends.[86]

Arriving back in Albuquerque on June 3, McIntire entered the jail that had held Milt Yarberry before his compatriot of Texas Ranger days was "jerked to Jesus" only two years earlier. Unable to raise bail, initially set at $10,000, McIntire remained jailed several days. He was visited by a number of New Mexican friends who supplied him with cigars, chewing tobacco, a cot and blankets, and hotel meals.[87] When his lawyers, H. B. Ferguson and Thomas Phelan, got the bail reduced to $5,000, his friends provided surety, and he was released to join them on the streets.

By the time his case came to trial on October 15, 1885, two and a half years after the double murder in American Valley, prosecution witnesses had scattered. Aware that he had no case, the district attorney reluctantly dropped the charges.[88]

The outcome was praised by McIntire's supporters and some in the press, including the editors of the *Albuquerque Evening Journal*, who applauded the decision as "McIntire's vindication," labeled the entire case "malicious persecution," and charged that he "was indicted on the evidence of a gang of scoundrels, all of whom are serving long terms in the penitentiary for various crimes or have died with their boots on." Extolling McIntire as "a noble-hearted, brave, fearless man," the paper's editors rejoiced that he was now a free man and that "justice, tardy as it is, has been done at last."[89]

An interview McIntire gave to a reporter for another Albuquerque paper was replete with self-pity and tinted with a hint of revenge. His life for two years, he said, had almost broken him, for the strain had been terrible. "I have tried to bear up . . . , but when people [look] at you as if you were a wild beast, and not a man of heart, and soul, and feeling, it is enough to make you forget that you possess such a thing as honor. . . . If I had been guilty, it would have been different." Those who had insulted him and hurt his feelings, he said, "had better watch out."[90]

When Jim Courtright, who had been hiding out with his family at Walla Walla, Washington, learned that the case against McIntire had been dropped, he surrendered to face the New Mexico charges. In 1886 the case against him, as expected, was also dismissed. He returned to Fort Worth, where on February 8, 1887, he faced gambler Luke Short in a memorable gunfight, came out second-best, and died in the street.

Following his release, McIntire, the self-proclaimed "man of heart, and soul, and feeling," resumed his gambling career, first at El Paso del Norte, Mexico, and later at his old stomping grounds, Mobeetie, in the Texas panhandle, where for some time he was a familiar figure around the gambling saloons and race track. At one time he owned two fine racehorses that won forty-two races for him without a loss. Or he so claimed. "My pockets were bulging out with money," he said.[91]

These were prosperous, fun-filled days, but McIntire, being McIntire, could not avoid trouble and brushes with the law. In 1886 he was hauled into a Mobeetie court and charged with "disturbing the quietude of the bystanders in a public place." He pleaded guilty, but the case was later dismissed.[92]

About this time he was involved in a more serious matter, a shooting affair.

The terminus of the Fort Worth & Denver City Railway, then building across Wilbarger County, was at Harrold, and the little town was enjoying a short-lived boom, with sixteen gambling saloons running full-bore. Of course McIntire and his current partner, Jim Wilkinson, headed there to get in on the excitement. They were engaged in a game of craps, and, as McIntire told it, the "bones were rolling right" when one of the losers began a verbal attack on Wilkinson. "As he would not stop," McIntire recalled, "I knocked him down. That 'stirred up his animals,' and was the beginning of a 'hot time.'"

The disgruntled crapshooter and his brother-in-law, John David-son, departed, muttering threats. McIntire and Wilkinson bellied up to the bar to celebrate their winnings. McIntire was raising his glass when in the back-bar mirror he saw the barrel of a rifle protruding from a doorway behind. Dropping his glass, he ran to the door and grappled with the rifle-wielder, who turned out to be Davidson. In the darkness outside Davidson jammed the muzzle of his rifle against McIntire's midsection and pulled the trigger.

"I was too quick for him, however," said McIntire, "and ducked my stomach back and he missed me." McIntire got off a shot from his six-shooter that broke one of his adversary's arms. Davidson backed off into the darkness, but kept on firing. McIntire said he was at a dis-advantage as he could only locate his opponent by the flash of his gun, while he himself was framed in the light from the doorway and made a first-class target. But after an exchange of shots one of his bullets broke Davidson's other arm and "shot a nipple away." This finished the fight for Davidson.

Someone dispatched an erroneous telegram from Harrold that McIntire had killed John Davidson, and a number of Davidson's friends came to town to exact revenge. McIntire said he kept a close watch and never let them "get the drop" on him.[93]

Arrested in Tascosa for the shooting, McIntire gave bond, and remained there until court convened in Vernon, county seat of Wil-barger County. He traveled there with a party that included the judge, several attorneys, and lawmen. On the way they killed a mountain lion measuring nine feet eight and a half inches in length.[94] At Ver-non, the shooting charge against him was dismissed, he said, but the judge fined him $35 for "rolling the bones."[95]

During the 1880s and 1890s McIntire was a familiar figure in Tas-cosa, Amarillo, Panhandle City, and other northwestern Texas towns, where he raced horses and frequented the gambling saloons. "In this early day," a Panhandle City historian noted, "saloons flourished, each with a gambling hall adjoining." Helping to make the town notorious were "two famous gamblers," Jim McIntire and "Smoky Jim" McIntire,[96] who also reportedly operated a hotel in Panhandle City;[97] but like McIntire's "hotel" in Mobeetie, this may have been merely a front for a brothel.

In 1889 at Amarillo he stepped in to aid Potter County Sheriff James R. ("Jim") Gober in the arrest of a dangerous miscreant. After an altercation in a saloon in which Deputy Sheriff Eben F. True was stabbed, Gober went in search of R. M. ("Mack") Moore, one of the assailants. McIntire, described by the sheriff as "a very dependable friend," accompanied him. They went to the house of a man named Mel Thompson, where they believed Moore was hidden. Spotting Thompson running away, McIntire chased him down and ordered him to unlock the door of the house. "Moore is in there," said Thompson, "but I don't intend to get my head shot off by opening this door."

Gober directed McIntire to throw his weight at the door and knock it in. "McIntyre [sic] was six feet tall, weighed two hundred pounds, and was a cool level-headed man," said the sheriff. "When he hit the door running at full speed, it flew wide open." Startled by the sudden assault, the wanted man quickly surrendered.[98]

McIntire joined the September 1893 Cherokee Strip land run. He and Kittie lived for a while at Woodward, Oklahoma Territory, where he opened a saloon and cold storage facility.[99] In March 1898 he received a nice offer for his business and sold out. The *Woodward News* of March 25 reported: "Mr. and Mrs. Jim McIntyre [sic] have moved to Hot Springs, Arkansas, where they will make their future home."

Hot Springs was one of the hottest gambling towns in the country, and there, said McIntire, "I lived high and 'blew in' my money, playing the races and almost living over a gambling-table. I lost considerable money and after awhile grew tired of the place."[100] Kittie returned to Woodward while Jim checked out the gambling prospects at Guthrie. Finding them agreeable, he sent for Kittie, as the *News* dutifully reported: "Mrs. Kittie McIntire left Sunday to make her home in Guthrie, where she and her husband, Jim McIntire, will reside."[101]

In 1900 the McIntires were living in Ponca City, Kay County, Oklahoma, where they were enumerated in the U.S. Census. Jim, forty-six years old, gave his occupation as "speculator." Catherine ("Kittie") age thirty-six, was a native of "French Canada." A twenty-year-old niece, Flora L. McIntire, daughter of one of Jim's Ohio brothers, lived with them.

McIntire was running a profitable gambling house in Mountain View, Kiowa County, Oklahoma, when he fell victim to the black smallpox epidemic that struck the community in 1901.[102] He managed to survive, but in his delirium had what is now called a "near-death experience" in which he thought his spirit left his body and visited both hell and heaven. After recovery he was so impressed by the memory of his hallucinatory visions and convinced of their reality that he wrote down his remembered experiences in the afterlife and included this as the final chapter in his autobiography, published in 1902.

After writing his book McIntire dropped out of sight. He was variously reported as having died in El Paso; Kansas City; Canadian, Texas; and Woodward, Oklahoma, sometime between 1910 and 1916.

# — 10 —

## JIM MASTERSON
### 1855–1895

*I can still shut my eyes and see him walking down the street, six-shooter under his coat, hat tilted to one side, a cigar in the corner of his mouth and his face as impassive as an Indian's. I maintain he was the most deadly man with a gun outside of Harvey Logan, the executioner of the Wild Bunch in Wyoming. If Jim Masterson had ever met either Logan or that buck-toothed little Billy the Kid, my chips would have been on Jim.*

— George Bolds

Brother combinations, operating on both sides of the law, contributed largely to the rich gunfighting history of the Wild West. Celebrated frontier lawmen brothers were almost as numerous as brother-dominated outlaw gangs. The brothers Pinkerton of detective agency fame were prominent in the fight to establish law and order in the West for decades. Perhaps best remembered today were the five Earps — James, Virgil, Wyatt, Morgan, and Warren — all of whom, with the exception of James, who was partially incapacitated by a Civil War injury, wore the badge in frontier towns. The Mastersons were five in number also, and three brothers — Edward, "Bat," and Jim — became noted lawmen.

Quite often, through greater personal charisma or opportune publicity, the fame of one member of the family has largely overshadowed his sibling or siblings. Thus the name of Jesse James is far better remembered today than that of his older brother, Frank, and Wyatt

Earp has long left the memory of his lawmen brothers in the wake of his celebrity (or notoriety).

This curious phenomenon is particularly manifest in the case of the Masterson brothers. The name of W. B. ("Bat") Masterson, the subject of several biographies and a successful television series, is recognizable today throughout much of the United States and parts of the Western world, but the public knows little of Bat's older brother, Edward, who, as city marshal of turbulent Dodge City, was gunned down in the line of duty, and even less of brother James, who followed his older siblings into law enforcement and wore the star in more localities and engaged in more gunfights than either of them.

Like his older brothers, Jim Masterson was a Canadian by birth, entering this world in the town of Henryville, Quebec, on September 18, 1855.[1] While Jim was still small, his father, Thomas Masterson, Sr., a farmer, brought the growing family to the United States and began a decade-long westward trek to the frontier state of Kansas, with periodic stops at farmlands in New York, Illinois, and Missouri.[2] Whatever schooling young Jim received was minimal, according to surviving written records in his hand, which show only a faint claim to literacy.

In June 1871 Thomas Masterson settled on an eighty-acre farm in Grant Township, Sedgwick County, Kansas, in close proximity to the Chisholm Trail and midway between the infant communities of Newton and Wichita. In the next few years both towns would become centers of the Texas cattle trade, an industry that would profoundly influence the careers of the Masterson boys.

But of more immediate concern to them in 1871 was another fast-developing industry, buffalo hide hunting on the plains just to the west. In the fall of 1871, after helping their father build a sod house and plant and harvest an initial crop, Ed and Bat left to take part in that great hunt. Jim, only sixteen, was not allowed to accompany them, but the following year, when he turned seventeen, nothing could prevent him from joining his brothers on the buffalo range.

Over the next five or six years he divided his time between the buffalo hunting grounds and Dodge City, the hide capital of western Kansas. When Dodge City began attracting the Texas cattlemen, he spent his summers in the town and his winters on the hunting trails.[3] In the spring of 1877, in anticipation of the cattle season, he partnered Dodge City entrepreneur Ben Springer in the operation of a combination saloon and dance hall they called the "Lady Gay."[4]

When business flagged with the end of summer, Jim returned to hide hunting. A Dodge City newspaper noted he was back in town in February 1878 after an absence of four months.[5] After disposing of his hides, he headed back to the buffalo range, and so was not in town when tragedy struck only a few weeks later.

By early 1878 his older brothers had become the top law enforcement officers in Dodge, Ed as city marshal and Bat as Ford County sheriff. On April 9 both brothers figured in a deadly gunfight with Texas cowboys. Ed was killed, and Bat downed two of his assailants, killing one and severely wounding the other.[6]

Returning to Dodge, Jim followed the lead of his brothers and pinned on a badge. In March, as a deputy under his sheriff brother, he rode in a posse led by Bat that ranged south in an unsuccessful search for outlaw Mike Roark, wanted for the holdup of a Santa Fe train in January.[7] He continued to serve as a deputy sheriff of Ford County throughout April and May and then on June 1 accepted an additional appointment as city policeman under Charlie Bassett, successor to Ed as city marshal.[8]

In the early morning hours of July 26 Policeman Masterson and Deputy City Marshal Wyatt Earp were patrolling the streets of Dodge when a couple of cowboys, full of spirit, both boisterous and alcoholic, got their attention. Galloping through town on the way to their prairie campgrounds, the herders unlimbered pistols and fired in all directions. At least one bullet tore through the flimsy siding of the Comique Theater and Dance Hall, sending folks inside, including performer Eddie Foy, Sheriff Bat Masterson, and gambler John H. ("Doc") Holliday, scurrying for cover.[9]

Earp and Masterson opened fire on the shootists, and one, shot in the arm, tumbled from his horse. George Hoy, the wounded cowboy, lingered almost a month before dying in August.[10]

Over the next year Jim Masterson and the man destined to become a Western lawman legend, Wyatt Earp, worked closely together policing Dodge. In a January 1879 editorial Nicholas B. Klaine, probate judge and editor of the *Dodge City Times*, complimented Sheriff Bat Masterson, Under Sheriff Bassett, and Deputies William Duffy and James Masterson for "making things lively for lawbreakers."[11]

The following month Bat and Jim Masterson, together with Charlie Bassett, entrained for Fort Leavenworth, where they picked up seven Cheyenne Indian prisoners charged with atrocities committed during the Dull Knife raid through Kansas the previous September, and brought them back to Dodge City for trial.[12]

Jim spent a week's vacation at home with his parents and younger siblings in early May 1879, but returned in time to assist Wyatt Earp in running down a horse herder who had cheated a black man out of money due him for services rendered. Backed by six of his pals, the accused cheat defied the officers in a tense confrontation, but when the lawmen showed no signs of weakening, the seven backed off, and the debt was paid.[13]

On June 9 Jim Masterson was one of the officers involved in a row with some drovers who defied the city ordinance requiring them to check their weapons while in town. "War was declared," said the *Ford County Globe*. "Several shots were fired, and one of the cow boys was wounded in the leg." According to additional details provided by the *Dodge City Times* and the *National Police Gazette*, after the cowboys were disbursed, one of them, a man named Martin, was seen "hovering around the room" of Jim Masterson, apparently bent on revenge. Discovering his stalker first, however, Jim shot and "dangerously wounded" him. Martin's condition was given as "critical," but whether he survived went unreported.[14]

At least one visitor to Dodge that summer recognized and commented on the success of the Dodge City officers in riding herd on the rowdy Texas cowboys. A resident of Topeka, after witnessing the work of the Dodge City police, wrote the *Ford County Globe*: "With Charley Basset [*sic*] for Marshal, Wyatt Earp for deputy, and Jas. Masterson as an officer . . . , an offender might as well be beneath the nether mill stone."[15]

As the end of the 1879 cattle shipping season neared, some of the leading lawmen of Dodge City sought other venues. Earp left in early September, and Bat Masterson, defeated for reelection as sheriff in November, departed Dodge shortly thereafter. Bassett also resigned as city marshal in November, a move that provided an opportunity for Jim Masterson. On November 4 the city council promoted him to the chief marshalship, with Neal Brown his assistant. The salary for each was $100 a month.[16]

For a year City Marshal Jim Masterson kept a tight lid on the explosive cow town; it is noteworthy that not a single incidence of violence involving the Dodge constabulary was significant enough during this period to be recorded in the two local newspapers. George Bolds, a young man who came to Dodge City a few months before Jim became city marshal, was greatly impressed by the demeanor of the town's top lawman.

"As far as I am concerned," he said, "Jim Masterson could outdraw his brother Bat and Wyatt Earp and could match them in courage. I've seen him bash a man in the face who had a gun turned on him and take that same gun and break the barrel on the bar. I've seen him in Dodge buffaloing a bunch of drunken, hooting cowhands by simply walking up, staring at them coldly and ordering them out of town."[17]

A new administration taking over the reins of the city in the spring of 1880 acknowledged the success of Masterson and Brown by reappointing them to their respective positions at the same salary.[18]

On June 22, 1880, Jim Masterson was enumerated in the U.S. Census at Dodge City as twenty-four years old, occupation "city marshal." Living with him was Minnie Roberts, age sixteen, whose occupation was given as "concubine."[19] Jim's relationship with Minnie, a strikingly handsome girl, was not casual. She remained with him during his eventful career in Kansas, Colorado, New Mexico, and Oklahoma. No record of a formal marriage has been found, but for years she used the name "Minnie Masterson," and she and Jim apparently lived together in a common law arrangement.[20] Gossipmongers in Dodge City spread the rumor that Bat also took a shine to Minnie, leading to a rift between the brothers.[21]

As the cattle shipping season of 1880 neared an end and the summer influx of hell-raising Texas cowboys dwindled, the city council of Dodge slashed the pay of its law officers in half, reducing the salaries of Jim and Neal Brown to $50 a month, effective November 1.[22] This drastic reduction in pay necessitated for Jim a return to the saloon business, and he again entered into a partnership in the Lady Gay operation, this time with A. J. Peacock. It was an unfortunate decision, one that ultimately led to a gun battle and his expulsion from Dodge.

Leading up to that explosive event was a rather farcical affair a month earlier. On March 4, 1881, the agent for the Adams Express

Minnie Roberts, paramour of Jim Masterson, claimed to be his wife.
From the author's collection.

Company in Dodge, M. C. Ruby, wrote a letter to the editor of his hometown newspaper ripping the Dodge City officials, including the police officers. He accused them of immorality, venality, hooliganism, and criminality. Calling Mayor "Dog" Kelley "a flannel mouthed Irishman" and the keeper of a gambling saloon and a woman, he said that City Marshal Masterson and Assistant Brown also were gamblers, each with a "kept woman."[23]

When news of this letter got back to Dodge City, the city officials did not scalp Ruby, but they did demonstrate their displeasure with his remarks in a spectacular manner. "Mr. Ruby," reported the *Ford County Globe*, "was taken out to the railroad water tank last Wednesday, and drenched with water by Mayor Kelley and his policemen, for writing an article to an Iowa newspaper reflecting discreditably upon said officials."[24]

Ruby was publicly chastised, but many citizens of Dodge shared his displeasure with the city officers. At an election held only five days after Ruby's dunking the voters threw Kelley and the entire city council out of office, and two days later the new administration, led by Mayor Alonzo B. "Ab" Webster, owner of the Old House Saloon, a competitor of the Lady Gay, fired Jim Masterson and Neal Brown. Webster appointed himself acting marshal and named Fred Singer, a bartender in his saloon, his deputy.[25]

Enraged by this turn of events, Jim turned his anger against his saloon partner, A. J. Peacock, whom he suspected of working against him in the recent election. Peacock's hiring of Al Updegraff, his brother-in-law, as a bartender in the Lady Gay was also a bone of contention between the partners. On April 6 the dispute erupted in gunfire. The Dodge City papers were strangely silent regarding the affair, but the *Caldwell Commercial* reported that Jim was "shot at a number of times and slightly wounded."[26]

Al Updegraff some time later presented the Peacock-Updegraff side of the story in a letter to the *Ford County Globe*. When Peacock refused to oust him from the job as bartender, he said, "Masterson, having claimed to be a killer, then undertook the job of killing me, and attempted it on the following evening by coming into the saloon and cocking his revolver in my face. I got the best of him by a large majority, and, notwithstanding his reputation as a killer, he hid out and was next morning arrested upon my complaint."[27]

Updegraff's claim that while looking down the barrel of a cocked revolver in the hand of a reputed killer he had somehow gotten "the best of him by a large majority" may have raised some eyebrows among Dodge Citians, but this little skirmish was soon overshadowed by ensuing events.

Someone fired off a telegram to Bat Masterson, then working the gamblers' circuit. It read: "Come at once. Updegraff and Peacock are going to kill Jim."[28]

Despite friction between the Masterson brothers — over the affections of Minnie Roberts as some believed, or some other cause — Jim was still his brother, and, having already lost one brother in a Dodge City shootout, Bat did not intend to lose another if he could prevent it. He immediately headed back to the Cowboy Capital. On the morning of April 16 he swung down from the eastbound train and found Peacock and Updegraff waiting. Pistols appeared, and a gunfight was on. Bat dropped down behind a railroad embankment and traded shots with his adversaries, who took cover around the corner of the county jail. Errant bullets ripped into business buildings north of the tracks, and soon others, believed to be Jim Masterson and cronies Charlie Ronan and Tom O'Brien, joined in the battle from vantage points in the houses. Updegraff went down with a bullet through the lung, and Masterson and Peacock had emptied their pistols before Mayor Webster and his assistant, Fred Singer, brandishing shotguns, came running. They disarmed Bat, placed him under arrest, and took him before a police judge, who fined him $10 and costs for disturbing the peace. The officers saw that Updegraff received treatment for his wound, but took no action against him or Peacock for their part in the gunfight.[29]

Later that day warrants were issued for the arrest of Jim Masterson, Ronan, and O'Brien, but prosecution was postponed on the condition that they would leave Dodge City, together with Bat Masterson, and not return. Nick Klaine, in his April 21, 1888, *Times*, accused the Masterson brothers and their friends of inciting the "reckless affair" and believed they would "never darken Dodge City any more." In another column he noted that "Jim Masterson and Charley Ronan have gone west to grow up with the country."[30]

Dodge City had not seen the last of the Masterson brothers, however. Both would be back to figure prominently in the later history of the town. For the time being, however, all four of those banished from Dodge settled in Trinidad, Colorado, a tough little town on the Santa Fe Railroad line, just north of the New Mexico border.

Within a few months Jim returned to law enforcement in Trinidad, pinning on a policeman's badge under the well-respected city marshal, Lou Kreeger. He also became a deputy of Las Animas County Sheriff Juan Vigil. In January 1882 the *Trinidad Daily Times* commended him for his "good work Thursday night by 'running in' five of the numerous vags and bunco steerers who are hanging around town."[31]

But Jim also came under criticism in some quarters for his lack of patience with miscreants and his propensity to wield his six-shooter as a bludgeon on little provocation. He had already been indicted for one such episode when he and Marshal Kreeger were called one night in March to break up a fight. One of the combatants resisted arrest, and "Officer Masterson, without many words, struck him full in the face with his .45 and the men were marched to jail without further trouble."[32]

Again accused of unnecessary brutality for this action, Masterson was vigorously defended by Marshal Kreeger and Olney Newell, editor of the *Trinidad Daily News*. "The man was drunk and surrounded by a drunken party," said Kreeger. "He was getting ready for a fight in which his companions would have joined. The only thing to do was to drop him. Masterson was nearest to him and hit him. If he had not done so I would." Newell agreed: "If a man resists arrest we say bring him to time, and if it is necessary to hit him, hit him hard."[33] On March 10 Jim was charged with assault and battery, but charges were dropped the next day. The case was later reopened, but a jury found the defendant not guilty, and a county judge dismissed the case with all costs assessed against the complainant.[34]

In April 1882 John Conkie, newly elected mayor, took office in Trinidad, and one of his first acts was to appoint Bat Masterson to replace Kreeger as city marshal. To the surprise of many, no doubt, one of Marshal Masterson's first acts was to discharge brother Jim from the police force. During Bat's tenure in the job he enlisted Kreeger, Feliciano Vigil, H. E. Hardy, and George Goodell to serve on the city police force, but ignored Jim.[35] When, eight months later, Goodell resigned as policeman, a newspaper editor touted Jim for the job.[36] Marshal Masterson refused to employ his brother, however, and hired Jose Y. Alirez instead.[37] Bat's stubborn refusal to work with Jim is the best evidence we have that the brothers were indeed alienated, whether over rivalry for the affection of Minnie Roberts, who had come to Trinidad with Jim, or some other cause of hostility is not known.

After losing his policeman's position, Jim took a job dispensing drinks in P. L. Beatty's Grand Central Bar and continued on as deputy sheriff. Then in October he received another county appointment. "Jim Masterson is fully clothed with the power and authority of constable . . . , invested with these honors by the board of commissioners," reported the *Trinidad Weekly News*.[38]

Due to a change in municipal rules, Bat Masterson, who had been appointed to his post as city marshal, was required to stand for reelection in April 1883. He ran as a candidate of the Citizens' Party, and the voters of Trinidad rejected the entire ticket. Elected in his stead was Lou Kreeger, the man Bat had replaced the year earlier and who would serve the town of Trinidad and the county of Las Animas during a notable law enforcement career of more than thirty years.[39] Marshal Kreeger at once named Jim Masterson to his police force, and Jim helped Kreeger keep a tight rein on Trinidad's unruly element.[40]

In late 1884 a smoldering decades-old battle between managers of the Maxwell Land Grant Company and settlers in northern New Mexico Territory threatened to burst forth with renewed violence. The latest trouble was centered in Raton, Colfax County, New Mexico, about fifteen miles south of Trinidad, where an outlaw named Dick Rogers had organized a gang of gunmen, ostensibly to support the side of the small settlers in the dispute. Rogers was soon involved in several shootings, and when Colfax County Sheriff John Hixenbaugh attempted to arrest him he dropped the officer with a bullet in the leg that necessitated amputation.[41]

What prompted Jim Masterson to involve himself in the Colfax County troubles is not apparent. Perhaps it was indignation at the temerity of Rogers to come into his bailiwick at Trinidad and gun people down. Perhaps it was a thirst for danger and excitement for which he appears to have developed a taste. Or perhaps it was simply a hankering for the $500 reward New Mexico Governor Lionel A. Sheldon had offered for the arrest and conviction of Dick Rogers. At any rate, in the early days of 1885 Masterson turned up in Raton and on January 23 accepted appointment as undersheriff to the incapacitated Sheriff Hixenbaugh.[42]

Many ordinary citizens, as well as officials of the Maxwell Land Grant Company, were outraged by the violent tactics of Rogers and his gang. Feeling the need for a gunfighter of demonstrated ability to deal with the Rogers threat, they welcomed Masterson's arrival. In announcing Masterson's appointment, the *Raton Comet* described him as "a man of tried courage [who] will prove a terror to the would-be bad men."[43] Future New Mexico governor George Curry, who was allied with those opposed to the company, simply called Jim "a notorious gunman."[44]

Only one week after his appointment the "notorious gunman" suffered a miserable humiliation. On the night of January 30 Rogers and six members of his gang rode into Raton from their hideout in the hills. They were disporting themselves in Williams & Sargent's dance hall when Jim Masterson, unaware of their presence, wandered into the establishment and immediately found himself surrounded by outlaws with drawn guns. To the delight of his friends and supporters, Rogers disarmed Masterson, beat him unmercifully, and made him dance a jig in the middle of the floor.[45]

Thus embarrassed, Jim might have turned in his badge, packed up his gear, and quietly slipped back to Trinidad, but he still had the confidence of county officials, who urged him to stay on. Determined to finish the job he had started, and fuming with anger against the Rogers bunch, he decided to remain. It was a decision he would come to regret.

Two weeks after the dance hall fiasco Governor Sheldon increased the bounty on Dick Rogers to $1,000. At Sheldon's request, Adjutant General Edward L. Bartlett ordered the formation of a territorial militia company at Raton to deal with the increasing violence there, and placed Jim Masterson in command. Commissioned as captain of Company H of Colonel Max Frost's regiment, Masterson enlisted Deputy Sheriff Jesse W. Lee as second lieutenant and John M. Cavanaugh as first sergeant. He was authorized to enroll sufficient privates to bring the muster roll to a maximum of forty men. On February 18 the commissions were dispatched to the new captain, and the following day two cases containing forty rifles and ammunition, marked to the attention of Captain James Masterson, arrived at the Raton express office.[46]

George Curry claimed that Masterson's militia recruits were, with the exception of a few, "professional gunmen and gamblers." He also said that Masterson was commissioned a deputy U.S. marshal with orders to evict settlers in Colfax County at the behest of Maxwell Land Grant Company officials.[47]

On February 21 Captain Masterson and a party of militiamen set out in search of Dick Rogers and his cohorts. They were only successful in collaring Bob Lee, a known associate of the gang who was under indictment for an earlier shooting. When a man named J. Osfield interfered in the apprehension, Masterson arrested him also and took both men to Springer, where Osfield was released and Lee furnished bond.[48]

While Masterson's militiamen continued their search, opponents of the Maxwell Land Grant Company, appalled by what they viewed as the company's heavy-handed political machinations, opened a counteroffensive. On February 25 *Raton Independent* editor J. C. Holmes called on the governor with a petition signed by eighty-eight Raton businessmen, protesting the formation of the militia company and Masterson's appointment as commander. Attached were affidavits from ten men whose names appeared on the muster rolls, placed there, it was claimed, without their knowledge or consent.[49]

In a statement to the press Holmes said that the petition signers first learned of the militia company formation when the arms arrived at the depot addressed to Masterson, "a pretty hard man." They feared his militia company would be the cause of more bloodshed.[50]

Holmes's arguments convinced the governor. He immediately issued a special order suspending Masterson's commission and disbanding the company.[51]

Assured by this turn of events that he would be protected from the wrath of Masterson, Dick Rogers surrendered on February 28, and taken before a magistrate entered "not guilty" pleas to charges of murder, attempted murder of Hixenbaugh, and assault on Masterson, and was released on $1,000 bond.

Masterson was in Cimarron when he received the disastrous news that the two cases of arms marked for his attention had disappeared from the Raton depot, and, even worse, the governor had revoked his commission and disbanded his company. Boiling with anger, he returned to Raton on March 2.

He was still in an ugly moody when he ran into J. E. Herndon, one of the so-called paper members of his militia who had signed the affidavit of protest leading to the company's disbandment. Pulling a gun, Masterson threatened Herndon's life and the life of "every son of a bitch who signed the affidavit."[52]

He was reportedly even more violent when he met D. F. Stevens, chairman of the board of county commissioners and another petition signer, on the street and struck him over the head with his pistol.[53]

Emboldened by the change of events, the forces opposed to the Maxwell Land Grant Company mobilized. A vigilante group of several hundred, organized by George Curry, rounded up remnants of Masterson's militia company, disarmed them, and held them under arrest in the Raton skating rink, where the vigilantes had established their headquarters.[54] Masterson and two of his cohorts retreated to the Moulton Hotel, barricaded the doors, and prepared for battle, but after personal assurances by George Curry that they would not be murdered, agreed to come out and join their comrades in custody at the skating rink.[55]

There, Osfield, the man Masterson had arrested with Bob Lee, presided over a mass meeting, attended by some six hundred anti–land grant partisans, including Dick Rogers and his pals. A decision was made with regard to the members of the now defunct militia. Jim Masterson and those not residents of New Mexico were to be expelled from the territory. Oddly enough, given the animosity only recently raised by the formation of a militia company, the assembly chose to form another military unit to carry out the expulsion. Dick Rogers, a man under indictment for murder, was elected captain. Charles F. Hunt was made first lieutenant; Thomas F. Gable, second lieutenant; and George Curry, first sergeant.[56]

On the afternoon of March 3, 1885, Masterson led a procession of his followers on foot out of Raton and began the arduous, seven-mile-long uphill march through Wootton Pass to the Colorado line. Behind them rode notorious outlaw Dick Rogers at the head of his newly formed military company. At the state line Rogers turned back after a stern warning to Masterson and the others to stay out of New Mexico on pain of death.[57]

The editor of a Trinidad paper on March 4 reported simply: "Mr. James Masterson of Raton, undersheriff of Colfax County, N.M., is in the city," but suggested wryly in another column, "If you want to get paralyzed, just ask Ed Stone [one of the Masterson crew] how far it is from here to Raton by wagon road."[58] A few days later the editor referred sarcastically to the "Raton Walking Militia," a derisive appellation that stuck to its members for years.[59]

The humiliations he suffered at the hands of Dick Rogers during the Raton episode smarted fiercely for Jim Masterson, but he must have felt some sense of satisfaction when, only two weeks after supervising the ignominious march of the "walking militia" out of New Mexico, Rogers and two of his henchmen were shot to death in a bitterly fought gun battle with officers at Springer.

Jim Masterson stayed clear of New Mexico after his exile from the territory in March 1885. Later that year he was enumerated in the Colorado census as a resident of Trinidad. His occupation was given as "saloon keeper," while "keeping house" for him was Minnie, his "wife." By late 1888 he was back in Dodge City, another locality from which he had once been banished. Those enemies who had driven him out seven years earlier were still in control, he found. They had since joined forces with the prohibitionists to shut down drinking establishments in the town once famous as "the Bibulous Babylon." Alcoholic beverages could only be purchased — for medicinal purposes, of course — at "drugstores," which happened to be owned and operated by the controlling clique.

Jim quickly got into trouble again. On December 30 officers arrested him on a charge of "selling, bartering, and giving away intoxicating liquors" from a Front Street basement. As evidence the officers confiscated two bottles of sherry and two bottles of beer.[60]

Masterson soon became involved in more serious business than this farcical arrest. During the later 1880s county seat wars broke out in western Kansas as town promoters, convinced that capture of the seat of county government was the key to prosperity, rapid growth, and personal quick fortune, fought doggedly, both in the courts and in the streets, for that prize. At special county seat elections they imported gunfighters to protect friendly voters and intimidate the opposition. Dodge City, long known as a rendezvous of gunmen, became a major source of gunfighting recruits — including Jim Masterson — who suddenly found their services in demand at high wages.

In newly organized Gray County, just west of Dodge, the towns of Cimarron and Ingalls contended for the county seat prize. When Ingalls founder Asa T. Soule, a New York millionaire, having invested heavily in an irrigation project in that section, announced he wanted his town as the county seat, the war was on.

As a result of earlier voting Cimarron held the county records, but Ingalls emerged victorious from another election held on November 6, 1888, winning both the county seat and the important county clerk and sheriff offices. Cimarron backers contested the election, however, and A. T. Riley, county clerk pro tem, refused to turn over the records to newly elected county clerk Newton F. Watson of Ingalls. Soule's lawyers secured a directive from the Kansas Supreme Court, ordering the record transfer. Armed with the court order and Soule's promise of a $1,000 bounty, Watson enlisted a corps of Dodge City gunmen to take the records by force.[61]

Jim Masterson was an early recruit. Other veteran lawmen of Cowtown Capital days — Bill Tilghman, Ben Daniels, Neal Brown, and Fred Singer — signed on. Filling out the ranks were three youngbloods, George W. Bolds, Edward D. ("Ed") Brooks, and William H. ("Billy") Allensworth. Accompanying the eight, all specially deputized Gray County sheriff's deputies, would be Watson with his legal papers and Ingalls coal dealer Charles Reicheldeffer, hired to convey the raiders in one of his heavy wagons.

On the morning of January 12, 1889, the wagon rolled into Cimarron and halted outside Charles J. Dixon's grocery store, where the county records were held in an upstairs storeroom serving as a temporary courthouse. The other raiders stood guard outside while Watson, Masterson, Allensworth, and Singer entered the building; ran up the steps to the second floor; held A. T. Riley and J. Q. ("Jake") Shoup, chairman of the board of county commissioners, at gunpoint; and began removing the records.[62]

Suddenly a shot rang out from below, and the gunfight that would make headlines across the country as the "Battle of Cimarron" was on. Aroused Cimarron citizens, recognizing that their courthouse was under siege, grabbed weapons and began shooting at the Ingalls invaders, who returned the fire. One newspaper later reported that as many as a thousand shots were fired during the battle,[63] but the total was probably closer to forty.[64]

Cimarron resident "Will" English was killed and several others wounded in the exchange of gunfire. The Ingalls men in the street took cover behind the wagon as Cimarron residents of both sexes, numbering as many as two hundred, poured lead at them.[65] "The bullets began to fly," said George Bolds, like "the frantic buzzing of angry bees." He "saw two women, each armed with a rifle, rush out a side street. . . . Horses were flailing at the air with their hooves, wounded ones were screaming in pain, men were shouting, the air was heavy with gunpowder."[66]

Driver Charlie Reicheldeffer struggled mightily to control his frightened horses until a bullet stuck him in the hip. Falling backward into the bed, he struck his head and was knocked unconscious. His horses bolted, leaving Tilghman, Daniels, Brown, Bolds, and Brooks exposed to the Cimarron fire. They ran for the cover of an irrigation canal at the end of the street. The *Cimarron Jacksonian* said the five "scattered like so many birds," stopping at times to return fire at the citizens, who "were 'pumping' lead into them thick and fast."[67]

Ed Brooks fell, shot through the body and both legs. Bill Tilghman hobbled along, having suffered some kind of leg injury.[68] Bolds was hit in the leg, went down, got up, and stumbled on a few yards before crashing to the ground again with a bullet in the head. Somehow he got to his feet and, using his Winchester as a crutch, made it to the canal.[69]

Reicheldeffer, meanwhile, had regained consciousness and control of his team of horses. He drove to the canal where Daniels and Brown, who had run the gauntlet unscathed, loaded the wounded in the bed and hightailed it for Ingalls.

Masterson, Watson, Allensworth, and Singer, the beleaguered Ingalls partisans in the courthouse, held out all day under sporadic fire from below. They piled office furniture against the door to prevent forcible entry by Cimarron fighters, and took refuge atop a steel safe when shots were fired up through the ceiling. They were trapped, but the Cimarron folks didn't know what to do with them.

Telegrams describing the fight flew over the nation's wires all that day. Another flurry of messages between Cimarron and Ingalls finally resulted in Cimarron's agreement to turn over the four besieged men to the custody of Gray County Sheriff J. N. ("Buffalo Joe") Reynolds. A special train with Reynolds, Ford County Sheriff Hamilton Bell, and a number of deputies pulled into Cimarron about six that evening. While townspeople stood silently watching, Reynolds disarmed and arrested the four Ingalls fighters and took them under heavy guard to the train for return to Ingalls.[70]

Responding to appeals for intervention by the state militia to prevent further violence, Governor John A. Martin ordered General Murray Myers and two companies of the Kansas National Guard to the scene. The troops camped between the rival towns and remained two days, and their presence seemed to have a calming effect.[71]

The Ingalls fighters were released on their own recognizance to await any legal action against them. On June 12, 1889, six months to the day after the Cimarron battle, Sheriff Reynolds, acting on a complaint filed by two Cimarron partisans, arrested Masterson, Singer, Allensworth, and Watson, the men who had been besieged in the courthouse, as suspects in the murder of Will English. At a hearing before a justice of the peace the four waived preliminary examination and were released on bail.[72]

The trial of these four men began on July 10 before Judge A. J. Abbott and lasted a week. At its conclusion a jury brought in a verdict of not guilty, and the defendants were released.[73]

For Jim Masterson, 1889 was an eventful year. In addition to his participation in a daylong gun battle and the resulting trial for murder in Kansas, he would take part in a historic land rush and stand trial in Oklahoma for assault.

In April of that year, while awaiting trial for the Cimarron affair, he and nearly eight thousand other "boomers," including Bill Tilghman, gathered at Arkansas City, Kansas, to make the wild run into the Unassigned Lands of Indian Territory. At high noon on April 22 cavalryman blew bugles and fired carbines to signal the start, and the rush was on.

Masterson and Tilghman made the run aboard one of eleven trains the Santa Fe line dispatched from Arkansas City. Their destination

Officers of early-day Guthrie, Oklahoma, pose in front of the city marshal's office. Jim Masterson, fourth from left with a pistol stuck in his waistband, waves a hat at the photographer. From the author's collection.

was Guthrie, which before the opening consisted simply of a railroad water tank and a land office shack, but after April 22 it quickly blossomed into a good-size town of ten thousand people. In the mad rush to claim city lots, boomers pitched tents everywhere, and soon passage through town was impossible. Mayor D. B. Dyer of the provisional government had a street survey taken and issued a proclamation ordering those camped on the rights-of-way to evacuate, an edict those affected met with contemptuous sneers. Dyer called on Tilghman and Masterson for help, and they came up with a plan. Hauling two heavy logs from a nearby creek to the top of the hill where a street designated Oklahoma Avenue began, they hitched four mules to the ends.

Mounted and well-armed, with a pair of six-guns at the waist and a rifle at the saddle, they started down the hill, riding ahead of this huge drag. Men had been sent ahead with warnings that tents and belongings had to be removed before they were ridden over. Many in the path of the drag protested loudly, but none chose violent resistance, and with an hour Oklahoma Avenue was cleared, and "for the first time since the occupation of Guthrie you could stand on the hill and look straight down the avenue to the Santa Fe station."[74]

Masterson and Tilghman refused payment for this service and also turned down Dyer's offer of police positions. Tilghman was busy dabbling in real estate, and Masterson was concentrating on gambling, his major source of income the past few years. Later both would wear badges and become deeply involved in the war against the outlaws who congregated in the new territories.

After his acquittal for murder in July, Masterson the following month was charged with another crime. On August 21 a complaint was filed alleging that on the previous day in Guthrie James Masterson, Jerome Fitzgerald, and one John Doe assaulted W. M. Gardner with "deadly instruments . . . revolver, knucks, stone and pistol." Masterson and Fitzgerald were arrested and released on $500 bond each.[75] At a hearing on August 29 W. M. Allison, commissioner of the U.S. Circuit Court, after hearing testimony from witnesses to the altercation, discharged the case.[76]

During this period Masterson earned his living gambling professionally,[77] tending bar, and working intermittently as a deputy under John W. Hixon, the first elected sheriff of Logan County.[78] The Guthrie city directory for 1892 showed his occupation as deputy sheriff and his residence as 701 Cleveland.[79] In July of that year he joined Sheriff Hixon, City Marshal Ed Kelley, and Deputy Morris Robacker in a search for the notorious desperado Nelson Ellsworth "Zip" Wyatt, who, among his other crimes, had killed a deputy sheriff in Kansas and escaped from the Logan County jail. On a tip that the outlaw was staying at the home of "Old Man" Wyatt, fifteen miles north of Guthrie, Hixon's posse raided the place but found their quarry had flown.[80]

Jim and Minnie Roberts had split up by this time, although she was still using his surname. "Minnie Masterson" was enumerated in the 1890 Oklahoma Territorial Census as a resident of Beaver County in Oklahoma's panhandle, where she and her sister ran a restaurant.

On September 26, 1892, Jim Masterson wrote a remarkable self-recriminating letter to his brother Tom, referencing a woman with whom he apparently had a disastrous relationship: "That dark lady you spoke of in your letter was at one time a very nice lady and if she has gone rong [sic] I am to blame for it all. She is one among many . . . girls who wished to do right but the Devil part in me would not allow her to do so. . . . I am sorry for her for I am to blame for what . . . part she is playing now."[81]

Masterson's belligerent nature, "the Devil side" of him, is evident in the records of the Guthrie police court. In June 1890 he was arrested by City Marshal Ed Kelley,[82] charged with assault, and fined $5. A year later, in June 1891, he was involved in a fight with a man named Barton Smith. When they were arrested by Kelley, the two men entered complaints against each other. Masterson, with Kelley as a co-complainant, charged Smith with "unlawfully and willfully disturbing the peace by assaulting this complaining witness by threatening to fight and by assaulting him by pulling him off a chair by the legs and using loud and boisterous language contrary to the ordnance . . . and against the peace and dignity of said city." Smith charged that Masterson did "unlawfully and willfully disturb the peace of this complaining witness by fighting and striking him on the head and in the face with a six-shooter or revolver." At a hearing Judge C. W. Goodrich fined the defendants $10 each.[83]

In July 1893 Evett Dumas Nix, a wholesale grocer in Guthrie with no background in law enforcement but with strong political ties to Democratic president Grover Cleveland, received appointment as

U.S. marshal for Oklahoma Territory. Well aware of his own inexperience, Nix enlisted a roster of deputies with wide-ranging expertise in battling the criminal element, including Jim Masterson, John Hixon, and three who would gain renown as the "Three Guardsmen" of Oklahoma — Bill Tilghman, "Heck" Thomas, and Chris Madsen.

The most troublesome outlaw band operating in the territory at the time was the Bill Dalton–Bill Doolin gang, which included in its membership many of the most hardened criminals and killers in the West: George ("Bitter Creek") Newcomb, William ("Tulsa Jack") Blake, Roy Daugherty (alias "Arkansas Tom") Jones, Charles ("Cock-eyed Charley") Pierce, George ("Red Buck") Waightman, and Charles ("Dynamite Dick") Clifton. Among their many crimes the gang had carried out raids in localities familiar to both Jim Masterson and Bill Tilghman, holding up a bank in Spearville, near Dodge City, in November 1892, and robbing a train at Cimarron, Kansas, in June 1893. Following these crimes they fled back to hideouts in the wilds of Oklahoma Territory.

In response to a tip that the gang was using the little village of Ingalls, thirty-five miles northeast of Guthrie, as a rendezvous, two deputy marshals unknown to the outlaws, Orrington ("Red") Lucas and W. C. ("Doc") Roberts, went undercover to check out the report. Posing as surveyors of a proposed railroad route, they pitched a tent outside Ingalls and took their recreation in the town's O.K. Hotel and Ransom Saloon, taking note of the comings and goings of patrons whom they recognized as gang members.

On August 30, 1893, Roberts rode to Guthrie and alerted John Hixon, the deputy marshal in charge, that the entire gang was disporting in the Ransom Saloon. Hixon immediately organized a strike force to attack the town. At dusk the next day a canvas-covered wagon pulled out of Stillwater carrying seven deputy marshals: brothers Thomas J. ("Tom") and Hamilton B. ("Ham") Hueston, Richard ("Dick") Speed, Henry Keller, George Cox, M. A. Iauson, and H. A. ("Hi") Thompson. About the same time a similar wagon, driven by Jim Masterson, left Guthrie with Deputy Marshals John Hixon, "Doc" Roberts, Isaac A. ("Ike") Steel, J. S. ("Steve") Burke, and Lafayette ("Lafe") Shadley.[84]

The wagon from Stillwater reached the outskirts of Ingalls about eleven that night. As Hi Thompson told the story years later: "We expected to surround the hotel at midnight and capture the desperadoes, but the Guthrie wagon was delayed and did not join us till daybreak. . . . This delay caused us to revise our plan. [In the morning] Lucas went in to restudy the situation and returned at nine o'clock. He reported Doolin, Dalton, Newcomb, Dynamite Dick, and Tulsa Jack had gone to Ransom's saloon for their early-morning drinking and game of poker. Pierce, Waightman, and Arkansas Tom were 'not on deck.' "[85]

Even with thirteen heavily armed and experienced deputy marshals under his command Hixon thought he needed more firepower to take on the outlaws. He dispatched Iauson to Stillwater on a fast horse with a request for reinforcements. Chief Deputy John M. Hale, Payne County Sheriff Frank M. Burdick, and Stillwater City Marshal O. W. Sollers rounded up eleven men "known to be good shots," and set out for the scene of battle.[86]

But before they arrived all hell broke loose in Ingalls.

Hixon deployed his men around town in an effort to cut off avenues of escape. Dr. Jacob Hiram Pickering of Ingalls, who recorded a full account of the events of that day in his diary, said that at first no one took particular notice of the "hundreds of Boomers" on the move in the vicinity.[87]

While the deputies were still seeking advantageous positions, Bitter Creek Newcomb came out of the saloon and strolled toward the blacksmith shop where his horse, "Old Ben," was having a shoe tightened. He was riding "Old Ben" back when he saw a stranger carrying a rifle step into the street and speak to Dell Simmons, a fourteen-year-old boy passing by. The man was Deputy Marshal Dick Speed.

"Who is that man?" Speed asked, pointing to Newcomb.

"Why, that's Bitter Creek," the boy exclaimed, surprised that anyone would not recognize such a famous man.

Hearing the boy's response, Newcomb jerked his rifle from its scabbard, but Speed swung his Winchester up first and fired the initial shot in what would become one of the deadliest gun battles of the West.[88]

Speed's bullet struck the magazine of Newcomb's rifle and ricocheted into his leg and groin. The outlaw wheeled his horse to escape. Speed levered another round into the chamber of his rifle and took aim at Newcomb for a killing shot. But at that instant Roy Daugherty, who had heard the first shot from his second floor bedroom in the O.K. Hotel, cut loose from a window. His first rifle shot struck Speed's shoulder; his second sent the officer reeling to the ground with a bullet in the chest. He would die within minutes. Newcomb, bent over the neck of his horse and in great pain, galloped out of town in a hail of bullets from other deputies. Covering fire from his pals in the Ransom Saloon helped him make it to the timber on the edge of town without suffering further damage. When he disappeared into the trees, the lawmen turned their barrage on the saloon and Daugherty's upper window vantage point.

Young Dell Simmons was struck in the cross fire and died later that day. At least four noncombatants were also hit.

When the shooting was over Dr. Pickering was a very busy man ministering to the wounded. Someone later counted 172 bullet holes in the Ransom building alone.[89]

Finding their position in the saloon untenable, the outlaws made a break for their horses in the stable. Bill Doolin led the way. Crouched low, ducking and dodging, he ran safely to the stable. From there he kept up a withering fire to cover the gauntlet runs of Dalton, Clifton, and Blake.

While moving to a more advantageous position to bring fire on the stable, Tom Hueston came under Arkansas Tom's deadly rifle fire. From his upper window roost Daugherty pumped two bullets into the deputy, mortally wounding him.

In the stable Doolin and Clifton quickly saddled four horses while Dalton and Blake kept the officers pinned down with heavy fire. Dr. Pickering said he saw Jim Masterson behind a blackjack tree "little more than half as thick as his body," with outlaw lead clipping bark from its trunk, cutting off limbs, and "tearing holes in the ground all around him." Masterson, he said, "stood his ground until his ammunition was exhausted," then raced back to his wagon for a fresh supply of cartridges.[90] According to a newspaper account, Masterson was deliberate to the point of foolhardiness. He carried on the fight from behind the tree until he ran out of ammunition and then "walked under heavy fire to the wagon, filled his pockets with cartridges and returned. He sat down in front, saying that he would 'take things easy.' The tree was soon gashed with bullets that struck above Masterson's head, and twigs and limbs fell everywhere around him. Not a bullet hit him."[91]

Suddenly four horsemen exploded from the livery stable, Dalton and Blake from the front, Doolin and Clifton from the rear. They all headed for a gully beyond the town. A bullet from Hixon's rifle hit Dalton's horse in the jaw, and the frantic animal wheeled around in a circle. When Dalton got his mount under control, he spurred him after the others, but before he had gone many yards a bullet from Lafe Shadley's rifle broke the horse's leg, and he went down. Dalton jumped clear and ran after the other outlaws, who had stopped their flight at a wire fence. After a few feet he turned back, remembering that the gang's only wire-cutters were stowed in his saddlebag. Seeing the gang leader afoot and seemingly confused, Lafe Shadley ran forward to make the arrest. From his sniper's position high above the street, Roy Daugherty took a bead on Shadley and dropped him with a fatal wound.

Securing his wire-cutters, Dalton ran to the fence and, quickly snipping the wires, dropped with his friends into a draw on the other side.

Jim Masterson in a newspaper interview several months later remembered Dalton's escape somewhat differently.

> As he rode away we let him have it. As we fired, he dropped his Winchester. "Hell," says I, "fellers, we've got him. Let his horse have it." So I aims for his horse and down he comes. Bill was thrown over and over and rolled into a gully out of sight. Now, this here gully, while I didn't know it, was about ten feet deep, and two of the gang rides up to get him. We didn't know it till I saw their hats as they went down the gully.
>
> "Hell, fellers," I says. "They've gone up and got him." As they came out of the gully on the jump, Dalton was up behind Bill Doolin. Dynamite Dick was the other man. Well, we blazed away at them and Dalton tumbled off. Then they stopped, lifted him in the saddle, and Doolin got up behind. I raised my sight to 500 yards, but I couldn't get 'em, and they went off on the run.[92]

The officers all believed they had wounded Dalton in the exchange, but learned later that Dynamite Dick Clifton, not Dalton, had been hit in the neck.

The outlaws fled southeast and were pursued unsuccessfully by the reinforcement party from Stillwater. Other officers, including Deputy Masterson, Sheriff Burdick, and City Marshal Sollers, mounted a siege of the hotel, where Arkansas Tom still perched behind an upstairs window with the deadly rifle that had downed three of their number. Sollers said later that he and Burdick identified themselves and pleaded with Daugherty to surrender, but, still full of fight, he responded, "If I come out, I'll come out shootin'!"[93]

In his book *Oklahombres* U.S. Marshal Evett Dumas Nix tells a fanciful story, repeated by many others, of how Jim Masterson pulled from his shirt several sticks of dynamite, "which he had brought along for just such an emergency," and ordered Arkansas Tom to come out or he would "blow the house into the middle of next week."[94]

The version of Hi Thompson, who was there, was not quite as dramatic: "Masterson was hot for revenge over the shooting of Shadley, but none of us dared venture near the hotel and we had no dynamite. Masterson said if he could get some at the hardware store he would blow the place plumb to hell and Jones with it. . . . Hixon nixed the idea."[95]

Finally, after several hours of stalemate, Daugherty surrendered to a preacher named Mason.[96]

The capture of a single outlaw had come at a terrible price—two civilians and three officers dead—but the gunfight at Ingalls really was the beginning of the end for the Doolin-Dalton gang. Over the next four years one after another gang member—seven in all—were gunned down by the deputy marshals. Ironically, Arkansas Tom Daugherty, the man who had personally killed three deputy marshals in the Ingalls battle, and the only prize the officers had to show for their efforts that day, outlived his fellow gang members by many years. In and out of prison, he continued his life of crime and finally died in a hail of gunfire in 1924.[97]

Only two weeks after the Ingalls battle, Jim Masterson participated in another land rush, the opening to white settlement of the Cherokee Outlet, an expanse of some eight million acres added to Oklahoma Territory by an act of Congress. On September 16, 1893, as bugles sounded and rifles cracked, one hundred thousand people surged forward from Kansas and the extant Oklahoma Territory to populate more than a dozen new towns and seven new counties. As in earlier land rushes, "sooners" had sneaked in to claim prime sites before the official send-off. A dispatch from Perry, one of the new towns, named Jim Masterson as a leading "sooner," saying he rode in shortly after noon, "mounted on Bill Dalton's famous horse," at the head of two hundred early arrivals.[98]

Masterson was still in Perry two months later when he was interviewed by a correspondent of the *Kansas City Times*, who numbered him among the lawmen with "an enviable record at quickness with the trigger" keeping a lid on the town. Identified, as usual, as "a brother of the famous Bat," Jim was described as "a slender, blue-eyed fellow and bundle of nerves."[99]

By early 1894 Jim Masterson was back in Guthrie, working out of the U.S. marshal's office. A newspaper there reported in May that he and Deputy Marshal Forrest Halsell, scouting through the Indian country, ran across Bill Dalton, Bill Doolin, and another outlaw they did not recognize. Since they were outnumbered, three to two, the deputies decided rewards offered for the outlaws were insufficient to risk a gun battle. "The meeting was a stand-off, neither party making any break."[100]

The trial of Arkansas Tom Daugherty for the murder of Deputy Marshal Tom Hueston was coming up in Stillwater that month. Frank Dale, judge of the first judicial district and chief justice of the territorial supreme court, would preside. Hearing reports that the Dalton gang would attempt a rescue of Arkansas Tom during the trial, and having received threats against his own life, Judge Dale requested special bodyguards from the U.S. marshal's office. "Judge Dale is not a nervous man and it is thought if he thinks it necessary to send down for help the situation must be critical," said the *Oklahoma State Capital*. Jim Masterson was one of four deputies dispatched to Stillwater, and the trial proceeded without incident.[101]

Ten months later, Jim Masterson, at the age of thirty-nine, was struck down, not by an enemy's bullet, but by a dreaded killer of the nineteenth century, tuberculosis. He contracted the most virulent form of the disease, commonly called "galloping" or "quick" consumption. On March 31, 1895, he died at his home in Guthrie. "Jim Masterson, a first day settler of Guthrie and a well known figure about town, died last night about 11 o'clock," reported the paper.

The cause of his death was quick consumption. He was conscious to the last. He was even out Saturday, but last night about 11 o'clock he called to have some of his friends come to see him, and died an hour later.

The deceased was at one time a well known figure in western Kansas [and] was reputed to be a brave man. He came to this city the first day and has been acting as deputy marshal since. He was considered here the bravest of all the marshals. Whenever a big raid was to be made on any stronghold of outlaws, like that at Ingalls, he was always asked to be one of the party. When every man would flinch, he would still be found in the front rank. Every man has his virtues and his faults. Jim Masterson was a man who never went back on a friend, and never forgot an obligation. He never pretended to keep up the conventional social amenities; but yet there was a man whom money could absolutely never make break a trust, and who would have done a kind act to a man on the gallows after all the world had given him the cold shoulder, and where there was no chance of any personal reward. Many who walk the conventional paths of social life are not as honorable in their obligations to their fellow men as he was. He was so proud that in his last moments he would not let his condition be known to his relatives. He is a brother of Bat Masterson, a man of national reputation as backer of athletic sports, and quite rich, but he would not apply to him for aid.

The body will be shipped to relatives in Wichita in the morning for interment.[102]

Although the piece was laudatory on the whole, the author could not resist noting that Jim was "a brother of Bat Masterson, a man of national reputation," an addendum that had followed the publication of Jim's name throughout his life and would continue after his death. When word reached Dodge City that a Masterson had expired in Guthrie of "quick consumption," it was immediately assumed that the famous gunfighter Bat Masterson had at last cashed in his chips and a wire went out across the country. The headline ran, "BAT MASTERSON IS DEAD," and the account went on to describe the daring career of "the most fearless official on the plains [who] never flinched or weakened [and] killed 28 men in his day."[103]

A bulletin issued the following day from Wichita corrected the error, but in so doing further maligned the exploits of Jim Masterson. "There is no truth in the reported death of Bat Masterson," ran the wire. "His brother is the man who died. The latter was simply a plain citizen who never attained notoriety."[104]

The *Herald* of El Paso, Texas, put it rather differently: "The obituary of Bat Masterson, the widely known plucky sport, has appeared in many papers of the land, his death having been confounded [*sic*] with that of Jim Masterson, a noted killer-brother at Guthrie, Oklahoma, the other day."[105]

And so Jim Masterson was depicted at his passing as both "a plain citizen who never attained notoriety" and "a noted killer-brother" of Bat Masterson. In either case, his eventful and colorful career on the frontier was largely ignored, and he joined the growing list of the Old West's forgotten gunfighters.

# — 11 —

## ED SHORT
1864–1891

*A dead shot, quick as a flash with a gun, yet he was not a man killer*
*by choice.*
— Thompson B. Ferguson, former governor of
Oklahoma Territory

Ed Short left his rural Indiana home at the age of nineteen following
his fatal shooting of another young man, a sensational murder trial,
and the resultant notoriety. Full of vitality and adventurous spirit, he
headed west. There, in the frontier settlements of Kansas and Oklahoma, he found plenty of excitement over the next seven years, and, at
the age of twenty-six, he also found an early death in an exchange of
bullets with a deadly killer.

Born and christened Charles Edwin Short on October 27, 1864, at
New Marion, Indiana, the first of four children and the only son of
Charles Cassel Short and Lucinda Mink Short, he was always called
Ed to avoid confusion with his father.[1] He grew up in Osgood, Ripley
County, a small community in southeast Indiana near the Ohio and
Kentucky lines. In 1881 tragedy struck the Short family. His father, a
collector of revenue for the state whose health had deteriorated since
his Union army service in the Civil War, died, leaving seventeen-
year-old Ed responsible for his ill mother and three younger sisters.
To help support the family, he worked in a stone quarry and as a clerk
in a store, even as he continued his school studies. In 1883 he was
graduated from high school in Osgood.

For years Ed Short had been harassed by a schoolmate named Frederick Wagner, who was something of a bully. Tiring of Wagner's annoyance, Short began to carry a gun. On the evening of May 12, 1883, the two met on the platform of the Osgood train depot. Short was accompanied by his friend Newt Smith; a young man named Col Harlan was with Wagner. Obviously spoiling for a fight, Wagner advanced on Short, taunting him. Short backed off, warning his tormenter that he was armed and would shoot if he had to. Wagner paid no attention and, carrying a heavy stone in his hand, continued his advance. After retreating some 140 feet, according to eyewitnesses, Short stood his ground. Wagner was in the act of throwing the stone at him from a distance of 15 or 20 feet when Short pulled his pistol and fired two shots. Wagner staggered and fell. Two days later he died from his wounds.[2]

Released on $2,000 bail provided by his mother and six reputable citizens of Ripley County, Ed Short was almost killed less than a month later when a tornado struck Osgood. He was standing outside his home on June 10 when the twister picked him up and threw him to the ground. Two other men were killed by the storm, but young Ed escaped with only a severely sprained shoulder.[3]

On September 6 Short was indicted on two counts, murder in the second degree and carrying a concealed weapon. For three days he was jailed in the county lockup.

The trial began on November 20, with William G. Holland conducting the prosecution and Jud Berkshire presenting the defense. Said a newspaper of the time: "The indictment was for murder in the second degree, and no criminal case for many years at this place was more ably prosecuted and defended, and no case in the history of the county elected so much interest. This may account from the fact that the dead Frederick Wagner and Charles E. Short, the defendant, both belonged among the best families in the community."[4]

After deliberating eight hours, the jury returned a verdict of not guilty. The trial was well publicized by newspapers throughout the area. After the jury's decision, a reporter for a Cincinnati paper wrote that there was talk in Osgood of lynching young Ed Short. The editor of the *Ripley County Journal* rejected this suggestion as a "bare and bold falsehood." Peter Wagner, the victim's father, he said, would have been the first and fiercest in denouncing it. "Everybody acquiesces in the verdict."[5]

Following the trial, which must have been a harrowing experience for the entire Short family, Ed tried to return to a quiet life in peaceful Osgood.

Blond-haired, compactly built, and of pleasing appearance, if not handsome, Short would always be known as a fellow with an eye for the ladies and they for him. "Ed Short," commented the editor of the *Ripley County Journal* in January 1884, "changes his love like his winter clothes & chooses a new mate every Valentine's Day."[6]

Contemporary newspaper descriptions of Short's physical appearance are in agreement. He was "of medium height and good-looking" according to one,[7] while another said he was "small in stature, quiet in manner, dudish in dress."[8] But some later writers depicted him quite differently. He was described by one noted historical writer as "a blond man of large, robust physique and commanding appearance."[9]

In May 1884 Ed Short turned his face to the sunset and headed west. In the remaining seven years of his short life he would build a reputation as a gunfighter, "a dead shot, quick as a flash with a gun."[10]

He stopped for a while in Emporia, Kansas, and then Topeka, where he drove a laundry wagon for a while. People there remembered him "as a quiet man who never sought a quarrel and never backed out of one."[11] He reportedly drifted down to the cow towns of Hunnewell and Caldwell, Kansas, where he cowboyed and may have pinned on a lawman's badge for the first time.[12]

Late in the year 1886 he was in Dodge City, where he met and came under the spell of Samuel Newitt Wood, a nationally known lawyer, politician, newspaper publisher, and fire-eating crusader for anything that interested him, from the abolition of slavery to town promotion.

A sixty-year-old native of Indianan Short's neighboring state of Ohio, Wood was thickset, charismatic, and pugnacious, with flashing black eyes and a booming voice that demanded attention. The son of Quakers, he had none of the peace-loving characteristics for which the sect was renowned. While still in his teens he had been a strong and vocal opponent of slavery. He had helped form the antislavery Liberty Party in 1844 and in the 1850s was a staunch supporter of

Charles Robinson, leader of the Free State movement in Kansas and the state's first governor. In the "Bleeding Kansas" years prior to the Civil War he was active in the underground railroad movement transporting slaves to the Northern states and, as a commissioned officer in the Kansas Rangers, continually battled slave state proponents. He served in the both houses of the Kansas legislature. Commissioned a captain at the outbreak of the Civil War, he fought with distinction, suffered several wounds, and rose in the ranks. By war's end he had acquired the title of "Colonel," and a decided limp, both of which he retained to the end of his life.

Admired by many, Wood had more than his share of enemies, whose name for him was not "Colonel" but "Dirty Sam Wood," an appellation attributable either to his notoriously soiled shirtfronts or his reputation for political and financial skullduggery or both.[13]

When Ed Short met him in 1886 Sam Wood was deeply involved in his latest venture, establishment and promotion of a town in newly organized Stevens County in the southwest corner of Kansas. Wood had platted a town that he called Woodsdale after himself and was bending every effort to win its selection as the seat of the new county. Approval as the center of government for these newly created counties was believed by town promoters of the day to ensure business investment and quite possibly that certain key to future prosperity and riches, the acquisition of a railroad.

Mesmerized by Wood's oratory and his prophesies of the glorious future envisioned for Woodsdale, Ed Short decided to move on to Stevens County and the infant town. In so doing he involved himself in one of the bitterest and bloodiest battles of a period of violent county seat struggles in western Kansas.

The schemes of Sam Wood, he found, were aggressively opposed by the founders and businessmen of Hugoton, another aspirant for the county seat. At one point in the summer of 1886 Hugoton supporters arrested Wood and Isaac Price, another Woodsdale boomer, on very flimsy charges and kept them confined for several days just before a crucial election. It amounted to a kidnapping.[14]

In the early months of 1887 Woodsdale boomed as entrepreneurs moved in and set up businesses. Wood led the way with a newspaper, the *Woodsdale Democrat*, which, from its initial edition of March 11, trumpeted the wonders of Woodsdale and castigated Hugoton and its residents. Sam Robinson, a thirty-five-year-old Kentuckian who was destined to be an important figure in Ed Short's life, erected a hotel he called the Great Western. The Fancy Grocery and the OK Feed Barn held grand openings. Doctor S. S. Wilbur hung out his shingle. There was a lumber, flour, and feed dealer and a feed and coal retailer. The Noble brothers opened adjoining establishments—Joe had the Palace Barber Shop and Albert the Palace Drug Store in partnership with another doctor, D. C. Gamble. Real estate dealers and lawyers opened offices. Ed Short opened a billiard and pool hall.[15]

To no one's surprise Sam Wood became mayor of Woodsdale. His selection for city marshal was hotel proprietor Sam Robinson, who carried a reputation as a fighting man, handy with a gun. A Stevens County pioneer described Robinson as "tall, with snapping black eyes and black mustache, a man of little learning but with a volatile temper. He wore a white broad-brimmed hat, and his tight jaws were usually set upon a quid of tobacco. He dressed well, was pleasant enough to his patrons, but had few close friends in the town. [He] went armed, as was the custom of many men of that day, but he was so secretive in his manners that it was whispered around town that he had been a gunman in his day, and had killed men."[16]

Some did not confine their remarks to whispers. A veteran Kansas newspaperman said that when Robinson turned up in Woodsdale, he "had already made a record for himself as a six shooter artist in Pratt and Barber Counties and . . . was probably about as cold blooded a murderer as ever drew a gun."[17]

But he was just the kind of man Sam Wood wanted to back him in his fight with Hugoton, and Wood took every opportunity as editor of the *Woodsdale Democrat* to throw free publicity and plaudits in the direction of Robinson and his hotel. "On the northeast side of the square will be found the Great Western Hotel," he wrote in April 1887. "This house is growing more popular every day. Sam Robinson, the proprietor, is a jolly, good-natured fellow and never fails to entertain his guests. The house has recently received several coats of paint, which makes it look as though Sam is going to put on some metropolitan airs."[18]

That same month the Woodsdale city council met and, at the urging of Mayor Wood, appointed Sam Robinson city marshal.[19] To assist Robinson the council appointed Ed Short, who would later be characterized in the press as having "a record as an all around tough man and expert twirler of the '4.' "[20]

Robinson and Short were not only teamed up in law enforcement, they entered into a business partnership as well. In August Robinson turned over management of his hotel to another firm, while retaining ownership of the building, and Short disposed of his pool hall. As partners the two men went into the meat market business. They ran an ad in the *Democrat*:

THE CITY MEAT MARKET.

ROBINSON & SHORT, PROP.

FRESH AND SALT MEATS.

FAT CATTLE WANTED. CASH FOR HIDES.

CALL AND SEE THEM.[21]

Ed Short entered into another partnership that September; he got married. He and Fannie Culver were joined in matrimony on September 25. Said editor Wood of the *Democrat*: "We join their many friends in wishing them a peaceful life and hope they will live 'long' and have many little 'shorts.' "[22]

The wishes and hopes of their friends were not to be fulfilled, however. The lives of the newlyweds would be neither peaceful nor long, and there would not be any little Shorts. Only five months after the wedding, on Sunday, February 27, 1888, Fannie committed suicide. She left a note: "Eddie, stay with me until I am gone from earth. Meet me in heaven. Live a Christian the balance of your life. Goodbye, my darling husband. Eddie, my darling, goodbye. Oh! That last sweet kiss you gave me I will take to Heaven with me."[23]

Meanwhile, the battle between Woodsdale and Hugoton raged on. An election was scheduled for November 1887, and the office of sheriff was most hotly contested. Sam Robinson badly wanted the job and seemed to have the endorsement of Sam Wood's *Democrat*. In an editorial in September Wood opined: "This week Samuel Robinson comes out with his announcement as candidate for the office of Sheriff of Stevens county. Sam is one of the best rustlers [go-getters] in the state of Kansas. He served in the capacity of under sheriff of Meade county for a term of two years, and certainly discharged his duties with credit. If Sam would not make a good sheriff, then we don't know how to look for one."[24]

But by the time the "People's Party" convention was held a month later Wood had thrown his support to a coalition ticket with John M. Cross the candidate for sheriff. Furious at what he considered a betrayal, Robinson dissolved his meat market partnership with Short, resigned his position as Woodsdale city marshal, and, taking his wife, his child, and his hotel with him, moved out of Woodsdale. He had the hotel jacked up and pulled on wagons eight miles to the main street of the rival town of Hugoton, where he was warmly welcomed and almost immediately presented with the star of city marshal. Bert Noble, a sycophantic pal of Robinson's, sold his drugstore and followed in his wake.[25]

In his newspaper columns Sam Wood attacked the defectors with all the vitriol at his command, and he always kept a large stock on hand. "Woodsdale had a foul stomach and was compelled to vomit, not having any other vessel handy, used Hugoton," he wrote. "What Hugoton will do with the filthy stuff we cannot imagine. Perhaps vomit it into Macon City, and in this way drown out the prairie dogs."[26]

Wood was fully cognizant of the fact that Ed Short, although evidently still on good terms with his former partner, had remained loyal to Woodsdale and had not, like Bert Noble, followed Robinson in his desertion. Wood quickly moved to reward that loyalty by promoting Short to the city marshal's position.

In a public ceremony he presented Short with a nickel-plated, ivory-handled Colt's six-shooter and a handsome leather gun belt and holster. The revolver bore the inscription: "Presented by the citizens of Woodsdale to C. E. Short, city marshal, Oct. 25, 1887." Never one to pass up an opportunity to orate, Wood delivered a speech admonishing the city marshal to use the weapon he had been given with care, concluding: "Do not kill any one if possible to prevent it, but if it comes to a question whether you are to be killed or kill the other fellow, give yourself the benefit of the doubt and kill the other fellow." A similar pistol, but without an inscription, was presented to William I. Lynn, who was to become assistant marshal.[27]

Ed Short, it became obvious, was a favorite of the entire Sam Wood family. Some months later Samuel's son David, a resident of Montrose, Colorado, shipped Short another weapon, a handsome 50-caliber Winchester rifle, as a token of his admiration for the Woodsdale city marshal.[28] And, after the death of his wife, Short spent a good deal of time socializing with Mary Elvira Wood, Sam's niece, who spent the summer of 1888 at the home of her aunt and uncle in Woodsdale.[29]

The November 1887 election for Stevens County sheriff was so close that it was not until February 1888 that the winner was announced. After several challenges and recounts a three-judge panel finally announced that Wood's candidate, John M. Cross, had defeated his opponent, J. T. Dalton, by two votes. While Wood and his political allies celebrated, Sam Robinson, convinced that the shrievalty plum had been snatched from his grasp by the duplicitous Sam Wood and his gang, fumed in his marshal's office in Hugoton.

Another election over a bond issue scheduled for June 1, 1888, produced some heated political meetings, including one in Voorhees in which Sheriff Cross and his deputy, Jim Gerrond, completely lost control. Hotheads on both sides of the issue shouted down speakers, and the meeting ended in chaos, with Sam Robinson waving a revolver and shouting oaths and Deputy Gerrond going to the floor with a bloody gash on his head from a pistol blow. Predictably, editor Wood of the *Democrat* blamed the riot on the "Hugoton mob," and said Sheriff Cross would have been completely justified had he "shot a half dozen of them like dogs."[30]

The election held on June 1 was inconclusive, with both sides claiming victory. The board of county commissioners claimed they could not canvass the vote because Hugoton had become an armed camp, with two hundred armed men defying Woodsdale supporters to enter their town. Threats against the life of Wood, Short, and Cross were openly voiced. Sheriff Cross wired the Kansas governor that he had been driven from Hugoton on election day and could only return to serve writs or keep the peace at the risk of his life. He asked for a company of state militia to assist him in enforcing the law.

At the very height of this turmoil, a man named George Byers went before justice of the peace D. W. Walker in Woodsdale and filed a complaint, charging Sam Robinson with striking him on the head with a revolver at the meeting in Voorhees. Walker promptly issued a warrant for the arrest of Robinson on a charge of assault with intent to kill, and handed it to City Marshal Ed Short to make the arrest.

On the afternoon of June 5 Short, mounted on a fleet horse owned by Sam Wood and carrying the arrest warrant, rode into Hugoton, a town that had been described as an "armed camp." Accompanying him in a light spring wagon were Deputy Sheriff Jim Gerrond and Bill Housley, a gunfighter of note specially deputized for the mission. They did not find "200 armed men" awaiting them, although there were a few fellows lounging quietly on benches in front of the post office. Gerrond dropped off the wagon and sat down with them, while Housley turned the wagon around, facing it north, back in the direction of Woodsdale.

Ed Short rode on down the street to the office of the city marshal. Sam Robinson was seated on a chair in the doorway. The two former friends and business partners, now city marshals of towns locked in an escalating county seat war, eyed each other for a few moments. And then Short, still mounted, said, "Sam, I have a warrant for your arrest."

It is not exactly clear what happened next, as reports from the warring towns varied considerably, but guns were pulled and shots fired from either side. Although both Short and Robinson were men of high gunfighting repute, none of the shots took effect.

At the sound of gunfire, Jim Gerrond, down the street, leaped up, pulled his pistol, and also pumped bullets in the direction of Robinson. He, too, missed his target. Robinson, taking fire from two directions, scurried back into the building.

Gerrond jumped up into the wagon, and Housley whipped the horses into a gallop as Short also spurred his mount back toward Woodsdale. Robinson reportedly emptied his pistol and fired both a shotgun and Winchester rifle in the direction of the fleeing Woodsdale officers. It was claimed by Hugoton supporters that in his flight, Short snapped off two ineffectual rounds into the store of J. B. Chamberlain, Sam Wood's deadly enemy. And Woodsdale partisans said that the three retreating officers received fire from marksmen in buildings along the street, but, again, no bullet found its target.

A few men of Hugoton saddled horses and mounted a pursuit. Short, on his racehorse, easily escaped, but the pursuers caught up to Gerrond and Housley in their slower wagon before they reached Woodsdale and safety. While Gerrond held off the Hugoton men with rifle fire, Housley unhitched the horses. Together they mounted and rode off, abandoning the wagon and a single Winchester rifle, which the Hugoton men confiscated as the spoils of war.

The gun battle in Hugoton was not a banner day for western gunmen, extolled in legend for firearm accuracy. An estimated thirty shots had been fired in the exchange, and the only casualty was an elderly farmer, one of the loungers in front of the post office. One of Robinson's bullets, intended for Gerrond, struck the heel of his boot, bruising his foot slightly.[31]

The battle triggered a barrage of editorial volleys from the newspapers of the rival towns. Sam Wood of the *Woodsdale Democrat* blamed Robinson for precipitating the exchange. Short fired first, he said, but only after Robinson went for his gun: "Short was not required to wait until Robinson fired — and Short fired instantly, he was not a second ahead of Robinson."[32]

Editor C. M. Davis of the *Hugoton Hermes*, on the other hand, said that the three Woodsdale officers were merely tools of Sam Wood, who ordered the attack on Robinson, whom he feared "as the coward fears an avenger, as a cold blooded murderer fears the gallows, as a child fears an imagined ghost. . . . The attack on our citizens was an attempt at murder, coolly planned and failed only because the matter was entrusted to parties who were not used to such big game and took a bad spell of ague, spoiling their marksmanship and defeating their purpose."[33] Editor Davis did not offer an excuse for the equally poor marksmanship of Robinson and the other Hugoton shooters.

The war of words continued unabated. In an editorial column Wood staunchly defended Ed Short and charged that five Woodsdale partisans — Short, Sheriff Cross, Gerrond, Housley, and himself — had been targeted for assassination by the Hugoton forces:

> The idea that C. E. Short, our city marshall, is an outlaw and desperado is supremely ridiculous. True, Ed is brave and fearless in the discharge of his duties, but in no sense does he possess a single trait of character which goes to make up the outlaw and desperado. He is quiet, unostentatious and very gentlemanly in his deportment, and is as free from boisterous and rowdy conduct as his defamers are free from truth and honesty. . . .
>
> Nat Campbell . . . is the self-appointed executioner of S. N. Wood, editor of this paper. Sam Robinson is loaded for Ed

Short, and swears that he will kill him in a "holy minute," if he (Short) ever gets in range. Sheriff Cross, Under Sheriff Gerrond and Will Housley are the other victims whose blood seems necessary to propitiate the wrath of Hugoton ruffianism. We have not learned the names of the marksmen selected to put daylight through each one. They are probably considered lawful game for who[ever] gets the first crack at them.[34]

In another column Wood quoted a report in the *Hugoton Hermes* that in only ten minutes the town had raised $50 to buy a racehorse for Sam Robinson and added: "Hugoton understands how to fit out her kidnappers and highwaymen, Robinson openly declares his intention to shoot Ed Short, and Hugoton will give him every facility to do the deed."[35]

Recognizing the escalating tension in Stevens County and the likelihood of an outbreak of violence, Kansas Governor John A. Martin ordered two companies of militia to the location and had them set up camp between the two towns. Under the protection of the military the county commissioners canvassed the votes on the bond issue and announced the measure had been defeated. Tempers then cooled somewhat, and the militia companies withdrew.

As a kind of peace apparently settled over the county, Sam Robinson and a group of Hugoton adherents and their wives and children on Saturday, July 21, set out on a recreational trip into No Man's Land (also called the "Public Lands" or the "Neutral Strip"), that stretch of territory lying south of Kansas, north of the Texas panhandle, east of New Mexico, and west of Oklahoma. Called No Man's Land because no governmental authority was responsible for it, this tract of territory had long been a favorite hangout of outlaws and desperadoes.

Shortly after the party passed through Voorhees on their excursion, Ed Short rode into town. Learning that Robinson, for whom he still held an arrest warrant, was out of the friendly confines of Hugoton, Short decided to go after him. The fact that he had no legal authority in No Man's Land bothered him not at all; the same lack of law that attracted outlaws to the area gave lawmen the freedom to arrest anyone there they were capable of collaring. Short returned to Woodsdale, enlisted Bill Housley and Dick Wilson as possemen to help him arrest Robinson, and rode back south to No Man's Land.

He had no trouble following the trail and caught up with the Hugoton party soon after its members went into camp on Goff Creek. Seeing women and children in the camp, Short was reluctant to make any move that might precipitate a gunfight. By means of a passing cowboy, he sent word to Robinson that he had the camp surrounded, intended to serve his warrant, and demanded Robinson's surrender.

Correctly guessing that Short was running a bluff, Robinson saddled the fleet horse the residents of Hugoton had bought him and galloped off, with Short and his posse in pursuit. Robinson on his thoroughbred drew away at first, but as the race progressed the horse gradually tired, and his three pursuers closed in on him. The Hugoton marshal was forced to pull up, take cover, and make a fight of it. There was an exchange of gunfire in which Robinson received a minor wound, a bullet crease across the calf of his leg. Short, aware that he could never take his quarry without help, sent Wilson back to Woodsdale for reinforcements. During the night Robinson slipped away.[36]

The rest of the Hugoton party, meanwhile, had deserted their camp on Goss Creek and hurried back across the state line to spread the word of Short's pursuit of Robinson. Soon Hugoton scouting parties were in the field to assist their beleaguered marshal. Dick Wilson, on his way north to enlist aid for Short, ran into one group of Hugoton horsemen. Spotting them before they saw him, he hid his Winchester and cartridge belt in a cornfield and then denied knowledge of any Short and Robinson encounter. The men of Hugoton permitted him to go on.[37]

Another Hugoton scouting party stumbled across Short and Housley leaving No Man's Land after Robinson's escape. A running fight ensued. Greatly outnumbered and outgunned, the two Woodsdale men barely escaped. In his haste to get away Short dropped the beautiful revolver given him recently by his Woodsdale admirers, and the weapon became a Hugoton trophy. To avoid any further clashes with Hugoton partisans, who seemed to be everywhere, Short and Housley took a long, circuitous route back home.[38]

After slipping away from Short's posse, Robinson linked up with the main body of Hugoton men. Riding in this group were many of the leading men of the town. Having succeeded in rescuing their marshal, they should have reversed directions and returned to Hugoton, but Robinson, seething with anger and hell-bent on vengeance, led them deeper into the wilds of No Man's Land in search of anyone from hated Woodsdale.

When news of Short's difficulties below the border reached Woodsdale, Sheriff John Cross organized a posse to go to the relief of the Woodsdale marshal. Four men were deputized: Bob Hubbard, Rolland Wilcox, Cyrus ("Ted") Eaton, and Herbert Tonney. Only Hubbard, recently arrived in Woodsdale from Beer City, a tough outlaw rendezvous in the Neutral Strip, had previous law enforcement experience; he had formerly been city marshal of Saratoga, Pratt County, Kansas. The others were all young men — Tonney was only nineteen — with a youthful lust for thrills and adventure. Well armed and mounted, they followed Sheriff Cross out of Woodsdale on the night of July 24, headed for No Man's Land.

Unable to find Short the following day, they stopped for the night at a hay camp near a depression in the prairie called Wild Horse Lake.

During the night they were rudely jarred from sleep. Encircling them with pointed rifles was the Hugoton party led by Sam Robinson. Mercilessly, Robinson and his cohorts gunned down the sheriff and his four possemen as they stood with their hands in the air. All died within moments except young Tonney, who took a bullet that passed through the neck, just missing the carotid artery, and exited his left shoulder. He feigned death and lived to tell the tale. The shooting, which came to be called the Hay Meadow Massacre, inflamed Stevens County again and became front-page news across the country.

Governor Martin dispatched Simeon Briggs Bradford, adjutant general of the state, to investigate the matter. After interviewing a number of people from both towns, Bradford, in his report to the governor, recommended, among other measures, that the respective mayors of Woodsdale and Hugoton immediately discharge the current city marshals, Ed Short and Sam Robinson, as they seemed to be at the center of all the trouble.

A reporter for the *New York Times* who was carrying out his own on-site investigation reached much the same conclusion. Most of the Stevens County troubles, he wrote, could be attributed to "a couple of land speculators and two border desperadoes, who are Town Marshals [Ed Short and Sam Robinson]."[39]

Acting on Bradford's recommendation, Governor Martin activated the entire Second Regiment of the Kansas National Guard. He ordered eight companies, totaling six hundred men, supported by an artillery battery with a Gatling gun, to Stevens County. The military declared martial law in the opposing towns, disarmed the population, and remained on hand for a month. Federal marshals arrested Sam Robinson and seven other Hugoton men for participation in the Hay Meadow Massacre. Taken under military guard to Leavenworth, they were indicted by a federal grand jury and released on bond. The case would drag on in the courts for years, but in the end no one was ever punished for the brutal murders committed that hot July night at Wild Horse Lake.[40]

In spite of General Bradford's suggestion that Mayor Wood fire his city marshal, Ed Short retained that position in Woodsdale several months longer. But in late 1888 he resigned and left for Colorado. There, according to newspaper reports, he was busy recruiting men to join him in the land rush into the Indian Territory scheduled for April 22, 1889. Two months earlier the *Woodsdale Democrat* predicted that he would come through Stevens County on his way east and perhaps use the opportunity to reclaim his prized presentation six-shooter that was still being held in Hugoton: "It is no secret that Ed Short is arranging a company of 200 cow boys in Colorado to invade Oklahoma. They will come through Stevens county and the time of coming no man knows. We presume they will go south of the sand hills. Ed wants his revolver. There is blood on the moon. We would whisper to the people of Hugoton: 'Better be honest,' return the stolen property and make the murderers leave and avoid the wrath to come."[41]

There was no raid on Hugoton by Short and those who came with him from Colorado, and apparently he never did recover his revolver.

Short did make the run into the Unassigned Lands of Indian Territory with Bill Tilghman, Ben Daniels, Jim Masterson, and other notable Kansas peace officers. He settled in the new town of Hennessey, where the residents elected him city marshal at the first municipal election. With the establishment of Oklahoma Territory the next year, William Grimes was named U.S. marshal for the new territory. He quickly appointed Ed Short one of his deputies.

In the summer of 1890 Short was one of 245 witnesses called to the federal court at Paris, Texas, to testify in the case of the men charged with the Hay Meadow murders. He must have been pleased when on July 8, four weeks after the trial began, the jury found six defendants guilty of the murder of Sheriff Cross and to hear ten days later a sentence of death imposed by the judge.[42] The death sentence would never be carried out, but Short did not live long enough to suffer that disappointment.

Neither did Sam Wood, the nemesis of the Hugoton defendants. On June 23, 1891, Wood walked out of a Methodist church in Hugoton, which was serving as a temporary courthouse, and was shot to death in front of his wife and witnesses. His killer was Jim Brennan, a gunman who had been hired as a bodyguard for Judge Theodosius Botkin, Wood's bitter enemy.[43] When he heard the news, Short hurried to Kansas and caught the train at Newton that was carrying the body of Sam Wood to Cottonwood Falls, where he was to be buried. Margaret Wood, Sam's widow, later wrote: "[Ed Short's] sorrow at the loss of his old friend was deep and sincere. He said Col. Wood had been a true friend to him, and more like a father than any one he had ever known after his own father died; and that if he had known that Col. Wood was compelled to go to Hugoton, he would have come prepared to go with him and protect him."[44]

According to sensational newspaper reports, Short threatened to kill Judge Botkin if he presided over the trial of Jim Brennan, Wood's killer, and Botkin, in fear of his life, fled to Topeka.[45] But one paper quoted U.S. Marshal R. L. Walker of Kansas and his deputies as denying the report. "Short was not that kind of man," said Deputy Marshal Leon DeBost. "If he had shot Botkin I should not have been surprised but he never told what he was going to do until it was done. He feared neither man nor the devil."[46]

Two months to the day after Sam Wood was killed, Short himself died in a roar of gunfire.

In August 1891 Charles Bryant, an extremely dangerous member of the Dalton outlaw gang then terrorizing the Southwest, rode into Hennessey and took a room in the Rock Island Hotel. Called "Black-Faced Charley" because of the grains of black powder an early shooting affair had left imbedded in his face, Bryant was obviously unwell, either from sickness or, as some believed, from the effects of a fistfight in which he had come out second-best.[47] He kept to his bed and had his meals brought to his room.

When Short, who knew Bryant from years earlier when the two had worked cattle together, learned that the sick man at the hotel was a wanted member of the Dalton gang, he determined to take him into custody. As one old-timer told the story,

> Ed Short had seen Bryant not long before he became ill. Short and Bill Miller rode east of town one day, and as they rode along they looked over their list of pictures of men, and the warrants for men Short was hunting. He read a description of Bryant and remarked to Miller, "I am going to Hennessey and arrest that man Bryant."
>
> "If you do, you had better watch out or he will get you, Ed," answered Miller.
>
> Ed Short returned to the hotel and watched Jean Thorne, the nurse who waited on Bryant. . . . Short wanted to take in Bryant's meals or medicine, but Miss Thorne refused to let him do so. One day, just a few minutes before she was to take in Bryant's dinner, Short went to the door, opened it, and, leveling a six-shooter at Bryant, ordered him to throw up his hands. Bryant reached for his gun, but Short had him and he surrendered.[48]

All that night Short remained awake to guard his prisoner. The next day, Sunday, August 23, he caught a few hours sleep while S. R. Overton, the Rock Island Railroad agent at Hennessey, kept watch over Bryant.

Having arrested the dangerous outlaw, Short still faced a problem. None of the jails in Hennessey or surrounding towns were strong enough to hold Bryant if his outlaw friends decided to spring their pal. Short believed it would be folly to attempt to take his prisoner overland to Guthrie, as gang members would almost surely be lying in wait to rescue Bryant. The Rock Island Railroad line passed through Hennessey, and a northbound train was scheduled to stop at Hennessey at five that afternoon. Short decided that the best strategy was to take his prisoner by train to the federal jail at Wichita, where he could be safely incarcerated.

Shortly before five o'clock that Sunday afternoon, Short, armed with a pair of six-shooters and a Winchester rifle, escorted Bryant, hands manacled at his back, from the hotel to the Hennessey depot. There he consulted with conductor Jim Collins and made arrangements to segregate his prisoner from the other passengers and ride with him in the mail and baggage car. The only companion of the officer and his prisoner in the car would be the postal agent. When

Bryant complained after boarding that his arms ached from having been shackled so long behind his back, Short relented and cuffed his hands in front.

As the train slowed for Waukomis, its first stop, Short spotted several riders galloping across the prairie toward the depot. Thinking that the horsemen might have rescue in mind, he handed the postal agent one of his revolvers and instructed him to watch Bryant while he investigated. Rifle in hand, Short stepped onto the depot platform and warily eyed the oncoming riders. The agent, with no experience guarding dangerous outlaws, and more concerned with the sorting of the mail to be dropped at Waukomis, casually stuck the pistol in one of the letter pigeonholes and concentrated on his job.

Seizing his opportunity, Black-Faced Charley leaped to his feet and snatched up the revolver in his manacled hands just as conductor Jim Collins entered the car. Backing both men to the rear of the car with their hands held high, Bryant carefully slid open the car door. There stood Short, rifle in hand, a few feet away on the platform. Short turned to find himself looking into the yawning muzzle of a cocked six-shooter in Bryant's cuffed hands. For a split second as he swung his rifle up, the eyes of lawman and outlaw locked over their leveled weapons.

Then began what one historian has called "the most spectacular gun duel between two men of iron nerve in the history of the West."[49]

They fired at each other at point-blank range, Bryant cocking and triggering his revolver until all six chambers were empty, and Short levering and firing eight shots from his Winchester.[50] Bullets from both weapons struck vital parts. Bryant, hit in the heart and spinal cord, fell forward and, gasping his last breath, tumbled down the steps. Although one of the outlaw's bullets had struck Short in the left shoulder, gone through his body, and exited his back under his right arm, and another had torn into his right arm, he stayed on his feet. Dropping his rifle, he grabbed Bryant's legs and yelled for help. Conductor Collins came to his assistance and helped him pull the outlaw's body back onto the platform. Short then collapsed and died within ten minutes.[51]

Stretched out on the platform beside the body of Black-Faced Charley Bryant, Ed Short, dying, looked up at Collins. "The damn bastard got me, but I got him," he whispered. "I wish I could see Mother."[52]

Ed Short, who died, together with his adversary, in a blaze of gunfire. From the author's collection.

The bodies of outlaw and lawman were prepared for burial by the Schaeffer Undertaking Parlor of Caldwell, Kansas. Bryant's remains were shipped to Arkansas City, Kansas, where relatives claimed the body for burial in Decatur, Texas.[53] U.S. Marshal W. C. Grimes paid his deputy's undertaking bills, bought a $150 casket, and shipped Short's body to Osgood, Indiana, where it was received by Lucinda Mink Short, the mother Ed never got to see again, and three of his sisters. Funeral services were held in the Short home on the afternoon of August 27, and the body of twenty-six-year-old Charles Edwin ("Ed") Short was laid to rest beside the grave of his father in the Osgood Cemetery.[54]

A week later G. M. Foulk, general claim agent for the Santa Fe Railroad at Topeka, Kansas, wrote a letter to U.S. Marshal Grimes. He had that day, he said,

> made voucher in favor of Mrs. L. M. Short of Osgood, Ind., for $500, the amount of the reward offered by this company for the arrest and conviction of each and every one engaged in the robbery of our train No. 403 near Wharton, O. T. May 9th.
>
> While the conditions under which the reward was to be paid were for the arrest and conviction, yet the company concluded not to stand on any technical point in the case, having sufficient proof to lead them to believe that Bryant was one of the men engaged in the robbery, and for the further fact that C. E. Short lost his life in his efforts to bring Bryant to justice, the Co. concluded to pay the amount to the mother, Mrs. Short, regardless of any legal rights they may have in the matter.[55]

In commenting on the passing of Ed Short, the editor of the *Oklahoma Daily Times Journal* of Oklahoma City commented: "The west has produced many such characters such as Ed Short. His class was a shade higher than that of a desperado, yet he was a bad man. He was a bad man in the sense that he was a dangerous man. There was little of the bravado about him. He was totally unlike the dime novel hero, yet he reveled in deeds of blood, and more than one man in Oklahoma will breathe easier now that he is dead."[56]

In an interview given twenty-nine years after Ed Short died, former Oklahoma governor Thompson B. Ferguson was much more effusive in his praise of the man, eulogizing him as "a martyr to law enforcement." Said Ferguson:

He gave his life to a commonwealth in an effort to protect society, and organized government. Among the many tragedies of the border, when brave men were risking their lives, and giving their all in defense of the law, there is none sadder than the one connected with the passing on of Ed Short. He was one man who died too soon. He was a man the people could not afford to lose. Brave, cool and ever ready to take the lead in time of danger but never following in the rear. While on the marshal's force in Oklahoma, if bad men were to be hunted, he was among the first to volunteer for the task.

A dead shot, quick as a flash with a gun, yet he was not a man killer by choice. His plan was to capture without shooting when it could be done, yet there was not a "bad man" on the border that he was afraid to go up against under any kind of circumstances, favorable or unfavorable.[57]

# — 12 —

# HILL LOFTIS
1870–1929

*He was a killer and he got to be a bad one.*
— W. M. ("Bob") Beverly

At birth he was named Hillary N. Loftis. He lived the greater part of his life and gained widespread notoriety in Texas and New Mexico under the name Tom Ross. When he died with a bullet in his brain, he was known as Charles Gannon. He was one of the last of the Old West gunfighters.

Born in Sanford (now Lamar) County, Alabama, on January 11, 1870, he was the fourth-born child of Samuel Jemison Loftis and his wife, Jane.[1] Samuel Loftis cultivated crops on both sides of the Alabama-Mississippi state line. From an early age Hillary, or "Hill" as he was called by everyone, toiled with his brothers on that farmland. Headstrong and rebellious, Hill detested the discipline of farm work and the schoolroom, and at the age of thirteen ran off to become a cowboy in Texas.[2] His departure may have been hastened by a lack of desire to testify in court when a family dispute over a property boundary escalated into violence and a brother-in-law shot one of his brothers.[3]

In north Texas young Loftis found employment on the ranches of Dan Waggoner and other pioneer cattlemen of the region. Ever restless, he changed job locations four times in the first six years after leaving home.[4]

He never had any trouble finding friends and admirers, however. Range inspector Frank L. Campbell, who knew Hill Loftis well as a boy and a young man, attested: "In those days he was a good enough young fellow, and I never heard nothing against him until he got in with a certain outfit of bad men. He was a lively youth, fond of fun, and a bright one."[5]

At some point Hill's eldest brother, Jerome, joined him, and the two lived together. Some believed Jerome, nine years the elder, exerted a steadying influence on his impetuous younger brother, but he, too, would run afoul of the law. In 1889 Jerome was indicted in New Boston, Bowie County, Texas, for stabbing a man. Ten years would pass before Texas Ranger Sergeant W. John Sullivan arrested him in Vernon, Wilbarger County. By that time witnesses were scarce, and he came clear. After this brush with the law Jerome lived a commendable life, while brother Hill's career took the opposite direction.[6]

Finding cowboy life too tame for him, Hill in 1895 threw in with an outlaw band headed by George ("Red Buck") Waightman, a criminal and killer so mean and unpredictable that Bill Doolin had booted him out of his Indian Territory gang. Others joining Waightman included Joe P. Beckham, former sheriff of Motley County, Texas, who, having killed his successor and absconded with county funds,[7] was a fugitive from the law, and Elmer ("Mysterious Kid") Lewis, a nineteen-year-old already acquiring a bad reputation.[8] Lewis had cowboyed with Loftis on the Waggoner range and was probably responsible for enlisting him in the gang.

On Christmas Eve, 1895, these four stormed into the company store operated by Dan Waggoner and brutally pistol-whipped the clerk when he refused to disclose where the money was kept. A short time later they robbed the store and post office of Alf Bailey, about four miles away, making off with cash, stamps, and merchandise worth some $700.[9]

Texas Ranger Captain William J. ("Bill") McDonald was notified of the attacks. Personally unable to head pursuit of the outlaws because of a recent injury, McDonald ordered Sergeant W. J. L. Sullivan to give chase. Sullivan gathered a posse that included Rangers Bud Hardin, Jack Harvell, Bob McClure, Billy McCauley, and Lee Queen, as well as Sheriff Richard P. ("Dick") Sanders of Wilbarger County and his deputy, John T. Williams;[10] Billy Moses, former Motley County sheriff;[11] Vernon City Marshal Charley Sanders; and Constable Tom Pickett of Wichita Falls.[12] On Christmas Day Sergeant Sullivan took the outlaws' trail.

As he later related, "a big blue norther blew up," slowing their progress. It was bitterly cold. At dusk they came upon a line rider dugout, "half rock and half dirt." Horses tethered outside indicated that riders had taken cover from the storm in the shelter of the dugout. Unsure whether the dugout was occupied by his quarry or simply a party of hunters, Sullivan hesitated before making a move. But as darkness fell and the temperature dropped he ordered a charge.

The outlaws were indeed in that dugout, and a gun battle erupted. Accounts of the battle have been left from the perspective of either side — by Sergeant Sullivan, leader of the attacking lawmen outside in the freezing cold, and by Byrd Cochrain, a cowboy who was living in the dugout when the outlaws took shelter there and who became the proverbial innocent bystander.

Sullivan said he and his men spurred their horses toward the dugout at a gallop. When they were within seventy-five yards, four outlaws he identified as Waightman, Beckham, Loftis, and Kid Lewis opened fire, hitting none of the lawmen, but killing three of their horses. Sullivan had difficulty pulling his rifle from the scabbard as his terrified mount reared and plunged. Finally, grasping the weapon, he fell to the ground.

Seeing Waightman in the doorway of the dugout, he fired. The bullet struck the outlaw over the heart, and he fell backward, but an iron breastplate he was wearing saved him, and he was simply stunned by the shot. Red Buck rejoined the fight until another shot hit him above the armor, shattering his collarbone and shoulder blade. Beckham was also struck by a bullet, which killed him.[13]

Cochrain was in the dugout "making some biscuits and trying to keep from freezing to death," when all hell broke loose. "A bullet struck my pan of biscuits shattering them all over the place." As he crouched in a corner behind a wood stack, Cochrain watched Waightman "brazenly standing in the open door, swearing at the officers" until Sullivan's bullet hit his breastplate, knocking him down. Later he saw the outlaw struck again by a bullet and "heard the sickening splat of a slug as it hit Joe [Beckham] in the eye."[14]

After killing the outlaws' horses to prevent their escape, the officers maintained a siege of the dugout. There was sporadic fire from both sides until eleven o'clock that night. "Finally," said Sullivan, "we got so cold we couldn't pull a cartridge from our belts, and couldn't work the lever of our Winchesters, and we had to quit." None of the officers had been hit in the exchange, but stiff with cold and disheartened, they withdrew to a cattle ranch some twenty-five miles away.[15]

Three of the four outlaws had been hit in the fight. Beckham was killed, and Red Buck and Lewis were wounded. Only Hill Loftis emerged unscathed. Cochrain said that after the lawmen pulled out, "we made a cot from a bed in the dugout to carry the wounded Lewis on. We left Joe on the dirt floor, and headed out into the icy darkness."[16]

The gang broke up after this engagement, and within a few months two of the outlaw survivors of the dugout battle were dead.

On February 25, 1896, Kid Lewis and an accomplice, Foster Crawford,[17] robbed the City National Bank in Wichita Falls, Texas, getting away with $600 in gold and silver and killing cashier Frank Dorsey in the process. They hid out in the canebrakes of the Wichita River, but Ranger Captain McDonald quickly captured them and jailed them at Wichita Falls. Acting on a report that Hill Loftis had been involved in the robbery, he made an unsuccessful search for the former partner of Elmer Lewis. Fortunately for Loftis, he wasn't taken in, for folks in Wichita Falls, incensed over the murder of the popular bank cashier, stormed the jail, and took Lewis and Crawford out and hanged them from a telephone pole.[18]

Red Buck Waightman, returning to his haunts in Oklahoma Territory, met the end of the outlaw trail on March 5, 1896, when lawmen including the redoubtable Chris Madsen hunted him down and killed him near Arapahoe.

On February 12, 1896, a grand jury in Wilbarger County indicted Hill Loftis for "robbery by assault with the use of firearms," and he became a fugitive from justice.[19]

The 1900 "black book" of the Texas sheriffs described him as "about 32 years old, height 5 feet 9 inches, weight 160 pounds, hair dark, [and] a very peculiar shaped head, being very long behind, high forehead." His occupation was "cowboy," and he was believed to be in New Mexico. Sheriff John T. Williams offered a $25 reward for information leading to his capture.[20]

Others remarked on the unusual shape of Loftis's head. Byrd Cochrain said "Hill had flashing black eyes that could pierce through a man like cold steel, and a watermelon shaped head that was a feature one never forgot."[21]

And William Warren Sterling, who rose through the ranks of the Texas Rangers to become adjutant general of the state, wrote that "the size of [Loftis's] mis-shapen head with its shaggy hair, and the loose skin of his throat, which resembled the dewlap of a cow brute, caused some to call him 'Buffalo Head.'" He was, said Sterling, "a natural born outlaw, but it may not have been his fault. His elongated skull probably caused some pressure on the brain, and might account for his vicious tendencies."[22]

"If you once saw that man you never could forget him," Range Inspector Frank L. Campbell, who had watched Loftis grow up, told a reporter. "He couldn't change the shape of his head, a most remarkably shaped head, full of brains that might have put him far forward in life if he had used his brains right." When the reporter remarked that Loftis bore a striking resemblance to William E. Borah, the famous U.S. senator from Idaho, a lawyer rejoined, "Yes, and he's got just as much brains as Bill Borah, too."[23]

Byrd Cochrain admitted riding with Loftis for "a spell" after the dugout fight, but said they then went their separate ways. Loftis, he said, "was shielded by old man Cobb," but then left the state for the Kansas City stockyards, where he remained several weeks with William Lawrence ("Lod") Calohan, an inspector for the cattlemen's association.[24]

Loftis's movements over the next six years are hazy, and as a wanted fugitive from justice he tried to keep it that way.[25] He took a new name, Charles Gannon, and, according to Cochrain, spent some time in South America. But that locale did not appeal to him; years later he remarked to Cochrain that he would "rather be in a pen in Texas than a free man in South America."[26] Rumor had him in Colorado, Wyoming, Montana, Alaska, and Canada, always working in some phase of the cattle industry.[27]

But he yearned for the Lone Star State, and around the turn of the century reportedly wrote a lawman he trusted, Jeff D. Harkey, sheriff of Dickens County, Texas, saying he would like to return and stand

Hill Loftis, also known as Tom Ross and Charles Gannon. Courtesy of the Panhandle-Plains Historical Museum, Canyon, Texas.

trial in Wilbarger County, but nothing came of this overture.[28] About 1902 he did return, however, and now using the name Tom Ross, signed on as a ranch hand for the Halff brothers in Gaines County, Texas.[29]

Ownership of four sections of land in Gaines County he had purchased ten years earlier certainly served as an inducement to bring Loftis back to that section of Texas. Another incentive, perhaps even more powerful, was in the person of twenty-two-year-old Lillian ("Trixie") Hardin, whom he had known and admired as a teen-ager six years earlier. Trixie, the daughter of a prosperous Wichita Falls couple, had been partially blind from birth, but that did not deter "Tom Ross" from courting her. On December 9, 1903, the couple applied for a marriage license at Stanton, county seat of Martin County, Texas, and on January 24, 1904, Justice of the Peace Samuel P. Ford united them in marriage in the tiny hamlet of Gomez in unorganized Terry County. An Indian friend known only as "Chief" acted as best man.[30] Ross and his bride set up a home and established a ranch on land in the northwestern section of Gaines County that extended over the line into New Mexico. In 1908 a daughter, Bessie, their only child, was born.

Wilbarger Sheriff John T. Williams in June 1905 got a tip that Hill Loftis, now known as Tom Ross, was working a cattle roundup in the western counties of Texas, a region beyond the sheriff's jurisdiction. He enlisted the help of Martin County Sheriff Charles Tom and Captain John H. Rogers of the Texas Rangers to apprehend the fugitive and return him to Wilbarger County for prosecution on the old charges.

Captain Rogers and Sheriff Tom rode a hundred miles to the sand dunes country near the New Mexico line, where Ross was reported to be working. On June 17 they came across him suddenly. Ross, recognizing them as lawmen instantly and divining their purpose, wheeled his horse and galloped off. Rogers fired one shot with his Winchester, aiming at Ross's horse, but missed. Since the lawmen had earlier traded their exhausted mounts for "very inferior ridden-down horses," as Rogers described them, they chose not to chase their quarry. Returning to a nearby ranch, they ate a meal and returned to the trail again in the early evening.[31]

As they entered the dunes, the ranger captain, some distance ahead of the sheriff, dropped temporarily out of his companion's sight. But he was directly in the sights of a Winchester in the hands of a waiting Tom Ross. A bullet from that rifle grazed the jaw of Rogers's mount, cut the reins, and narrowly missed the Ranger. The horse reared, and Rogers, unable to control him without the reins, tumbled to the ground. What happened next Rogers explained in his official report:

> As I fell to the ground he fired at me. About the same time I hit the ground I slipped and hurt my back. I felt confident that I was ruined [killed]. He kept me covered with the Winchester, giving me no opportunity to draw my pistol or even to get a hand on it. . . . I lay on my back with my hands up and in spite of all I could do or say it looked as though he would kill me, saying that I had tried to murder him one and one-half hours previous. Finally he said he [would] not kill me, but only for the regard of some cowmen that had ridden up in the mean time. He took my pistol from me and unloaded it, returning it to me empty. He also relieved me of the balance of my ammunition.[32]

Sheriff Tom rode up, and, as Rogers put it, Ross also "throwed down" on him and disarmed him. As the sheriff later told the story, when Rogers fell off his horse he yelled, "I'm shot! I'm shot!" and Ross snorted that if he did not get up he certainly would be shot.[33]

Ross had the officers at his mercy and might have killed them both but for the intercession of Ross's good friend Billy Connell, who was driving the roundup wagon. Connell pulled up at this critical moment and talked Ross out of any murderous intention. After demanding and receiving a promise from the lawmen to quit stalking him, Ross returned their empty weapons and let them go.[34]

It must have been difficult for Captain John Rogers, extolled in Texas Ranger lore as one of the "four great captains" of the turn-of-the-century period,[35] to relate the ignominy of his encounter with Ross. He said as much in his official report: "It is very humiliating to me, this being the first report of this kind in 22 years of service, but I feel that to have made fight under the condition, being out of range of effective work with a pistol and having a man with a Winchester thrown down on me, I would better have attempted suicide."[36]

Rogers said that Ross demanded the arrest warrant and he complied, but Dee Harkey described an even more humiliating scene. Ross, he said, "made the officers eat the warrant."[37]

Captain Rogers had agreed to quit tracking Ross, and as far as he was concerned personally, he kept that promise. He no longer rode out with search parties looking for the fugitive, but he did send others. Only three days after the embarrassing confrontation he sent a four-man scouting party with a month's rations and forage into the region, looking for Ross. But their search of the area, including surveillance of the Ross ranch dugout, proved unrewarding. It was concluded Ross had left the state.[38]

On July 15 the *Terry County Voice* of Brownfield, Texas, reported that sixteen Rangers had located Ross, but "went away empty." It was not clear if shots were exchanged, but the Rangers came on Ross practicing with his guns, "and it may be that his marksmanship was more or less suggestive of the propriety of their retiring without him."[39]

It is unlikely that sixteen tough Texas Rangers would have been intimidated by the pistol prowess of Tom Ross, and this yarn may well have been baseless. The paper seemed prejudiced in favor of Ross as the author of the piece opined that Ross "was not so bad . . . as one might think from reports," and was willing to surrender to a Wilbarger County officer, but never to the Texas Rangers.[40]

Another story of Ross's defiance of lawmen was related in an article written by Mary Whatley Clarke, a schoolteacher of Knowles, New Mexico, who taught Ross's daughter, Bessie. "Tom Ross and his family lived a few miles distant," she said.

> It was whispered around even then that he was "a bad man of the West," and rumors were rife about him. It was said that he had killed a man in the past and that officers had ridden out to the range to arrest him. Ross told them he would return with them if they would ride by the camp and let him pick up a clean shirt. They agreed. When they reached the roundup camp, Ross unrolled his bedroll, took out a clean shirt and put it on. By then the officers were less vigilant and before they realized it Ross had pulled a gun on them.
>
> He disarmed them and stuck the guns down a prairie dog hole. Then, taking the bridles off their horses, he slapped the animals over the rumps and started them off on the run. He warned the officers if they ever came back after him again they would not return. It was said Ross could hit a quail on the wing with a six shooter, so the officers never attempted to arrest him again.[41]

Anna Beth Curry Erickson, another West Texas neighbor of the Ross family, remembered Tom's wife, Trixie, as "a small, heavy set, short lady with graying hair and beautiful eyes. Bess was short and had beautiful black hair and the same brown eyes. Bess was a very sweet girl." As for the husband and father, "There never was a time," said Erickson, "when I was not aware of the name TOM ROSS. He was short and heavily built, his head sitting right on top of his wide shoulders."[42]

Ross struck Mary Clarke as "a jovial, friendly type [who] had scores of friends throughout that section of Texas and New Mexico. . . . A heavy-set, dark-haired, black-eyed handsome man, [he] was a graceful dancer . . . , an exceptional waltzer"[43]

John R. Erickson, who grew up years later in Tom Ross country, heard many stories from his mother, grandmother, and great-uncles about the notorious cowman and gunfighter. His grandmother remembered Ross as "a nice looking man, some say part Indian, a good dancer, good company, and a crack shot." He was a good neighbor to those he liked, but he had many enemies, real or imagined, and when "sundown came, if he were home, he would draw the window shades for fear some stray bullet might come along."[44]

While acknowledging that Ross "had a wonderful personality and was a man that carried a lot of influence [and] could have been a useful citizen," other family members said he was feared by everyone in Gaines County. "No one deliberately displeased him. He left you alone if you left him alone, but woe to anyone who angered him!"[45]

Generally, by this time in the West cowboys no longer went armed, but an uncle told Erickson that Ross was never without a weapon. "The authorities knew he would carry a gun anyway, and since nobody wanted to cross him, they made him a game warden. He carried a pistol and sometimes used it on people's heads."[46]

Ross was renowned for his remarkable marksmanship with a handgun. Texas folklorist J. Frank Dobie said that Ross kept in constant practice, riding his "horse at full speed along a fence, hitting every post center."[47] Bessie told friends she loved to watch her father practice shooting. He preferred the new automatic pistol to the old-fashioned revolver, she said, "because it is quicker and doesn't jam." He could bring down pheasants and prairie chickens on the wing with his pistol, and she couldn't recall him ever missing a bird. "It was feats such as this that gave Tom Ross the reputation of being the best shot in Texas."[48]

Ross confirmed his preference for the Colt .45-caliber automatic pistol in a newspaper interview: "I use the automatic pistol. The automatic is to the old six-shooter what lightning is to the wind. The automatic doesn't jam."[49]

After his dust-up with the Texas Rangers, Ross kept out of sight for two years. Then in early 1906 he turned up in Stanton, Martin County, Texas, with his father-in-law, Frank Hardin, and, surprisingly, spent the night at the home of Sheriff Charles Tom, whom he had threatened to kill back in the sand dunes. He wanted assurance of safe passage to Wilbarger County to answer that ten-year-old indictment against him. Sheriff Tom gave him that assurance and on May 28 accompanied him to Vernon, Wilbarger County, where Ross surrendered to Sheriff John Williams. Released on $2,000 bond posted by Frank Hardin and William Waggoner, son of his former employer, Ross returned to his Gaines County home to await trial the following September.[50]

After ten years of dodging the law and coming very close to compounding his crimes by murdering two highly respected and popular peace officers who were trying to arrest him, Hill Loftis, alias Charles Gannon, alias Tom Ross, quickly was cleared of the robbery charges against him. When the case was called, his lawyer, L. P. Bonner, filed a motion maintaining that the charges were "vague, indefinite and uncertain," failed "to give a description of the alleged stolen property," and, in addition, did not "aver the ownership of the property." The judge concurred in this argument and dismissed the case.[51]

Ross returned to his little ranch straddling the Texas–New Mexico boundary. On his ten-section property, watered by six windmills, he ran about two hundred head of cattle.[52] Ross, by all accounts, was completely devoted to his wife and daughter, but marriage and fatherhood did little to curtail his lawless behavior, and his legal problems continued. Over the course of the next dozen years or so he was arrested and cited for a number of offenses, including fighting, carrying a gun in public, and assault.

Near Carlsbad, New Mexico, in 1912 he bulldozed a man named William J. ("Jack") Russell, forcing him at gunpoint to write out a

$750 check as repayment for money Ross had put down in a failed cattle deal, and refused to release Russell until the check was cashed. Arrested on Russell's complaint, Ross was charged with highway robbery and assault.[53] Dee Harkey sat on the grand jury that handed down the indictment. Having always liked Ross and gotten on well with him, he advised his friend to get a continuance and settle with Russell out of court. "In the meantime," Harkey continued, "Jack Russell got scared of Tom and went to Arizona. I do not think Tom meant to kill him, but only to force him to settle the case out of court. [Tom] went out to see Russell, so he told me so himself, and made arrangements to pay Russell $2,700 if he would stay away from Carlsbad until he got this case settled. Tom's lawyer finally got a compromise with the district attorney, by Tom paying a fine and costs."[54]

A case brought against Ross about this time became the cause of great animosity between the defendant and Judge Charles R. Brice, a highly respected jurist of New Mexico's Fifth District. Ross wanted a trial in Lovington, where he had many friends, some of whom would undoubtedly sit on the jury, but Judge Brice, on his own motion, moved the case to Roswell, where Ross's pals were not nearly as numerous. According to Dee Harkey, this infuriated Ross, who threatened the judge's life if he did not return the case to Lovington. Undaunted, Brice refused.[55]

A fearless judge was not the only officer of the law Tom Ross found himself up against. William Davis ("Dave") Allison and Horace Lorenzo ("Hod") Roberson, an intrepid pair Texas & Southwestern Cattlemen's Association inspectors, were also hot on his trail, building cattle theft cases against him. Both were veteran lawmen of the southwestern cattle ranges.

Dave Allison, a five-term sheriff of Midland County, Texas, spent four years as a Texas Ranger in the company commanded by celebrated Ranger Captain John R. Hughes. Joining the Arizona Rangers in 1903, Allison quickly rose through the ranks to sergeant and finally lieutenant. When the organization was disbanded, he settled in Roswell, New Mexico, where he served as city marshal for two years. At the age of fifty-six he took employment with the cattlemen's association as a range inspector and detective. He also held commissions as a special Texas Ranger and deputy U.S. marshal.[56]

Hod Roberson, fifteen years younger than Allison, had cowboyed in Texas, fought with the U.S. Army in the Philippines, managed ranches in the Texas–New Mexico border country, and served also as a Ranger in Captain Hughes's company. He was a big, burly man, feared and respected as a gunman. Stories that he had gunned down thirty-eight men were greatly exaggerated, but he had killed several, including two cowboys in a 1915 shooting at a Sierra Blanca, Texas, stockyard. A five-year-long legal battle ensued in which Roberson was found guilty of murder and given a twenty-year sentence. Retried, he was convicted of manslaughter and sentenced to five years. Retried once more, he was convicted again of manslaughter and given a two-year sentence. At a fourth trial he finally won an acquittal. While this interminable court battle dragged on, Roberson was hired as a cattle inspector and detective by the cattlemen's association. He also held commissions as a special Texas Ranger; deputy sheriff of Midland County, Texas; and deputy U.S. marshal.[57]

Working together in their capacity as investigators for the cattlemen's association, Allison and Roberson developed a strong case of cattle theft against Tom Ross, which they presented to a grand jury in Gaines County, Texas, leading to an indictment in October 1922. Two months later they gave evidence of cattle theft committed by Ross in New Mexico and succeeded in getting a grand jury at Lovington, Lea County, to hand down an indictment against the man there also.

Plainly the two inspectors were out to get Ross, whom they had suspected of rustling activities for some time. As the *Roswell Record* reported, "bad feelings had existed between these men [and Ross] for years."[58] Ross had openly sworn that if a cattle inspector ever set foot on his property, the man would never live to tell about it.[59]

At the same time the two cattle detectives were working up their cases against Tom Ross they were building similar cases against a man named Milton Paul ("Milt") Good.

Milt Good came from a family with a long history of violence and problems with the law dating back to the 1870s. His father, Isham J. Good, and uncle John Good were notorious fighting men in Texas and later New Mexico, where Milt was born in 1889. Raised with cattle and horses, Milt worked as a cowboy, ran his own ranch, and eventually became a top-notch rodeo performer. Specializing in steer roping, he finished first in fourteen of the fifteen contests he entered in 1920, was awarded $4,000 in prize money, and claimed the world's championship.[60]

His financial fortunes took a downward turn when he returned to ranching, and by 1922 he was in dire financial straits. He began rustling cattle and soon caught the attention of range detectives Allison and Roberson. After a lengthy investigation over a period of nine and a half months the inspectors secured indictments against Good for theft of 516 cattle in four Texas counties.

Veteran cattleman Bob Beverly was well acquainted with all four principals in this affair: Dave Allison and Horace Roberson, the accusers, and Tom Ross and Milt Good, the accused. Aware that all were fighting men of the Old West school, he recognized the cases presented a potential for explosive violence. At one point, when the indictments against Good were handed down, he prevented a shooting clash between Good and Allison at the courthouse at Midland. "Both had their guns," said Beverly, "and I stood between them, one in each hand, and held them apart. I said: 'Neither one of you men won't kill me and I won't let you kill each other.' "[61]

Beverly tried to stay clear of the blowup he saw coming. Both sides wanted him as a witness, but he refused to testify for either.[62]

Others feared that blood would be shed before the cases were settled. It was rumored that Roberson, on hearing of Ross's threats, said he was ready to settle their differences with guns. He was quoted as saying he had heard Ross was fast with a gun, but if it came to a showdown, he would have to be even faster.[63] He reportedly sent word to Ross that "if he wanted to shoot it out, to come down the street with a pistol in his hand."[64] If that defiant challenge ever reached the ears of Tom Ross, he evidenced no desire to meet the big detective, reputed slayer of thirty-eight men, in a six-shooter face-off.

Ross and Good got together and nursed their grievances. Given the generational disparity between them — Ross was almost two decades older than Good and had much more experience defying the law and lawmen — there can be little doubt that Ross was the leader and author of the audacious course upon which they embarked.

A grand jury was scheduled to hear charges against Tom Ross at Seminole, Texas, on Monday, April 2, 1923. Gathered in the lobby of the Seminole's Gaines Hotel at eight o'clock the evening of April 1 were a group of men deeply interested in that proceeding:[65] District Judge N. R. Morgan; District Attorney Gordon B. McGuire; Gaines County Sheriff R. L. Britton; former state senator and district judge George E. Lockhart, who would represent Ross at the hearings; and Inspectors Dave Allison and Horace Roberson. Two prominent local citizens, Bill Birdwell and "Billy Bill" Williamson, also joined in a discussion dominated by talk about the forthcoming grand jury session.

Suddenly the front door flew open, and Milt Good, brandishing a shotgun, and Tom Ross, pistol in hand,[66] burst into the lobby. Without a word, both gunmen cut loose. There was a deafening roar of gunfire, and the room quickly became engulfed in smoke. Allison toppled to the floor, struck eight times with bullets and buckshot. He died instantly. Roberson was blown back in his chair, dead from multiple gunshot wounds before he had a chance to draw a weapon. As the others in the room watched in horror, Ross barked a command: "Milt, do your duty!" and the two gunmen pumped additional rounds into the lifeless bodies of their victims.[67] Ross himself would later admit under oath that in shooting Roberson, he "aimed at his head, at his neck, at his heart, and his hip."[68]

With the exception of Judge Morgan, the witnesses to this shocking double murder fled in a panic from the scene. The sixty-nine-year-old jurist, who had almost been a victim himself as a bullet passed between his right arm and body, stood stock still, paralyzed with fear.[69]

Hearing the gunshots, Martha Roberson, Horace's wife, who had been reading in her second-floor bedroom, rushed downstairs in her nightdress. At a glance she saw the prostrate, blood-spattered forms of her husband and Allison, the frozen figure of the judge, and two armed men backing out the door. Martha, a nurse of long experience, knew immediately that Horace and Allison were dead. Realizing that the only help she could give them now was to attack their killers, she ran to her husband's slumped body and reached for the six-shooter in his hip scabbard. But the handle of the weapon had been shattered by a precisely aimed "hip" shot from Ross's pistol.[70]

Undeterred, the brave woman looked for and found the little back-up automatic she knew Horace always carried. She snapped off the safety and ran to the door in time to see the two gunmen about to enter a Model T Ford automobile. Taking deliberate aim, Martha fired two shots, one at each man. A bullet from the small caliber handgun struck the metal buckle of Ross's belt and glanced off, painting a red crease across his stomach.[71] The other struck Good in the left arm, passed through, and lodged in his hip. Painfully wounded, but still functioning, the killers climbed into their car and sped off.[72]

About ten miles northwest of Seminole they stopped at the ranch of Soon Birdwell and received first aid for their wounds. Although not life-threatening, those wounds proved so painful that Ross and Good decided to give themselves up in order to receive professional medical attention. They telephoned Sheriff Britton, one of those who had so precipitously fled the lobby of the Gaines Hotel when the bullets began flying. Britton still wanted no part of these vicious gunmen and refused to come get them. Finally a Birdwell neighbor volunteered to drive them back to Seminole, where they surrendered to the sheriff and turned over their handguns. Later Mrs. Birdwell brought in the rest of their weapons, two rifles and the shotgun that had been used in the shooting. Sheriff Britton locked the two men up in a new jail, which, ironically, Tom Ross had contributed generously to build.[73]

Instead of indicting Tom Ross for cattle theft as expected, the grand jury the next day brought first-degree murder indictments against Ross and Good. Clarke M. Mullican, judge of the Seventy-second Judicial Court, denied bail and scheduled separate trials for the two charged with the murder of Allison to be held in Lubbock in June. Trials for the murder of Roberson were to be held separately at Abilene in September.[74]

The Texas & Southwestern Cattlemen's Association spared no expense to secure convictions of the killers of their highly regarded inspectors. Dayton Moses, attorney for the organization, joined District Attorney Gordon B. McGuire, who had been an eyewitness to the shootings, and attorneys S. C. Rowe of Fort Worth and J. E. Vickers of Lubbock in the prosecution. When friends and supporters of Tom Ross made threats against Moses's life, he was kept under constant guard. An impressive battery of lawyers represented the accused: State Senator W. H. Bledsoe of Lubbock, Perry Spencer of Lubbock, John Howard of Pecos, and George E. Lockhart of Tahoka, who had also personally witnessed the shootings.[75]

Milt Good (*left*) and Tom Ross in handcuffs at trial. Courtesy of the Texas and Southwestern Cattle Raisers Foundation, Fort Worth, Texas.

Opening at Lubbock in June, Ross's trial for the murder of Allison was hailed as "the most important murder trial docketed in the Southwestern country since the twentieth century began."[76] Tensions ran high. Those opposed to the reported high-handed tactics of the cattlemen's association tended to forgive and support Ross, while others, appalled at the ferocity of the attack, wanted to see him punished by the full severity of the law. A total of thirty-two sheriffs and deputy sheriffs from all over Texas, as well as lawmen from beyond the state's borders, were on hand. Sheriff H. L. ("Bud") Johnston of Lubbock County took every precaution to prevent any violent outbreak. Robertus Love covered the trial for a St. Louis newspaper and wrote an extensive three-part series about it.[77] Sheriff Johnston, he said, allowed no one carrying a weapon in the courtroom. The sheriff posted seven or eight deputies on the stairway leading to the third-floor courtroom to frisk court attendees for guns. Women were sent to a separate entrance, where a matron conducted the search. Officers made an intensive search of the courtroom every morning before court opened.[78]

It was a huge trial. More than 400 men were called until a "special venire" of 125 could be chosen and a jury of 12 eventually selected. A total of 468 subpoenas were issued, and more than 250 witnesses from sixty-four West Texas towns and counties testified.[79]

Testimony began on June 21. Eyewitnesses to the bloody affair all said they recognized Tom Ross as the man who entered the hotel lobby with gun in hand and began shooting at once, giving Allison no chance to defend himself. A high point of the court proceedings was reached when Martha Roberson took the stand. Asked whom she had shot that night, she glared across at Ross and gritted through clenched teeth, "The man who killed my husband."[80] Throughout the entire proceedings Ross maintained "an air of indifference."[81]

Ross's lawyers offered a single argument in his defense: the old "Code of the West." They presented a parade of witnesses in an effort to depict Allison and Roberson as dangerous, vindictive men, out to get Tom Ross at any cost. One defense witness testified that he had heard Roberson boast that he had killed thirty-eight men. Ross, they contended, was in fear for his life and had to kill the cattle inspectors before they killed him. Their client, they argued, only fired when he saw Allison and Roberson reaching for their guns, and it was a clear case of self-defense.

Closing arguments for the prosecution were made by Dayton Moses, who spoke eloquently for two hours, denouncing the killings and the witnesses for the defense in "scathing" language. At one point he said, "It was a pity that [Martha Roberson] didn't have a .45 instead of the small pistol that she used" to wound the defendants.[82]

The judge instructed the jury that if the evidence indicated beyond a reasonable doubt that Ross "unlawfully and with malice aforethought" killed Allison, he should be found guilty of murder. Punishment, ranging from penitentiary confinement of five years to life or the death penalty, was to be determined by the jury.[83] It came as a surprise to no one that the jury, after twenty-seven hours of deliberation, found him guilty of first-degree murder. His guilt had never been at issue in the jury room, it seems, only the extent of his punishment, with several jurors insisting on the death penalty. Finally agreement was reached and the sentence set at thirty-five years in the penitentiary.

It had to be a moment of despair for Ross when the sentence was announced, but the charm that had won him so many friends over the years was still in evidence. One of the jurors, a young man, approached Ross, extended his hand, and actually apologized for the length of the sentence imposed.

"Oh, that's all right, son," said Ross with a smile. "You had to do your duty."[84]

The Good trial, which followed immediately, was something of an anticlimax, with the same lawyers and the same witnesses going over the same ground. Good, too, was found guilty, but his sentence was only twenty-six years. This figure was arrived at when one of the jurors insisted that a year be deducted from the thirty-five given Ross for Good's wife and eight children.[85]

Trials of the accused in the matter of Hod Roberson's death were held before Judge Walter R. Ely in Abilene three months later. Again Ross was tried first, and again witnesses for the prosecution described how the defendant shot the inspector down in cold blood, and defense witnesses trooped in to vilify Roberson's character and justify Ross in killing him. Everyone was surprised that the jury was out for ninety-six hours, but the cause of the delay was later learned: eleven jurors wanted a first-degree murder conviction and the death penalty, and one held out for a manslaughter conviction. In the end a compromise was reached; Ross was convicted of murder but sentenced to a prison term of only twenty years. Good's jury also found him guilty but, unaccountably, set his sentence at twenty-five years, five more than Ross's. The defendants were shocked when Judge Ely ordered that the sentences in the two murder convictions run consecutively. This meant that Ross, at age fifty-three, could look forward to fifty-five years in prison, or, in reality, a life term. Good, thirty-four years old in 1923, faced fifty-one years behind bars, until he was eighty-five.[86]

The convicted men were held in jail at Dallas for sixteen months awaiting decisions on appeals filed by their attorneys. When the last of the appeals was denied, officers transferred them to the Texas State Penitentiary at Huntsville, where they were received on January 24, 1925.[87]

Ross and Good immediately began planning an escape and within a year made their break. Joined by long-term convicts Clarence ("Red") Whalen and George Arlington, on November 29, 1925, they overpowered a guard, took his keys and a pair of bolt cutters, and made their way to the prison ballpark. There they used a fire ladder to scale a wall and ran to a car where a man and a woman whose identities were never disclosed awaited them with guns and coveralls to pull over their prison clothes. They roared off in the car and made a clean getaway.[88]

Taking turns driving, they crossed Texas, New Mexico, Arizona, and California, and continued up the West Coast through Oregon and Washington. After parting with Whalen and Arlington, they stopped finally at the little town of Blaine, snuggled conveniently next to the Canadian border. There they took employment at a sawmill and waited for the uproar over their daring escape to subside.[89]

Early in 1926, homesick and longing to see their families, the two fugitives began the long trip back. They retraced their route to New Mexico, where they holed up in Ross's ranch house for three days. Ross remained with his wife and daughter while Good went on to reunite with his family."[90]

Then they split up. Good said they parted on good terms, and Ross declared him the best friend he ever had. "When he left, I gave him a

30-30 Winchester. As he told me goodbye, he said that the man who took that Winchester from him would take it after he was dead and gone. I never saw Tom again."[91]

Ross then headed north alone. In May 1926, using the name "Charles Gannon," he turned up in the Great Falls region of northwestern Montana, where he hired on with the Frye Cattle Company. His well of range experience and skill with cattle soon earned him a promotion to foreman. He was doing the work he enjoyed and gaining the respect and friendship of other cowmen, but he could not be happy, separated as he was from his family, and constantly in dread that cattle association detectives or Texas Rangers had gotten on his trail.

He had reason to worry, for those organizations were indeed relentless in their hunt for him, even following up leads as far away as Mexico and Canada.[92]

In December 1928 they got a tip that their quarry, using the alias "Charles Gannon," was employed by the Frye Cattle Company in Montana. Ranger Captain Tom Hickman, who had taken the lead in the Tom Ross search, notified Sheriff Richard J. ("Dick") Croff of Glacier County, Montana, to keep Gannon under surveillance.[93]

When Sheriff Croff notified managers of the Frye Cattle Company that their foreman was believed to be a convicted murderer and prison escapee from Texas, they sent range detective Ralph W. Hayward to their winter cow camp, 120 miles north of Great Falls, just beyond the Canadian border, to keep an eye on Gannon. In a move that infuriated Ross, they went a step further and demoted him, putting Hayward in his place.[94]

On February 3, 1929, Hill Loftis, alias Tom Ross, alias Charles Gannon, exploded violently once again. On that bitterly cold Sunday afternoon — the mercury dropped to thirty degrees below zero — Ross and Hayward had words in the company cabin. While three other cowboys watched, the angry discussion escalated into shouted insults and cursing. Suddenly Ross whipped out a pistol and emptied it into Hayward's body, drilling a "tight little circle over his heart," and killing him instantly.[95]

Waving his gun at the horrified cowboys, Ross ordered them out into the cold. He then made preparations to die, burning all his personal papers and writing a suicide note devoted primarily to excoriating the man he had just killed. "This fellow," he wrote, "is a new man in the cow business. He might be allright [sic] among Dagoes but not among cow punchers." Concluding, "Good bye to the world," he lay down on his bunk, put the pistol to his temple, and pulled the trigger.[96]

When it became known that the cowboy "Charley Gannon" was in fact the desperate southwestern outlaw and prison escapee Tom Ross, north country newspapers gave the murder-suicide extensive coverage. A Canadian paper suggested that Ross, reverting to his old ways, was responsible for a recent wave of cattle thefts in the region and had killed Hayward when the detective got too close. [97] Another Montana paper printed an item charging Ross with another regional murder: "A special to the *Havre Daily News* from Browning [Montana] says that it has been quite definitely established that when Gannon left Texas he went to Canada and that in a rage one day at a Canadian cattle camp, he killed a Chinese cook with a club. He then drifted south to the United States and to the Rimrock ranch of the Frye Company where he had been working."[98]

Ed Reagan and his wife, who had befriended Ross in Montana, escorted his body back to his family in New Mexico. They were met at Lubbock by Trixie Ross, who, still half-blind, had asked former Gaines County sheriff Cleve Cobb to help her identify the body as that of her husband. The facial features were badly disfigured, but Cobb confirmed the dead man was indeed Ross, mainly because his boots had a worn pattern unique to those worn by Ross.[99]

Walter McGonagill, an old Ross friend, had died in Carlsbad that same week, and a double funeral for the two men was held in Lovington, New Mexico, on February 11, 1929. The Reverend William M. Beauchamp, who conducted the services, deemed it probably the largest gathering ever assembled at a funeral in the town's history.[100] Reported a dispatch from Lovington to the *Fort Worth Star-Telegram*:

Three thousand persons, friends and relatives of the two men, assembled from all over Texas and New Mexico for the double funeral. The little church could not hold a fourth of the crowd.

Ross and McGonagill . . . were separated by the laws of Texas and only Providence brought them back together, but both were in their caskets. Ross was 59 years old and McGonagill was about 55.

After the double funeral, two hearses drove side by side to the small cemetery and the bodies were lowered into their graves at the same time.

This caused the greatest assembly of old-time Texas–New Mexico cattlemen that New Mexico has ever known. Cowboys acted as pall bearers for each casket. Gray-haired cattlemen and cattle women stood silently with bowed heads and many bitter tears were shed.[101]

Not all who attended the funeral shed tears, for many sworn enemies of Tom Ross were there. A man named Mathis Wilhoit, who had brought one of the original charges of rustling against Ross back in 1922, a charge that eventually led to the double murder in Seminole, and many of his friends and supporters were there, apparently to make absolutely certain that the deadly gunmen Tom Ross was indeed dead. Rev. Beauchamp recalled watching in horror as Wilhoit approached the Ross casket and examined the body, looking for identifying marks. He even reached inside and turned the head of the corpse to see if a disfigured ear that had been one of Ross's distinguishing features was visible. It was, and Wilhoit was satisfied. The clergyman said tensions were high in Lovington that day, and "he really sighed with relief when the body was buried" because "he knew that a lot of men on both sides were carrying pistols and he was deathly afraid that a shooting would start any second." As a student of Ross's life has noted, had shooting erupted, "it would have been [an] appropriate setting for the last rites of a man who was as controversial in death as he had been in life."[102]

In reporting his passing, a writer for an Abilene paper penned a line that would have made a fitting gravestone epitaph: "Ross died as he had lived, a pistol in his hand and defiant."[103]

# *Afterword*

My aim in writing this series of *Deadly Dozen* books was to call attention to some of the Old West gunfighters overlooked by later writers in the field. I deliberately chose subjects whose careers had never been the subjects of full-length biographies. But as I wrote and prepared my books for publication, other authors were discovering some of the same colorful figures and recording their lives in other volumes. Even before my first book, *Deadly Dozen*, appeared in 2003 with a chapter on Dan Tucker, a full-length biography of Tucker was published.[1] This was followed by a biography of Barney Riggs, who had provided another chapter in my book.[2] So far none of the twelve gunmen in *Deadly Dozen*, Volume 2, published in 2007, has, to my knowledge, been given a book-length treatment by another author, but after completing the research and writing of this volume, I became aware that the central character in one of my chapters, Jim "Whispering" Smith, was also the subject of a new biography, published in 2007.[3]

I welcome these additions to the historical literature and hope in the coming years to see more full-length biographies of some of the thirty-six gunfighters' lives I have sketched in my three books.

In this "Age of Political Correctness," when the achievements of women and minorities must be emphasized, readers wondering why all of the gunfighters covered in my books were white males may ask: "Weren't any blacks, Indians, Hispanics, or women handy with shooting irons in the Wild West?" The answer is yes, there were a few, but very few. The American West in the late nineteenth century when the gunfighter flourished was a society dominated by white males, and the gunfighting class was no exception.

Since minority and female gun wielders were unusual, their stories have caught the attention of writers who have related those tales in earlier books. The career of Belle Starr, the best-known pistol-packing member of the distaff set, was nationally publicized as early as 1889,[4] and her life has been related in detail by several fine authors, including Burton Rascoe[5] and Glenn Shirley.[6]

The exploits of Apache Kid, Ned Christie, and Rufus Buck, three of the very few full-blooded Indians known as gunfighters, have been recorded in book form.[7] A number of mixed-bloods, including Zeke Proctor, Sam Sixkiller, and Henry Starr, have also been recounted by recent writers.[8]

When selecting possible candidates for this volume, I seriously considered relating the amazing story of Bass Reeves, the black deputy U.S. marshal of Indian Territory, undoubtedly one of the deadliest gunfighters of the frontier West, whose remarkable life had long been neglected. But before I had even begun in-depth research I became aware that other writers were working on the Reeves story, and I dropped his name from my list. In 2005 and 2006 no less than three biographies of Reeves were published, and his story has at last received the recognition it had so long deserved.[9]

There were several notable gunfighters of Hispanic origins, including Elfego Baca, whose famous 1884 gun battle against enormous odds is one of the legendary feats of New Mexico history. His story has been recounted in at least two biographies.[10] The amazing career of the gunfighting Texas Ranger Captain M. T. Gonzaullas has also been related in two life histories.[11] Hispanic outlaws of pistol-wielding notoriety, including Joaquin Murrieta, Juan Soto, and Tiburcio Vasquez, figured prominently in early California history, and their exploits have been recounted in many books, most notably in the recent works of California authors William B. Secrest and John Boessenecker.[12] I have left to these two eminent outlaw/lawman historians, both good friends of mine, the task of recording the stories of the California bandoleros and pistoleros.

The stories of hundreds, if not thousands, of other forgotten gunfighters lie buried in old newspapers, court records, and archives, waiting to be unearthed and retold by a new generation of researchers and writers. In the hope that my three *Deadly Dozen* books have contributed to our fund of knowledge of that most fascinating period of American history, the Wild West, and motivated others, I look forward to their discoveries.

# *Notes*

## INTRODUCTION

1. The story of John Bull is provided in the opening chapter of *Deadly Dozen*, my initial book in this series.

2. Smith was seventy-six when he committed suicide; Loftis was fifty-nine. Considering that the average age at death of the other seven who met violent ends was only thirty-one, the two who chose to take their own lives had long surpassed the life expectancy of a western gunfighter. Perhaps they had simply tired of the strenuous and precarious profession they had chosen.

## CHAPTER 1. FARMER PEEL

1. U.S. Army enlistment papers for Langford M. Peel, National Archives. Other years and locations have been cited for Peel's birth. Bill O'Neal, in his *Fighting Men of the Indian Wars* (181), gives the year 1826 without a location. Inferring from misinformation on a headboard placed at Peel's grave that he was born in Liverpool and died in 1867 at the age of thirty-six, some writers have given his nationality as English and his date of birth as 1831. Charles D. Greenfield, in "There Was Something About Him" (30), said he was born in Pennsylvania in 1829. The date of 1829 is consistent with all of Peel's military records, which all give Belfast, Ireland, as his place of birth. Thirty years after his death newspapers as distant as Elko, Nevada, and New York City still ran stories on Peel. The *Aspen (Colorado) Tribune* of August 31, 1897, reprinted an article about him taken from the *New York Sun*.

2. U.S. Census, 1850, St. Louis County, Missouri; Lowe, *Five Years a Dragoon*, 90.

3. U.S. Army enlistment papers for Langford M. Peel.

4. Ibid.

5. Description and Historical Register of Enlisted Soldiers of the Army, 1841–42, National Archives.

6. O'Neal, *Fighting Men of the Indian Wars*, 181; Gorenfeld to DeArment, April 30, May 2, 2007. "Dragoons theoretically were troops trained to fight both on foot and on horseback. A dragoon was armed with a musketoon, which was a short, smooth-bore musket, a horse pistol, also smooth-bore, and a sabre. . . . The dragoons formed a separate branch of service. . . . Each of the ten companies [in the regiment] had a captain, a first lieutenant, and a second lieutenant. Enlisted men were four sergeants, four corporals, two buglers,

one farrier-and-blacksmith, and fifty privates" (Lowe, *Five Years a Dragoon*, xvii).

7. Lowe, *Five Years a Dragoon*, 82–83, 90; O'Neal, *Fighting Men of the Indian Wars*, 181–82.

8. Lowe, *Five Years a Dragoon*, 90.

9. Ibid.; O'Neal, *Fighting Men of the Indian Wars*, 182.

10. Lowe, *Five Years a Dragoon*, 30–31.

11. U.S. Census, 1850, St. Louis, St. Louis County, Missouri. Peel's enumeration as "Langford P. Lyon" may well have been a census-taker's error, mistakenly assuming the son of Rachel Lyon was also named Lyon. No other instance of Langford's use of a surname other than Peel has been found. The census of 1860 reveals that Rachel and her soldier husband, John Lyons, were back in the East, residing in New York City. When he was fifty-two in 1870, Lyons was still in the army and stationed at the Allegheny Arsenal at Pittsburgh. Rachel, now fifty-eight, lived with him. He may have died in the next ten years, for he was no longer enumerated in the 1880 census, but Rachel was still at the same location, living with a thirty-one-year-old stepson, John Lyons, who, according to the census, was born in Germany (U.S. Census, 1860, New York County, New York; U.S. Census, 1870, Allegheny County, Pennsylvania; U.S. Census, 1880, Allegheny County, Pennsylvania).

12. Marriages, St. Louis, 1804–76; *Sacramento (California) Union*, August 9, 1867; Greenfield, "There Was Something About Him," 30.

13. U.S. Census, 1860, Leavenworth County, Kansas; Lowe, *Five Years a Dragoon*, 141. Peel was one of only two married men in the troop, a Sergeant Espy being the other (Lowe, *Five Years a Dragoon*, 140).

14. Lowe, *Five Years a Dragoon*, 89–94.

15. Ibid., 137.

16. Ibid., 121–22; "Description and Historical Register of Enlisted Soldiers of the Army, 1853–55."

17. Langford, *Vigilante Days and Ways*, 429.

18. Rucker was reported to be the wayward son of a former Tennessee governor (Greenfield, "There Was Something About Him," 32), but if that was true, he was using an alias since Tennessee never had a governor named Rucker.

19. Langford, *Vigilante Days and Ways*, 429.

20. Ibid., 430.

21. A well-known sporting man in later years, A. B. Miller owned several famous racehorses and the steamer *Octavia* (*Sacramento [California] Union*, August 9, 1867; DeArment, *Knights of the Green Cloth*, 61–62, 309, 311).

22. DeArment, *Knights of the Green Cloth*, 430–33.

23. Angel, *History of Nevada*, 357.

24. Greenfield, "There Was Something About Him," 32, 49.

25. Affidavit of Richard J. Ackley, September 29, 1858.

26. Langford, *Vigilante Days and Ways*, 433–34.

27. *Sacramento (California) Union*, August 9, 1867.

28. Langford, *Vigilante Days and Ways*, 434.

29. Twain, *Roughing It*, 339.

30. Ibid., 343–45.

31. Lyman, *Saga of the Comstock Lode*, 160.

32. Ibid. Lyman said that Peel was "a dead shot," but also mentioned, without attribution, that he was a college man, "a Cambridge graduate" (ibid). William R. Gillis, who was at Virginia City and presumably knew Peel personally, was impressed by his appearance and demeanor. Peel was, said Gillis, a man of "magnificent physique, six feet high and finely proportioned, a graduate of Harvard, highly cultured. . . . A man of noble presence, courteous and gracious" (Gillis, *Gold Rush Days with Mark Twain*, 42). Of course, Peel was no college graduate. His formal education had been minimal. He had received U.S. Army training in bugle blowing and military matters, but the rest of his learning had been acquired in the School of Hard Knocks.

33. Davis, *History of Nevada*, 245–47. An earlier Nevada historian described Peel differently, saying he did not look or act "like the typical 'bad man.' He was mild-mannered . . . , quiet in his ways, drank lightly and never became boisterous" (Angel, *History of Nevada*, 357).

34. *Gold Hill (Nevada) News*, January 2, 1877.

35. Angel, *History of Nevada*, 357.

36. *San Francisco Alta*, October 1, 1863.

37. "Pistol Pockets in the United States."

38. Ibid.; DeArment, *Knights of the Green Cloth*, 298.

39. Angel, *History of Nevada*, 345. Although Peel was probably unaware of it, the date was coincidentally the twenty-first anniversary of his first discharge from the U.S. Army.

40. Lyman, *Saga of the Comstock Lode*, 160–61.

41. Langford, *Vigilante Days and Ways*, 435–36.

42. Gillis, *Gold Rush Days with Mark Twain*, 45.

43. Angel, *History of Nevada*, 357.

44. Langford, *Vigilante Days and Ways*, 436.

45. Lyman, *Saga of the Comstock Lode*, 161–62.

46. Davis, *History of Nevada*, 246–47.

47. Angel, *History of Nevada*, 357.

48. *Aspen (Colorado) Tribune*, August 31, 1897.

49. Drury, *Editor on the Comstock Lode*, 169–70. In another version of this incident, De Quille went after Peel with a stiletto knife and, crowding against him at a bar, put the point of the blade to the gunman's throat and demanded to know if he had any complaints about his writing. Peel denied he had and complimented the newsman, saying he was the first man to ever get the drop on him (Greenfield, "There Was Something About Him," 32; DeArment, *Knights of the Green Cloth*, 299–300).

50. *Aspen (Colorado) Tribune*, August 31, 1897.

51. *Gold Hill (Nevada) News*, March 6, 1865.

52. *Sacramento (California) Union*, August 9, 1867.

53. Greenfield, "There Was Something About Him," 49.

54. Ibid.

55. Ibid.

56. *Helena (Montana) Independent*, July 23, 1882.

57. The *Montana Post*, quoted in the *Sacramento (California) Union*, August 9, 1867.

58. Ibid.; *Helena (Montana) Independent*, July 23, 1882.

59. *Montana Post*, quoted in the *Sacramento (California) Union*, August 9, 1867.

60. Ibid.

61. Greenfield, "There Was Something About Him," 50.

62. Sanders, *X. Beidler*, 140.

63. Curtin, "Passing of Farmer Peel," 9. The notion that Peel could not be killed in a fair fight was echoed by James Marber, who had known and admired Peel in Virginia City but was not in Helena when he was killed. "Farmer Peale [*sic*] died with his boots on, but no man killed him in open fight," he said, adding a sentence that contained at least three errors of fact: "An assassin waylaid him and killed him with a shotgun as he was walking with his wife on a Sunday afternoon" (*Aspen [Colorado] Tribune*, August 31, 1897).

64. *Helena (Montana) Independent*, July 23, 1882. The editor described Bull as "gentlemanly looking [with] nothing noticeable about the man save the eagle eye. Quick, restless and full of light, indicating nerve and courage combined with much mental activity."

65. For an account of the remarkable life of John Bull, see DeArment, *Deadly Dozen*, vol. 1, 6–18.

66. Curtin, "Passing of Farmer Peel," 10. The headboard is still held by the Montana State Historical Society.

## CHAPTER 2. CHARLIE HARRISON

1. Ancestry.com, MyFamily.com.inc; U.S. Census, 1860, Denver, Arapahoe County, Kansas Territory.

2. Parkhill, *Law Goes West*, 61.

3. The exact date of Harrison's arrival in Denver is not known. Eugene Teats, his father, and the rest of the Teats family were enumerated as residents of McComb County, Michigan, in the U.S. Census taken in June 1860. But Eugene, by his own account, left home in the early spring of that year to join his father in Denver and arrived there in March (Teats, "Recollections of a Pikes-Peaker"). By August Charles Harrison was well established in Denver with property valued at $4,000 (U.S. Census, 1860, Denver, Arapahoe County, Kansas Territory), so he evidently arrived sometime between March and August.

4. Richardson, *Beyond the Mississippi*, 187–88.

5. Willison, *Here They Dug the Gold*, 85.

6. Ibid.

7. Ibid., 86.

8. Richardson, *Beyond the Mississippi*, 186.

9. Raine, *Guns of the Frontier*, 77.

10. Willison, *Here They Dug the Gold*, 85–86.

11. Masterson, "Famous Gun Fighters of the Western Frontier."

12. See chapter 4.

13. Dial, *Saloons of Denver*, 14; Raine, *Guns of the Frontier*, 77; Willison, *Here They Dug the Gold*, 86. All these authors ascribe Masterson's comments to Harrison of Denver, a man who was killed when Bat Masterson was a farm boy of ten in Illinois.

14. Asbury, *Sucker's Progress*, 165.

15. Willison, *Here They Dug the Gold*, 85.

16. Stark was described as "the Mexican negro" in the *Rocky Mountain News* (Denver), July 25, 1860, and as "a mulatto" in news dispatches (*Janesville [Wisconsin] Daily Gazette*, July 21, 1860).

17. *Rocky Mountain News* (Denver), July 25, 1860; *Janesville (Wisconsin) Daily Gazette*, July 21, 1860; Willison, *Here They Dug the Gold*, 103–104; Zamonski and Keller, *Fifty-Niners*, 119–21; DeArment, *Knights of the Green Cloth*, 48–50; Dial, *Saloons of Denver*, 14; Leonard, *Lynching in Colorado*, 21.

18. Willison, *Here They Dug the Gold*, 104.

19. Dial, *Saloons of Denver*, 13–14; Zamonski and Keller, *Fifty-Niners*, 145. After selling the Criterion to Harrison, Ed Jump left Denver to pursue a career as an artist. His work appeared in *Frank Leslie's Illustrated News* and historical works of the period including A. D. Richardson's *Beyond the Mississippi*. Jump committed suicide in Chicago in 1883 (Dial, *Saloons of Denver*, 10).

20. *Rocky Mountain News* (Denver), July 25, 1860.

21. Ibid., August 1, 1860.

22. Zamonski and Keller, *Fifty-Niners*, 132.

23. Ibid., 133–40; Hill, *Tales of the Colorado Pioneers*, 54–57.

24. Willison, *Here They Dug the Gold*, 106.

25. Zamonski and Keller, *Fifty-Niners*, 191.

26. Ibid., 192.

27. Ibid.

28. In his account Thomas later elaborated on the alleged killing of Hill's friend. Only a week earlier, he said, Harrison had murdered "an inoffensive young German" who understood little English: "Harrison had met the Dutchman in a saloon . . . and ordered him to come to the bar and have a drink, flourishing his six-shooter as he did so, which so frightened the poor devil . . . that he fell on his knees and lifting his clasped hands began to supplicate for mercy. Harrison grabbed him by the hair, and saying, 'No damned Dutchman shall refuse to drink with me and live to blow about it!' shot him through the head, scattering his brains about the floor" (Thomas, "In the Days of the Overland Trail"). Thomas did not claim to have personally witnessed this murder, and, since no mention of it can be found in any

other source, this tale, like the story of Harrison's killing of another "German" in Leavenworth, is undoubtedly apocryphal.

29. Ibid.

30. Zamonski and Keller, *Fifty-Niners*, 210–11. From a card dated December 11, 1860, and published in the *Rocky Mountain News* (Denver). It is interesting that Harrison referred to the smoke that obscured his vision even as he was firing. Black powder cap and ball pistols created a great deal of smoke when fired, contributing to the inaccuracy of many gunfight participants, but this is rarely mentioned in accounts of shootings and is never shown in television or motion picture depictions of gunfights.

31. Zamonski and Keller, *Fifty-Niners*, 196–98.

32. Ibid., 198–99.

33. Ibid., 199–200.

34. Thomas, "In the Days of the Overland Trail."

35. Zamonski and Keller, *Fifty-Niners*, 201–208.

36. Also known as Mrs. Sheridan, Ada LaMonte was reportedly a former rider in a circus (Parkhill, *Wildest of the West*, 29). Dr. O. D. Cass, who practiced in early-day Denver, said he was approached by a man "about five feet nine inches in height, bearded like a pard, trousers in bootlegs, his dark hair covered by a black slouch hat beneath which I saw a pair of gleaming black eyes," who wanted him to treat "his woman." When Cass informed him his fee was $25, with payment up front, the man "whipped out an ugly looking six-shooter," thrust it in the doctor's face, and snapped, "Damn your fee; follow me, sir, and be quick about it." Thus encouraged, Cass said he stood not upon the order of his going, but hastened to obey. He attended the woman for a week and cured her. Then one day the stranger strode into Cass's office "with the air of a cavalry brigadier," placed five twenty-dollar gold pieces on his desk, and asked if that would cover his services. When assured by the doctor, the man said: 'See here, doctor. I've taken a notion to you. There's a good many rough fellows about town, who drink and fight and make trouble for honest people. If any of 'em ever interfere with you, you send for me. My name is Charlie Harrison'" (quoted in Secrest, *Hell's Belles*, 67). Ada LaMonte remained in Denver long after Harrison left. She later operated a brothel in Georgetown but in the early 1870s returned to Denver, where her house was the scene of a sordid murder (Bancroft, *Denver's Lively Past*, 13).

37. Willison, *Here They Dug the Gold*, 102.

38. Noel, *City and the Saloon*, 34.

39. Thomas, "In the Days of the Overland Trail."

40. *Rocky Mountain News* (Denver), December 10, 1860.

41. Ibid., December 11, 1860.

42. Ibid.

43. Ibid., December 28, 1860.

44. Dial, *Saloons of Denver*, 17; Perkin, *First One Hundred Years*, 182.

45. Zamonski and Keller, *Fifty-Niners*, 212.

46. Ibid., 213–17.

47. Willison, *Here They Dug the Gold*, 103.

48. Zamonski and Keller, *Fifty-Niners*, 217.

49. *Rocky Mountain News* (Denver), December 21, 1860; Leonard, *Lynching in Colorado*, 26.

50. Zamonski and Keller, *Fifty-Niners*, 218.

51. Ibid., 250–54; DeArment, *Knights of the Green Cloth*, 60–62; Willison, *Here They Dug the Gold*, 89–94.

52. The story of the dramatic events in Denver that summer of 1861 and the central role played by Harrison are detailed in Zamonski and Keller, *Fifty-Niners*, 255–69; and Perkin, *First One Hundred Years*, 239. The Criterion, following Harrison's departure, never again held the exalted position it enjoyed during his management. "Count" Henri Murat, who claimed to be the nephew of the king of Naples, and his wife, the "Countess," ran the place for a time and, in an effort to make people forget the place's notoriety, renamed it the Mozart Billiard Hall. But it was all in vain. The once great saloon, gambling hall, and theater continued its decline and in time suffered the humiliation of becoming a grocery store (Dial, *Saloons of Denver*, 18–29).

53. Cox, "Battle of Cane Hill in Depth"; Cox, "Battle of Cane Hill—Confederate Reports."

54. Zamonski, "Colorado Gold and the Confederacy," 99.

55. Quoted in ibid., 100–101.

56. Ibid., 102; DeArment, *Knights of the Green Cloth*, 65–66; Perkin, *First One Hundred Years*, 250.

57. Zamonski, "Denver's Godfather."

58. Bartles, "Massacre of Confederates," 64.

59. Zamonski, "Colorado Gold and the Confederacy"; Willison, *Here They Dug the Gold*, 110; Brown: *Empire of Silver*, 46.

### CHAPTER 3. WHISPERING SMITH

1. Oddly enough, as at least one historian has pointed out, the exploits of Frank Spearman's fictional "Whispering" Smith were based more upon the career of Joe LeFors of Wyoming than that of James L. Smith (Prassel, *Western Peace Officer*, 250).

2. *Denver Times*, February 7, 1905.

3. *Rocky Mountain News* (Denver), August 27, 1914.

4. In his physical description of Smith, Bronson failed to comment on his prominent aquiline nose, a feature that earned him the name of "Hawkbill," according to one historian "Hawkbill," she added, "was noted as a cold, cunning and relentless individual, absolutely insensible to fear" (Klock, *Black Hills Outlaws*, 8).

5. Bronson, *Red-Blooded Heroes*, 77–78.

6. Hurley, *Jungle Patrol*.

7. Bartholomew, *Western Hard-Cases*, 72–88.

8. U.S. Census, 1840, Anne Arundel County, Maryland; Rybolt, "Whispering Smith," 18. In a letter written in 1887 Smith said his age was fifty-one,

which would indicate an 1836 year of birth (Bailey, "Wyoming Stock Inspectors and Detectives," 79).

9. Bronson, *Red-Blooded Heroes* (77): "Of Captain Smith's early history nothing was known, except that he had served with great credit as a captain of artillery in the Union Army." Diligent Smith researcher Robert T. Rybolt admitted that confirmation of the report could not be found in the National Archives, but he remained "certain" that Smith was a Civil War veteran (Rybolt, "Search for 'Whispering Smith,' " 7).

10. *Rocky Mountain News* (Denver), August 27, 1914.

11. Records of Volunteer Officers, Civil War, National Archives.

12. *Edwards New Orleans Directory, 1873*, 409.

13. The marriage was performed by Rev. Father J. J. Duffo in the Church of the Immaculate Conception. *New Orleans Parish Recorder*, Book 4, Folio 272; Rybolt, " 'Whispering Smith,' " 6.

14. *New Orleans Times*, May 25, 1874; Transcript, New Orleans Municipal Police Court, May 23, 1874.

15. Transcript, New Orleans Municipal Police Court, May 25, 1874.

16. *Edwards New Orleans Directory, 1874*, 706.

17. *New Orleans Republican*, November 14, 25, 1875; State of Louisiana, New Orleans Grand Jury Report, January 10, 1876. Thomas Devereaux was later tried for the murder of a former police detective and acquitted. After serving in the state legislature he was made chief of detectives at New Orleans. In 1881 he was killed in a gunfight with two of his detectives (Rousey, *Policing the Southern City*, 171).

18. *Wolfe's Omaha, Nebraska, Directory for 1876–77*, 188. The Smith residence was listed as at 557 Eleventh Street in Omaha. James was employed by the Union Pacific Railroad Company. Anna'a occupation was given as "washerwoman."

19. Prassel, *Western Peace Officer*, 140.

20. Hutton, *Doc Middleton*, 254.

21. Minutes of the Cheyenne City Council, February 12, 1878.

22. McGillycuddy, *Blood on the Moon*, 128.

23. Ibid.

24. Rybolt, " 'Whispering Smith' Still a Mystery," 5.

25. *Black Hills Journal* (Rapid City, Dakota Territory), July 5, 1879.

26. *Black Hills Daily Times* (Rapid City, Dakota Territory), July 8, 1879.

27. *Sidney (Nebraska) Telegraph*, July 12, 1879.

28. McGillycuddy, *Blood on the Moon*, 129. Irma H. Klock, in *Black Hills Outlaws* (8–9), alleges that Jim Smith "never saw the necessity of taking a wrongdoer to jail when the miscreant could be hanged before then, with no further expense to the taxpayers." According to this story, Lame Johnny, who "knew Hawkbill's reputation," told his pal Harris before leaving that he did not expect to get to Rapid City alive. "It was [Boone] May who opened the door and said, 'Get out, Johnny.' Smith gave him a push. Johnny begged to have his shackles removed but ended up tumbling out of the coach with Smith

closely following him — and the stage drove on. Said one gentleman many years later, 'That was Smith alright — bet he fixed the rope himself.'"

29. Folks suspected Brown's involvement because he had played a role in a similar lynching less than a year earlier. On October 31, 1878, while he and Jim May were transporting suspected stagecoach robbers Billy Mansfield and Archie McLaughlin from Fort Laramie to Deadwood for trial, masked men stopped and disarmed them and hanged their prisoners (*Cheyenne Daily Leader*, November 5, 1878).

30. John B. Furay to A. D. Hazen, January 8, 1880, quoted in Spring, "Who Robbed the Mail Coach?" 25.

31. John B. Furay to D. B. Parker, July 7, 1880, quoted in ibid., 58.

32. *Sidney (Nebraska) Telegraph*, July 12, 1879; *Black Hills Journal* (Rapid City, Dakota Territory), August 30, 1879.

33. Born James M. Riley on February 9, 1851, at Bastrop, Texas, the outlaw leader was sentenced to prison in Texas in 1875, but escaped and adopted the alias David Charles Middleton. He signed his name with small circles after the initials "D. C." and thus became "Doc." Some writers have speculated that he was the Jim Riley involved in the famous "General Massacre" at Newton, Kansas, on August 20, 1871, but his biographer discounts the notion (Hutton, *Doc Middleton*; Rybolt, "'Whispering Smith' Still a Mystery," 3).

34. *Cheyenne Daily Sun*, March 14, 1879.

35. Rybolt, "Whispering Smith," 37; Rybolt, "'Whispering Smith' Still a Mystery," 4; Hutton, *Doc Middleton*, 70–71.

36. Rybolt, "'Whispering Smith' Still a Mystery," 4.

37. Ibid., 5–6; Hutton, *Doc Middleton*, 132–34. The *posse comitatus* act prohibited military forces from aiding in the apprehension of civilian malefactors, but in this instance, as in others, the excuse was given that the army personnel were in the field looking for deserters.

38. "Doc Middleton: Road Agent and Bandit."

39. *Cheyenne Daily Sun*, September 30, 1879. Middleton served three and a half years of his sentence. After his release he settled in Gordon, Nebraska, and became a deputy sheriff. In 1893 a horse race from Chadron, Nebraska, to Chicago was run as a feature of the Columbian Exposition held in Chicago. Middleton competed and finished, but did not win (Hutton, *Doc Middleton*).

40. *Cheyenne Daily Leader*, November 12, 1879.

41. Ibid.

42. Lee, *Wild Towns of Nebraska*, 91.

43. "The county judge was a farro [*sic*] dealer in the Capital [*sic*] saloon, where the county clerk was lookout and the sheriff kept cases" (Yost, *Call of the Range*, 65).

44. Rybolt, "'Whispering Smith' Still a Mystery," 7.

45. Ibid.; *Sidney (Nebraska) Telegraph*, January 8, 1881.

46. Rybolt, "'Whispering Smith' Still a Mystery," 7. Edgar Bronson, in his *The Red-Blooded Heroes of the Frontier* (79–81), gives a greatly distorted ac-

count of Smith's six-shooter adventures in Sidney. Called to the town after the attempted bullion heist, Smith, said Bronson, announced "he was going to clean out the town, and purposed killing McCarthy [McCarty] on sight." That night he was asleep in his room when suddenly awakened by McCarty standing over him with a pistol in his hand. Smith talked McCarty out of shooting him then and there, but followed him when he left the room and shot him dead. "During the day Jim got two more scalps."

47. Ibid.; *Sidney (Nebraska) Telegraph*, June 19, 1951; Shumway, *History of Western Nebraska*, 154;

48. *Cheyenne Daily Leader*, April 5, 1881. It should be remembered that an editor of the newspaper reporting this story was J. G. Mills, the man he had once challenged to a duel and the same man who had once accused him of cowardice in the pages of his paper.

49. Yost, *Call of the Range*, 66.

50. Rybolt, " 'Whispering Smith' Still a Mystery," 7; Roster of Agency Employees, 1853–1909.

51. *Commissioner of Indian Affairs Annual Report*, 1881, 16.

52. *Rio Grande Republican* (Las Cruces, New Mexico), September 16, 25, 1881.

53. Bronson, *Red-Blooded Heroes*, 83. Bronson added: "This was the last time we ever met, and lucky it will probably be for me if we never meet again; for if Jim still lives and there is aught in this story he sees occasion to take exception to, I am sure to be due for a mix-up I can very well get on without" (84). This was published in 1910, and Whispering Smith, still very much alive, evidently took no exception to Bronson's remarks.

54. Harris, "Hawkbill."

55. Rybolt, " 'Whispering Smith' Still a Mystery," 7. However, Llewellyn's boasts about the $10,000, as cited in Hutton, *Doc Middleton*, 261–62, seem to have been made years later in the *Rio Grande Republican* (Las Cruces, New Mexico), October 13, 1888, reprinted from the *Topeka Capital*.

56. Bailey, "Wyoming Stock Inspectors and Detectives," 183.

57. Cheyenne County, Nebraska, Court Records, Vol. 1, 169.

58. Bailey, "Wyoming Stock Inspectors and Detectives," 57–58.

59. Ibid., 74.

60. Bartlett Richards was one of the wealthiest cattlemen in Nebraska. In later years he was tried for evasion of the fence law and sentenced to one day in the custody of a U.S. marshal. When he celebrated with a big party, President Theodore Roosevelt heard about it and had him tried again. This time he received a jail term (ibid., 75).

61. Ibid., 114–15. Smith obviously took delight in bullying those he despised, and he admired that capability in others. In another letter to the WSGA secretary he praised the actions of association inspector Claude A. Talbot: "The association men done well here at the last term of court, especially Talbot who knocked down a shyster lawyer by the name of Risely for saying in court that the Association could hire him to swear to anything for six

bits a day. The knocking down of Risely was highly commended by everybody here as he is the most notorious shyster in the state" (ibid., 59).

62. Ibid., 118.

63. Ibid., 118–19.

64. Ibid., 61–62; Carroll, "Whispering Smith's Hundred Dollar Hit," 8–10; DeArment, "Wyoming Range Detectives," 15.

65. Bailey, "Wyoming Stock Inspectors and Detectives," 61–62. "Hoosier" in this instance was being used in its original meaning — that is, "hayseed" or "country bumpkin," not a native of Indiana.

66. Carroll, "Whispering Smith's Hundred Dollar Hit," 8–10.

67. Bailey, "Wyoming Stock Inspectors and Detectives," 62–63.

68. Ibid., 63.

69. Ibid., 73–74.

70. Ibid., 75.

71. Ibid., 77.

72. Ibid., 78.

73. Ibid., 79.

74. Yost, *Call of the Range*, 225.

75. *Eastern Utah Advocate* (Price), February 5, 1891.

76. Cause No. 551, Third District Court, Salt Lake County, Territory of Utah, November 4, 1889.

77. Ibid.

78. *Ogden (Utah) Standard*, October 7, 1890.

79. *Eastern Utah Advocate* (Price), February 5, 1891; September 17, 1914.

80. Baker, *Wild Bunch at Robbers Roost*, 48–49.

81. *Eastern Utah Advocate* (Price), October 7, 1897.

82. Ibid., January 6, 1898.

83. Ibid. Prosecutor Warf had a penchant for taking on experienced gunfighters in deadly clashes. A few months after the exchange of bullets with Jim Smith, Warf engaged in a battle with Jack Watson, another veteran of many shooting scrapes, and killed him. See chapter 3 of DeArment, *Deadly Dozen, Volume 2*.

84. Cause No. 14, Seventh District Court, Carbon County, Utah.

85. Murphy's Exchange, at 1617 Larimer in Denver, was known as the "Slaughterhouse" by the city's sports because of the number of killings committed there.

86. Lewis, "King of the Gun-Players."

87. *George's Weekly* (Denver), September 8, 1900.

88. The *Eastern Utah Advocate* of September 17, 1914, in reporting the passing of Jim Smith, mentioned that after leaving Price, Utah, he had "bodyguarded the two blackmailing proprietors of the *Denver Post*."

89. *Denver Times*, February 7, 1905.

90. DeArment, *Broadway Bat*. After departing Denver in 1902, not 1900, Masterson went to New York City, where he had a successful career as a sportswriter and editor over the next two decades.

91. *Rocky Mountain News* (Denver), September 6, 1914.

92. U.S. Census, 1910, Chaffee County, Colorado.

93. *Denver Post*, August 27, 1914.

94. *Rocky Mountain News* (Denver), August 27, 1914.

95. The popular 1906 novel *Whispering Smith* spawned no less than six motion pictures with the catchy name "Whispering Smith" in the title. The first, *Whispering Smith*, a 1916 silent feature, starred J. P. McGowan in the title role. Serving as assistant director was the soon-to-be famous silent screen comedian Harold Lloyd. Another silent feature of the same title appeared in 1926 with H. B. Warner in the starring role. A ten-episode silent serial entitled *Whispering Smith Rides* followed in 1927. The first sound feature, *Whispering Smith Speaks*, with George O'Brien in the title role, came out in 1935. Then in 1948 Alan Ladd starred in the first big-budget *Whispering Smith*. In 1951 *Whispering Smith Hits London*, with Richard Carlson in the lead role, was a brazen exploitation of the memorable name. Audie Murphy, the most highly decorated World War II hero turned actor, starred in twenty-six thirty-minute episodes of *Whispering Smith*, a 1961 television series (www.thrilling detective..com/eyes/whispering_smith.html).

## CHAPTER 4. JIM LEVY

1. See chapters on Irish-born Pat Desmond and Mart Duggan in De-Arment, *Deadly Dozen*.

2. Secrest, "Jim Levy," 25.

3. 1820–1850 Passenger and Immigration Lists Record, Ancestry.com.

4. U.S. Census, 1860, Sacramento County, California.

5. Quoted in Ashbaugh, *Nevada's Turbulent Yesterday*, 21–22.

6. Ibid., 21.

7. Sasser, "Pioche, Nevada," 24.

8. Ashbaugh, *Nevada's Turbulent Yesterday*, 21.

9. Quoted in ibid., 22.

10. *Pioche (Nevada) Daily Record*, August 3, 1873.

11. *Territorial Enterprise* (Virginia City, Nevada), November 15, 18, 1868.

12. Lillard, *Desert Challenge*, 198; Earl, "Violent Life of a Nevada Badman," 9.

13. Earl, "Violent Life of a Nevada Badman," 10.

14. Ibid.

15. *Territorial Enterprise* (Virginia City, Nevada), March 3, 4, 28, 1871.

16. Hopkins, "Morgan Courtney," 11.

17. Sasser, "Pioche, Nevada," 27.

18. *Ely (Nevada) Record*, September 6, 1872; *Pioche (Nevada) Daily Record*, September 24, 1872.

19. *Pioche (Nevada) Daily Record*, September 24, 25, October 2, 3, 15, 1872; *Territorial Enterprise* (Virginia City, Nevada), September 28, October 17, 1872; August 8, 1873.

20. *Eureka (Nevada) Daily Sentinel*, November 10, 1872.

21. *Pioche (Nevada) Daily Record*, August 2, 3, 1873; Hopkins, "Morgan Courtney," 48. The statement was signed by five witnesses, including John Manning, a staunch Courtney admirer and professional fighting man who a month later, on September 2, 1873, engaged in a shooting duel with an Irish policeman named W. L. "Fat Mac" McKee. Manning came out second-best and joined Courtney in the Pioche graveyard (Hopkins, "Morgan Courtney," 48).

22. *Pioche (Nevada) Daily Record*, August 3, 1873.

23. *Reese River Reveille* (Austin, Nevada), August 4, 1873.

24. Ibid.

25. *Pioche (Nevada) Daily Record*, September 14, 1873.

26. Ibid., September 20, 1873.

27. Hopkins, "Morgan Courtney," 10–11.

28. Ashbaugh, *Nevada's Turbulent Yesterday*, 30; Secrest, "Jim Levy," 25.

29. *Territorial Enterprise* (Virginia City, Nevada), June 6, 1871, quoting the *Pioche (Nevada) Daily Record*.

30. Ibid.

31. Ibid. As examples of the inaccuracy of western gunfight reporting the following might by cited: the *San Francisco Examiner* of August 7, 1896, stated that Dave Neagle shot Levy while the latter was in a pistol duel with Morgan Courtney; Denis McLoughlin, in his *Wild and Woolly: An Encyclopedia of the Old West* (299), said that Levy was shot dead by Neagle in Arizona.

32. *Territorial Enterprise* (Virginia City, Nevada), June 6, 1871, quoting the *Pioche (Nevada) Daily Record*.

33. Ibid.

34. Ibid.

35. Secrest, "Jim Levy," 25.

36. Ibid., 26.

37. *Pioche (Nevada) Daily Record*, January 17, 23, 31, 1873.

38. Metz, *Encyclopedia of Lawmen, Outlaws, and Gunfighters*, 154.

39. Sasser, "Pioche, Nevada," 28.

40. *Manitowok (Wisconsin) Pilot*, March 8, 1877, quoted in Fattig, *Wyatt Earp*, 73.

41. John Bull was a prominent frontier gambler-gunman for a half a century. His career is related in DeArment, *Deadly Dozen*.

42. There were several "Billy" Allens with gunfighting renown in the West, including William G. Allen, later of Tombstone, Arizona, and William J. Allen of Leadville, Colorado. It is not clear if the "Billy" Allen cited by Peirce was either of these or another man entirely.

43. Before coming to Deadwood, where he operated as a gambler, Hardwick led a gang of whiskey peddlers and wolf hunters in northern Montana and Canada and was known as the "Green River Renegade." The murder of about forty friendly Assiniboine by Hardwick and his followers in 1872 led

to the formation of the Northwest Mounted Police in Canada (DeArment, *Knights of the Green Cloth*, 339–40).

44. Joel Collins and Sam Bass were leaders of an outlaw gang that committed a number of stagecoach robberies near Deadwood in 1877. On September 18, 1877, they pulled off a hugely successful train robbery, netting a haul of some $60,000 in gold coins. Collins was killed a week later in Kansas (Miller, *Sam Bass & Gang*).

45. Samuel S. ("Laughing Sam") Hartman was associated with the "bummers" of Leadville, the lower class of sneak thieves, footpads, and tin-horn gamblers, but he was considered dangerous. Like Joel Collins, he turned to highway robbery. Late in 1877 he was captured, convicted, and sentenced to eight years in the penitentiary (Secrest, *I Buried Hickok*, 112; Spring, *Cheyenne and Black Hills Stage and Express Routes*, 220–21).

46. According to Peirce, Clifton, "one of Quantrel's [*sic*] old band in Missouri, was another bad hombre [who] cashed in down in the Indian Territory." A "Sam Clifton" has been listed as one of William Clarke Quantrill's notorious Confederate irregulars (Breihan, *Quantrill and His Civil War Guerrillas*, 167).

47. D. Boone May was one of the most famous and feared express guards on the dangerous Cheyenne and Black Hills Stage and Express Route.

48. In an October 18, 1925, letter from Peirce to Frank J. Wilstach, quoted in Wilstach, *Wild Bill Hickok*, 267–68.

49. Walter Scott ("Quick Shot") Davis was a highly regarded express guard of the era (see chapter 3).

50. Brawler and gunman Mulqueen reportedly knocked out Wyatt Earp in a San Francisco saloon altercation a quarter century later (*San Francisco Call*, April 28, 1900).

51. Dosier was a noted Omaha gambler (DeArment, *Knights of the Green Cloth*, 315).

52. Rich, a Cheyenne gambler, was one of the three men playing cards with Hickok when Hickok was killed by Jack McCall.

53. Bill Hillman, Charley Rich, Tom Dosier, and Johnny Oyster were all pallbearers at Hickok's funeral. The other two were Jerry Lewis and Charles Young (Rosa, *They Called Him Wild Bill*, 301).

54. Storms would achieve a kind of fame by falling five years later to the deadly pistol of gambler Luke Short in Tombstone, Arizona.

55. The "pard" of Wild Bill Hickok, Utter took charge of Hickok's funeral and placed the first tombstone on his grave (Spring, *Colorado Charley*, 102).

56. Lake, *Wyatt Earp*, 158. "Doc" Peirce prepared the body for burial (Wilstach, *Wild Bill Hickok*, 283, 289).

57. Howard, *"Doc" Howard's Memoirs*, 20.

58. Masterson, "Famous Gun Fighters of the Western Frontier." It is suspected that Masterson, who lived for many years in Denver during the 1880s and 1890s, confused the Charley Harrison, the gunman he had seen in Cheyenne in 1877, with stories he heard from Denver old-timers about

Charley Harrison, the gunman who had dominated the "Bummers" of Denver in 1860–61, long before Masterson's time. See chapter 1.

59. *Cheyenne Daily Leader*, March 10, 1877.

60. "It looked like 100 to 1 that Harrison would win the fight because of his well-known courage and proficiency in the use of the pistol. . . . [He] was made a hot favorite in the betting" (Masterson, "Famous Gun Fighters of the Western Frontier").

61. *Cheyenne Daily Leader*, March 10, 1877.

62. Ibid., March 15, 1877.

63. Howard, *"Doc" Howard's Memoirs*, 20.

64. *Cheyenne Daily Leader*, March 11, 1877.

65. *Cheyenne Weekly Leader*, March 29, 1877.

66. Masterson, "Famous Gun Fighters of the Western Frontier."

67. According to historian Bill O'Neal, Masterson was no longer in Cheyenne at the time of the gunfight, the date of which O'Neal gives as March 16 rather than March 9 (*Cheyenne*, 114).

68. *Cheyenne Daily Leader*, March 10, 1877.

69. O'Neal, *Cheyenne*, 116.

70. *Cheyenne Daily Sun*, June 21, 1877.

71. Ibid.

72. *Deadwood (Dakota) Weekly Pioneer*, June 22, 1877; *Cheyenne Daily Leader*, June 20, 21, 22, 1877.

73. *Phoenix Herald*, March 4, 1881; Roberts, *Doc Holliday*, 138, 448; Jay, "Gambler's War in Tombstone," 26.

74. Roberts, *Doc Holliday*, 135.

75. Ibid., 135–36.

76. Gifford, who accepted appointment as a deputy U.S. marshal in February 1881, served in the Arizona Territory House of Representatives in the early 1880s. In 1886, together with other Tucson sporting men, he donated the land upon which the University of Arizona was built. Later he partnered Wyatt Earp in horseracing enterprises in California (DeArment, *Knights of the Green Cloth*, 131).

77. Secrest, "Jim Levy," 57.

78. *Arizona Daily Star* (Tucson), June 6, 1882.

79. Ibid.

80. Ibid.

81. Ibid., June 9, 1882.

82. Ibid., June 8, 1882.

83. Ibid., June 9, 1882.

84. Ibid.

85. Ibid., June 9, 10, 1882.

86. Ibid., June 11, 1882.

87. Ibid., June 7, 1882.

88. Ibid., October 24, 1882.

89. Ibid., October 28, 1882.

90. Quoted in ibid., November 21, 1882.

91. Carmony, *Next Stop*, 25; "PROFESSIONAL GAMBLER IS KILLED IN UNEX-PECTED ATTACK."

92. Banta (1843–1924) certainly qualified as an Arizona pioneer. He came to the territory in 1863, began work at the *Tucson Citizen* in 1870, established five newspapers, and was a scout and Indian fighter, deputy sheriff of Pima County, district attorney of Apache County, and probate judge (Banta, *Albert Franklin Banta*).

93. *Arizona Republican* (Phoenix), April 18, 1925, quoting a memoir written by Banta, March 30, 1924.

## CHAPTER 5. DAVE NEAGLE

1. U.S. Census, 1850, Suffolk County, Massachusetts; U.S. Census, 1860, San Francisco County, California; Death Certificate of David Butler Neagle; Secrest, *Lawmen and Desperadoes*, 252.

2. Bailey, *Tombstone, Arizona*, 142; Secrest, *Lawmen and Desperadoes*. 252.

3. Testifying under oath at a court hearing in August 1896, Neagle recounted in detail his mining camp peregrinations (*San Francisco Examiner*, August 6, 1896). A miner named David Neagle was enumerated in the 1870 U.S. Census at Treasure City. His age was given as twenty-nine and his birthplace as Ireland. Census records are notoriously inaccurate, however, and no doubt this was David B. Neagle, age twenty-three in 1870 and born in Massachusetts.

4. Louisa, born on April 14, 1870, died on February 15, 1875 (*San Francisco Daily Evening Bulletin*, February 16, 1875). Emma was born on October 7, 1871, and died on October 21, 1876 (*Gold Hill [Nevada] News*, October 23, 1876).

5. U.S. Census, 1900, San Francisco County, California; U.S. Census, 1910, 1920, Alameda County, California. Bertha, described as having "hair and eyes as black as those of an Andalusian," was reportedly born to French parents aboard the "old brig Moses" sailing around Cape Horn from France to San Francisco in 1854 (*San Francisco Examiner*, August 18, 1889).

6. *Territorial Enterprise* (Virginia City, Nevada), June 6, 1871, quoting the *Pioche (Nevada) Daily Record*; Metz, *Encyclopedia of Lawmen, Outlaws, and Gunfighters*, 154.

7. Wilson, *Silver Stampede*, 74.

8. Secrest, *Lawmen and Desperadoes*. 253.

9. Osgood, "Life and Times of David Neagle," 9.

10. Wilson, *Silver Stampede*, 77, 142, 179.

11. Ibid., 100.

12. Ibid., 179.

13. Ibid., 141–42.

14. Secrest, *Lawmen and Desperadoes*, 253.

15. Wilson, *Silver Stampede*, 199–200; Osgood, "Life and Times of David Neagle," 9.

16. *Pioche (Nevada) Daily Record*, August 15, 1875; U.S. Census, 1920, Alameda County, California.

17. Osgood, "Life and Times of David Neagle," 9.

18. *Pioche (Nevada) Daily Record*, March 24, 1876.

19. Secrest, *Lawmen and Desperadoes*, 253; *San Francisco Examiner*, August 6, 1896.

20. *Prescott (Arizona) Weekly Miner*, July 13, 1877.

21. Osgood, "Life and Times of David Neagle," 10; *San Francisco Examiner*, August 7, 1896.

22. *Territorial Enterprise* (Virginia City, Nevada), January 16, 1878.

23. Testimony of David Neagle at a court hearing in San Francisco, September 6, 1889, quoted in the *San Francisco Chronicle*, September 7, 1889.

24. *Tombstone (Arizona) Daily Epitaph*, September 15, 1880.

25. Breakenridge, *Helldorado*, 118.

26. Lake, *Under Cover for Wells Fargo*, 39. "I had known Dave Neagle in Nevada," said Dodge, "before either of us had thought of Tombstone."

27. Lake, *Wyatt Earp*, 252.

28. Neagle was one of a number of officers in search of the highwaymen. Accounts vary as to which officers made the arrests. Billy Breakenridge said that he and Neagle collared Spence and Stilwell (Breakenridge, *Helldorado*, 140). Fred Dodge said that he and Wyatt Earp arrested Stilwell and Morgan Earp and that Neagle nabbed Spence (Lake, *Under Cover for Wells Fargo*, 14).

29. Gatto, *Real Wyatt Earp*, 83; Shillingberg, *Tombstone A.T.*, 270.

30. *Tombstone (Arizona) Nugget*, January 31, 1882. It took some courage to ride into the Earp camp and arrest one of the members. As the paper noted, "Contrary to the expectations of some, no resistance was offered to the arrest, and the plucky deputy returned to town with his prisoner."

31. Fattig, *Wyatt Earp*, 507; DeArment, *Knights of the Green Cloth*, 79.

32. Shillingberg, *Tombstone A.T.*, 290–91; Fattig, *Wyatt Earp*, 466. Neagle reportedly spent $2,000 to win this election (Osgood, "Life and Times of David Neagle," 10).

33. Bailey, *Tombstone, Arizona*, 142–43.

34. Ibid., 143–44; *Tombstone (Arizona) Daily Epitaph*, May 11, 13, 1882; Traywick, *Tombstone's Boothill*, 91–92. A San Francisco newspaper years later, in an attempt to denigrate Neagle's courage and ability as a gunfighter, alleged that Figueroa was armed only with a .22 pistol and that Neagle dropped him with a shot from a Winchester rifle at a distance of 250 yards (*San Francisco Examiner*, August 5, 1896).

35. *Tombstone (Arizona) Daily Epitaph*, July 17, 1882; Bailey, *Tombstone, Arizona*, 144.

36. Alexander, *John H. Behan*, 205.

37. Lake, *Under Cover for Wells Fargo*, 41.

38. *Tombstone (Arizona) Weekly Epitaph*, October 21, 1882.

39. Ibid.; Bailey, *Tombstone, Arizona*, 145; Shillingberg, *Tombstone A.T.*, 330.

40. *Tombstone (Arizona) Weekly Epitaph*, November 13, 1882; Fattig, *Wyatt Earp*, 798.

41. U.S. Census, 1910 and 1920, Alameda County, California. John Behan had earlier named his son Albert; it is not known if that carries any significance.

42. *Daily Miner* (Butte, Montana), March 2, 1884; *Helena (Montana) Independent*, March 5, 1884; *Prescott (Arizona) Weekly Courier*, September 5, 1884; *Arizona Daily Star* (Tucson), August 20, 1884; Bailey and Chaput, *Cochise County Stalwarts*, 35–36; Osgood, "Life and Times of David Neagle," 11.

43. *San Francisco Examiner*, August 5, 7, 1896; Wilson, *Silver Stampede*, 309.

44. *San Francisco Examiner*, August 7, 1896.

45. Osgood, "Life and Times of David Neagle," 11. Buckley, who lost his eyesight in his thirtieth year, "was in absolute control of San Francisco for some twenty years, probably the most corrupt period in the history of the city" (Asbury, *Barbary Coast*, 193).

46. Secrest, *Lawmen and Desperadoes*, 254.

47. Osgood, "Life and Times of David Neagle," 11. The entire Sharon-Hill-Terry-Fields-Neagle story is covered in detail in Gould, *Cast of Hawks*.

48. *Freeborn County Standard* (Albert Lea, Minnesota), September 12, 1888.

49. Ibid.

50. *San Francisco Examiner*, August 6, 1896.

51. *Freeborn County Standard* (Albert Lea, Minnesota), September 12, 1888.

52. Ibid.; *Morning Oregonian* (Portland), September 4, 1888; *Idaho Daily Statesman* (Boise), September 23, 1888.

53. *Reno (Nevada) Evening Gazette*, September 17, 1888.

54. *San Francisco Examiner*, August 6, 1896.

55. Gould, *Cast of Hawks*, 299.

56. "Like many veteran gunfighters," Neagle's weapon of choice was the "old fashioned single action Colt six-shooter" (*Chicago Tribune*, August 17, 1889). Commenting on the man's armament, the *San Francisco Examiner* of August 6, 1896, reported that "Neagle carries two heavy revolvers. The favorite weapon among killers is a Colt's 44 or 45. The bore is only a matter of choice for a 44 will bore a hole big enough to cause death. The barrel is sawed off for convenience in carrying. Neagle is left-handed but shoots equally well with either hand. As he carried a pistol in each hip pocket he has an advantage over the ordinary man. He knows all the tricks."

57. Quoted in Gould, *Cast of Hawks*, 301–302.

58. Ibid., 302; Osgood, "Life and Times of David Neagle," 16. These were certainly dangerous days for judges in California. Only the day earlier Judge W. L. Pierce of San Diego's Supreme Court had been shot and seriously injured in that city by a man named W. S. Clendenin, who objected to the judge's ruling in Clendenin's divorce action against his wife (*Reno [Nevada] Evening Gazette*, August 15, 1889).

59. It was reported in a dispatch from San Francisco that "the marshals believe Mrs. Terry took a weapon from her husband's body" (*Sandusky [Ohio] Daily Register*, August 16, 1889). No weapon was found when Terry's body was examined moments after the shooting, and Sarah later claimed that her husband had left his weapons on the train before going to the dining room (Gould, *Cast of Hawks*, 303).

60. Ibid., 302.

61. Osgood, "Life and Times of David Neagle," 16.

62. Gould, *Cast of Hawks*, 305.

63. Ibid., 307–308.

64. Ibid., 308.

65. Dispatches from Lathrop and San Francisco published in the *Reno (Nevada) Evening Gazette*, August 17, 1889.

66. *Salt Lake Tribune*, August 20, 1889.

67. Osgood, "Life and Times of David Neagle," 16.

68. Quoted in Roberts, "Pursuit of Duty," 33.

69. Quoted in Secrest, *Lawmen and Desperadoes*, 255.

70. *San Francisco Examiner*, August 18, 1889.

71. *Reno (Nevada) Evening Gazette*, August 14, 1889.

72. Ibid.

73. Quoted in Roberts, "Pursuit of Duty," 33.

74. Quoted in Gould, *Cast of Hawks*, 320.

75. *Sandusky (Ohio) Daily Register*, September 6, 7, 1889. Neagle's version of the shooting given later to friends and acquaintances was contradictory in several respects. Harry Gorman, an old friend from the Comstock, ran into Neagle some years later when Neagle returned to Virginia City to visit his sister. Pulling out "a well-worn six-shooter which showed the friction of many years of use," Neagle said it was the gun he used to kill Terry. Gorman noticed he drew it from his left side with his left hand. "The action was so fast that it was all over in a moment or two," said Neagle. When Terry struck Fields, "I arose and, with my right hand forward, told him, 'Step back, I am a United States officer.' He was not three feet away. It appeared as if he saw me for the first time. . . . I have never seen such an expression of anger and hate in the face of any human being. His eyes blazed. In spite of his more than seventy years, he presented a most formidable appearance. . . . As he saw me a look of recognition was blended with the other expressions, and he reached for the knife. I knew that in a moment either he or I would be a dead man." Neagle said he drew his gun with his left hand, but grasped it also with his right "to prevent its being grasped or deflected," and fired. "As he fell I fired again, and under my breath, as he sank slowly to the floor, I muttered to myself, 'That one is for Broderick.'" Gorman believed Neagle to be "as cold and calm under stress as any man that ever lived, and when Terry raised his hand in menace and defiance, he sealed his death warrant; he was doomed to die" (Gorman, *My Memories of the Comstock*, 170–72). As a young man in San Francisco, Jeffrey Schweitzer often saw Neagle, who was friendly with

Schweitzer's father. "A quiet, gentlemanly fellow who did little talking," Neagle on one occasion described the Terry shooting. "He said that after Judge Terry had assaulted Justice Field, he [Neagle] jumped between them pushing Judge Terry back with his right hand, keeping his left hand in his pants pocket. Judge Terry did not know Dave was left-handed and when the judge made the motion assumed by Dave that he (Terry) was about to pull a knife, Dave shot him with the pistol concealed in his left pants pocket. As the judge was falling Dave shot him a second time through the eye, the pistol still being concealed in his pocket. The impression that Dave gave me was that the second shot was not necessary but that he wanted to be positive the judge would cause no more trouble" (Schweitzer, "Letter to the Editor").

76. In the August 20, 1889, issue of the *San Francisco Examiner* a writer speculated that in shooting Terry, Neagle may have employed the "Pioche Trick," which he went on to describe: "[The shooter] looks the man in the face and he talks to him, and the man seeing his right hand is empty feels safe. If he pushed him with the left hand the man might look to see what he was doing with his right. As he throws the right hand across the man's breast and says, 'Stop!' he slides his gun out with his left, and keeping it under cover of the right hand gets it against the man's body and fires. The victim drops, and as he falls one or two more shots can be got in. It is one of the safest ways to shoot a man at close range, because if he does not see the weapon he cannot grab it and perhaps disarm the shooter. Of course I do not say that Neagle did shoot that way because I did not see him, but I think he knew of the trick, having lived over in Pioche and being familiar with the use of pistols as a man had to be in those days" (*New York Times*, September 4, 1889).

77. *Fitchburg (Massachusetts) Sentinel*, September 17, 1889; *Reno (Nevada) Evening Gazette*, September 16, 1889.

78. Gould, *Cast of Hawks*, 322.

79. Ibid., 327. Neagle evidently did not go across the country to Washington to hear the arguments in his case. In the last week of February 1890 he was in Nevada, visiting friends in Reno and Virginia City. On February 23 Alfred Doten, a longtime resident of Virginia City, noted in his journal that Neagle, whom he had known for years, had arrived from San Francisco, and the two old friends spent an "evening about town" and did not get to bed until one o'clock (Doten, *Journals of Alfred Doten*, 1759). The *Daily Nevada State Journal* of Reno on February 25 commented that Neagle had arrived in that town the night before from Virginia City.

80. Gould, *Cast of Hawks*, 327.

81. Ibid.; Osgood, "Life and Times of David Neagle," 16.

82. Quoted in Gould, *Cast of Hawks*, 328.

83. *Daily Nevada State Journal* (Reno), August 15, 1896.

84. Reprinted in the *Arizona Republican* (Phoenix), August 8, 1896.

85. Ibid., August 5, 1896; *Daily Nevada State Journal* (Reno), August 5, 1896.

86. *San Francisco Examiner*, August 5, 1896.

87. *Arizona Republican* (Phoenix), August 8, 1896.

88. Ibid. The *Reno (Nevada) Weekly Gazette and Stockman* three years earlier (July 13, 1893) had said that Neagle had "considerable notoriety as a gun fighter." James Barry would later publish a book in which the author included Neagle, "the gunfighter, who numbered among his accomplishments the slaying of Judge Terry," among the unsavory characters of San Francisco (Shillingberg, *Tombstone A.T.*, 361).

89. *Reno (Nevada) Evening Gazette*, August 7, 1896.

90. Ibid., April 12, 1896; *Daily Nevada State Journal* (Reno), August 15, 1896; *San Francisco Call*, August 13, 1896.

91. *San Francisco Call*, August 14, 1896.

92. The articles under the byline "Wyatt S. Earp," but no doubt written by a ghostwriter, probably ace reporter Robert Chambers, appeared in the *Examiner* issues of August 2, 9, and 16, 1896.

93. In a letter to Neagle's widowed sister, Mrs. M. J. Kelly of Virginia City, July 18, 1886, Stewart referred to "your brother, Mr. David Neagle . . . , an old friend of mine." Neagle called on the senator for political favors in at least two letters, February 14, 1901, and October 2, 1901 (William M. Stewart records, Nevada State Historical Society).

94. Secrest, *Lawmen and Desperadoes*, 255; Bailey and Chaput, *Cochise County Stalwarts*, 37.

95. U.S. Census, 1910, 1920, Oakland, Alameda County, California.

96. *Oakland (California) Daily Evening Tribune*, November 30, 1925.

## CHAPTER 6. BILLY BROOKS

1. Sifakis, *Encyclopedia of American Crime*, 100.

2. Goodnight et al., *Pioneer Days in the Southwest*, 35.

3. Rideout, *Six Years on the Border*, 98.

4. Streeter, *Prairie Trails and Cow Towns*, 139.

5. U.S. Census, 1860, Clermont County, Ohio; U.S. Census, 1870, Butler County, Kansas.

6. Sandoz, *Buffalo Hunters*, 161; Streeter, *Prairie Trails and Cow Towns*, 139.

7. Bentley, *History of Wichita and Sedgwick County, Kansas*, 457.

8. Brooks was "reputed to have killed several men in gunfights in the 1860s" (Sifakis, *Encyclopedia of American Crime*, 100).

9. *Kansas Daily Commonwealth* (Topeka), June 14, 1872.

10. Ibid.; Rosa and Koop, *Rowdy Joe Lowe*.

11. *Wichita (Kansas) Eagle*, June 14, 1872.

12. Roberts, *From Tin Star to Hanging Tree*, 15–16; Miller and Snell, *Why the West Was Wild*, 51–52.

13. Roberts, *From Tin Star to Hanging Tree*, 16.

14. Miller and Snell, *Why the West Was Wild*, 52.

15. Quoted in Wright, *Dodge City*, 144.

16. *Leavenworth (Kansas) Daily Commercial*, October 5, 1872.

17. "From Mrs. Anthony's Diary," *Dodge City Globe-Republican*, June 30, 1898, quoted in Roberts, *From Tin Star to Hanging Tree*, 19–20.

18. Rideout, *Six Years on the Border*, 100.

19. Rath, *Early Ford County*, 264.

20. *Newton Kansan*, November 21, 1872.

21. *Leavenworth (Kansas) Daily Commercial*, November 21, 1872.

22. *Kansas City (Missouri) Times*, November 22, 1872.

23. *Herald and Torch Light* (Hagerstown, Maryland), December 4, 1872, reprinted from the *Kansas City (Missouri) Times*.

24. *Topeka (Kansas) Daily Commonwealth*, November 22, 1872.

25. Raymond to Beeson, September 25, 1936.

26. Goodnight et al., *Pioneer Days in the Southwest*, 35.

27. Raine, *Famous Sheriffs and Western Outlaws*, 7.

28. Goodnight et al., *Pioneer Days in the Southwest*, 36–38. Stuart Lake, in his biography of Wyatt Earp, repeats, without attribution, Dubbs's reminiscences uncritically. Unlike his contemporary writer William MacLeod Raine, he accepts Dubbs's statement that Brooks killed fifteen men in his first thirty days as "marshal" at Dodge. He even expanded on Dubbs's tale of this gunfight, writing that Brooks "single-handed[ly]" shot it out with the four brothers and killed "all four with as many shots from his sixgun while they cut loose at him ineffectively" (Lake, *Wyatt Earp*, 138–39).

29. Roberts, *From Tin Star to Hanging Tree*, 26.

30. Ibid., 27.

31. *Wichita (Kansas) Beacon*, February 19, 1873.

32. Ibid., February 26, 1873.

33. Edwards to Simpson, November 18, 1925.

34. *Wichita (Kansas) Eagle*, January 2, 1873.

35. Jesse Drew, a nineteen-year-old prostitute, was enumerated in the organization census taken at Dodge in January 1873. Also enumerated was Henry Brown, age twenty-one, who may have been Brooks's shooting victim (Rath, *Early Ford County*, 261–64).

36. Wright, *Dodge City*, 170.

37. *Kansas Daily Commonwealth* (Topeka), December 31, 1872.

38. *Dodge City (Kansas) Democrat*, June 19, 1903.

39. Wright, *Dodge City*, 171.

40. Dykstra, *Cattle Towns*, 113.

41. Young, *Dodge City*, 45.

42. Roberts, *From Tin Star to Hanging Tree*, 20.

43. Young, *Hard Knocks*, 167.

44. Drago, *Wild, Woolly and Wicked*, 282; Carter, *Cowboy Capital of the World*, 42.

45. Snell, "Diary of a Dodge City Buffalo Hunter," 262.

46. Ibid.

47. Vestal, *Queen of Cowtowns*, 95.

48. Wright, *Dodge City*, 171.

49. Snell, "Diary of a Dodge City Buffalo Hunter," 262.
50. Roberts, *From Tin Star to Hanging Tree*, 40.
51. Snell, "Diary of a Dodge City Buffalo Hunter," 262.
52. Beeson to Campbell, May 1951.
53. Lake, *Wyatt Earp*, 186.
54. Roberts, *From Tin Star to Hanging Tree*, 43–44. After meticulous research Earp biographer Lee Silva states flatly: "I have found no record of a shootout between Morgan Earp and Billy Brooks, or ANYONE, ANYWHERE in Montana" (Silva, *Wyatt Earp*, Vol. 1, 661).
55. DeArment, " 'Hurricane Bill' Martin."
56. *Denver Field and Farm*, March 10, 1900.
57. Kirk Jordan was later convicted of horse stealing. On his way to prison he reportedly jumped from a moving train and broke his neck (Roberts, *From Tin Star to Hanging Tree*, 49–50).
58. DeArment, " 'Hurricane Bill' Martin."
59. McLean kept a saloon on the road just south of Caldwell with a sign reading "Last Chance" for travelers heading toward Indian Territory, and "First Chance" for those arriving from the territory. It was for years a notorious rendezvous for outlaws and bad men (Roberts, *From Tin Star to Hanging Tree*, 71).
60. Named as members of the conspiracy were Henry Hall, Jerry Williams, Jasper Marion (alias "Granger"), Dave Terrill, William Brandon, William Watkins, and three others known only by their nicknames: "Red," "Bob," and "Jim" (*Sumner County Press* [Wellington, Kansas], August 6, 1874; Roberts, *From Tin Star to Hanging Tree*, 61).
61. *Sumner County Press* (Wellington, Kansas), July 2, 1874.
62. *Kansas Daily Commonwealth* (Topeka), July 17, 1874.
63. Roberts, *From Tin Star to Hanging Tree*, 64–65.
64. *Sumner County Press* (Wellington, Kansas), July 30, 1874.
65. Ibid.
66. Ibid.
67. There were reportedly two other men in the dugout with Brooks, but there were no charges against them, and they were later released (Roberts, *From Tin Star to Hanging Tree*, 77).
68. Rideout, *Six Years on the Border*, 98–100.
69. Ibid., 100–101.
70. Roberts, *From Tin Star to Hanging Tree*, 77.
71. *Sumner County Press* (Wellington, Kansas), July 30, 1874.
72. Ibid. The news of the hangings went out over the press wires. The *Burlington (Iowa) Hawkeye* of July 31, 1874, printed a dispatch datelined St. Louis that vigilantes near Wellington had hanged three men "Bell, Brooks and Smith," who, before their demise, had confessed to horse stealing, and said twenty others were involved.
73. Rideout, *Six Years on the Border*, 106–107.
74. Roberts, *From Tin Star to Hanging Tree*, 85.

## CHAPTER 7. PORT STOCKTON

1. U.S. Census, 1850, Upshur County, Texas; U.S. Census, 1860, Hopkins County, Texas; Wahl to DeArment, January 16, 2006. The U.S. Census of 1880 gave the ages of both Port and Ike as twenty-nine years, leading one author to erroneously conclude that the brothers were twins (Peters, "Vengeance of Bert Wilkinson," 45).

2. *Fort Worth (Texas) Daily Democrat*, March 19, 1881, quoting the *Durango (Colorado) Record*.

3. In a 1973 article for a western magazine a writer asserted that at the age of twelve Port killed a man who had abused him, but he went free as nothing could be proved. It appears nothing can be proved about this claim as well. Belief in the author's credibility is strained when, in the space of two short sentences, several factual errors appear, the writer erroneously stating that Port was the younger brother and was born in Erath County, Texas, in 1851 (Jones, "New Mexico's Stockton Gang," 39). The canard that Port killed his first man at the age of twelve is repeated in Hawk, "He Lived by the Sword," 3.

4. Those providing his bail were J. R. O'Neal, W. C. Bibb, and John Alsup.

5. *List of Fugitives from Justice, 1878*; Cause No. 179, *Erath County, State of Texas v. Porter Stockton, Assault with Intent to Murder*.

6. Stanley, *Desperadoes of New Mexico*, 173–75.

7. Tom Bicknell, who has researched the Thompson brothers for years, has found no contemporary reference to a Stockton in Ellsworth (Bicknell to DeArment, February 26, 2006), and Ellsworth historian Jim Gray has "never come across any mention of anyone by the name of Stockton being in Ellsworth" (Gray to DeArment, March 1, 2006).

8. Emily Jane Cowan evidently married a man named Marshall before marrying Port. U.S. Census, 1860, Erath County, Texas; U.S. Census, 1880, Rio Arriba County, Colorado; Peters, "Vengeance of Bert Wilkinson," 45–46; Wahl to DeArment, February 28, 2006; Peters to DeArment, March 1, 2006.

9. *Las Vegas (New Mexico) Optic*, January 16, 1881.

10. Nunis, "Biographical Notes," 345–47; Nunis, "Place Notes," 353.

11. Conard, *"Uncle Dick" Wootten*, 436.

12. Schoenberger, *Gunfighters*, 5.

13. Wootten said the shooting took place "two days before Christmas," or December 23. The date has also been given as December 27 (Parsons, *Clay Allison*, 13).

14. Possemen accompanying Stockton, it is said, were Mason T. Bowman, later a noted New Mexico lawman who was then going under the name "Matt Mason," and Nick Camblin (Parsons, *Clay Allison*, 13). Stockton may have been legally deputized to lead this posse. According to a later newspaper report the posse was led by a Las Animas County, Colorado, deputy sheriff (*Aspen [Colorado] Weekly Times*, September 27, 1884, quoting the *Rocky Mountain News*), but he certainly acted illegally when he pursued his quarry into New Mexico.

15. Conard, *"Uncle Dick Wootten,"* 436–37.

16. Parsons, *Clay Allison*, 14–15; Rasch, "Sudden Death in Cimarron," 14–16; Hornung, "By the Banks of the Cimarron."

17. Hornung, "By the Banks of the Cimarron."

18. The famous gunfighter John Wesley Hardin also allegedly killed a man to still his snoring. Writers intent on sensationalism seem to have been attracted to this apocryphal story.

19. Ibid.; Rasch, "Sudden Death in Cimarron," 14–16; Criminal Cause No. 416, Colfax County, New Mexico. Brother Ike Stockton told a reporter in 1881 his version of the killing and insisted that, despite newspaper reports that Port had downed eighteen or nineteen victims, this was the only person he ever killed (*Denver Republican*, August 12, 1881).

20. Governor's Correspondence, New Mexico Territorial Archives, Santa Fe.

21. Ibid.; *Colorado Daily Chieftain* (Pueblo), September 3, 1876.

22. *Santa Fe New Mexican*, September 18, 1876; Hornung, "By the Banks of the Cimarron"; Rasch, "Sudden Death in Cimarron," 16.

23. *Rocky Mountain News* (Denver), March 31, 1881.

24. Stanley, *Desperadoes of New Mexico*, 178; O'Neal, *Encyclopedia of Western Gunfighters*, 302.

25. Stanley, in his *Desperadoes of New Mexico* (178), relates this story, and again it is repeated in O'Neal, *Encyclopedia of Western Gunfighters*, 302.

26. Howe, *Timberleg of the Diamond Tail*, 45.

27. DeArment, "Revenge!" 58.

28. Rasch, "Sudden Death in Cimarron," 7; Hornung, "By the Banks of the Cimarron."

29. Quoted in Chesley, *Adventuring with the Old-timers*, 94. In other reports the Withers killed was William (Rasch, "Sudden Death in Cimarron," 7; Hornung, "By the Banks of the Cimarron").

30. Rasch, "Sudden Death in Cimarron," 7.

31. Ibid.; Hornung, "By the Banks of the Cimarron."

32. Haley, *Charles Goodnight*, 343; *Fort Griffin (Texas) Echo*, April 10, 1880; *Las Vegas (New Mexico) Daily Gazette*, April 14, 1880; Rasch, "Alias Whiskey Jim"; Goodnight to Haley, April 8, 1927.

33. One report had it that for a short time Port held the city marshal post at Rico in the adjoining county of Dolores (O'Neal, *Encyclopedia of Western Gunfighters*, 301), but this has not been confirmed.

34. *Ouray (Colorado) Times*, February 28, 1880. Animas City was about two miles north of the new town of Durango, which would eventually swallow it up.

35. *Dolores News* (Rico, Colorado), September 18, 1880.

36. *La Plata Miner* (Silverton, Colorado), July 17, 1880, quoting the *Animas City Southwest*.

37. Ibid.; *Dolores News* (Rico, Colorado), July 10, 1880.

38. Coe, *Frontier Fighter*, 258.

39. Bechner, *Guns along the Silvery San Juan*.

40. *Santa Fe New Mexican*, April 9, 1881; Rasch, "Tom Nance," 25.

41. U.S. Census, 1880, Taos County, New Mexico.

42. *Santa Fe New Mexican*, April 9, 1881.

43. Ibid.; *Dolores News* (Rico, Colorado), September 18, 1880.

44. *La Plata Miner* (Silverton, Colorado), September 25, 1880, quoting the *Animas City Southwest*.

45. Ibid.

46. Englin was also publisher of the town's paper, the *Animas City Southwest*.

47. *Dolores News* (Rico, Colorado), September 18, 1880.

48. Ibid.; *Dolores News* (Rico, Colorado), September 18, 1880; Charles Naeglin interview, January 17, 1934.

49. Quoted in Bechner, *Guns along the Silvery San Juan*. Stanley has written that after leaving Las Animas, Port went to Rico, Colorado, where he applied for and received appointment as city marshal, but soon was discharged when he got into an argument with a man and "used a shotgun to blast his head off" (*Private War of Ike Stockton*, 93). The author provided no source for this assertion, however, and, like many other stories in his book, this one seems to be fictional.

50. Rasch, "Sudden Death in Cimarron," 8.

51. Rasch, "Tom Nance," 25.

52. Naeglin, interview.

53. *Dolores News* (Rico, Colorado), June 26, 1880, quoted in Benson, "Port Stockton," 25.

54. George Coe identifies this man as "Halford" (*Frontier Fighter*, 239).

55. McHenry to Wallace, March 30, 1881.

56. Ibid.; *Dolores News* (Rico, Colorado), September 4, 1880; March 19, 1881; Rasch, "Tom Nance," 25; Bechner, *Guns along the Silvery San Juan*.

57. Rasch, "Feuding at Farmington"; Rasch, "Tom Nance," 25.

58. Erastus Thompson interview, July 31, 1934.

59. Bechner, *Guns along the Silvery San Juan*. The battle delayed the dedication of a new hotel scheduled for that day, but more than fifty years later visitors to the city were being shown bullet marks where chunks of brick had been shot from the face of the building (ibid.).

60. *Dolores News* (Rico, Colorado), February 5, 1881; Peters, "Vengeance of Bert Wilkinson," 47.

61. F. Stanley, in *The Private War of Ike Stockton* (100–104) and *Desperadoes of New Mexico* (180), has Port at the head of this group and taking the lead in the gunplay that followed, but none of the contemporary papers mention him as being present. Significantly, Jasper Coe, a bitter enemy of the Stocktons, in a letter to the *Daily Gazette* of Colorado Springs, Colorado (March 27, 1881), also does not place Port at the scene. Oscar's name was spelled "Pruett" in some newspaper reports, but editor Jones of the *Dolores News* (Rico, Colorado), who claimed to know the man well, consistently spelled it "Puett."

62. *Dolores News* (Rico, Colorado), April 30, 1881.
63. *Colorado Springs (Colorado) Daily Gazette*, March 27, 1881.
64. Reprinted in the *La Plata Miner* (Silverton, Colorado), January 8, 1881.
65. McHenry to Wallace.
66. *Dolores News* (Rico, Colorado), January 22, 1881; *Freeborn County Standard* (Albert Lea, Minnesota), February 3, 1881; *Bismarck (Dakota Territory) Daily Tribune*, February 4, 1881; *Fort Worth (Texas) Daily Democrat*, March 19, 1881, reprinted from the *Durango (Colorado) Record*.
67. *Denver Republican*, August 12, 1881; McHenry to Wallace; Rasch, "Tom Nance," 25.
68. *Daily Gazette* (Colorado Springs, Colorado), March 27, 1881. Emily Stockton was more than "slightly hurt," according to the *Dolores News* (Rico, Colorado) of April 30, 1881: "One shot fired at her passed through the right hand and on through the left arm, paralyzing that limb, and rendering both limbs useless. Another shot entered the lower part of the left breast, ranging downward into the left side, where it is now lodged."
69. *Dolores News* (Rico, Colorado), April 23, 1881.
70. From the *Durango (Colorado) Record*, reprinted in a number of papers.
71. *San Francisco Bulletin*, March 31, 1881, and papers from Baltimore; Trenton, New Jersey; and New Haven, Connecticut, in the East, to Chicago and Owyhee, Idaho, in the West.
72. *Dolores News* (Rico, Colorado), January 22, 1881.
73. *Denver Republican*, August 12, 1881.
74. Naeglin, interview.
75. *Dolores News* (Rico, Colorado), January 22, 1881.
76. From the *Durango (Colorado) Record*, repeated in a number of papers.
77. *Las Vegas (New Mexico) Daily Gazette*, January 16, 1881.
78. Gilbreath, *Death on the Gallows*, 217.
79. Stanley, *Private War of Ike Stockton*, 105.

## CHAPTER 8. IKE STOCKTON

1. U.S. Census, 1850, Upshur County, Texas; U.S. Census, 1860, Hopkins County, Texas; Wahl to DeArment, January 16, 2006.
2. Both girls had been raised in the same household, that of stock farmer Isaac Robinson and his wife of Stephenville, Erath County, Texas. Their mother was Sarah Hickey (U.S. Census, 1860, Erath County, Texas; U.S. Census, 1880, Rio Arriba County, Colorado; Peters, "Vengeance of Bert Wilkinson," 45–46; Wahl to DeArment, February 28, 2006; Peters to DeArment, March 1, 2006).
3. U.S. Census, 1880, Animas City, La Plata County, Colorado.
4. O'Neal, *Encyclopedia of Gunfighters*, 301; Bechner, *Guns along the Silvery San Juan*.
5. Bechner, *Guns along the Silvery San Juan*.
6. Mullin, *Maurice Garland Fulton's History of the Lincoln County War*, 159.

7. Zamonski, "Rougher Than Hell," 301. Tom Lacy was said to be a first cousin to the Stockton boys (*Dolores News* [Rico, Colorado], May 28, 1881). The middle name of Dick Wootten, who owned and operated a toll road and roadhouse at Raton Pass, was Lacy. There may have been a family connection with Wootten also.

8. Coe, *Frontier Fighter*, 242.

9. Rasch, "Feuding at Farmington;" Rasch, "Tom Nance," 25.

10. *Dolores News* (Rico, Colorado), July 24, 1880. Wilkinson, said to be "a highwayman and murderer" at the age of nineteen, reportedly came from one of the best families in the nation. His grandfather "was for many years a member of the Indiana legislature," and his father, who held posts as Indian agent for the Upper Missouri Sioux and register of the U.S. Land Office at Vermillion, Dakota Territory, was a cousin of Hon. James F. Harlan of Iowa (*Durango [Colorado] Herald*, September 8, 1881).

11. *Arizona Weekly Star* (Tucson), April 21, 1881.

12. *Dolores News*, February 5, April 23, 1881.

13. *Santa Fe New Mexican*, March 1, 1881.

14. Ibid., March 12, 1881.

15. *Denver Republican*, August 12, 1881.

16. *Colorado Springs (Colorado) Daily Gazette*, March 27, 1881.

17. *Dolores News* (Rico, Colorado), April 23, 1881.

18. *La Plata (Silverton, Colorado) Miner*, March 12, 1881. Although the paper reported Radigan was "doing well," surgeons amputated his leg at Fort Lewis, where he remained for two months (*Dolores News* [Rico, Colorado], September 10, 1881).

19. Rasch, "Other Allison," 14. The bullet evidently traversed an erratic course down Allison's leg, causing a great deal of damage. When he entered the Colorado State Penitentiary seven months later, the injury was described as a "gunshot wound below the left groin and on inside of thigh, and one above the knee, and two on back of leg — all on left leg" (Dugan, *Bandit Years*, 69).

20. *Dolores News* (Rico, Colorado), March 19, 1881.

21. Early New Mexico historian George B. Anderson, while portraying the Stocktons and their followers as "cattle thieves," noted that the Farmington cowboys, "while honest, ran wild at times. . . . 'Shooting up the town' — such town as there was at Farmington at the time — was a not an uncommon form of diversion" (*History of New Mexico*, 863).

22. The phrase "Reign of Terror" was picked up and repeated in a wire dispatch reprinted in newspapers as widely dispersed as the *San Francisco Bulletin*, March 31, 1881; *Chicago Daily Inter-Ocean*, April 1, 1881; *Baltimore Sun*, April 2, 1881; *New Haven (Connecticut), Register*, April 2, 1881; *Trenton (New Jersey) State Gazette*, April 4, 1881; and *Owyhee (Idaho) Avalanche*, April 23, 1881.

23. *Colorado Springs (Colorado) Daily Gazette*, March 27, 1881.

24. McHenry to Wallace.

25. *Aspen (Colorado) Weekly Times*, May 21, 1881; Rasch, "Other Allison."
26. *Denver Republican*, August 12, 1881.
27. Dugan, *Bandit Years*, 71; Rasch, "Other Allison," 14.
28. Quoted in the *Dolores News* (Rico, Colorado), July 2, 1881.
29. *Dolores News* (Rico, Colorado), July 2, 1881.
30. Ibid., April 16, 1881; Rasch, "Tom Nance," 49.
31. *Dolores News* (Rico, Colorado), April 16, 1881.
32. Ibid.
33. Ibid., April 30, 1881, reprinted from the *Ouray (Colorado) Times*.
34. *Daily Nevada Sate Journal* (Reno), April 2, 1881.
35. *Atchison (Kansas) Globe*, April 15, 1881.
36. *Wellsboro (Pennsylvania) Agitator*, April 19, 1881.
37. *La Plata Miner* (Silverton, Colorado), April 9, 1881; *Dolores News* (Rico, Colorado), April 9, 1881.
38. *Santa Fe New Mexican*, April 8, 1881.
39. This report was repeated in the "New Mexico News" section of the April 21, 1881, edition of the *Arizona Weekly Star* (Tucson), which added the additional inflammatory information that Stockton was at Durango, Colorado, "awaiting reinforcements from Texas, when he expects to descend on Rio Arriba county."
40. The dispatch, printed in the *Denver Republican*, April 14, 1881, was picked up and reprinted in newspapers as far away as Butte, Montana (*Daily Miner*, April 16, 1881).
41. *Dolores News* (Rico, Colorado), April 23, 1881, quoting the *Durango (Colorado) Record*.
42. Ibid., April 30, 1881.
43. Ibid.
44. *Santa Fe New Mexican*, April 27, 1881.
45. Ibid.
46. *Santa Fe New Mexican*, May 6, 1881. The incident in which "one citizen was killed and one outlaw wounded" must have been the gunfight on the La Plata where Barker lost his life and Radigan was injured.
47. *Atlanta Constitution*, May 6, 1881, printing a bulletin from Durango dated May 5.
48. *Dolores News* (Rico, Colorado), May 14, 1881.
49. Ibid.
50. *Santa Fe New Mexican*, May 19, 1881, quoted in Stanley, *Ike Stockton*, 127.
51. Reprinted in the *Aspen (Colorado) Weekly Times*, May 21, 1881.
52. Ibid., May 28, 1881.
53. Jones, "Lynching of Bert Wilkinson."
54. *Dolores News* (Rico, Colorado), May 21, 1881.
55. Ibid., May 28, 1881.
56. Quoted in Jones, "Lynching of Bert Wilkinson."
57. *Santa Fe New Mexican*, June 4, 1881.

58. *La Plata Miner* (Silverton, Colorado), January 25, May 17, 1879; May 14, 1881.

59. Ibid., May 28, 1881.

60. *Dolores News* (Rico, Colorado), June 4, 1881.

61. One historian postulated that the operations of "a notorious band of cattle thieves" led by the Stockton brothers "were primarily responsible for the so-called war between the white settlers and the Indians" (Anderson, *History of New Mexico*, 863).

62. In a "special telegram" to the *Chicago Daily Inter-Ocean* of June 25, 1881, a correspondent reported that "Ike Stockton and J. H. Eskridge, two of the so-styled outlaws of Durango, were also killed, the latter being shot six times."

63. *Chicago Daily Inter-Ocean*, October 1, 1881.

64. Quoted in Bechner, *Guns along the Silvery San Juan.*

65. *Dolores News* (Rico, Colorado), July 18, 1881.

66. Ibid.

67. *Santa Fe New Mexican*, August 7, 1881.

68. *Dolores News* (Rico, Colorado), August 13, 1881.

69. Ibid., August 27, 1881.

70. *Denver Republican*, August 12, 1881.

71. Bechner, *Guns along the Silvery San Juan.*

72. A gambler named Edwards was wounded by a stray bullet in the saloon, and two rounds ripped through the clothes of the bartender (*Dolores News* [Rico, Colorado], August 27, 1881; Peters, "Vengeance of Bert Wilkinson," 47).

73. *San Juan Herald* (Silverton, Colorado), August 25, 1881.

74. Ibid.

75. Ibid., September 1, 1881.

76. *San Juan Herald* (Silverton, Colorado), September 1, 1881.

77. *Dolores News* (Rico, Colorado), August 27, 1881.

78. *Ouray (Colorado) Times*, August 27, 1881.

79. *Durango (Colorado) Record*, September 1, 1881.

80. *Rocky Mountain News* (Denver), September 1, 1881.

81. David J. Cook, founder and head of the Rocky Mountain Detective Agency, called Hawley "one of the most courageous as well as one of the shrewdest members of the association" (Cook, *Hands Up*, 86).

82. *Rocky Mountain News* (Denver), September 1, 1881.

83. Ibid.

84. *Durango (Colorado) Southwest*, August 31, 1881, quoted in the *Dolores News* (Rico, Colorado), September 3, 1881.

85. Ibid.

86. Quoted in the *Dolores News*, September 3, 1881.

87. *Colorado Springs (Colorado) Daily Gazette*, September 1, 1881.

88. *La Plata Miner* (Silverton, Colorado), quoted in the *Dolores News* (Rico, Colorado), September 10, 1881.

89. Ibid.

90. *San Juan Herald* (Silverton, Colorado), September 8, 1881.

91. *Durango (Colorado) Herald*, September 8, 1881.

92. *Dolores News* (Rico, Colorado), September 10, 1881.

93. Ibid.

94. Jones, "Lynching of Bert Wilkinson."

95. *Colorado Springs (Colorado) Daily Gazette*, September 16, 1881.

96. Durango had long been in need of a sturdy jail. Ten months earlier, in its issue of December 11, 1880, the *La Plata Miner* of Silverton had commented: "What Durango needs most just at present is a good strong calaboose, as the town is filled up with professedly bad men, who need to be tied down occasionally to keep them within bounds. Mr. James Sullivan, who is acting as deputy sheriff, although a very efficient officer, is rendered almost powerless from the fact that if he does arrest a man for a breach of the peace, he has no place to confine him unless he takes him to Animas City. Consequently the only thing he can do is to knock down and rag out, which he does successfully."

97. The *Dolores News* (Rico, Colorado), October 1, 1881, reported that Dr. H. A. Clay performed the amputation, assisted by Drs. Davis, Smith, Tracy, Griffith, Bellinger, and Folsom.

98. *Atlanta Constitution*, September 28, 1881; *Denver Tribune*, September 28, 1881; *Durango (Colorado) Herald*, September 29, 1881; *Colorado Springs (Colorado) Daily Gazette*, September 30, 1881; *Dolores News* (Rico, Colorado), October 1, 1881; *San Juan Herald* (Silverton, Colorado), October 6, 1881. In *An Empire of Silver* (117), author Robert L. Brown gives a particularly fallacious account of Ike Stockton's final days. His accomplice in the treacherous arrest of Wilkinson, according to this story, was not M. C. Cook but, amazingly, Jim Sullivan, and "the citizens took the case out of [Marshal Watson's] hands and summarily executed both Stockton and Sullivan by the good old cottonwood route."

99. *Colorado Springs (Colorado) Daily Gazette*, September 30, 1881.

100. *Dolores News* (Rico, Colorado), October 1, 1881.

### CHAPTER 9. JIM MCINTIRE

1. A new edition, with annotations and notes by Robert K. DeArment, published in 1992 by the University of Oklahoma Press, is cited throughout this chapter.

2. Siringo, *Riata and Spurs*, 189.

3. Cunningham, *Triggernometry*, 208.

4. Hunter and Rose, *Album of Gunfighters*, 158.

5. U.S. Census, 1850, 1860, Brown County, Ohio; U.S. Census, 1870, Lawrence County, Ohio; Donaldson, *Brown County, Ohio, Marriage Records*; Colletta and Puckett, *Tombstone Inscriptions of Brown County, Ohio*, 273.

6. McIntire, *Early Days in Texas*, 11–16, 120–21.

7. Ibid., 16–17, 121.

8. Ibid., 20–27, 123–24.

9. Ibid., 52–53. Interviewed years later by army captain W. S. Nye, a Kiowa named Hunting Horse, who was in the fight, admitted that the Indians mutilated the Ranger's body, but mentioned no cannibalism: "Lone Wolf got off his horse and chopped the man's head to pieces with his brass hatchet-pipe. Then he took out his butcher knife and cut open the man's bowels. Everybody who wanted to shot arrows into it or poked it with their lances" (Nye, *Carbine and Lance*, 257).

10. McIntire, *Early Days in Texas*, 55–56. This action took place on May 8, 1875. The woman was later identified as the wife of the Comanche leader, Black Coyote (Nye, *Carbine and Lance*, 303–304).

11. Gilson's favorite weapon was reportedly "a sawed-off shotgun mounted on a pistol handle . . . loaded with buckshot and capable of deadly execution at short range" (Rye, *Quirt and the Spur*, 76). Fortunately for McIntire's skinner, Gilson had loaded his gun with birdshot on this occasion.

12. McIntire, *Early Days in Texas*, 38–39.

13. Ibid., 40–41.

14. The career of Milton J. Yarberry is recounted in DeArment, *Deadly Dozen*, 52–65.

15. McIntire, *Early Days in Texas*, 65.

16. Lieutenant G. W. Campbell to Major John B. Jones, February 17, 1877, Adjutant Generals' Files, Texas State Library, Austin.

17. Texas Ranger Monthly Returns, Muster Rolls and Payment Records, Adjutant Generals' Files, Texas State Library.

18. DeArment, *Bravo of the Brazos*, 131–39; Adjutant Generals' Files, Texas State Library.

19. McIntire, *Early Days in Texas*, 65.

20. Ibid.

21. Ibid., 66.

22. Ibid., 68.

23. Originally a buffalo hunters' camp called Hidetown, the name was changed to Sweetwater after an adjacent creek when the U.S. Army established Fort Elliott nearby. Since a town named Sweetwater was already established in Nolan County, the name was again changed in 1879 to Mobeetie, the Indian name for the creek (Sheffy, "Old Mobeetie," 5).

24. *Dodge City (Kansas) Times*, April 26, 1879.

25. DeArment, "Frontier Adventures of Jim McIntire," 13.

26. Mobeetie saloonkeeper McIntire may well have caught the attention of Bat Masterson, whose fame as a gunfighter had its genesis in the town when it was called Sweetwater. Three years earlier Masterson had been involved in a bloody gunfight with an army corporal named Melvin King in one of the town's saloons. King and a woman named Mollie Brennan were killed, and Masterson received a severe wound (DeArment, *Bat Masterson*, 62–66).

27. This was one of many aliases (John J. Mont, John Longmont, Barney Longmont, John Long, "Long John," Frank Roberts, Frank Ridden, Frank Rivers) adopted by the buffalo hunter turned gambler. Lawman Pat Garrett,

who knew him well, described Longhurst as "a six-footer, a splendid shot," but "a boisterous bully" who "coveted the reputation of a 'bad man.'" After hiring out his gun in New Mexico's Lincoln County War, Longhurst had hooked up with the Larn-Selman criminal combine in Shackelford County, Texas. He was under indictment for the murder of Alexander McSween in New Mexico and was wanted for two killings at Fort Griffin (DeArment, "Great Outlaw Confederacy," 14; Nolan, *Pat F. Garrett's The Authentic Life of Billy the Kid*, 94, 96).

28. DeArment, "Great Outlaw Confederacy," 14.

29. Sworn statement of James McIntire before Moses Wiley, June 30, 1879.

30. Wiley to Jones, July 1, 1879.

31. Metz, *John Selman*, 112; Nolan, *Pat F. Garrett's The Authentic Life of Billy the Kid*, 96.

32. Sheffy, "Old Mobeetie," 13.

33. Ibid.

34. Ibid.; Haley, *Charles Goodnight*, 359; DeArment, "Frontier Adventures of Jim McIntire," 13.

35. McIntire, *Early Days in Texas*, 70. The best analysis of McIntire's assertion is found in Lee Silva's *Wyatt Earp*, Vol. 1, *The Cowtown Years*, 651–56.

36. McIntire, *Early Days in Texas*, 69–70; Harris, *Hide Town in the Texas Panhandle*, 25–27; DeArment, *Jim Courtright of Fort Worth*, 102–105; Nolan, *Tascosa*, 66–68.

37. Poe followed one gang member to Trinidad, Colorado, where the local sheriff not only refused to let him arrest the suspect but threw Poe himself into jail (Poe, *Buckboard Days*, 98).

38. McIntire, *Early Days in Texas*, 70–71, 141; Bryan, *Wildest of the Wild West*, 130–34; Nolan, *Tascosa*, 283–84.

39. McIntire, *Early Days in Texas*, 71.

40. Belle Hindes was no doubt "Belle Hines," the chippie who filed the ridiculous bad language charge against McIntire back in Mobeetie.

41. Ibid., 72–74; James H. East, interviewed by J. Evetts Haley, Douglas, Arizona, September 27, 1927.

42. Callon, *Las Vegas, New Mexico*, 108.

43. *Las Vegas (New Mexico) Optic*, February 9, 1881.

44. McIntire, *Early Days in Texas*, 72.

45. *Las Vegas (New Mexico) Optic*, January 21, 1881.

46. McIntire, *Early Days in Texas*, 74. McIntire's autobiography is riddled with incorrect dates as his memory was exceedingly faulty with regard to time. For instance, he said he "threw up" the marshal's job in Las Vegas "after two years' experience," when actually he served in that capacity only about two months.

47. U.S. Census, 1900, Ponca City, Kay County, Oklahoma Territory.

48. *Las Vegas (New Mexico) Optic*, November 15, 1882.

49. Ibid.; *El Paso (Texas) Lone Star*, December 20, 1882.

50. *El Paso (Texas) Lone Star*, December 30, 1882.

51. McIntire, *Early Days in Texas*, 77–78.

52. Reprint of a *Lake Valley Herald* story in the *Dallas Daily Herald*, April 1, 1883.

53. McIntire said the pay of $10 a day was offered him directly by General Logan, but the cattlemen Casey and Moore were undoubtedly the employers.

54. DeArment, *Jim Courtright of Fort Worth*, 132.

55. The story of the murders is drawn from ibid., 127–41; *Albuquerque Morning Journal*, May 11, 18, October 10, 18, 1883; *Albuquerque Daily Democrat*, May 17, 1883; Westphall, "American Valley Murders." McIntire, in his autobiography, obfuscates the American Valley murder story, saying that some cattle thieves he had arrested and taken to jail in Albuquerque "made an affidavit stating that Jim Courtright and I killed some Mexicans while scouting with Logan, and that gave the Territory Militia another chance at me" (*Early Days in Texas*, 78).

56. DeArment, "Mystery of Outlaw Bill," 20.

57. *Albuquerque Daily Democrat*, May 30, 1883; DeArment, *Jim Courtright of Fort Worth*, 142–43.

58. McIntire, *Early Days in Texas*, 83–84. The $1,000 reward offered for the fugitives was mentioned in the *El Paso (Texas) Lone Star*, June 2, 16, 1883.

59. *Dallas Daily Herald*, June 21, 1883.

60. Ibid., June 30, 1883.

61. Westphall, "American Valley Murders," 128; Rasch, "Murder in American Valley," 4–5. Newspapers reported that the jury stood at eleven to one for conviction in the first trial and eleven to one for acquittal in the second (DeArment, *Jim Courtright of Fort Worth*, 154, 258).

62. McIntire, *Early Days in Texas*, 84.

63. Ibid., 84–85. The *Will Kyle* struck a log near Australia, Mississippi, and sank on November 15, 1883 (Way, "Way's Directory of Western Rivers Packets," 315).

64. McIntire, *Early Days in Texas*, 85.

65. Kelly, *Wichita County Beginnings*, 253.

66. DeArment, *Jim Courtright of Fort Worth*, 155–59.

67. McIntire, *Early Days in Texas*, 86.

68. DeArment, *Jim Courtright of Fort Worth*, 164–67.

69. McIntire, *Early Days in Texas*, 87.

70. DeArment, *Jim Courtright of Fort Worth*, 169.

71. *San Antonio (Texas) Daily Express*, October 24, 1884.

72. Ibid., October 25, 1884.

73. Monthly Return, October 31, 1884, Company C, Frontier Battalion, Texas Rangers.

74. Schmitt to King, November 22, 1884.

75. *Dallas Weekly Herald*, December 13, 1884.

76. McIntire, *Early Days in Texas*, 87–89.

77. Ibid., 90.

78. *San Antonio (Texas) Daily Express*, December 13, 1884.

79. McIntire, *Early Days in Texas*, 90.

80. The fallacious rumor that Courtright and McIntire went to Latin America was picked up and stated as fact in "Long-Haired Jim Courtright" by Eugene Cunningham in 1929. He later repeated the fable in his widely read book *Triggernometry* (212). Many later writers have followed his lead, including Hunter and Rose, *Album of Gunfighters* (158); Cox, *Luke Short and His Era* (155); and Metz, *Shooters* (170).

81. *New Orleans Times-Democrat*, April 22, 1885.

82. *New Orleans Daily Picayune*, April 23, 1885.

83. McIntire, *Early Days in Texas*, 90–91; DeArment, *Jim Courtright of Fort Worth*, 178–79.

84. McIntire, *Early Days in Texas*, 92–93.

85. *New Orleans Daily Picayune*, April 21, 23, 1885; *New Orleans Times-Democrat*, April 21, 23, 1885; *Denver Tribune-Republican*, April 27, 1885; Rasch, "Murder in American Valley," 6.

86. *Albuquerque Morning Journal*, June 8, 1885.

87. Ibid.

88. *Albuquerque Evening Democrat*, October 15, 1885.

89. *Albuquerque Evening Journal*, October 19, 1885.

90. *Albuquerque Evening Democrat*, October 15, 1885.

91. McIntire, *Early Days in Texas*, 97.

92. Porter, *Memory Cups*, 155.

93. McIntire, *Early Days in Texas*, 97–98.

94. Ibid., 98–99.

95. Ibid., 99. No record of the case can be found in the county or district court files of Wilbarger County (Kennon to DeArment, October 29, 1989).

96. Paul, "Early Days in Carson County, Texas," 3.

97. Crocchiola to DeArment, March 20, 1990.

98. Gober, *Cowboy Justice*, 130–32.

99. McIntire, *Early Days in Texas*, 102.

100. Ibid.

101. *Woodward (Oklahoma) News*, June 3, 1898.

102. "The town of Mountain View was almost completely wiped out by [smallpox] in 1901. They had a place there where they took those having the dread disease, who didn't have anyone to care for them" (Clem A. Trotter, interview by Ruby Wolfenberger, January 19, 1938).

### CHAPTER 10. JIM MASTERSON

1. Birth certificate of James Patrick Masterson, County of Iberville, Canada; Penn, "Note on Bartholomew Masterson," 11–12; DeArment, "*True West* Legends: Jim Masterson," 31.

2. Following the older three boys were Nelly, born in 1857; Thomas, in 1858; George, in 1860; and Emma, in 1862 (DeArment, *Bat Masterson*, 10).

3. He did get home to "Sunny Dale," the family farm occasionally, as in April 1874 when he and his brother Ed went back to attend the wedding of Theo Raymond, a buffalo-hunting friend. He was called "that old buffalo slayer, 'Cheyenne Jim'" in the society item in the *Wichita (Kansas) Eagle* of April 30.

4. *Dodge City (Kansas) Times*, March 31, 1877. At the same time Springer was a partner with Bat Masterson in the Lone Star Dance Hall in Dodge (Myers, "Lawman James P. Masterson," 2).

5. *Dodge City (Kansas) Times*, February 23, 1878.

6. DeArment, *Broadway Bat*, xii.

7. *Dodge City (Kansas) Times*, March 16, 1878.

8. *Larned (Kansas) Press*, May 30, 1878; *Dodge City (Kansas) Times*, July 6, 1878. It was not unusual for western lawmen of the period to hold multiple positions. Bat Masterson, for instance, while serving as sheriff of Ford County also held a commission as a deputy U.S. marshal, and City Marshal Charles Bassett also held the county position of undersheriff. Jim Masterson's salary as policeman ranged from $75 to $100 a month, depending on the season. At times, additionally, the city council allowed $2 per arrest. For his work as a sheriff's deputy he was generally paid on a per diem basis.

9. DeArment, *Bat Masterson*, 114–15. According to the account in the *Ford County (Kansas) Globe* of July 30, 1878, "A general scamper was made by the crowd, some getting under the stage, others running out the front door, and behind the bar; in the language of the bard, 'such a gittin up stairs never was seed.'"

10. *Dodge City (Kansas) Times*, July 27, 1878; *Ford County (Kansas) Globe*, August 27, 1878.

11. *Dodge City (Kansas) Times*, January 11, 1879.

12. Ibid., February 15, 1879; *Ford County (Kansas) Globe*, February 17, 1879.

13. *Dodge City (Kansas) Times*, May 10, 24, 1879.

14. *Ford County (Kansas) Globe*, June 10, 1879; *Dodge City (Kansas) Times*, June 14, 1879; *National Police Gazette*, June 21, 1879; Myers, "Lawman James P. Masterson," 4.

15. *Ford County (Kansas) Globe*, July 22, 1879.

16. *Dodge City (Kansas) Times*, November 15, 1879.

17. Horan, *Across the Cimarron*, 58, 76.

18. *Dodge City (Kansas) Times*, May 8, 1880.

19. As listed by census-taker W. C. Shinn, there were several "concubines" enumerated in the Dodge City census of 1880, including Annie Ladue, age nineteen, "keeping house" for Bat Masterson, and Laura Campbell, age twenty-three, doing the same for Charles Ronan, a twenty-five-year-old bartender and pal of the Masterson brothers. There was also one "paramour," twenty-nine-year-old George Anderson, whose occupation was "driving cattle" and who was cohabitating with a twenty-seven-year-old laundress. A number of single females, all in their twenties, gave their occupation as "sporting."

20. In the Oklahoma Territorial Census of June 1890 Minnie was enumerated in Beaver County, where she and her sister had opened a restaurant. She gave her name as "Minnie Masterson," her age as twenty-two, and her family status as "wife." Common law marriage was a not unusual practice during the period. Two of Jim Masterson's more famous law enforcement associates, his brother Bat and Wyatt Earp, had similar relationships, each paired with a woman for decades, and diligent efforts by researchers to find records of formal marriages have been unsuccessful.

21. Myers to DeArment, May 26, 2001; DeArment, "Bat Masterson's Femmes Fatales," 60. After Jim's death in 1895, Minnie married a man named Joseph Bryson and later moved to Liberal, Kansas, where she died on June 30, 1940. The death record shows her date of birth as August 3, 1865, which indicates that she had not yet turned fifteen years old when enumerated in the 1880 census at Dodge City, and was actually twenty-four, not twenty-two as shown in the June 1890 census (Myers to DeArment).

22. *Dodge City (Kansas) Times*, December 11, 1880.

23. *Oskaloosa (Iowa) Herald*, March 17, 1881.

24. *Ford County (Kansas) Globe*, April 5, 1881.

25. *Dodge City (Kansas) Times*, April 7, 1881; Haywood, *Merchant Prince of Dodge City*, 142; Faulk, *Dodge City*, 167.

26. *Caldwell (Kansas) Commercial*, April 21, 1881. The *Ford County (Kansas) Globe* (April 19, 1881) reported that "pistols were drawn and several shots fired, but no one was hurt."

27. *Ford County (Kansas) Globe*, May 10, 1881.

28. DeArment, *Bat Masterson*, 204. Some mystery surrounds this call for Bat's help regarding who sent it and where Bat received it. Stuart Lake, in his biography of Wyatt Earp, indicated Bat had already left Tombstone at the time of Jim's trouble (*Wyatt Earp*, 359), and Alfred Henry Lewis, who knew Bat best and most likely heard the story directly from his lips, wrote that he got the wire in Deming, New Mexico ("King of the Gun-Players"). Stanley Vestal, in *Queen of Cowtowns* (219), also placed Bat in New Mexico when he received the telegram, as did the *Dodge City (Kansas) Times* of April 21, 1881. None of these sources mentions the author of the appeal for help, but Odie B. Faulk, in *Dodge City* (167), states that Jim sent the wire himself. Walter Noble Burns, in *Tombstone* (57), quotes Earp as saying: "Bat showed me the message he received in Tombstone and it was not from his brother." George Goodell, who was in Dodge City at the time and was later closely associated with both Masterson brothers in Colorado, claimed to have sent the telegram (DeArment, *Deadly Dozen*, 83).

29. *Ford County (Kansas) Globe*, April 19, 1881; *Caldwell (Kansas) Commercial*, April 21, 1881. In a wildly exaggerated feature story on Bat Masterson and his exploits, the *Journal* of Kansas City, Missouri, in its issue of November 15, 1881, said that "Bat's second brother [Jim] was killed in Dodge City by two men named Updegraff and Peacock" and that Bat came from Tombstone and shot them dead.

30. According to a report in a Trinidad paper, Ronan had little time to "grow up," falling victim to tuberculosis and dying only six weeks after leaving Dodge City (DeArment, *Bat Masterson*, 219), but the former Dodge City gambler and gunman evidently continued his uproarious career for the balance of that year. The *Ford County (Kansas) Globe*, in issues of December 20, 1881, and January 3, 1882, gave details of shootings in which Ronan, then a resident of Albuquerque, killed two or more men.

31. *Trinidad (Colorado) Daily Times*, January 28, 1882.

32. *Trinidad (Colorado) Daily News*, March 17, 1882.

33. Ibid.

34. *People v. James Masterson*, Las Animas County District Court Book #2, 113.

35. DeArment, *Bat Masterson*, 239.

36. *Trinidad (Colorado) Daily Democrat*, November 25, 1882.

37. Ibid., November 28, 1882.

38. *Trinidad (Colorado) Weekly News*, October 26, 1882.

39. DeArment, "Kreeger's Toughest Arrest," 14–19.

40. DeArment, *Bat Masterson*, 249.

41. Otero, *My Life on the Frontier, 1882–1897*, 151; Peters, "Masterson's Militia," 56.

42. Peters, "Masterson's Militia," 56.

43. *Raton (New Mexico) Comet*, December 26, 1884.

44. Curry, *George Curry*, 49.

45. Otero, *My Life on the Frontier, 1882–1897*, 152; Peters, "Masterson's Militia," 56.

46. *New Mexico Adjutant General's Annual Report for 1885*; Peters, "Masterson's Militia," 57.

47. Curry, *George Curry*, 49.

48. Peters, "Masterson's Militia," 21.

49. *New Mexico Adjutant General's Annual Report for 1885*.

50. Otero, *My Life on the Frontier, 1882–1897*, 152–53.

51. *New Mexico Adjutant General's Annual Report for 1885*.

52. Peters, "Masterson's Militia," 24.

53. Curry, *George Curry*, 49.

54. "Leadership displayed by George Curry in organizing the Vigilantes and marking out a peaceful program for them in connection with the Jim Masterson militia incident marked the first step in a career which brought him fame in later years and the friendship of many noted men" (Keleher, *Maxwell Land Grant*, 101).

55. Ibid., 102; Curry, *George Curry*, 50.

56. Curry, *George Curry*, 50.

57. Ibid. According to Miguel Otero, other prominent businessmen and county officials, including T. A. Schomberg, Harry Whigham, and District Attorney Melvin W. Wells, in fear of their lives, fled New Mexico for Trinidad, also, but returned later (Otero, *My Life on the Frontier, 1864–1882*, 105).

58. *Trinidad (Colorado) Daily Advertiser*, March 4, 1885.
59. Ibid., March 6, 1885.
60. Cause No. 1837, *State of Kansas v. James Masterson*.
61. Shirley, *Guardian of the Law*, 178.
62. *Cimarron (Kansas) Jacksonian*, January 18, 1889.
63. *Dodge City (Kansas) Times*, January 17, 1889.
64. *Atchison (Kansas) Daily Globe*, January 14, 1889.
65. *Atlanta Constitution*, January 26, 1889.
66. Horan, *Across the Cimarron*, 272–73.
67. *Cimarron (Kansas) Jacksonian*, January 18, 1889.
68. Bill Tilghman's wife, Zoe, in her biography of her husband, said that he had been struck in the calf of his leg by a bullet, "the only time he was ever touched by gunfire" (Tilghman, *Marshal of the Last Frontier*, 275), but in its account of the battle the *Dodge City (Kansas) Times* (January 17, 1889) said Tilghman only suffered a sprained ankle.
69. Horan, *Across the Cimarron*, 274–75.
70. Newspapers throughout the country carried the story of the "Battle of Cimarron," including papers in Atchison and Topeka, Kansas; Trenton, New Jersey; Atlanta; and of course Dodge City, Ingalls, and Cimarron.
71. DeArment, *Ballots and Bullets*, 57–59.
72. Cause No. 18, *State of Kansas v. N. F. Watson, et al.* Ben Daniels and Neal Brown were later arrested, but the case against them was ultimately dismissed.
73. Ibid.
74. Quoted in Shirley, *Guardian of the Law*, 190–91.
75. Cause No. 33, *United States of America v. Jerome Fitzgerald, James Masterson, and John Doe*, assault, August 21, 1889. Thomas E. Kelly and James Shearer were sureties.
76. Ibid. The witnesses were Frank Biggs, W. R. Lobaugh, and Dolph Byers.
77. On June 17, 1891, James Masterson paid a $10 fine in the Guthrie Police Court for conducting a gambling game. Typically, ruling bodies of frontier towns, as a sop to churchgoing reformers, regularly fined gamblers and prostitutes, the purveyors of vice, rather than assessing license fees.
78. Shirley, *Guardian of the Law*, 195.
79. *Business and Resident Directory of Guthrie and Logan County, OK. For the Years Commencing Sept. 1st, 1891.*
80. *Oklahoma State Capital* (Guthrie), July 16, 1892.
81. James Masterson to Thomas Masterson, September 26, 1892.
82. Ed P. Kelley saw service as Guthrie's first city marshal, chief of police under the town's first organized government, deputy U.S. marshal, and finally clerk of the Sixth District U.S. Court from 1902 until statehood. At this time he was a partner with Bill Tilghman in the operation of the Alpha saloon in Guthrie, where Jim Masterson frequented the back room poker table (Shirley, *Guardian of the Law*, 194–95).

83. Megehee to Ernst, April 2, 1981; Cause Nos. 81 and 83, Police Judge's Docket, Guthrie, Oklahoma.

84. Shirley, *Gunfight at Ingalls*, 71.

85. Quoted in ibid.

86. Ibid.

87. Quoted in ibid., 72.

88. One of the earliest contemporary newspaper stories recounting the battle appeared in the *Cherokee Advocate* of Tahlequah, Oklahoma, on September 16, 1893, in a letter from "Minco Minstrel."

89. Shirley, *Gunfight at Ingalls*, 78.

90. Quoted in ibid., 80–81.

91. *Stillwater (Oklahoma) Gazette*, July 20, 1906.

92. *Kansas City Times*, November 15, 1893.

93. Shirley, *Gunfight at Ingalls*, 84.

94. Nix, *Oklahombres*, 110–11; Shirley, *Six Gun and Silver Star*, 94–95.

95. Quoted in Shirley, *Gunfight at Ingalls*, 85.

96. Pickering's diary, as quoted in ibid. Said the *Oklahoma State Capital* (Guthrie) of September 8, 1893: "Nothing much is known of Arkansas Tom, or Tom Jones, the man who did such fatal shooting from the hotel garret at the recent Ingalls fight between the noted outlaws and United States marshals, and so Sheriff [William W.] Painter and Deputy Marshal Jim Masterson got photographer Flower to take a picture of him."

97. Shirley, *Gunfight at Ingalls*, passim.

98. *Dodge City (Kansas) Democrat*, September 23, 1893. This story, a telegram, also appeared in newspapers as far-flung as the *Idaho Daily Statesman* (Boise) of September 17, 1893, and the *Chicago Daily Inter-Ocean* of September 18, 1893. The *Guthrie (Oklahoma) Daily Leader* of September 19, 1893, said that Jim Masterson was one of the first horsemen to reach Perry, and he "rode Dalton's fiery steed." If he was indeed a "sooner," Masterson was not riding "Bill Dalton's famous horse." That poor animal had received two gunshot wounds, including a broken leg, in the Ingalls fight, and presumably had been destroyed.

99. *Kansas City Times*, November 15, 1893.

100. *Oklahoma State Capital* (Guthrie), May 11, 1894.

101. *Oklahoma Daily Press Gazette*, May 23, 1894; *Oklahoma State Capital* (Guthrie), May 19, 1894. When Judge Dale wrote Attorney General Richard Olney on May 21, 1894, requesting payment of $100 ($25 each) for the three days and nights his guards had spent on guard duty, the attorney general denied the request on May 28, and suggested the judge bill the U.S. marshal's office. "It is possible that the marshal will have no money for this purpose," he said. "The appropriation is exhausted. It is believed, however, that Congress will make during the present session a deficiency appropriation that will cover the expenses" (Attorney Generals' Files, National Archives).

102. *Oklahoma State Capital* (Guthrie), April 1, 1895.

103. *Evening Democrat* (Warren, Pennsylvania), April 10, 1895; *Hornellsville (New York) Weekly Tribune*, April 12, 1895.

104. *Evening Democrat* (Warren, Pennsylvania), April 11, 1895.

105. *El Paso (Texas) Herald*, April 15, 1895.

## CHAPTER 11. ED SHORT

1. Dugan, *Tales Never Told Around the Campfire*, 80; U.S. Census, 1870, Center Township, Ripley County, Indiana.

2. Dugan, *Tales Never Told Around the Campfire*, 81–82; Cause No. 1231, *State of Indiana v. Charles E. Short*, Ripley County Circuit Court.

3. *Ripley County Journal* (Versailles, Indiana), June 14, 1883.

4. *Versailles (Indiana) Republican*, December 6, 1883.

5. *Ripley County Journal* (Versailles, Indiana), December 6, 1883.

6. Ibid., January 10, 1884.

7. *State Journal* (Topeka, Kansas), August 24, 1891.

8. *Oklahoma Daily Times Journal* (Oklahoma City), August 26, 1891.

9. Shirley, *Six Gun and Silver Star*, 35. Shirley gave almost the same word-for-word description in *Heck Thomas* (157).

10. Former Oklahoma governor Thomson B. Ferguson in an interview published in the *Daily Oklahoman* (Oklahoma City), February 29, 1920.

11. *State Journal* (Topeka, Kansas), August 24, 1891.

12. DeArment, *Ballots and Bullets*, 107. Sam P. Ridings, author of *The Chisholm Trail*, said that Short "had spent much time at Caldwell, Kansas . . . , and the writer knew him well" (464).

13. DeArment, *Ballots and Bullets*, 89–91.

14. Ibid., 94–97.

15. Ibid., 104.

16. Chrisman, *Call of the High Plains*, 77.

17. McNeal, *When Kansas Was Young*, 173.

18. *Woodsdale (Kansas) Democrat*, April 8, 1887.

19. Ibid., April 29, 1887.

20. *Kansas City (Missouri) Star*, August 24, 1891.

21. *Woodsdale (Kansas) Democrat*, August 26, September 2, 1887.

22. Ibid., September 30, 1887.

23. Ibid., March 2, 1888.

24. Ibid., September 2, 1887.

25. Ibid., October 28, November 4, 1887; *Hugo Herald* (Hugoton, Kansas), October 27, 1887.

26. *Woodsdale (Kansas) Democrat*, October 28, 1887.

27. Ibid., November 18, 1887.

28. Ibid., July 13, 1888.

29. Ibid., June 29, July 20, 1888.

30. Ibid., June 8, 1888.

31. Ibid., June 8, 29, 1888; *Hugoton (Kansas) Hermes*, June 11, 1888; Chrisman, *Call of the High Plains*, 80.

32. *Woodsdale (Kansas) Democrat*, June 29, 1888.

33. *Hugoton (Kansas) Hermes*, June 11, 1888.

34. *Woodsdale (Kansas) Democrat*, June 15, 1888.

35. Ibid.

36. Snell, "Stevens County Seat Controversy," 59, 61; *Hugo Herald* (Hugoton, Kansas), July 26, 1888.

37. *Hugoton (Kansas) Hermes*, July 26, 1888.

38. Ibid.; Snell, "Stevens County Seat Controversy," 59–60.

39. *New York Times*, August 6, 1888.

40. DeArment, *Ballots and Bullets*. Sam Robinson fled Kansas in 1889 accompanied by his shadow, Bert Noble. In Colorado the two soon ran afoul of the law. With another criminal named Thompson they held up a Florissant store. The proprietor and several customers resisted, and Thompson was killed. The others escaped, only to engage in another gunfight with pursuing officers. When Robinson was wounded slightly, they surrendered. Convicted of armed robbery, Robinson was sentenced to fourteen years in prison while Noble got off with only a seven-year sentence. Released in 1894, Noble returned to a life of crime. In an abortive attempt to rob a Trinidad gambling hall in 1895 he and several others killed a police officer. Noble and two accomplices were hanged for the murder on June 26, 1896, at the Canon City prison. The execution took place only a few yards from the cell of Robinson, who was still serving his time for the Florissant robbery. Paroled on January 30, 1898, Robinson, perhaps chastened by the inglorious end of his friend, evidently avoided further trouble with the law and disappeared from history (ibid., 173–76).

41. *Woodsdale (Kansas) Democrat*, February 22, 1889.

42. DeArment, *Ballots and Bullets*, 179.

43. Ibid., 194–95.

44. Wood, *Memorial of Samuel N. Wood*, 170. Like the Hay Meadow murderers, Jim Brennan, the killer of Sam Wood, never was punished for his crime. He was never even brought to trial (DeArment, *Ballots and Bullets*, 201).

45. *Kansas City Star*, August 8, 18, 1891; *Oklahoma Daily Times Journal* (Oklahoma City), August 26, 1891.

46. *State Journal* (Topeka, Kansas), August 24, 1891.

47. Sam Ridings, in *The Chisholm Trail* (465), said Bryant was suffering from malaria. Thomas R. Holland, in *Oklahombres Revisited* (82), favored the fistfight story.

48. Barnard, *Rider of the Cherokee Strip*, 194.

49. Shirley, *West of Hell's Fringe*, 66.

50. *Chicago Herald*, August 25, 1891; *Dallas Morning News*, August 25, 1891.

51. *Dallas Morning News*, August 25, 1891; *Macon (Georgia) Daily Telegraph*, August 25, 1891; *Chicago Daily Inter-Ocean*, August 25, 1891.

52. Detailed accounts of the dramatic gunfight between Ed Short and

Charley Bryant have appeared in a number of books and magazines, but many contain inaccuracies. The most reliable sources, from which this version is drawn, are the contemporary newspapers cited and the *Kingfisher (Oklahoma) Free Press*, August 27, 1891; and *Hennessey (Oklahoma) Clipper*, August 28, 1891. The best secondary sources are Shirley, *West of Hell's Fringe*, 63–67; Holland, *Oklahombres Revisited*, 82–83; Rainey, *Cherokee Strip*, 255–61; and Dugan, *Tales Never Told Around the Campfire*, 90–92.

53. Dugan, *Tales Never Told Around the Campfire*, 92. "A number of Bryants are buried in Decatur Cemetery, but there is no marker for Charley" (Browning, *Violence Was No Stranger*, 36).

54. Dugan, *Tales Never Told Around the Campfire*, 92; Browning, *Violence Was No Stranger*, 228.

55. Quoted in Shirley, *West of Hell's Fringe*, 67.

56. *Oklahoma Daily Times Journal* (Oklahoma City), August 26, 1891.

57. *Daily Oklahoman* (Oklahoma City), February 29, 1920.

### CHAPTER 12. HILL LOFTIS

1. U.S. Census, 1860, Lowndes County, Mississippi; U.S. Census, 1870, Sanford County, Alabama; U.S. Census, 1880, Monroe County, Mississippi.

2. Herders of cattle in nineteenth-century Texas were called "cowboys" for good reason, for many, perhaps the majority, were indeed adolescent boys. The term "cowman" was reserved for older cattle owners and ranchers.

3. Fenton, "Staked Plains' Legendary Feudist," 6.

4. Fenton, "Tom Ross," 32.

5. *St. Louis Post-Dispatch*, July 15, 1923.

6. Fenton, "Tom Ross," 32–33; Sullivan, *Twelve Years in the Saddle*, 134–36.

7. Beckham was the first elected sheriff of Motley County, serving from February 5, 1891, until he was removed from office in early 1894. Charged with fraud in connection with the disappearance of county funds, he shot and killed the next elected sheriff, G. W. Cook, in June 1895 (Tise, *Texas County Sheriffs*, 385).

8. Fenton, "Tom Ross," 22; Burton, "Mysterious Kid." The notorious pseudo-outlaw Al Jennings said that Lewis rode the Owl Hoot Trail with him (Jennings and Irwin, *Beating Back*, 76–81), but everything Jennings ever claimed should be viewed with skepticism.

9. Fenton, "Tom Ross," 23; Sullivan, *Twelve Years in the Saddle*, 119–21; Paine, *Captain Bill McDonald*, 176–77.

10. Dick Sanders served two terms as Wilbarger County sheriff, 1894–98, and was succeeded by his deputy, John Williams, who served six terms, 1898–1910 (Tise, *Texas County Sheriffs*, 542).

11. Billy Moses was appointed Motley County sheriff by a district judge in 1894 after Joe Beckham was deposed.

12. Not the outlaw of the same name who rode with Billy the Kid nor Tom M. Pickett, a notorious gunman in Arizona's Pleasant Valley War, this Tom

Pickett was the sometime lawman and always faithful friend and bodyguard of cattle baron Burk Burnett and was with Burnett when his boss killed a man in a celebrated shootout in 1912 (see DeArment, *Deadly Dozen, Volume 2*).

13. Sullivan, *Twelve Years in the Saddle*, 123–24.

14. Owen, *Byrd Cochrain*, 36–38.

15. Sullivan, *Twelve Years in the Saddle*, 125.

16. Owen, *Byrd Cochrain*, 38.

17. Crawford a few years earlier had cowboyed with twenty-one-year-old George Lewis ("Tex") Rickard, who would go on to become one of the great gamblers of the era and the world's first million dollar fight promoter (Samuels, *Magnificent Rube*, 25).

18. Fenton, "Tom Ross," 26–29; Paine, *Captain Bill McDonald*, 199–213. There is some confusion about the identity of these two criminals. Dan Thrapp, in a sketch of Elmer Lewis in his monumental *Encyclopedia of Frontier Biography* (Vol. 2, 851), reports that under the alias Foster Holbrook, Lewis had been implicated with Robert and William Christian and gang member John Mackey in the killing of Pottawatomie County Deputy Sheriff William C. Turner on April 27, 1895, in Oklahoma Territory. Astute English historian Jeff Burton, in *Black Jack Christian* (3), records that the Christian brothers and Mackey received prison sentences, but Holbrook was acquitted. The foremost historian of Oklahoma outlaw history, Glenn Shirley, however, asserts that Foster Holbrook and Foster Crawford were one and the same individual (*West of Hell's Fringe*, 347, 480).

19. Cause No. 901, *Wilbarger County, State of Texas v. Hill Loftis*. In the stilted jargon of the law, the indictment alleged that "Hill Loftis, on or about the 26th day of December in 1895 by assault and by violence to Alf Bailey by the use [of] firearms and by putting the said Alf Bailey in fear of his life and bodily injury, fraudulently and without the consent of the said Alf Bailey did take from the person and possession of him. . . about seventy dollars in money, paper money commonly called greenbacks, and silver coins of the United States and gold coins of the United States . . . , also about three hundred dollars worth of men's clothing, hats and other dry goods and groceries. tobacco, coffee, leather quirts and other articles of dry goods and groceries to tedious to mention . . . , with the intent to deprive the said Alf Bailey of the same and appropriate the same to his said Hill Loftis' own use, contrary to the statute in such cases made and provided and against the peace and dignity of the State."

20. *List of Fugitives from Justice, 1900*. As a deputy Williams had participated in the shootout at the dugout against Loftis and his cohorts.

21. Owen, *Byrd Cochrain*, 43.

22. Sterling, *Trails and Trials of a Texas Ranger*, 377.

23. *St. Louis Post-Dispatch*, July 15, 1923.

24. Owen, *Byrd Cochrain*, 38, 43; *St. Louis Post-Dispatch*, July 15, 1923.

25. It has been suggested that in 1899 he was a member of an outlaw gang

in New Mexico led by James Knight, or Nite (Burton, *Deadliest Outlaws*, 148; Tanner and Tanner, *Last of the Old-Time Outlaws*, 155), but little evidence has emerged to support this.

26. Owen, *Byrd Cochrain*, 38.

27. Fenton, "Tom Ross," 34.

28. Harkey, *Mean as Hell*, 206. Dee Harkey was a brother of Jeff D. Harkey, who served as Dickens County sheriff from March 1891 to November 1900 (Tise, *Texas County Sheriffs*, 159).

29. Mayer and Solomon Halff, the sons of Jewish parents, were born in Alsace-Lorraine, France, and immigrated to America in the 1850s. At one time the brothers owned more than a million acres of ranchland in Texas (Tyler, *New Handbook of Texas*, Vol. 3, 412).

30. Marriage License Records, Martin County, Texas. The year of Trixie's birth as indicated by the U.S. Census of 1920 was 1883, which would have made her only nineteen when Ross reunited with her in 1902, but ages reported on census records are notoriously inaccurate. The age of Tom Ross given on that 1920 census report was forty-six when his actual age was fifty.

31. Texas Ranger Monthly Returns, Muster Rolls and Payment Records, Adjutant Generals' Files, Texas State Library.

32. Ibid.

33. Smithson and Hull, *Martin County*, 15.

34. Ibid.; Fenton, "Tom Ross," 39; Harkey, *Mean as Hell*, 206.

35. Utley, *Lone Star Justice*, 253. The others were Captains J. A. Brooks, John R. Hughes, and W. J. McDonald. Ross had already had some dealings with McDonald back in 1895–96.

36. Monthly Returns for June 1904, Company C, Texas Rangers.

37. Harkey, *Mean as Hell*, 206. Harkey, of course, was not there to witness this alleged indignity. He may have gotten the story from Billy Connell (certainly not the ranger or sheriff), or he may have simply made it up to enliven his account, something he was not averse to doing.

38. Fenton, "Tom Ross," 20.

39. Quoted in ibid.

40. Ibid.

41. Clarke, "Bad Man . . . Good Man?" 43.

42. Erickson, *Prairie Gothic*, 136, 140.

43. Clarke, "Bad Man . . . Good Man?" 60.

44. Erickson, *Prairie Gothic*, 137.

45. Ibid.

46. Ibid.

47. Dobie, "Within the Code," 47.

48. *St. Louis Post-Dispatch*, July 29, 1923.

49. Ibid., July 15, 1923.

50. Fenton, "Tom Ross," 41–42; Cause No. 901, *Wilbarger County, State of Texas v. Hill Loftis*; Harkey, *Mean as Hell*, 206.

51. Fenton, "Tom Ross," 42; Cause No. 901, *Wilbarger County, State of Texas v. Hill Loftis.*

52. Fenton, "Staked Plains' Legendary Feudist," 12.

53. Ibid., 13.

54. Harkey, *Mean as Hell*, 208.

55. Ibid., 208–209; Owen, *Byrd Cochrain*, 44.

56. Alexander, *Fearless Dave Allison*; DeArment, "Bloody Easter," 12–13.

57. DeArment, "Bloody Easter," 13–14.

58. *Roswell (New Mexico) Record*, April 2, 1923.

59. *Lubbock (Texas) Avalanche-Journal*, September 25, 1949.

60. DeArment, "Bloody Easter," 16; Good, *Twelve Years in a Texas Prison*, 8–11.

61. Bob Beverly, interviewed by J. Evetts Haley, March 24, 1945.

62. Ibid.

63. *Dallas Morning News*, June 23, 1923.

64. Clarke, "Bad Man . . . Good Man?" 62.

65. Ironically, the day was both Easter Sunday and April Fool's Day.

66. There is some disagreement over the weapons Ross used in the shooting. Ross told a reporter he used his favorite handgun, the .45 automatic (*St. Louis Post-Dispatch*, July 15, 1923), but other sources said he used a .45 caliber Smith and Wesson revolver (Fenton, "Staked Plains' Legendary Feudist," 17).

67. *St. Louis Post-Dispatch*, July 22, 1923; Owen, *Byrd Cochrain*, 48.

68. "Cattle Thieves Kill Two Association Inspectors."

69. Fenton, "Tom Ross," 106.

70. "Cattle Thieves Kill Two Association Inspectors"; Devereaux, "Gentle Woman, Tough Medicine," 27.

71. "Many secondary accounts make mention that Martha Roberson used a .25 caliber pistol to shoot Tom Ross and Milt Good. During her testimony at the murder trial of Tom Ross, she testified the handgun was a Colt, .380 caliber, confirmed by stipulation made by Texas & Southwestern Cattle Raisers Association attorney Dayton Moses, who was assisting with the prosecution. An argument over the caliber of the weapon is historically nonproductive; the important fact is she stood her ground and shot both Ross and Good" (Devereaux, "Gentle Woman, Tough Medicine," 33).

72. Ibid.; *Seminole (Texas) Sentinel*, April 5, 1923.

73. Fenton, "Tom Ross," 108.

74. *Mexia (Texas) Daily News*, April 13, 1923.

75. Clarke, "Bad Man . . . Good Man?" 62; "Prison Gates Await Slayers of Inspectors Allison and Roberson."

76. *St. Louis Post-Dispatch*, July 15, 1923.

77. Three years after covering the Ross trial at Lubbock, Robertus Love published *The Rise and Fall of Jesse James*, acknowledged by perceptive western outlaw-lawman bibliophile Ramon Adams as "probably the most reliable book written about Jesse James to that date" (*Six-Guns and Saddle Leather*, 406).

78. *St. Louis Post-Dispatch*, July 29, 1923.

79. *Mexia (Texas) Daily News*, June 26, 1923; *Seminole (Texas) Sentinel*, June 21, 1923; Pettey, "Seminole Incident," 139.

80. *Mexia (Texas) Daily News*, June 22, 1923.

81. Ibid., June 21, 1923.

82. *Dallas Morning News*, June 28, 1923.

83. *Mexia (Texas) Daily News*, June 27, 1923.

84. *St. Louis Post-Dispatch*, July 29, 1923.

85. Good, *Twelve Years in a Texas Prison*, 19.

86. Ibid., 21; *Mexia (Texas) Daily News*, September 14, 16, 19, 1923; "Ross and Good Found Guilty."

87. Prison Records of Tom Ross and Milt Good, Texas State Penitentiary, Huntsville. Ross, who gave his age incorrectly as fifty-two, was assigned convict number 52154. He also claimed incorrectly that he had never before been arrested. Described as "white with a dark complexion" and brown hair and eyes, he was five feet eight and a half inches tall, and weighed 205 pounds. "It was noted he had several gold crowns and gold bridges on his teeth." He had seven years of schooling. A self-employed "ranchman," he was a member of the Baptist Church and said he did not drink, gamble, or use tobacco.

Milt Good, assigned convict number 52153, was thirty-five years old, "white, with a fair complexion, brown hair and hazel eyes." He was the same height as Ross and weighed 186 pounds. He had completed eight years of schooling and was also a self-employed "ranchman." He was not a member of a church, but said he did not use tobacco, drink, or gamble and had never before been arrested.

88. *Mexia (Texas) Daily News*, November 30, 1925; Good, *Twelve Years in a Texas Prison*, 29–30. One newspaper printed the romantic report that the getaway car was driven by a woman who had fallen in love with Arlington during his Dallas trial (*Fort Worth [Texas] Star-Telegram*, November 30, 1925). Another rumor was that the car had been provided as part of "financial and political aid from powerful people Hill Loftis had served in bygone days" (Sterling, *Trails and Trials of a Texas Ranger*, 380). After an investigation of the escape at the prison two guards were dismissed for "laxity" (*Mexia [Texas] Daily News*, December 6, 1925).

89. Good, *Twelve Years in a Texas Prison*, 31–33. There was a persistent rumor that the escapees had gotten away to Mexico by means of a modern contraption, the airplane ("Escape of Tom Ross and Milt Good"). In a completely unbelievable account Dee Harkey said Ross and Good somehow acquired an airplane after escaping and came to the ranch of J. W. Wooten near Carlsbad, New Mexico. Who piloted the plane is left unexplained. According to this tale, Ross stopped there for the express purpose of enlisting Wooten's help in killing Judge Brice, against whom they both bore a grudge. Learning of the plot, Harkey said he gave Ross an ultimatum: leave in ten minutes or he was coming after him. The plane took off with Ross in it, and Good went his own way (Harkey, *Mean as Hell*, 209–10).

90. Good, *Twelve Years in a Texas Prison*, 35.

91. Ibid. The Texas authorities had not given up the hunt for Ross and Good. Several of them, including the noted man hunter Captain Frank Hamer of the Texas Rangers, who some years later would lead the posse that brought a sudden and grisly end to the criminal careers of the notorious Bonnie Parker and Clyde Barrow. In a letter from the Austin Police Department quoted in Good's *Twelve Years in a Texas Prison* (38–39) it is noted that "Captain Hamer is personally trying to apprehend these men [Ross and Good], and is financing his own way." On June 26, 1926, Good was captured near Antlers, Oklahoma, by Sheriff N. F. Kirkpatrick and his deputies Sam Thornton and Lee Pollock. The next day he was taken back to Texas by another storied Texas Ranger, Captain Tom Hickman, and jailed at Fort Worth ("Milt Good Is Captured"). Placed back within the walls of the prison at Huntsville, Good attempted another escape in October 1927. With several other convicts he dug a tunnel under the east wall of the prison, but an alert guard saw the escapees emerging from the tunnel and sounded the alarm, and they were soon captured ("Milt Good Makes Second Break for Freedom"). Good's wife worked tirelessly for years to obtain a pardon for her husband. Her efforts were strongly opposed by Dayton Moses of the cattlemen's association, who admitted in an August 4, 1932, letter to the Board of Pardons and Paroles that personal reasons affected his attitude. "I may be embittered against cold blooded murder," he wrote, "because my next oldest brother, Billy Moses, a sheriff in Montana, was murdered in 1914" ("Regarding the Milt Good Pardon"). Billy Moses, it may be remembered, was a member of the posse that engaged in the pitched battle with Hill Loftis and the Waightman gang back in 1895. At Huntsville, Good worked hard to gain the confidence of the warden, Lee Simmons, and was successful. Together they organized a popular prison rodeo, and Simmons chose Good as his personal driver (Simmons, *Assignment Huntsville*, 194). With the warden's assistance, the work of Mrs. Good was finally rewarded when Texas Governor Miriam A. ("Ma") Ferguson pardoned Milt Good on November 27, 1934, with his release to be effective January 20, 1935 (Good, *Twelve Years in a Texas Prison*, 74). Good continued to ranch in New Mexico and Texas until his accidental death on July 3, 1960, at his ranch near Cotulla, Texas. As he opened a gate, his car slipped into gear and crushed him against the fence (*Cotulla [Texas] Record*, July 8, 1960).

92. *Fort Worth (Texas) Star-Telegram*, February 6, 1929.

93. *Seminole (Texas) Sentinel*, February 7, 1929; *Lovington (New Mexico) Leader*, February 8, 1929; Fenton, "Tom Ross," 185–86.

94. Fenton, "Staked Plains' Legendary Feudist," 20–21.

95. Ibid., 21; *Cut Bank (Montana) Press*, February 8, 1929.

96. *Dallas Morning News*, February 6, 1929; Fenton, "Tom Ross," 187.

97. *Calgary Evening Herald* (Alberta, Canada), February 5, 1929.

98. *Cut Bank (Montana) Press*, February 8, 1929.

99. Pettey, "Seminole Incident"; Fenton, "Tom Ross," 190.

100. *Lovington (New Mexico) Leader*, February 15, 1929.
101. *Fort Worth (Texas) Star-Telegram*, February 12, 1929.
102. Fenton, "Tom Ross," 191–92.
103. *Abilene (Texas) Reporter*, February 6, 1929.

## AFTERWORD

1. Alexander, *Dangerous Dan Tucker*.
2. Lindsey and Riggs, *Barney K. Riggs*.
3. Bristow, *Whispering Smith*.
4. Anonymously published, this tome carried the ponderous title, *Bella Starr, The Bandit Queen, or The Female Jesse James. A Full and Authentic History of the Dashing Female Highwayman, With Copious Extracts from Her Journal. Handsomely and Profusely Illustrated.* It was published in New York by Richard K. Fox, owner and editor of the *National Police Gazette*.
5. Rascoe, *Belle Starr*.
6. Shirley, *Belle Starr and Her Times*.
7. Hayes, *Apache Vengeance*; Speer, *Killing of Ned Christie*; Shirley, *Thirteen Days of Terror*.
8. Steele, *Last Cherokee Warriors*; Burton, *Black, Red, and Deadly*; Shirley, *Henry Starr*.
9. Brady, *Black Badge*; Burton, *Black Gun, Silver Star*; Paulsen, *Legend of Bass Reeves*.
10. Crichton, *Law and Order*; Ball, *Elfego Baca in Life and Legend*.
11. Stephens, *Lone Wolf*; Malsch, *"Lone Wolf" Gonzaullas*.
12. Secrest, *Lawmen and Desperadoes*; Secrest, *Dangerous Trails*; Secrest, *Man from the Rio Grande*; Boessenecker, *Badge and Buckshot*; Boessenecker, *Lawman*; Boessenecker, *Gold Dust and Gunsmoke*.

# Bibliography

## GOVERNMENT DOCUMENTS

Adjutant Generals' Files, Texas State Library, Austin.

Affidavit of Richard J. Ackley, September 29, 1858, Utah State Archives, Utah History Research Center, Salt Lake City.

Birth Certificate of James Patrick Masterson, County of Iberville, Canada.

*Commissioner of Indian Affairs Annual Report*, 1881.

Death Certificate of Bertha Blanch Neagle, November 14, 1927, No. 2635, California State Board of Health.

Death Certificate of David Butler Neagle, November 28, 1925, No. 2448, California State Board of Health.

Description and Historical Register of Enlisted Soldiers of the Army, 1841–42, National Archives and Records Administration, Washington, D.C.

Governor's Correspondence, New Mexico Territorial Archives, Santa Fe.

*Journal of the Executive Proceedings of the Senate.* Vol. 36, 59th Congress, 1st Session.

Marriage License Records, Martin County, Texas.

Marriages, St. Louis, 1804–76.

Minutes of the City Council, Cheyenne, Wyoming, February 12, 1878.

*New Mexico Adjutant General's Annual Report for 1885.*

Passenger and Immigration Lists Record, 1820–50.

Records of Volunteer Officers, Civil War, National Archives and Records Administration, Washington, D.C.

Roster of Agency Employees, 1853–1909, Record Group 75, Bureau of Indian Affairs, National Archives and Records Administration, Washington, D.C.

Texas Ranger Monthly Returns, Muster Rolls and Payment Records, Adjutant Generals' Files, Texas State Library, Austin.

U.S. Army Enlistment Records, Langford M. Peel, National Archives and Records Administration, Washington, D.C.

## U.S. CENSUS

Alabama: Sanford County, 1870.

Arizona: Pima County, 1920.

California: Alameda County, 1910, 1920; Sacramento County, 1860; San Francisco County, 1860, 1900.

Colorado: Chaffee County, 1910; La Plata County, 1880; Rio Arriba County, 1880.

Indiana: Ripley County, 1870.

Kansas: Arapahoe County, 1860; Butler County, 1870; Ford County, 1880; Franklin County, 1870; Leavenworth County, 1860; Osage County, 1880.

Maryland: Anne Arundel County, 1840.

Massachusetts: Suffolk County, 1850.

Michigan: McComb County, 1860.

Mississippi: Lowndes County, 1860; Monroe County, 1880.

Missouri: St. Louis County, 1850.

Nevada: White Pine County, 1870.

New Mexico: Taos County, 1880.

New York: New York County, 1860.

Ohio: Brown County, 1850, 1860; Clermont County, 1860; Lawrence County, 1870.

Oklahoma Territory: Kay County, 1900.

Pennsylvania: Allegheny County, 1870, 1880.

Texas: Erath County, 1860; Gaines County, 1920; Hopkins County, 1860; Oldham County, 1880; Upshur County, 1850, 1860.

## STATE AND TERRITORIAL CENSUSES
Colorado Census, Las Animas County, 1885.
Oklahoma Territorial Census, Beaver County, 1890.

## COURT AND PRISON RECORDS
Colorado
*People v. James Masterson*, Las Animas County District Court Book #2.

Indiana
Cause Nos. 1231, 1235, *State of Indiana v. Charles E. Short*, Ripley County Circuit Court.

Kansas
Cause No. 18, *State of Kansas v. N. F. Watson, Fred Singer, Neil Brown, Ben Daniels, William Allensworth, and James Masterson*, June 12, 1889.
Cause Nos. 864, 887, *State of Kansas v. B. F. Daniels*, Criminal Appearance, Docket A.
Cause No. 1837, *State of Kansas v. James Masterson*, December 30, 1888.

Louisiana
New Orleans Municipal Police Court Transcript, May 23, 25, 1874.
State of Louisiana, New Orleans Grand Jury Report, January 10, 1876.

Nebraska
Cheyenne County Court Records, Vol. 1.

New Mexico
Criminal Cause No. 416, Colfax County.

Oklahoma
Cause Nos. 81, 83, Police Judge's Docket, Guthrie.

Texas
Cause No. 901, *Wilbarger County, State of Texas v. Hill Loftis.*
Cause No. 131, *Bosque County, State of Texas v. M. H. Galbreath.*
Cause No. 179, *Erath County, State of Texas v. Porter Stockton, Assault with Intent to Murder.*
Cause No. 4909, *Taylor County, State of Texas v. Tom Ross.*
Prison Records of Tom Ross and Milt Good, Texas State Penitentiary, Huntsville.

United States
Cause No. 33, *United States of America v. Jerome Fitzgerald, James Masterson, and John Doe*, assault, August 21, 1889.

Utah
Cause No. 14, Seventh District Court, Carbon County.
Cause No. 551, Third District Court, Salt Lake County, November 4, 1889.

## MANUSCRIPTS

Bailey, Rebecca Williamson. "Wyoming Stock Inspectors and Detectives." Master's thesis, University of Wyoming, 1948.
Fenton, James I. "The Staked Plains' Legendary Feudist, Tom Ross."
———. "Tom Ross: Outlaw and Stockman." Master's thesis, University of Texas at El Paso, 1979.
Hornung, Chuck. "By the Banks of the Cimarron."
Snell, Joseph W. "The Stevens County Seat Controversy." Master's thesis, Kansas University, 1962.
Teats, Eugene. "Recollections of a Pikes-Peaker." Denver Public Library, Denver.
Way, Frederick, Jr. "Way's Directory of Western Rivers Packets." Louisiana Department, Louisiana State Library, Baton Rouge.

## LETTERS AND UNPUBLISHED DOCUMENTS

Merritt Beeson to Walter S. Campbell, May 1951. Beeson Collection, Boot Hill Museum, Dodge City, Kansas.
Tom Bicknell to R. K. DeArment, February 26, 2006.
Billy M. Birmingham, Huntsville, Texas, Penitentiary to R. K. DeArment, April 19, 1993.
Msgr. Stanley Crocchiola [F. Stanley] to R. K. DeArment, March 20, 1990.

Dave Cruickshank to William B. Secrest, October 18, 1982. Secrest Collection, Fresno, California.

Chief Justice Frank Dale to A. G. Richard Olney, May 21, 1894. Attorney Generals' Files, National Archives and Records Administration, Washington, D.C.

J. B. Edwards to O. H. Simpson, November 18, 1925. Beeson Collection, Boot Hill Museum, Dodge City, Kansas.

Charles Goodnight to J. Evetts Haley, April 8, 1927. Haley Memorial Library, Midland, Texas.

Jim Gray to R. K. DeArment, March 1, 2006.

Jana Kennon, Deputy, Wilbarger County, Texas, to R. K. DeArment, October 29, 1989.

Robert H. Land to William Secrest, March 23, 1964. Secrest Collection, Fresno, California.

James Masterson to Thomas Masterson, September 26, 1892. Kansas State Historical Society, Topeka.

C. H. McHenry to Lew Wallace, March 30, 1881. New Mexico Territorial Archives, Santa Fe.

Mark Megehee, Curator, Oklahoma Territorial Museum, to Robert Ernst, April 2, 1981. Ernst Collection, Ponca City, Oklahoma.

Roger Myers to R. K. DeArment, May 26, 2001.

H. P. Myton to "To Whom It May Concern." Record Group 60, National Archives and Records Administration, Washington, D.C.

Dave Neagle to Senator William M. Stewart, February 14, October 2, 1901. Nevada State Historical Society, Carson City.

Richard Olney to Judge Frank Dale, May 28, 1894. Attorney Generals' Files, National Archives and Records Administration, Washington, D.C.

J. C. Paul, "Early Days in Carson County, Texas." Research Center, Panhandle-Plains Historical Museum, Canyon, Texas.

Chris Penn to R. K. DeArment, December 14, 2006.

Jim Peters to R. K. DeArment, February 20, March 1, 2006.

Henry H. Raymond to Merritt L. Beeson, September 25, 1936. Henry H. Raymond Collection, Kansas State Historical Society, Topeka.

Joseph G. Rosa to William B. Secrest, February 5, 1977. Secrest Collection, Fresno, California.

Captain George H. Schmitt to Adjutant General William H. King, November 22, 1884. Adjutant Generals' Files, Texas State Library, Austin.

James L. Smith to Thomas Sturgis, secretary of the W.S.G.A., March 20, 21, 22, 26, April 18, August 1, 7, 1886; January 8, 11, 1887. Wyoming Stock Growers Association Letter File, University of Wyoming, Laramie.

William M. Stewart to Mrs. M. J. Kelly, July 16, 1886. Nevada State Historical Society, Carson City.

Sworn statement of James McIntire before Moses Wiley, June 30, 1879. Research Center, Panhandle-Plains Historical Museum, Canyon, Texas.

Carol Wahl to R. K. DeArment, January 16, February 28, 2006.

Moses Wiley to Texas Ranger Major John B. Jones, July 1, 1879. Research Center, Panhandle-Plains Historical Museum, Canyon, Texas.

## INTERVIEWS

Bob Beverly. Interview by J. Evetts Haley, March 24, 1945, June 23, 1946. Nita Stewart Haley Memorial Library, Midland, Texas.

James H. East. Interview by J. Evetts Haley, September 27, 1927. Nita Stewart Haley Memorial Library, Midland, Texas.

Charles Naeglin. Interview, January 17, 1934. Library of the State Historical Society of Colorado, Denver.

Erastus Thompson. Interview, July 31, 1934. Library of the State Historical Society of Colorado, Denver.

Clem A. Trotter. Interview by Ruby Wolfenberger, January 19, 1938. *Indian Pioneer History* 103:344. Archives Division, Oklahoma Historical Society, Oklahoma City.

## NEWSPAPERS

*Abilene (Texas) Reporter*, February 6, 1929.

*Albuquerque Daily Democrat*, May 17, 30, 1883.

*Albuquerque Evening Democrat*, October 15, 1885.

*Albuquerque Evening Journal*, October 19, 1885.

*Albuquerque Morning Journal*, May 11, 18, October 9, 10, 18, 1883; June 8, 1885.

*Arizona Daily Star* (Tucson), June 6, 7, 8, 9, 10, 11, September 9, October 24, 28, 31, November 21, 1882; August 20, 1884; September 22, 1889.

*Arizona Republican* (Phoenix), August 5, 8, 1896; April 18, 1925.

*Arizona Weekly Star* (Tucson), April 21, 1881.

*Aspen (Colorado) Tribune*, August 31, 1897.

*Aspen (Colorado) Weekly Times*, May 21, October 15, 1881; May 31, September 27, 1884.

*Atchison (Kansas) Daily Globe*, April 15, 1881.

*Atlanta Constitution*, May 6, September 28, 1881.

*Baltimore Sun*, April 2, 1881.

*Bismarck (Dakota Territory) Daily Tribune*, February 4, 1881.

*Black Hills Daily Times* (Rapid City, Dakota Territory), July 8, 1879.

*Black Hills Journal* (Rapid City, Dakota Territory), July 5, August 30, 1879.

*Burlington (Iowa) Hawkeye*, July 31, 1874.

*Butte (Montana) Daily Mirror*, April 16, 1881; March 2, 1884.

*Caldwell (Kansas) Commercial*, April 21, 1881.

*Calgary Evening Herald* (Alberta, Canada), February 5, 1929.

*Cherokee Advocate* (Tahlequah, Oklahoma), September 16, 1893.

*Cheyenne Daily Leader*, March 10, 11, 15, 16, 23, 24, June 20, 21, 1877; November 5, 1878; March 14, November 12, 1879; April 5, 1881.

*Cheyenne Daily Sun*, June 21, 1877; September 30, 1879; June 14, 1882.

*Cheyenne Weekly Leader*, March 29, 1877.

*Chicago Daily Inter-Ocean*, April 1, June 25, August 25, 1881; September 18, 1893.
*Chicago Herald*, August 24, 25, 1891.
*Chicago Tribune*, August 17, 1889.
*Cimarron (Kansas) Jacksonian*, January 18, 1889.
*Cimarron (Kansas) West-Echo*, January 17, 1889.
*Colorado Daily Chieftain* (Pueblo), September 3, 1876; June 2, 1881; July 1, 1882.
*Colorado Springs (Colorado) Daily Gazette*, March 27, April 15, September 1, 16, 30, 1881.
*Colorado Springs (Colorado) Weekly Gazette*, May 7, 1881.
*Cotulla (Texas) Record*, July 8, 1960.
*Cripple Creek (Colorado) Morning Times*, May 17, 1898.
*Cut Bank (Montana) Press*, February 8, 1929.
*Daily Evening Expositor* (Fresno, California), August 14, 1889.
*Daily Independent* (Elko, Nevada), November 6, 1897.
*Daily Morning Republican* (Fresno, California), August 15, 17, 1889; March 5, 1890.
*Daily Nevada State Journal* (Reno), April 2, 1881; February 25, 1890; August 5, 15, 1896.
*Daily Oklahoman* (Oklahoma City), February 29, 1920.
*Dallas Daily Herald*, April 1, June 21, 30, 1883.
*Dallas Morning News*, August 25, 1891; June 23, 24, 28, 1923; February 6, 1929.
*Dallas Weekly Herald*, December 13, 1884.
*Deadwood (Dakota) Weekly Pioneer*, June 22, 1877.
*Defiance (Ohio) Democrat*, May 19, 1881.
*Denver Field and Farm*, March 10, 1900.
*Denver Post*, August 27, 1914.
*Denver Republican*, April 14, August 12, 1881.
*Denver Times*, February 7, 1905.
*Denver Tribune*, September 28, 1881.
*Denver Tribune-Republican*, April 27, 1885.
*Dodge City (Kansas) Democrat*, December 13, 1884; April 17; September 23, 1893; January 31, 1902; June 19, 1903.
*Dodge City (Kansas) Times*, March 31, 1877; February 23, July 6, 27, 1878; January 11, February 15, April 26, May 10, 24, November 15, 1879; May 8, December 11, 1880; April 7, 21, 1881; January 17, 1889.
*Dolores News* (Rico, Colorado), July 1880–1881.
*Durango (Colorado) Democrat*, January 10, 1906.
*Durango (Colorado) Herald*, September 8, September 29, 1881.
*Durango (Colorado) Record*, September 2, 1881.
*Durango (Colorado) Southwest*, August 31, 1881.
*Eastern Utah Advocate* (Price), February 5, 1891; October 7, 1897; January 6, 1898; September 17, 1914.

*El Paso (Texas) Herald,* April 15, 1895; January 7, 1902.
*El Paso (Texas) Lone Star,* December 20, 30, 1882; June 2, 16, 1883.
*Ely (Nevada) Record,* September 6, 1872.
*Eureka (Nevada) Daily Sentinel,* November 10, 1872.
*Evening Democrat* (Warren, Pennsylvania), April 10, 11, 1895.
*Fitchburg (Massachusetts) Sentinel,* September 17, 1889.
*Ford County (Kansas) Globe,* July 30, August 27, 1878; February 17, June 10, July 22, October 28, 1879; April 5, 19, May 10, 1881.
*Fort Collins (Colorado) Courier,* August 22, 1889.
*Fort Griffin (Texas) Echo,* April 10, 1880.
*Fort Wayne (Indiana) Sentinel,* March 1, 1890.
*Fort Worth (Texas) Daily Democrat,* March 19, 1881.
*Fort Worth (Texas) Star-Telegram,* November 30, 1925; February 6, 12, 1929.
*Freeborn County Standard* (Albert Lea, Minnesota), February 3, 1881; September 12, 1888.
*Fresno (California) Weekly Republican,* August 23, September 6, 1889.
*George's Weekly* (Denver), September 8, 1900.
*Gold Hill (Nevada) News,* October 23, 1876.
*Gunnison (Colorado) News-Democrat,* September 23, 1881.
*Guthrie (Oklahoma) Daily Leader,* September 19, 1893.
*Helena (Montana) Independent,* March 5, 1884.
*Hennessey (Oklahoma) Clipper,* August 28, 1891.
*Herald and Torch Light* (Hagerstown, Maryland), December 4, 1872.
*Hornellsville (New York) Weekly Tribune,* April 12, 1895.
*Hugo Herald* (Hugoton, Kansas), October 27, 1887.
*Hugoton (Kansas) Hermes,* June 11, July 26, 1888.
*Idaho Daily Statesman* (Boise), September 23, 1888; September 17, 1893.
*Ingalls (Kansas) Union,* January 17, 1880.
*Janesville (Wisconsin) Daily Gazette,* July 21, 1860.
*Kansas City (Missouri) Journal,* November 15, 1881; January 25, 1902.
*Kansas City (Missouri) Star,* August 8, 18, 24, 1891.
*Kansas City (Missouri) Times,* November 22, 1872; November 15, 1893.
*Kansas Cowboy* (Dodge City), August 16, 1884.
*Kansas Daily Commonwealth* (Topeka), June 14, December 31, 1872; July 17, 1874.
*Kingfisher (Oklahoma) Free Press,* August 27, 1891.
*La Plata Miner* (Silverton, Colorado), January 25, May 17, 1879; July 17, September 25, December 11, 1880; January 8, March 12, April 9, May 14, 28, 1881; September 30, October 14, 1882.
*Larned (Kansas) Press,* May 30, 1878.
*Las Animas (Colorado) Leader,* October 11, 1873.
*Las Vegas (New Mexico) Daily Gazette,* April 14, 1880; January 16, 1881.
*Las Vegas (New Mexico) Optic,* January 16, 21, February 9, 1881; November 15, 1882.
*Leavenworth (Kansas) Daily Commercial,* October 5, November 21, 22, 1872.

*Lovington (New Mexico) Leader*, February 8, 15, 1929.
*Lubbock (Texas) Avalanche-Journal*, June 22, 1923; September 25, 1949.
*Macon (Georgia) Daily Telegraph*, August 25, 1891.
*Mexia (Texas) Daily News*, April 3, 13, June 21, 22, 26, 27, September 14, 16, 19, 1923; November 30, December 6, 1925.
*Morning Oregonian* (Portland), September 4, 1888.
*National Police Gazette*, June 21, 1879.
*New Haven (Connecticut) Register*, April 2, 1881.
*New Orleans Daily Picayune*, April 21, 23, 1885.
*New Orleans Republican*, November 14, 25, 1875.
*New Orleans Times*, May 25, 1874.
*New Orleans Times-Democrat*, April 21, 22, 23, 1885.
*Newton Kansan*, November 21, 1872.
*New York Times*, August 6, 1888; September 4, 1889.
*Oakland (California) Daily Evening Tribune*, August 16, 17, 1889; April 14, 1890; February 8, 1905; November 30, 1925.
*Ogden (Utah) Standard*, October 7, 1890.
*Oklahoma Daily Press Gazette* (Oklahoma City), May 23, 1894.
*Oklahoma Daily Times Journal* (Oklahoma City), August 24, 26, 1891.
*Oklahoma State Capital* (Guthrie), July 16, 1892; September 8, 1893; May 11, 19, 1894; April 1, 1895.
*Oskaloosa (Iowa) Herald*, March 17, 1881.
*Otero (New Mexico) Optic*, June 5, 1879.
*Ouray (Colorado) Times*, February 28, 1880; August 27, 1881.
*Owyhee (Idaho) Avalanche*, April 23, 1881.
*Phoenix Herald*, March 4, 1881.
*Pioche (Nevada) Daily Record*, June 1, 1871; September 24, 25, October 2, 3, 15, 1872; January 17, 23, 31, July 8, August 2, 3, 21, September 14, 20, 1873; December 24, 1874; March 24, May 5, August 15, 1875; March 24, December 20, 1876.
*Prescott (Arizona) Weekly Courier*, September 5, 1884.
*Prescott (Arizona) Weekly Miner*, July 13, 1877.
*Raton (New Mexico) Comet*, December 26, 1884.
*Reese River Reveille* (Austin, Nevada), August 4, 1873.
*Reno (Nevada) Evening Gazette*, September 17, 1888; August 14, 15, 16, 17, 1889; April 12, August 7, 8, 1896.
*Reno (Nevada) Weekly Gazette and Stockman*, July 13, 1893.
*Rio Grande Republican* (Las Cruces, New Mexico), September 16, 25, 1881; October 13, 1888.
*Ripley County Journal* (Versailles, Indiana), June 14, December 6, 1883; January 10, 1884.
*Rocky Mountain News* (Denver), July 25, August 1, December 10, 11, 21, 28, 1860; March 31, September 1, 1881; August 27, 28, September 6, 1914; November 18, 1979.
*Roswell (New Mexico) Record*, April 2, 1923.

*Sacramento (California) Union*, August 9, 1867.
*St. Louis Post-Dispatch*, July 15, 22, 29, 1923.
*Salt Lake Tribune*, August 16, 20, 1889.
*San Angelo (Texas) Standard*, October 8, 1886.
*San Antonio (Texas) Daily Express*, October 24, 15, December 13, 1884.
*Sandusky (Ohio) Daily Register*, August 16, September 6, 7, 1889.
*San Francisco Alta*, October 1, 1863.
*San Francisco Bulletin*, March 31, 1881.
*San Francisco Call*, August 13, 14, 1896; May 4, 1897; April 28, 1900.
*San Francisco Chronicle*, September 7, 1889; August 6, 1896.
*San Francisco Daily Evening Bulletin*, February 16, 1875.
*San Francisco Examiner*, August 18, 1889; August 2, 5, 7, 9, 13, 16, 1896; May 3, 1898.
*San Francisco Star*, August 7, 1896.
*San Juan Herald* (Silverton, Colorado), August 25, September 1, 8, October 6, 1881.
*Santa Fe New Mexican*, April 16, 1873; September 18, 1876; March 1, 12, April 8, 9, 27, May 6, 19, June 4, August 7, 1881; September 27, 1882.
*Seminole (Texas) Sentinel*, April 4, 5, June 21, 1923; February 7, 1929.
*Sidney (Nebraska) Telegraph*, April 4, July 12, 1879; May 29, 1880; January 8, 1881; May 19, 1903; June 19, 1951.
*State Journal* (Topeka, Kansas), August 24, 1891.
*Stillwater (Oklahoma) Gazette*, July 20, 1906.
*Sumner County Press* (Wellington, Kansas), July 2, 30, August 6, 1874.
*Territorial Enterprise* (Virginia City, Nevada), November 15, 18, 1868; March 3, 4, 28, June 6, 1871; September 28, October 17, 1872; August 8, 1873; January 9, 16, 1878.
*Tombstone (Arizona) Daily Epitaph*, September 15, 1880; May 11, 13, June 10, July 8, 17, 1882.
*Tombstone (Arizona) Nugget*, October 15, 1881; January 31, 1882.
*Tombstone (Arizona) Weekly Epitaph*, October 21, November 13, 21, 28, 1882.
*Topeka (Kansas) Capitol-Commonwealth*, July 17, 1874.
*Trenton (New Jersey) State Gazette*, April 4, 1881.
*Trenton (New Jersey) Times*, January 14, 1889.
*Trinidad (Colorado) Daily Advertiser*, March 3, 4, 6, 1885.
*Trinidad (Colorado) Daily Democrat*, November 25, 28, 1882.
*Trinidad (Colorado) Daily News*, March 17, 1882.
*Trinidad (Colorado) Daily Times*, January 28, 1882.
*Trinidad (Colorado) Weekly News*, October 26, 1882.
*Tucson (Arizona) Citizen*, January 9, 1902; September 28, 1904; January 24, 1906.
*Versailles (Indiana) Republican*, December 6, 1883.
*Washington Post*, April 27, 1906.
*Wellsboro (Pennsylvania) Agitator*, April 19, 1881.
*Western Mountaineer* (Golden, Colorado), August 2, December 6, 1860.

*Wichita (Kansas) Beacon*, February 19, 26, 1873.

*Wichita (Kansas) Eagle*, June 14, 1872; January 2, 1873; April 30, 1874.

*Woodsdale (Kansas) Democrat*, April 8, 29, August 26, September 2, October 28, November 4, 18, 1887; March 2, June 8, 15, 29, July 13, 20, 1888; February 22, 1889.

*Woodward (Oklahoma) News*, March 25, June 3, 1898.

## BOOKS AND PAMPHLETS

Adams, Ramon. *The Adams One-Fifty: A Checklist of the 150 Most Important Books on Western Outlaws and Lawmen*. Austin, Tex.: Jenkins, 1976.

——. *Burs Under the Saddle: A Second Look at Books and Histories of the West*. Norman: University of Oklahoma Press, 1964.

——. *More Burs Under the Saddle: Books and Histories of the West*. Norman: University of Oklahoma Press, 1979.

——. *Six-Guns and Saddle Leather: A Bibliography of Books and Pamphlets on Western Outlaws and Gunmen*. Norman: University of Oklahoma Press, 1969.

Alexander, Bob. *Dangerous Dan Tucker: New Mexico's Deadly Lawman*. Silver City, N.Mex.: High-Lonesome Books, 2001.

——. *Fearless Dave Allison*. Silver City, N.Mex.: High-Lonesome Books, 2003.

——. *John H. Behan, Sacrificed Sheriff*. Silver City, N.Mex.: High-Lonesome Books, 2002.

——. *Lawmen, Outlaws and S.O.Bs*. Silver City, N.Mex.: High-Lonesome Books, 2007.

Anderson, George B. *History of New Mexico: Its Resources and Its People*. Los Angeles: Pacific States, 1907.

Angel, Myron, ed. *History of Nevada*. Oakland, Calif.: Thompson and West, 1881.

Asbury, Herbert. *The Barbary Coast: An Informal History of San Francisco*. New York: Alfred A. Knopf, 1933.

——. *Sucker's Progress: An Informal History of Gambling in America from the Colonies to Canfield*. New York: Dodd, Mead, 1938.

Ashbaugh, Don. *Nevada's Turbulent Yesterday: A Study in Ghost Towns*. Los Angeles: Westernlore Press, 1963.

Bailey, Lynn R. *Tombstone, Arizona, "Too Tough to Die": The Rise, Fall, and Resurrection of a Silver Camp, 1878 to 1990*. Tucson, Ariz.: Westernlore Press, 2004.

Bailey, Lynn R., and Don Chaput. *Cochise County Stalwarts: A Who's Who of the Territorial Years*. 2 vols. Tucson, Ariz.: Westernlore Press, 2000.

Baker, Pearl. *The Wild Bunch at Robbers Roost*. New York: Abelard-Schuman, 1971.

Ball, Larry D. *Elfego Baca in Life and Legend*. El Paso: Texas Western Press, 1992.

———. *The United States Marshals of New Mexico and Arizona Territories, 1846–1912.* Albuquerque: University of New Mexico Press, 1978.

Bancroft, Caroline. *Denver's Lively Past.* Boulder, Colo.: Johnson, 1959.

*Banditti of the Rocky Mountains and Vigilance Committee in Idaho.* Minneapolis: Ross & Haines, 1964.

Banta, Albert Franklin. *Albert Franklin Banta: Arizona Pioneer.* Ed. Frank D. Reeves. Albuquerque: Historical Society of New Mexico, 1953.

Barnard, Evan G. *A Rider of the Cherokee Strip.* Boston: Houghton Mifflin, 1936.

Bartholomew, Ed. *The Biographical Album of Western Gunfighters.* Houston: Frontier Press of Texas, 1958.

———. *Western Hard-Cases or Gunfighters Named Smith.* Ruidoso, N.Mex.: Frontier Book, 1960.

Bechner, Raymond M. *Guns along the Silvery San Juan.* Canon City, Colo.: Master Printers, 1975.

Beebe, Lucius. *Comstock Commotion: The Story of the Territorial Enterprise.* Stanford, Calif.: Stanford University Press, 1954.

*Bella Starr, The Bandit Queen, or The Female Jesse James. A Full and Authentic History of the Dashing Female Highwayman, With Copious Extracts from Her Journal. Handsomely and Profusely Illustrated.* New York: Richard K. Fox, 1889.

Bentley, O. H. *The History of Wichita and Sedgwick County, Kansas.* Chicago: C. F. Cooper, 1910.

Boessenecker, John. *Badge and Buckshot: Lawlessness in Old California.* Norman: University of Oklahoma Press, 1988.

———. *Gold Dust and Gunsmoke: Tales of Gold Rush Outlaws, Gunfighters, Lawmen, and Vigilantes.* New York: John Wiley & Sons, 1999.

———. *Lawman: The Life and Times of Harry Morse, 1835–1912.* Norman: University of Oklahoma Press, 1998.

Bonney, Cecil. *Looking Over My Shoulder: Seventy-five Years in the Pecos Valley.* Roswell, N.Mex.: Hall-Poorbaugh Press, 1971.

Brady, Paul L. *The Black Badge: Deputy United States Marshal Bass Reeves from Slave to Heroic Lawman.* Los Angeles: Milligan Books, 2005.

Breakenridge, William M. *Helldorado: Bringing Law to the Mesquite.* Glorieta, N.Mex.: Rio Grande Press, 1970.

Breihan, Carl W. *Quantrill and His Civil War Guerrillas.* Denver, Colo.: Sage Books, 1959.

Bristow, Allen P. *Whispering Smith: His Life and Misadventures.* Santa Fe, N.Mex.: Sunstone Press, 2007.

Bronson, Edgar Beecher. *The Red-Blooded Heroes of the Frontier.* New York: George H. Doran, 1910.

Brown, Robert L. *An Empire of Silver: A History of the San Juan Silver Rush.* Caldwell, Idaho: Caxton Printers, 1968.

Browning, James A. *Violence Was No Stranger: A Guide to the Grave Sites of Famous Westerners.* Stillwater, Okla.: Barbed Wire Press, 1993.

Bryan, Howard. *Wildest of the Wild West.* Santa Fe, N.Mex.: Clear Light, 1988.

Burns, Walter Noble. *Tombstone: An Iliad of the Southwest.* New York: Harcourt, Brace, 1928.

Burroughs, John Rolfe. *Guardian of the Grasslands.* Cheyenne, Wyo.: Pioneer Printing & Stationary, 1971.

Burton, Art T. *Black, Red, and Deadly: Black and Indian Gunfighters of the Indian Territory, 1870–1907.* Austin, Tex.: Eakin Press, 1991.

——. *Black Gun, Silver Star: The Life and Legend of Frontier Marshal Bass Reeves.* Lincoln: University of Nebraska Press, 2006.

Burton, Jeffrey. *Black Jack Christian: Outlaw.* Santa Fe: The Press of the Territorian, 1967.

——. *The Deadliest Outlaws.* Portsmouth, England: Palomino Press, 2007.

*Business and Resident Directory of Guthrie and Logan County, OK. For the Years Commencing Sept. 1st, 1891.* Guthrie, Okla.: Frank G. Prouty, n.d.

Callon, Milton W. *Las Vegas, New Mexico: The Town That Wouldn't Gamble.* Las Vegas, N.Mex.: Las Vegas Daily Optic, 1962.

Carmony, Neil B., ed. *Next Stop: Tombstone. George's Hand's Contention City Diary, 1882.* Tucson, Ariz.: Trail to Yesterday Books, 1995.

Carter, Samuel, III. *Cowboy Capital of the World.* Garden City, N. Y.: Doubleday, 1973.

Casey, Robert J. *The Black Hills and Their Incredible Characters.* Indianapolis: Bobbs-Merrill, 1949.

Chesley, Hervey E. *Adventuring with the Old-Timers: Trails Traveled — Tales Told.* Midland, Tex.: Nita Stewart Haley Memorial Library, 1979.

Chrisman, Harry E. *The Call of the High Plains: The Autobiography of Charles E. Hancock.* Denver, Colo.: Maverick, 1989.

Cochran, Keith. *American West: A Historical Chronology.* Rapid City, S.Dak.: Cochran, 1992.

Coe, George W. *Frontier Fighter.* Chicago: R. R. Donnelley & Sons, 1984.

Conard, Howard Louis. *"Uncle Dick" Wootten: The Pioneer Frontiersman of the Rocky Mountain Region.* Chicago: W. E. Dibble, 1890.

*Confidential Delinquent List of Virginia City, Gold Hill, Carson and Reno, Nevada, and Bodie, California.* Virginia City, Nev.: October 1880.

Cook, D. J. *Hands Up; or, Twenty Years of Detective Life in the Mountains and the Plains.* Norman: University of Oklahoma Press, 1958.

Coke, Tom S. *Caldwell: Kansas Border Cow Town.* Westminster, Md.: Heritage Books, 2005.

——. *The Life and Times of Lawman Joe Thralls.* Westminster, Md.: Heritage Books, 2006.

Colletta, Lillian, and Leslie Puckett. *Tombstone Inscriptions of Brown County, Ohio.* Denville, N.J.: Lillian Colletta, 1963.

Cox, William R. *Luke Short and His Era.* Garden City, N.Y.: Doubleday, 1961.

Crichton, Kyle S. *Law and Order, Ltd.: The Rousing Life of Elfego Baca of New Mexico,* Santa Fe: New Mexico Publishing, 1928.

Cunningham, Eugene. *Triggernometry: A Gallery of Gunfighters.* 1934. Reprint. Caldwell, Idaho: Caxton Printers, 1962.

Cunningham, Sharon, and Mark Boardman, eds. *Revenge! And Other True Tales of the Old West.* Lafayette, Ind.: ScarletMask, 2004.

Curry, George. *George Curry, 1861–1947: An Autobiography.* Albuquerque: University of New Mexico Press, 1958.

DAR Sarah Platt Decker Chapter, Durango, Colorado. *Pioneers of the San Juan Country.* Vols. 2–3. Durango, Colo.: Durango Printing, 1952.

Davis, Sam P. *The History of Nevada.* 2 vols. Reno: Elms, 1912.

DeArment, Robert K. *Ballots and Bullets: The Bloody Kansas County Seat Wars.* Norman: University of Oklahoma Press, 2006.

———. *Bat Masterson: The Man and the Legend.* Norman: University of Oklahoma Press, 1979.

———. *Bravo of the Brazos: John Larn of Fort Griffin, Texas.* Norman: University of Oklahoma Press, 2002.

———. *Broadway Bat: Gunfighter in Gotham. The New York City Years of Bat Masterson.* Honolulu, Hawaii: Talei, 2005.

———. *Deadly Dozen: Twelve Forgotten Gunfighters of the Old West.* Norman: University of Oklahoma Press, 2003.

———. *Deadly Dozen: Twelve Forgotten Gunfighters of the Old West, Volume 2.* Norman: University of Oklahoma Press, 2007.

———. *Jim Courtright of Fort Worth: His Life and Legend.* Fort Worth, Tex.: TCU Press, 2004.

———. *Knights of the Green Cloth: The Saga of the Frontier Gamblers.* Norman: University of Oklahoma Press, 1982.

———, ed. *Outlaws and Lawmen of the Old West: The Best of NOLA.* Laramie, Wyo.: National Association for Outlaw and Lawman History, 2001.

Dial, Scott. *Saloons of Denver.* Ft. Collins, Colo.: Old Army Press, 1973.

Donaldson, Patricia R. *Brown County, Ohio, Marriage Records, 1818–1850.* N.p.: Patricia R. Donaldson, 1986.

Dorset, Phyllis Flanders. *The New Eldorado: The Story of Colorado's Gold and Silver Rushes.* New York: Macmillan, 1970.

Doten, Alfred. *The Journals of Alfred Doten, 1849–1903.* Reno: University of Nevada Press, 1973.

Drago, Harry Sinclair. *Wild, Woolly and Wicked: The History of the Kansas Cow Towns and the Texas Cattle Trade.* New York: Clarkson N. Potter, 1960.

Drury, Wells. *An Editor on the Comstock Lode.* New York: Farrar & Rinehart, 1936.

Dugan, Mark. *Bandit Years: A Gathering of Wolves.* Santa Fe, N.Mex.: Sunstone Press, 1987.

———. *Tales Never Told Around the Campfire: True Stories of Frontier America.* Athens: Ohio University Press, 1992.

Dykstra, Robert R. *The Cattle Towns.* New York: Atheneum, 1972.

Earl, Phillip I. *Heroes, Badmen and Honest Miners.* Reno, Nev.: Great Basin Press, 1976.

——. *This Was Nevada*. Reno: Nevada Historical Society, 1986.

*Edwards New Orleans Directory, 1873*.

*Edwards New Orleans Directory, 1874*.

Engebretson, Doug. *Empty Saddles, Forgotten Names: Outlaws of the Black Hills and Wyoming*. Aberdeen, S.Dak.: North Plains Press, 1982.

Erickson, John R. *Prairie Gothic: The Story of a West Texas Family*. Denton: University of North Texas Press, 2005.

Ernst, Donna. *Sundance, My Uncle*. College Station, Tex.: Creative Publishing, 1992.

Ernst, Robert. *Deadly Affrays: The Violent Deaths of the U.S. Marshals*. N.p.: ScarletMask, 2006.

Erwin, Richard E. *The Truth About Wyatt Earp*. Carpinteria, Calif.: O.K. Press, 1992.

Fattig, Timothy W. *Wyatt Earp: The Biography*. Honolulu, Hawaii: Talei, 2002.

Faulk, Odie B. *Dodge City: The Most Western Town of All*. New York: Oxford University Press, 1977.

Freeman, G. D. *Midnight and Noonday, or The Incidental History of Southern Kansas and the Indian Territory, 1871–1890*. Norman: University of Oklahoma Press, 1984.

Gatto, Steve. *The Real Wyatt Earp*. Silver City, N.Mex.: High-Lonesome Books, 2000.

Gilbreath, West C. *Death on the Gallows: The Story of Legal Hangings in New Mexico, 1847–1923*. Silver City, N.Mex.: High-Lonesome Books, 2002.

Gillis, William R., *Gold Rush Days with Mark Twain*. New York: Albert & Charles Boni, 1930.

Glasscock, C. B. *The Big Bonanza: The Story of the Comstock Lode*. Indianapolis: Bobbs-Merrill, 1931.

Gober, Jim. *Cowboy Justice: Tale of a Texas Lawman*. Lubbock: Texas Tech University Press, 1997.

Good, Milt, as told to W. E. Lockhart. *Twelve Years in a Texas Prison*. Amarillo, Tex.: Russell Stationery, 1935.

Goodnight, Charles, Emanuel Dubbs, John A. Hart, et al. *Pioneer Days in the Southwest from 1850 to 1879*. Guthrie, Okla.: State Capital, 1909.

Gorman, Harry M. *My Memories of the Comstock*. Los Angeles: Sutton House, 1939.

Gould, Milton S. *A Cast of Hawks*. LaJolla, Calif.: Copley Press, 1985.

Haley, J. Evetts. *Charles Goodnight, Cowman and Plainsman*. Norman: University of Oklahoma Press, 1949.

Harkey, Dee. *Mean as Hell*. Albuquerque: University of New Mexico Press, 1948.

Harris, Sallie B. *Hide Town in the Texas Panhandle*. Hereford, Tex.: Pioneer Book, 1968.

Hayes, Jess G. *Apache Vengeance: True Story of the Apache Kid*. Albuquerque: University of New Mexico Press, 1954.

Haywood, C. Robert. *The Merchant Prince of Dodge City: The Life and Times of Robert M. Wright*. Norman: University of Oklahoma Press, 1998.

Hill, Alice Polk. *Tales of the Colorado Pioneers*. Glorieta, N.Mex.: Rio Grande Press, 1976.

Holland, Thomas R. *Oklahombres Revisited*. N.p., 1992.

Horan, James D. *Across the Cimarron*. New York: Crown, 1956.

Howard, James W. "Doc." *"Doc Howard's Memoirs*. N.p., n.d. (ca. 1930).

Howe, Charles Willis, *Timberleg of the Diamond Trail*, San Antonio, Tex.: Naylor, 1949.

Hunter, John Marvin, and Noah H. Rose. *The Album of Gunfighters*. Bandera, Tex.: Hunter and Rose, 1951.

Hurley, Victor. *Jungle Patrol: The Story of the Philippine Constabulary*. New York: E. P. Dutton, 1938.

Hutton, Harold. *Doc Middleton: Life and Legends of the Notorious Plains Outlaw*. Chicago: Swallow Press, 1974.

———. *Vigilante Days: Frontier Justice along the Niobrara*. Chicago: Swallow Press, 1978.

Jennings, Al, and Will Irwin. *Beating Back*. New York: D. Appleton, 1920.

Keleher, William A. *Maxwell Land Grant*. Santa Fe, N.Mex.: Rydal Press, 1942.

Kelly, Louise. *Wichita County Beginnings*, Austin, Tex.: Eakin Press, 1982.

King, Frank M. *Mavericks: The Salty Comments of an Old-Time Cowpuncher*. Pasadena, Calif.: Trail's End, 1947.

Klock, Irma H. *Black Hills Outlaws, Lawmen and Others*. Deadwood, S.Dak.: Dakota Graphics, 1981.

Lake, Carolyn, ed. *Under Cover for Wells Fargo: The Unvarnished Recollections of Fred Dodge*. Boston: Houghton Mifflin, 1969.

Lake, Stuart N. *Wyatt Earp: Frontier Marshal*. Boston: Houghton Mifflin, 1931.

L'Aloge, Bob. *Riders along the Rio Grande: A Collection of Outlaws, Prostitutes and Vigilantes*. Las Cruces, N.Mex.: Yucca Tree Press, 1992.

Langford, Nathaniel P. *Vigilante Days and Ways*. Boston: J. G. Cupples, 1890.

Lavash, Donald R. *Sheriff William Brady, Tragic Hero of the Lincoln County War*. Santa Fe, N.Mex.: Sunstone Press, 1986.

Lee, Wayne C. *Wild Towns of Nebraska*. Caldwell, Idaho: Caxton, 1988.

Leonard, Stephen J. *Lynching in Colorado — 1859–1919*. Boulder: University Press of Colorado, 2002.

Lillard, Richard G. *Desert Challenge: An Interpretation of Nevada*. New York: Alfred A. Knopf, 1942.

Lindsey, Ellis, and Gene Riggs. *Barney K. Riggs: The Yuma and Pecos Avenger*. N.p.: Xlibris Corporation, 2002.

*List of Fugitives from Justice, 1878*. Austin: Texas State Library, 1878.

*List of Fugitives from Justice, 1891*. Austin: Texas State Library, 1891.

*List of Fugitives from Justice, 1900*. Austin: Texas State Library, 1891.

Lowe, Percival G. *Five Years a Dragoon ('49 to '54) and Other Adventures on the Great Plains*. Norman: University of Oklahoma Press, 1991.

Lyman, George D. *The Saga of the Comstock Lode: Boom Days in Virginia City.* New York: Charles Scribner's Sons, 1934.

Malsch, Brownson. *"Lone Wolf" Gonzaullas, Texas Ranger.* 1980. Reprint. Norman: University of Oklahoma Press, 1998.

Mather, R. E. and F. E. Boswell. *Gold Camp Desperadoes: A Study of Violence, Crime, and Punishment on the Mining Frontier.* San Jose, Calif.: History West, 1990.

McGillycuddy, Julia B. *Blood on the Moon: Valentine McGillycuddy and the Sioux.* Lincoln: University of Nebraska Press, 1990.

McIntire, Jim. *Early Days in Texas: A Trip to Hell and Heaven.* 1902. Reprint. Norman: University of Oklahoma Press, 1992.

McLoughlin, Denis. *Wild and Woolly: An Encyclopedia of the Old West.* Garden City, N.Y.: Doubleday, 1975.

McNeal, T. A. *When Kansas Was Young.* New York: Macmillan, 1922.

Metz, Leon Claire. *The Encyclopedia of Lawmen, Outlaws, and Gunfighters.* New York: Checkmark Books, 2003.

———. *John Selman: Texas Gunfighter.* 1966. Reprint. Norman: University of Oklahoma Press, 1980.

———. *The Shooters.* El Paso, Tex.: Mangan Books, 1976.

Miller, Nyle H., and Joseph W. Snell. *Why the West Was Wild.* Topeka: Kansas State Historical Society, 1963.

Miller, Rick. *Sam Bass & Gang.* Austin, Tex.: State House Press, 1999.

Mullin, Robert N. *Maurice Garland Fulton's History of the Lincoln County War.* Tucson: University of Arizona Press, 1968.

Nash, Jay Robert. *Encyclopedia of Western Lawmen and Outlaws.* New York: Paragon House, 1992.

Nix, Evett Dumas. *Oklahombres, Particularly the Wilder Ones.* St. Louis: Eden, 1929.

Noel, Thomas J. *The City and the Saloon: Denver, 1858–1916.* Lincoln: University of Nebraska Press, 1982.

Nolan, Frederick. *Pat F. Garrett's The Authentic Life of Billy the Kid.* Norman: University of Oklahoma Press, 2000.

———. *Tascosa: Its Life and Gaudy Times.* Lubbock: Texas Tech University Press, 2007.

Nye, W. S. *Carbine and Lance: The Story of Old Fort Sill.* Norman: University of Oklahoma Press, 1937.

O'Neal, Bill. *Cheyenne: A Biography of the "Magic City" of the Old West, 1867–1903.* Austin, Tex.: Eakin Press, 2006.

———. *Encyclopedia of Western Gunfighters.* Norman: University of Oklahoma Press, 1979.

———. *Fighting Men of the Indian Wars: A Biographical Encyclopedia of the Mountain Men, Soldiers, Cowboys, and Pioneers Who Took Up Arms During America's Westward Expansion.* Stillwater, Okla.: Barbed Wire Press, 1991.

Otero, Miguel Antonio. *My Life on the Frontier, 1864–1882.* New York: Press of the Pioneers, 1935.

──. *My Life on the Frontier, 1882–1897: Death Knell of a Territory and Birth of a State.* Vol. 2. Albuquerque: University of New Mexico Press, 1939.

Owen, Valerie. *Byrd Cochrain of Dead Man's Corner.* Snyder, Tex.: Feather Press, 1972.

Paine, Albert Bigelow. *Captain Bill McDonald, Texas Ranger.* Austin, Tex.: State House Press, 1986.

Parkhill, Forbes. *The Law Goes West.* Denver: Sage Books, 1956.

──. *The Wildest of the West.* New York: Henry Holt, 1951.

Parsons, Chuck. *Clay Allison: Portrait of a Shootist.* Seagraves, Tex.: Pioneer Book, 1983.

Paulsen, Gary. *The Legend of Bass Reeves: Being the True and Fictional Account of the Most Valiant Marshal in the West.* New York: Wendy Lamb Books, 2006.

Perkin, Robert L. *The First One Hundred Years.* Garden City, N.Y.: Doubleday, 1959.

Poe, Sophie A. *Buckboard Days.* Caldwell, Idaho: Caxton, 1936.

Porter, Millie Jones. *Memory Cups of Panhandle Pioneers.* Clarenden, Tex.: Clarenden Press, 1945.

Prassel, Frank Richard. *The Western Peace Officer: A Legacy of Law and Order.* Norman: University of Oklahoma Press, 1972.

Raine, William MacLeod. *Famous Sheriffs and Western Outlaws.* Garden City, N.Y.: Doubleday, Doran, 1929.

──. *Guns of the Frontier.* Boston: Houghton Mifflin, 1940.

Rainey, George. *The Cherokee Strip.* Guthrie, Okla.: Co-Operative Publishing, 1933.

Rasch, Philip J. *Warriors of Lincoln County.* Laramie, Wyo.: National Association for Outlaw and Lawman History, 1998.

Rascoe, Burton. *Belle Starr, "The Bandit Queen."* New York: Duell, Sloan and Pearce, 1941.

Rath, Ida Ellen. *Early Ford County.* North Newton, Kans.: Mennonite Press, 1964.

Richardson, Albert D. *Beyond the Mississippi.* New York: American Publishing, 1867.

Rideout, Mrs. J. B. *Six Years on the Border, or, Sketches of Frontier Life.* Philadelphia: Presbyterian Board of Publication, 1883.

Ridings, Sam P. *The Chisholm Trail: A History of the World's Greatest Cattle Trail, Together With a Description of the Persons, a Narrative of the Events, and Reminiscences Associated With the Same.* Guthrie, Okla.: Co-Operative Publishing, 1936.

Roberts, Gary L. *Doc Holliday: The Life and Legend.* Hoboken, N.J.: John Wiley & Sons, 2006.

──. *From Tin Star to Hanging Tree: The Short Career and Violent Times of Billy Brooks.* Topeka, Kans.: H. M. Ives & Sons, 1975.

Rockwell, Wilson. *Sunset Slope: True Epics of Western Colorado.* Denver: Big Mountain Press, 1956.

Rosa, Joseph G. *The Gunfighter: Man or Myth?* Norman: University of Oklahoma Press, 1969.

——. *They Called Him Wild Bill: The Life and Adventures of James Butler Hickok.* Enlarged and rev. ed. Norman: University of Oklahoma Press, 1974.

Rosa, Joseph G., and Waldo E. Koop. *Rowdy Joe Lowe: Gambler with a Gun.* Norman: University of Oklahoma Press, 1989.

Rousey, Dennis C. *Policing the Southern City: New Orleans, 1805–1889.* Baton Rouge: Louisiana State University Press, 1996.

Rye, Edgar. *The Quirt and the Spur.* 1909. Reprint. Austin, Tex.: Steck-Vaughn, 1967.

Samuels, Charles. *The Magnificent Rube: The Life and Gaudy Times of Tex Rickard.* New York: McGraw-Hill, 1957.

Sanders, Helen Fitzgerald, ed. *X. Beidler: Vigilante.* Norman: University of Oklahoma Press, 1957.

Sandoz, Mari. *The Buffalo Hunters: The Story of the Hide Men.* New York: Hastings House, 1954.

Schoenberger, Dale T. *The Gunfighters.* Caldwell, Idaho: Caxton, 1971.

Secrest, Clark. *Hell's Belles: Denver's Brides of the Multitudes.* Aurora, Colo.: Hindsight Historical Publications, 1996.

Secrest, William B. *Dangerous Trails: Five Desperadoes of the Old West Coast.* Stillwater, Okla.: Barbed Wire Press, 1995.

——, ed. *I Buried Hickok: The Memoirs of White Eye Anderson.* College Station, Tex.: Creative Publishing, 1980.

——. *Lawmen and Desperadoes: A Compendium of Noted Early California Peace Officers, Badmen and Outlaws, 1850–1900.* Spokane, Wash.: Arthur H. Clark, 1994.

——. *The Man from the Rio Grande: A Biography of Harry Love, Leader of the California Rangers Who Tracked Down Joaquin Murrieta.* Spokane, Wash.: Arthur H. Clark, 2005.

Shillingberg, William B. *Tombstone A.T.: A History of Early Mining, Milling, and Mayhem.* Spokane, Wash.: Arthur H. Clark, 1999.

Shirley, Glenn. *Belle Starr and Her Times: The Literature, the Facts, and the Legends.* Norman: University of Oklahoma Press, 1982.

——. *Guardian of the Law: The Life and Times of William Mather Tilghman (1854–1924).* Austin, Tex.: Eakin Press, 1988.

——. *Gunfight at Ingalls: Death of an Outlaw Town.* Stillwater, Okla.: Barbed Wire Press, 1990.

——. *Heck Thomas: Frontier Marshal.* Norman: University of Oklahoma Press, 1962.

——. *Henry Starr: Last of the Real Badmen.* New York: David McKay, 1965.

——. *Six Gun and Silver Star.* Albuquerque: University of New Mexico, 1955.

——. *Thirteen Days of Terror: The Rufus Buck Gang in Indian Territory.* Stillwater, Okla.: Barbed Wire Press, 1996.

———. *West of Hell's Fringe: Crime, Criminals, and the Federal Peace Officer in Oklahoma Territory, 1889–1907.* Norman: University of Oklahoma Press, 1978.

Shumway, Grant L. *History of Western Nebraska and Its People.* Lincoln: Western, 1921.

Sifakis, Carl. *Encyclopedia of American Crime.* New York: Smithmark, 1992.

Silva, Lee. *Wyatt Earp: A Biography of the Legend.* Vol. 1, *The Cowtown Years.* Santa Ana, Calif.: Graphic, 2002.

Simmons, Lee. *Assignment Huntsville: Memoirs of a Texas Prison Official.* Austin: University of Texas Press, 1957.

Siringo, Charles A. *Riata and Spurs.* Expurgated ed. Boston: Houghton-Mifflin, 1927.

Smithson, Fay Eidson, and Pat Wilkinson Hull. *Martin County: The First Thirty Years.* Hereford, Tex.: Pioneer Book, 1970.

Sonnichsen, C. L. *Tularosa: Last of the Frontier West.* New York: Devin-Adair, 1963.

Spearman, Frank H. *Whispering Smith.* New York: Charles Scribner's Sons, 1912.

Speer, Bonnie Stahlman. *The Killing of Ned Christie, Cherokee Outlaw.* Norman, Okla.: Reliance Press, 1990.

Spellman, Paul N. *Captain John H. Rogers, Texas Ranger.* Denton, Tex.: University of North Texas Press, 2003.

Spring, Agnes Wright. *The Cheyenne and Black Hills Stage and Express Routes.* Lincoln: University of Nebraska Press, 1948.

———. *Colorado Charley, Wild Bill's Pard.* Boulder, Colo.: Pruett Press, 1968.

Stanley, F. *Desperadoes of New Mexico.* Denver, Colo.: World Press, 1953.

———. *The Private War of Ike Stockton.* Denver, Colo.: World Press, 1959.

Steele, Phillip. *The Last Cherokee Warriors: Zeke Proctor, Ned Christie.* Gretna, La.: Pelican, 1974.

Stephens, Robert W. *Captain George H. Schmitt, Texas Ranger.* N.p, n.d.

———. *Lone Wolf: The Story of Texas Ranger Captain M. T. Gonzaullas.* Dallas: privately published, 1979.

Sterling, William Warren. *Trails and Trials of a Texas Ranger.* Norman: University of Oklahoma Press, 1959.

Streeter, Floyd Benjamin. *Prairie Trails and Cow Towns.* New York: Devin Adair, 1963.

Sullivan, W. J. L. *Twelve Years in the Saddle; Twelve with the Texas Rangers.* Lincoln: University of Nebraska Press, 2001.

Sutley, Zack T. *The Last Frontier.* New York: Macmillan, 1930.

Tanner, Karen Holliday, and John D. Tanner, Jr. *Last of the Old-Time Outlaws.* Norman: University of Oklahoma Press, 2002.

Taylor, Morris F. *O. P. McMains and the Maxwell Land Grant Conflict.* Tucson: University of Arizona Press, 1979.

Tefertiller, Casey. *Wyatt Earp: The Life Behind the Legend.* New York: John Wiley & Sons, 1997.

Thrapp, Dan L. *Encyclopedia of Frontier Biography*. Glendale, Calif.: Arthur H. Clark, 1988.

Tilghman, Zoe A. *Marshal of the Last Frontier*. Glendale, Calif.: Arthur H. Clark, 1949.

Tise, Sammy. *Texas County Sheriffs*. Albuquerque, N.Mex.: Oakwood, 1989.

Traywick, Ben T. *John Henry (The Doc Holliday Story)*. Tombstone, Ariz.: Red Marie's Bookstore, 1996.

———. *Tombstone's Boothill*. Tombstone, Ariz.: Red Marie's Bookstore, 1994.

Twain, Mark. *Roughing It*. Hartford, Conn.: American Publishing, 1872.

Tyler, Ron, ed. *The New Handbook of Texas*. 6 vols. Austin: Texas State Historical Association, 1996.

Utley, Robert M. *Lone Star Justice: The First Century of the Texas Rangers*. New York: Oxford University Press, 2002.

Vestal, Stanley. *Queen of Cowtowns: Dodge City*. New York: Harper and Brothers, 1952.

Watson, Margaret G. *Silver Theatre: Amusements of the Mining Frontier in Early Nevada, 1850 to 1864*. Glendale, Calif.: Arthur H. Clark, 1964.

White, Donald. *The Border Queen: A History of Early Caldwell, Kansas*. Wyandotte, Okla.: Gregath, 1999.

Willison, George F. *Here They Dug the Gold*. New York: Reynal & Hitchcock, 1946.

Wilson, Neill C. *Silver Stampede: The Career of Death Valley's Hell-Camp, Old Panamint*. New York: Macmillan, 1937.

Wilstach, Frank J. *Wild Bill Hickok*. Garden City, N.Y.: Doubleday, Page, 1926.

*Wolfe's Omaha, Nebraska, Directory for 1876–77*.

Wood, Margaret L. *Memorial of Samuel N. Wood*. Kansas City, Mo.: Hudson-Kimberly, 1892.

Wright, Robert M. *Dodge City. The Cowboy Capitol and the Great Southwest*. Wichita, Kans.: Wichita Eagle Press, 1913.

Yost, Nellie Snyder. *The Call of the Range: The Story of the Nebraska Stock Growers Association*. Denver: Sage Books, 1966.

Young, Frederic R. *Dodge City: Up through a Century in Story and Pictures*. Dodge City, Kans.: Boot Hill Museum, 1972.

Young, Harry (Sam). *Hard Knocks: A Life Story of the Vanishing West*. Chicago: Laird & Lee, 1915.

Young, Roy B. *Cochise County Cowboy War: A Cast of Characters*. Apache, Okla.: Young & Sons, 1999.

Zamonski, Stanley W., and Teddy Keller. *The Fifty-Niners: A Denver Diary*. Denver: Sage Books, 1961.

### ARTICLES

Ammerman, Ada Schulz. "Lawmen of Cheyenne County, NE." NEGen-Web, 2004.

Bartles, W. L. "Massacre of Confederates by Osage Indians in 1863." *Kansas State Historical Collections*, 1904, Vol. 8.

Bean, Tom. "Cattle Inspector Said He Shot Only in Self Defense." *Livestock Weekly*, January 30, 1992.

Benson, Maxine. "Port Stockton." *Colorado Magazine* 18, no. 1 (1966).

Burton, Jeff. "The Mysterious Kid." *English Westerners Tally Sheet*, July 1974.

"Capture of Good Cost $800.00." *Cattleman*, August 1926.

Carroll, Murray. "Whispering Smith's Hundred Dollar Hit." *Quarterly of the National Association for Outlaw and Lawman History* (Summer 1987).

Carson. John. "Iron Man Llewellyn. *Frontier Times*, January 1972.

"Cattle Thieves Kill Two Association Inspectors." *Cattleman*, May 1923.

Clarke, Bridget. "Robert Dwyer, Pioneer Sheriff, Related to Bridget Clarke." *Pioneers of the San Juan Country*, Vol. 2.

Clarke, Mary Whatley. "Bad Man . . . Good Man?" *Cattleman*, December 1971.

Cox, Dale A. "Battle of Cane Hill — Confederate Reports." *www.exploresouthernhistory.com*.

———. "Battle of Cane Hill in Depth." *www.exploresouthernhistory.com*.

Cunningham, Eugene. "Long-Haired Jim Courtright." *Frontier Times*, February 1929.

Curtin, Walter R. "The Passing of Farmer Peel." *Pony Express Courier*, May 1943.

DeArment, Robert K. "Bat Masterson and the Boxing Club War of Denver." *Colorado Heritage*, Autumn 2000.

———. "Bat Masterson's Femmes Fatales." *True West*, October 2001.

———. "Bloody Easter." *Old West*, Spring 1994.

———. "The Frontier Adventures of Jim McIntire." *True West*, February 1999.

———. "The Great Outlaw Confederacy." *True West*, September 1990.

———. "Gunfighters and Lawmen: Lawman Neagle Ably Defended a Judge." *Wild West*, June 2007.

———. " 'Hurricane Bill' Martin, Horse Thief." *True West*, June 1991.

———. "Kreeger's Toughest Arrest." *True West*, June 1986.

———. "The Mystery of Outlaw Bill." *True West*, January 1992.

———. "*True West* Legends: Jim Masterson." *True West*, March 1999.

———. "Wyoming Range Detectives." *Old West*, Fall 1993.

Devereaux, Jan. "Gentle Woman, Tough Medicine." *Quarterly of the National Association for Outlaw and Lawman History* (April-June 2003).

Dobie, J. Frank. "Within the Code." *True West*, November-December 1965.

"Doc Middleton: Road Agent and Bandit." American Local History Network Wyoming Web site, www.rootsweb.com/wyoming/ar-middleton.htm.

Earl, Phillip I. "Violent Life of a Nevada Badman." *Quarterly of the National Association for Outlaw and Lawman History* (Winter 1988).

"Escape of Tom Ross and Milt Good." *Cattleman*, December 1925.

Fenton, James. "The Staked Plains' Legendary Feudist, Tom Ross." *West Texas Historical Association Year Book*, October 2003.

———. "Tom Ross: Ranger Nemesis." *Quarterly of the National Association for Outlaw and Lawman History* (Summer 1990).

Green, W. M. "Breaking Up the Lawless Element in Texas." *Frontier Times*, May 1924.

Greenfield, Charles D. "There Was Something About Him." *The West*, February 1967.

Harris, Kenneth. "Hawkbill." *The Teepee Book*, November-December 1915.

Hawk, G. K. "He Lived by the Sword." *Badmen*, Fall 1974.

Holben, Dick. "Ike Stockton's Revenge." *Westerner*, March 1971.

———. "The Vengeance Vendetta of the Stockton Terror." *Frontier West*, August 1973.

Hopkins, A. D. "Morgan Courtney, Gunfighter from Pioche." *Old West*, Spring 1981.

Hornung, Chuck. "Wyatt Earp's New Mexico Adventures." *Old West*, Summer 1999.

"Inspectors Allison and Roberson Murdered." *Cattleman*, April 1923.

Jay, Roger. "The Gambler's War in Tombstone: Fact or Artifact?" *Journal of the Western Outlaw-Lawman History Association* (Spring 2005).

Johnson, Fred M. "Gunman of Durango." *True West*, May 1984.

Jones, Calico. "New Mexico's Stockton Gang." *Real West*, July 1973.

Jones, Charles A. "The Lynching of Bert Wilkinson." *Pioneers of the San Juan Country* 3:68–76.

Kelly, Bill. "The Odyssey of Kid Lewis." *Real West*, March 1977.

Lewis, Alfred Henry, "The King of the Gun-Players: William Barclay Masterson." *Human Life*, November 1907.

Masterson, W. B. "Famous Gun Fighters of the Western Frontier: Ben Thompson." *Human Life*, January 1907.

Mays, Carelton. "Those Amazing Mastersons, Conclusion." *Real West*, March 1964.

"Milt Good Is Captured." *Cattleman*, July 1926.

"Milt Good Makes Second Break for Freedom." *Cattleman*, November 1927.

"Milt Good Reward Paid." *Cattleman*, November 1926.

Myers, Roger. "Lawman James P. Masterson." www.larned.net/rogmyers/jimm.htm.

———. "The Third Masterson, Lawman Jim." *Wild West*, October 2000.

Nunis, Doyce B. "Biographical Notes." In George W. Coe, *Frontier Fighter*. Chicago: R. R. Donnelley & Sons, 1984.

———. "Place Notes." In George W. Coe, *Frontier Fighter*. Chicago: R. R. Donnelley & Sons, 1984.

Osgood, Stacy. "The Life and Times of David Neagle." *Brand Book of the Chicago Corral of the Westerners* 19, nos. 2–3 (April–May 1962).

Penn, Chris. "A Note on Bartholomew Masterson." *English Westerners' Brand Book*, April 1967.

Peters, J. S. "George Woods, Knight-Erroneous." *Journal of the Western Outlaw-Lawman History Association* (Summer 2001).

———. "Masterson's Militia: A Short Career for Bat's Brother." *Old West*, Fall 1983.

——. "Masterson's Militia, Company H." In *Incident on the Red River and Other True Stories of New Mexico*. Santa Fe, N.Mex.: n.p., 1971.

——. "The Vengeance of Bert Wilkinson." *True West*, April 1997.

Pettey, Weston A. "The Seminole Incident and Tom Ross." *West Texas Historical Association Year Book*, 1980.

Phillips, Lee. "The 'Other Masterson,' One Tough Lawman." *Tombstone Epitaph*, February 1996.

"Pistol Pockets in the United States." *National Detective Review*, July 1889.

"Prison Gates Await Slayers of Inspectors Allison and Roberson." *Cattleman*, July 1923.

"PROFESSIONAL GAMBLER IS KILLED IN UNEXPECTED ATTACK BY TRIO AFTER HE HAD OFFERED TO BATTLE TWO." Unidentified clipping, Arizona Historical Society, Tucson.

Rasch, Philip J. "Alias Whiskey Jim." *Panhandle-Plains Historical Review* (1963).

——. "Feuding at Farmington." *New Mexico Historical Review* (July 1965).

——. "Murder in American Valley." *English Westerners' Brand Book*, April 1965.

——. "The Other Allison." *Quarterly of the National Association and Center for Outlaw and Lawman History* (Spring 1986).

——. "Sudden Death in Cimarron." *Quarterly of the National Association and Center for Outlaw and Lawman History* (October 1979).

——. "Tom Nance: A Dangerous Man." *Real West*, March 1979.

"Regarding the Milt Good Pardon." *Cattleman*, January 1935.

Reno, Lawrence A. "Whispering Smith vs. Bat Masterson." *Journal of the Western History Outlaw-Lawman Association* (Fall 2002).

Rickards, Colin W. "Billy Brooks: Dodge City's First Marshal." *English Westerners' Brand Book*, April 1961.

Roberts, Gary L. "In Pursuit of Duty." *American West*, September 1970.

"Ross and Good Cases Affirmed." *Cattleman*, October 1924.

"Ross and Good Found Guilty of the Murder of Inspector Roberson." *Cattleman*, October 1923.

Rybolt, Robert. "Legend Becomes Reality—Whispering Smith Is Real." *True West*, February 1984.

——. "The Search for 'Whispering Smith.'" *Quarterly of the National Association for Outlaw and Lawman History* (Fall 1986).

——. "Whispering Smith." *Nebraskaland* (November 1986).

——. "'Whispering Smith': The Man, the Myths and the Mystery." *Quarterly of the National Association for Outlaw and Lawman History* (Winter 1985).

——. "'Whispering Smith' Still a Mystery." *Quarterly of the National Association for Outlaw and Lawman History* (Spring 1985).

Sasser, Charles W. "Pioche, Nevada: The Bloodiest Town in the Old West." *Old West*, Summer 1984.

Secrest, William B. "Jim Levy: Top-Notch Gunfighter." *True West*, July–August 1978.

———. "Quick with a Gun: The Story of Dave Neagle." *True West*, June 1995.

Schweitzer, Jeffrey. "Letter to the Editor." *Pacific Historian* (Winter 1970).

Sheffy, L. F. "Old Mobeetie—The Capital of the Panhandle." *West Texas Historical Association Yearbook* 6 (1930).

Smith, Kevin Burton. "Whispering Smith." www.thrillingdetective.com/eyes/whispering_smith.html.

Snell, Joseph W., ed. "Diary of a Dodge City Buffalo Hunter, 1872–1873." *Kansas Historical Quarterly* 31, no. 4 (Winter 1965).

Spring, Agnes Wright. "Who Robbed the Mail Coach?" *Frontier Times*, September 1967.

Thomas, J. J. "In the Days of the Overland Trail." *The Trail*, May 1910.

Turner, John W. "An Early Pioneer Family." *Pioneers of the San Juan Country*, Vol. 3.

"The Way of the Transgressor Is Hard." *Cattleman*, March 1929.

West, George E. "The Oldest Range Man." *Pioneers of the San Juan Country*, Vol. 2.

Westphall, Victor. "The American Valley Murders." *Ayer y Hoy en Taos* (Fall 1989).

Zamonski, Stanley W. "Colorado Gold and the Confederacy." *Brand Book of the Denver Westerners*, 1956.

———. "Denver's Godfather." *Rocky Mountain News*, November 18, 1979.

———. "Rougher Than Hell." *Brand Book of the Denver Westerners*, 1957.

# Index

Beard, Edward T. ("Red"), 133
Beatty, P. L., 238
Beauchamp, William M., 298–99
Beckham, Joe P., 278–80, 345n7, 345n11
Beer City, "No Man's Land," 269
Beeson, Chalkley M. ("Chalk"), 143
Beeson, Merritt, 143
Behan, Albert, 320n41
Behan, John H., 108, 109, 110, 112, 320n41
Beidler, Xavier ("X"), 25
Belcher (robber suspect), 184
Belfast, Ireland, 6, 303n11
Belknap, Tex., 206
Bell, Hamilton, 245
Bennett, Hiram P., 42
Bergstein, Henry, 87
Berkshire, Jud, 258
Bethers, William, 84, 88
Beverly, W. M. ("Bob"), 277, 290
Big Lost Valley, 202, 205
Birdwell, Bill, 291
Birdwell, Mrs. Soon, 292
Birdwell, Soon, 292
Bisbee, Ariz., 112
Bishop, Ben, 7
Blackburn, John L., 18
Blackburn, Leslie F., 110, 111
Black Hills, 60, 61, 66, 71, 91, 92
Blaine, James G., 215
Blaine, Wash., 296
Blair, A. S., 43
Blake, William ("Tulsa Jack"), 249–51
Blancett, Moses, 179
Bledsoe, W. H., 292
"Bleeding Kansas," 260
Blinn, Lewis, 110
Bliss, Z. R., 56
Bloomfield, N.Mex., 160–61, 163, 179
Boasso, T. J., 224
Bodie, Calif., 108
Boessenecker, John, 301
Bolds, George W., 229, 233, 243–44
Bonfils, Fred G., 77–78, 80
Bonner, L. P., 287
Bonney, William ("Billy the Kid"), 5, 169, 170, 183, 210, 211, 229
Books: *Album of Western Gunfighters*, 201–202; *Cheyenne City Directory*, 70;

*Deadly Dozen*, 300–301; *Deadly Dozen II*, 300–301; *Denver City Directory*, 80; *Early Days in Texas*, 201; *Hard Knocks*, 140; *History of Nevada, 1881*, 83; *Oklahombres*, 253; *Roughing It*, 15; *Vigilante Days and Ways*, 11; *Western Hard-Cases, or Gunfighters Named Smith*, 56; *Whispering Smith*, 55, 314n95
"Boot Hill," 135, 139, 140
Borah, William E., 281
Border Ruffian (horse), 30, 47–48
Boston, Mass., 104
Boswell, N. K., 59, 60
Botkin, Theodosius, 271
Bowen, L. L., 46
Bowie knife, 39, 115, 116, 118
Bowman, James, 58
Bowman, Mason T., 326n14
Boyle, Larry, 58
Bradford, Simeon Briggs, 269–70
Brady, William, 170
Brandon, William, 325n60
Breakenridge, William M. ("Billy"), 109, 112, 319n28
Brennan, Jim, 271, 344n44
Bresnahan, Lawrence R., 60
Brice, Charles R., 288, 349n89
Bridges, Jack, 139
Britton, R. L., 291–92
Broderick, David, 114, 115, 123, 132n75
Bronson, Edgar Beecher, 56, 70, 311n46
Brooks, Cynthia, 131
Brooks, Edmund, 131
Brooks, Edward D. ("Ed"), 243–44
Brooks, J. A., 347n35
Brooks, Matilda, 135, 144, 146, 147, 149
Brooks, William L. ("Buffalo Bill," "Bully Billy"), 4, 5, 130–31, *132*, 133–49, 323n8, 324n28, 325n54, 325n67, 325n72; described, 130–31
Brown, George, 165
Brown, Henry? ("Browney"), 139, 324n35
Brown, Jesse, 61, 62, 67, 311n29
Brown, John, 162
Brown, Mrs. Jessie, 61, 62
Brown, Neal, 232–33, 235, 243–44, 341n72
Brown, Sam, 14, 15, 16

Courtright, Timothy Isaiah ("Jim"), 210, 213, *214*, 215–22, 225, 336n55, 337n80
Cox, George, 249
Cox, John H., 177
Coyle, James, 111
Crawford, Foster, 280, 346n17
Crawford, Nebr., 71
Crittenden, T. T., 52
Croff, Richard R. ("Dick"), 297
Cromwell, C. A., 43
Cross, John M., 263–64, 266–67, 269, 271
Crouch (mob victim), 161
Crowley, Michael, 100
Cubery, W. O., 128
Cunningham, Eugene, 201, 337n80
Cunningham, Thomas, 119
Curry, George, 239, 240, 241, 340n54
Curtin, Walter R., 25, 27
Curtis, Zeneas, 157

Dale, Frank, 254
Dallas, Tex., 202, 222, 223, 296
Dalliba, James E., 42, 43, 50
Dalton, Bill, 249–254, 342n96
Dalton, J. T., 264
Dalton brothers gang, 150, 271, 272
Daniels, Ben, 243–44, 270, 341n72
Danielson, Jesse, 72, 73
Darling, First Lieutenant, 6
Daugherty, Roy ("Arkansas Tom"), 249–54, 342n96
Davenport, Judge, 18–19
Davidson, John, 226
Davis, C. M., 266
Davis, John G., 146–48
Davis, M. M., 95
Davis, Walter Scott ("Quick Shot"), 66, 67, 91–92, 316n49
Deadwood, Dak., 71, 91–92, 93, 94, 95, 100
Deal, D. L., 87
Death Valley, 106
DeBost, Leon, 271
Decatur, Tex., 158, 221–22, 275
Denison, Tex., 223
Dennis, John (editor), 87, 88
Dennis, John ("El Dorado Johnny"), 15, 17, 18

Denny, Lyman ("Cash"), 202
DeNormandie, Edward, 209
Denver, Colo., 4, 29–51, 52, 53, 77, 78, 80, 81, 155, 172, 174, 177, 178, 188, 193
Denver House. *See* Elephant Corral
DeQuille, Dan, 19–20, 305n49
Detective agencies: Pinkerton National Detective Agency, 59, 201, 229; Rocky Mountain Detective Agency, 193, 217, 332n81
Devereau, Thomas, 58–59, 310n17
Dillar, James A., 146, 148
Dixon, Charles J., 243
Dobie, J. Frank, 286
Dodge, Fred, 109, 112, 319n26, 319n28
Dodge City, Kans., 4, 134–43, 145, 151, 152, 156, 207, 208, 210, 230–33, 235–37, 242–43, 249, 255, 259
Dodge House, 135, 137
Donant, Gus, 76
Donohue, Cornelius ("Lame Johnny"), 60–63, 64, 65, 310n28
Doolin, Bill, 249–54, 278
Dorsey, Frank, 280
Dorsey, John, 210
Dosier, Tom, 92, 316n51, 316n53
Doten, Alfred, 322n79
Drew, Jessie ("Captain Drew"), 139, 324n35
Drew, John R., 24
Dry Lake, Dak., 61
Dubbs, Emanuel, 130, 137–38, 209, 324n28
Dubray, Chat, 43
Duffo, J. J., 310n13
Duffy, William, 231
Dull Knife raid, 232
Duncan, George H., 100
Dunn, Samuel, 37
Durango, Colo., 158, 162, 163, 166, 167, 170, 171, 173, 175, 176, 177, 178, 179, 180, 181, 182, 186, 187, 188, 189, 190, 193, 198–99
Dustin, Al, 162, 165
Dyer, D. B., 247

Earp, James, 229
Earp, Morgan, 109, 143, 229, 319n28, 325n54

Earp, Virgil, 109, 111, 229
Earp, Warren, 229
Earp, Wyatt, 91, 92, 96, 109, 110, 112,
    128, 134, 143, 151, 152, 209, 229–30,
    231, 232, 317n76, 319n28, 323n92,
    339n20, 339n28
Earp brothers, 3, 5, 110, 128, 319n30
East Las Vegas, N.Mex., 210–12
Eaton, Cyrus ("Ted"), 269
Edgefield County, S.C. 29
Edwards, J. B., 138
Eisley, George, 60
El Dorado, Kans., 131
Elephant Corral, 30
Elko, Nev., 86, 303n1
Ellsworth, Kans., 134, 135, 151, 152
El Paso, Tex., 70, 150, 213, 217–18,
    228
El Paso del Norte, Mexico, 225
Elsinger, Robert, 216–17
Ely, John, 83, 84
Ely, Walter R., 295–96
Emporia, Kans., 133, 259
Englin, Eugene, 160, 167, 328n46
English bulldog pistol, 116
English, J. W. ("Will"), 244, 245
Erickson, Anna Beth Curry, 296
Erickson, John R., 286
Eskridge, Dow, 184
Eskridge, Dyson, 163, 165, 166, 171,
    175, 181–82, 184, 186, 187, 190–93,
    195–98, 332n62
Eskridge, Harg, 171, 174, 175, 179, 180,
    183, 184, 186, 187, 192, 195, 197, 198
Essington House. See Dodge House
Eureka, Nev., 88, 108

Farley, Hugh, 99
"Farmington Mob," 159, 171, 174, 175,
    180, 184, 189, 198
Farmington, N.Mex., 159, 161, 162, 163,
    166, 167, 171, 172, 173, 175, 177, 178,
    179, 182, 184, 186, 187
Faulk, Odie B., 339n28
Female Orphan Asylum, San Francisco,
    Calif., 104
Ferguson, H. B., 224
Ferguson, Miriam A. ("Ma"), 350n91
Ferguson, Thompson B., 257, 275

Field, Stephen J., 115, 117–19, 121, 123,
    124, 125, 126, 128, 322n75
Figueroa, Antonio, 111–12
Fitch, Thomas, 100
Fitzgerald, Jerome, 247
Flannigan, Dennis L., 67–68, 80
Fleming, Henry, 209, 210
Flipper, H. O., 209–10
Flood, Barney, 84, 85, 88
Florence, Idaho, 105
Floto, Otto C., 77
Flynn, James, 110, 111
Folks, John H., 148–49
Foltz, Doctor, 89
Fonck, John, 110
Ford automobile, 292
Ford, Samuel P., 283
Forts: Atkinson, 7; Dodge, 134, 137,
    142; Elliott, 209; Hartstuff, 64; Kea-
    rny, 8; Lawrence, 51; Leavenworth,
    10, 11, 232; Lewis, 162, 172, 198;
    Robinson, 61, 63, 71; Sill, 145; Stan-
    ton, 70; Sumter, 48, 117; Union, 9
Fort Griffin, Tex. (town), 144, 156, 206,
    208, 210
Fort Smith, Ark. (town), 205
Fort Worth, Tex. (town), 152, 202, 213,
    218, 219, 220–22, 225, 292
Foulk, G. M., 275
Fountain, Albert J., 213, 215
Fox, George, 189
Fox, Mayor, 195
Foy, Eddie, 231
Franks, John C., 114–17, 119, 124
Freeman, Thomas, 45
Free State Movement, 260
Fremont, John C., 109
Fresno, Calif., 117
"Frog Mouth Annie," 209
Frost, Max, 176–77, 179, 180, 187, 239
Furay, John B., 62, 63

Gable, Thomas F., 241
Galbreath, M. H. ("Bud"), 183, 187,
    192–95, 197–99, 333n98
Gale, T. M., 100
Gallagher, Patrick ("Reddy"), 77–78
Gallo Springs, N.Mex., 216, 217
Gamble, D. C., 261

Gannon, Charles. *See* Loftis, Hillary U. ("Hill")
Gardner, W. M., 247
Garrett, James W. ("Jim"), 163, 165, 166, 171, 174, 175, 179, 181
Garrett, Pat, 210, 211
Gatling gun, 270
Georgetown, Colo., 308n36
Gerrond, Jim, 264–67
Gibson, Dave, 97, 99–102
Gifford, Eli B., 96, 100, 317n76
Gillis, William R., 305n32
Gilmore, Sheriff, 107
Gilpin, William, 47
Gilson, William C. ("Big Bill"), 205, 334n11
Give-Me-A-Horse (Apache fugitive), 70
Glacier County, Mont., 297
Glafcke, Herman, 95
Gober, James R. ("Jim"), 227
Godkin, E. L., 124
Golden City, Colo., 39
Gomez, Tex., 283
Gonzaullas, M. T., 301
Gonzolez, Juan, 155
Good, Isham J., 289
Good, John, 289
Good, Milton Paul ("Milt"), 289–92, 293, 295–97, 349n87, 349n89, 350n91; described, 349n87
Goode, Johnnie, 190
Goodell, George, 237, 339n28
Goodrich, C. W., 248
Gorman, Harry, 321n75
Gorson, Thomas, 88, 90
Governor's Island, N.Y., 7
Grant, Effie, 211
Grant Township, Kans., 230
Graves, Alfred U. ("Alf"), 162, 165, 177, 189
Gray, Mike, 112
"Greaser Militia." *See* New Mexico Territorial Militia
Great Falls, Mont., 297
Greathouse, Jim, 158
Greeley, Horace, 43
Green, John, 101
Greer, Bill, 43, 47–48
Grimes, Albert C., 220–21

Grimes, William C., 270, 275
Grossetete, Alexis, 216–17
Guatemala, 223
Guinan, Andy, 173
Guthrie, Okla., 227, 247–50, 254, 255, 256, 272

Hadley, Martin, 37
Haff, Corporal, 8
Haines, William P., 179
Hale, John M., 250
Halff, Meyer, 283, 347n29
Halff, Solomon, 283, 347n29
Hall, Benjamin F., 50
Hall, C. P., 46
Hall, Henry, 325n60
Halsell, Forrest, 254
Halter, August, 129
Hamblet, Francis M. ("Frank"), 162, 163
Hamblet, John, 162, 163, 189
Hamblet, Lee, 162, 163, 189
Hamer, Frank, 350n91
Hamilton, G. R., 205
Hamilton, Nev., 90
Hamlin, J. J., 72–73
Hanson, O. Henry, 161–62,
Hardin, Bud, 278
Hardin, Frank, 287
Hardin, John Wesley, 327n18
Harding, Oscar, 95
Hardwick, Tom, 91, 315n43
Hardy, H. E., 237
Harkey, Dee, 284, 288, 347n28, 347n37, 349n89
Harkey, Jeff D., 281, 347n28
Harlan, Col, 258
Harlan, J. J. ("Off Wheeler"), 110
Harris, Frank, 61, 62, 63, 65
Harris, Jack, 15
Harrison, Charles ("Charley," of Denver), 4, 5, 29–54, 306n3, 307n13, 307n28, 308n30, 309n52, 316n58; described: 31, 308n36; quoted: 29, 41
Harrison, Charles (of Cheyenne), 4, 32, 92–95, 103, 316n58, 317n60
Harrison, Mrs. Charles, 94
Harrison, Heartwell, 29
Harrison, Jack, 32
Harrison, Mary Ann Polly Key, 29

INDEX

Hunt, Tom, 29, 30, 33, 47
Hunter, J. Marvin, 201
Hunter, Luke, 175, 176, 190, 191, 193, 195
Hunter, "Texas Bill", 171, 174
Hunting Horse (Kiowa), 334n9
Huntington, Henry F., 126, 127
Huntsville, Tex., 296
Hurley, John. *See* Donohue, Cornelius ("Lame Johnny")

Iauson, M. A., 249–50
Iberville County, Quebec, Canada, 230
Indian tribes: Apache, 69–70, 188; Cherokee, 154; Cheyenne, 144, 146, 232; Comanche, 188, 203; Kiowa, 203; Osage, 5, 53–54; Pawnee, 8
Ingalls, Kans., 243–45
Ingalls, Okla., 249–50
Innes, James, 37
*In re Neagle* (court case), 126
Ireland, John, 218, 220, 221
Ireland, 6, 82, 84, 99
Ironton, Ohio, 202

Jacksboro, Tex., 203, 205
James, Frank, 229
James, Jesse, 229
James brothers (outlaws), 150, 229
Jefferson Territory, 39, 46
Jewett, G. H., 74
Johnson, G. A., 124, 126
Johnson, M. R., 99
Johnson, Robert, 60
Johnson, Walter, 209
Johnson (Utah rancher), 14
Johnston, H. L. ("Bud"), 294
Jones "Arkansas Tom." *See* Daugherty, Roy
Jones, Charles B., 167, 171, 173, 174, 176, 178, 180, 182, 183, 186–88, 195–200, 328n61
Jones, John B., 203, 205, 206, 208
Jordan, Kirk, 141–42, 144, 325n57
Jorud, Leslie, 27
Joseph, Doctor, 93
Joyce, Milt, 113
Jump, Ed, 34, 307n19

Kansas City, Mo., 224, 228, 281
Kansas counties: Barber, 261; Comanche, 143; Ford, 207, 231, 245; Gray, 243, 245; Harvey, 133; Pawnee, 7; Pratt, 261, 269; Sedgwick, 230; Stevens, 260–62, 264, 267, 269, 270; Sumner, 146, 148
Kansas Supreme Court, 243
Keller, Henry, 249
Kelley, Ed, 248, 341n82
Kelley, James H. ("Dog"), 235
Kelly, Mrs. M. J., 323n93
Kenny, James, 111
Ketchum brothers (outlaws), 150
Kilpatrick brothers (outlaws), 150
King, W. H., 221–22
Kingfisher Station, Kans., 146
Kingston, N.Mex., 215, 217
Kinney, John, 213
Kirk, John, 147, 148
Kirkpatrick, N. F., 350n91
Kistler, R. A. ("Russ"), 156
Klaine, Nicholas B., 231, 236
Knarf (shooting witness), 136–37
Knowlden, William, 23
Knowles, N.Mex., 285
Kreeger, Lou, 237–38

Lacy, Isaac W. ("Tom"), 177, 182, 186, 189, 330n7
Ladd, Alan, 55, 314n95
Ladue, Annie, 338n19
Lake, Stuart, 91, 143, 324n28, 339n28
Lake Valley, N.Mex., 212–13, 215, 217
"Lame Johnny." *See* Donohue, Cornelius ("Lame Johnny")
Lamont, Ada, 43, 49, 308n36
Langford, Nathaniel P., 11, 14, 17, 18, 27
Langley, Thomas B., 100
Lannan, Pat, 17, 18
Laramie County, Wyo., 94
Larimore, William, 50
Larn, John, 206, 334n27
Las Cruces, N.Mex., 69
Las Vegas, N.Mex., 158, 210–11, 212, 213
Latham, J. E., 100
Law, Robert, 66

318n5, USS *Baron DeKalb* (riverboat), 58; USS *Rattler* (riverboat), 58
Vestal, Stanley, 339n28
Vickers, J. E., 292
Vigil, Feliciano, 237
Vigil, Juan, 237
Vigilance committees, 5, 25, 32, 115, 127, 172, 175, 179, 195, 241; Denver, 37; Durango Committee of Safety, 175, 179; "Shotgun Brigade," 62; Sidney "Regulators," 68, 69
Virginia City, Nev., 3, 14–21, 28, 83, 84, 86, 91, 100, 105, 108
Voorhees, Kans., 264, 267

Waggoner, Dan, 277, 278, 287
Waggoner, Seymour W., 33, 35, 37
Waggoner, William, 287
Wagner, Frederick, 258
Wagner, Peter, 258
Waightmen, George ("Red Buck"), 249–50, 278–80
Walford, Judge, 162
Walker, D. W., 264
Walker, R. L., 271
Wallace, Lew, 161, 170, 174, 176, 177, 178, 183, 187
Walla Walla, Wash., 225
Waller, Walter (Walled, Walton?), 154
Waller, W. G., 151
Walters, Patrick H. ("Patsy"), 67, 68
Wanless, John, 45
Ward, H. 102
Ward, Jerome L, 112
Warf, J. W., 77, 313n83
Warner, H. B., 314n95
Warren's ferry, 39
"Washington and Creole Mining War," 85, 88
Washington, D.C., 215
Waters, Patrick ("Pat"), 45–46
Watkins, William, 145–46, 325n60
Watson, Barney, 195, 198–99, 333n98
Watson, Jack, 313n83
Watson, Newton F., 243–45
Watts, Henry, 174
Watts, John, 213
Waukomis, Okla., 273
Wave, Matilda, 209

Weatherford, Tex., 202
Webb, John Joshua, 211
Weber, Phil, 160
Webley pistol, 67
Webster, Alonzo B. ("Ab"), 235–36
Weir, W. D., 13
Welfoot, Seth, 171, 178
Wellington, Kans., 146, 147, 148
West, James, 210
West Point Military Academy, 209
West Wichita, Kans., 133
Weston, Kans., 10
Whalen, Clarence ("Red"), 296
Wharton, Okla., 275
*Whispering Smith* (movies and television), 55, 314n95
White, Avery C., 124
White, Jim ("Kid"), 183
White Pine, Nev., 100
Wichita, Kans., 131, 144, 148, 149, 151, 152, 230, 255, 256, 272
Wichita Falls, Tex., 219, 220, 221, 279, 280, 283
Wilbur, S. S., 261
Wilcox, Rolland, 269
"Wild Bunch, The" 76, 229
Wild Horse Lake, 269, 270
Wiley, Moses, 208
Wilhoit, Mathis, 299
Wilkinson, Bert, 163, 171, 183, 190–98, 330n10, 333n98
Wilkinson, Jim, 225–26
Williams, Frank, 192, 193
Williams, Jack, 15
Williams, Jerry, 325n60
Williams, John T., 278, 280, 283, 287, 345n10
Williamson, "Billy Bill," 291
Willsie, Charles, 148
Wilson, Billy, 211
Wilson, Dick, 267–68
Wilson, Jack, 199
Winchester rifles, 102, 111, 147, 166, 207, 244, 250, 252, 263, 265, 266, 268, 272, 273, 280, 283, 284, 297
Withers, Ed, 156–58
Withers, William ("Bill"), 156, 157, 327n29
Wood, David, 263